LEADERSHIP DEVELOPMENT

MATURITY AND POWER

By Lee and Norma Barr

D1359592

EAKIN PRESS ★ Austin, Texas

FIRST EDITION

Published in the United States of America
By Eakin Press
An Imprint of Sunbelt Media, Inc.
P.O. Drawer 90159 ★ Austin, TX 78709-0159

ISBN 0-89015-945-9

Library of Congress Cataloging-in-Publication Data

Barr, Lee.
      Leadership development : maturity and power/ by Lee and Norma Barr. – 1st ed.
      p.   cm.
      ISBN 0-89015-945-9
      1. Leadership. 2. Work groups. I. Barr, Norma. II. Title.
HD57.7.B36   1994
658.4'092–dc20
                                                                                    93-39943
                                                                                    CIP

Contents

vi

viii

Preface

Leaders are rare. Many of us are attracted to the idea of leadership, but few are willing to endure the discomfort, challenge, and risk required to become a leader. This book provides methods for developing leadership capability through systematically balancing natural style and learned skills.

Developing and maintaining leadership capabilities is costly in terms of pain, discomfort, and uncertainty. Leadership cannot be faked for long. Neither is it something that can be awarded by title, edict, or legislation. Leadership is a dynamic relationship between the leader and the led. It requires maturity that comes from growth, challenge, and struggle. Bonding comes when people believe in the leader's ability to know what to do and, as a consequence, they want to help do it.

Every one of us can safely say that we have had discomfort, challenge, and risk. We can reasonably support our assertions that we have struggled and been tested. The critical question, however, rests with how we respond to the tests. Do we just burrow in deeper to our safe and well-known ways of responding? Or do we experience the struggle, shed limited ways of behaving, and embrace a new way of seeing and responding? Do we diminish ourselves by becoming more set in our ways, or do we expand by growing and opening up to the disquieting effects of change and uncertainty? If we become more rigid and stubbornly cling to our comfortable ways of seeing and experiencing, we cannot develop the maturity that genuine leadership demands.

As long as the printed word has existed, we have had books about leadership. Prior to printing, stories and songs inspired people by describing leaders' courage, daring, and achievements. In primitive cultures, bards and their songs of heroism and valor were welcomed at any hearth. Bards as storytellers and bearers of culture could roam freely from place to place. They were welcomed and given safe passage.

Leadership has always been and continues to be a provocative idea. Our culture abounds with images of heroic ability to save the day. When has there ever been a more potent capability for destruction than we have today? When has there ever been a more complex culture with more sophisticated information systems and greater potential for destruction and control than we have today? When has there ever been a more urgent need for leadership?

We describe a leader this way: "One who is more fearless, more clear, more unlimited, more wise, and more courageous than anyone else around. A leader sees clearly, decides wisely and acts in others' best interests." In short, leaders can think clearly under fire.

We believe the leader (1) sees what needs to be done today without losing tomorrow's vision, (2) communicates clearly and powerfully the actions and possibilities of the vision, (3) inspires others to contribute their best by demonstrating trustworthiness, integrity, maturity, and caring, (4) motivates others to want to belong, (5) stretches and pushes people to develop their potential, and (6) demonstrates confidence in the victorious achievement of the vision.

Leaders affect our thoughts, our emotions, our behaviors; in effect, they penetrate and interact with us in our psychological space. They help to shape our ideas of what is possible. They see potential in us that we don't see. We find ourselves thinking about how the leader would see a situation, how the leader would react to certain ideas, what the leader's standards of behavior are. We experience a surge of energy and commitment as we re-experience how we feel when the leader sees us as a trusted fellow participant in a worthwhile risk. Our mind is filled with images of the leader's actions, values, beliefs, and instincts. Our attention flows where the leader goes.

Leaders influence our actions. They create fields of focused energy that tend to stimulate and encourage others to reach out beyond what is safe and comfortable. As we interact within a leader's force field, we attach ourselves to forward exploration of possibility, flexibility, and discovery. The leader is not drawing us into little mirror reflections, but into a generous, creative process of self-generating discovery. Genuine leaders perpetually help us to see clearly our choices while never stealing our individuality. The real leader encourages us on the difficult journey toward mature adulthood, while teaching us to accept full responsibility for our choices. The leader does not seek to dominate through creating dependency, but rather seeks to show us the road to independence, strength, and personal freedom.

Genuine leaders are more mature than those they lead. In short, leaders are extraordinary — not ordinary. They are clearer, wiser, more fearless and courageous than others. Can anyone reasonably expect to develop such leadership capability? We believe so; otherwise we wouldn't be writing this book!

Our purpose in this book is to provide a roadmap for the complex journey of developing or improving leadership capability. Our research supports the notion that *balance* is a key to maturity as well as leadership capability. Since leadership itself implies people relationships, we found a valid, reliable method for organizing the intricate, convoluted behaviors of human beings into a common-sense, practical approach to understanding people. We use the Myers-Briggs Type Indicator as the organizing basis for a roadmap to leadership development. The foundation for true leadership is understanding people, and that process requires self-understanding — clear, truthful acceptance of our own strengths and weaknesses is a necessary payment for clear perception and clear judgment. We also use the Barr & Barr power style model to complete that foundation.

The Myers-Briggs Type Indicator enables a manager to identify basic preferences, i.e., favorite, known, and comfortable routes on the map. From that basic information, we can then more readily identify those development routes people are more likely to avoid because they are unexplored, unknown, or appear to be risky.

The other critical framework for understanding people involves the way they use power. Power is defined as potential to influence. It comes in many forms, but we will refer primarily to personal power, position power, organizational power, and political power.

Personal power — individual's personality, intelligence, experience, and style

xi

Position power — the amount of influence that is attributed to the title and organizational position one holds

Organizational power — the contacts, relationships, knowledge of business systems as well as the knowledge of how to get things done

Political power — political savvy and abilities to acquire favors, trade-offs, coercive or obligatory chips from others, and the reputation to influence outcomes

Our rationale includes the following assumptions:

1. Leadership implies relationships between the leader and the led.

2. Relationships are dependent upon how people see (perceptual choice of Sensing or Intuiting), how they judge what they see (judgment of Thinking or Feeling), how they experience interactions (actions of Judging or Perceiving), and how they communicate with each other (Introverting or Extroverting).*

3. Relationships are dependent upon how people use power. Power players use power immaturely.

4. The leader must be more mature than those who follow.

5. Maturity requires that the leader accept complete responsibility for what s/he does, thinks, feels, and is.

6. Accepting complete responsibility for self requires the leader to avoid self-deception by doing continuous, brutal self-examination. We know of no other route to clear perception and judgment.

7. The Myers-Briggs identification of basic preferences enables the leader to more clearly self-monitor, self-develop, and use a common language for guiding the development of others. Using the Myers-Briggs typology of Extrovert-

---

*References to the eight aspects of the Myers-Briggs have been capitalized throughout the book for easy recognition (Extrovert-Introvert, Sensor-Intuitor, Thinker-Feeler, Judge-Perceiver). References to the stages of power have been capitalized throughout the book for easy recognition (Stage IV Leadership, Stage III Competitive Manipulator or Intimidator, Stage II Benevolent or Abusive Dictator, and Stage I Helpless Infant or Terrible Tyrant).

Introvert, Sensor-Intuitor, Thinker-Feeler, Judge-Perceiver development can be systematic and orderly.

8. Developing balance on the Myers-Briggs preferences does not guarantee leadership development; it does, however, enhance ability to respond situationally to what is needed and increases capacity to risk. The actual doing requires personal action.

9. Mature use of power is required for effective leadership, making it essential to recognize mature and immature behavior.

This leadership development book is not intended as a psychological or therapeutic approach to human behavior. We work with managers to develop practical skills and abilities for working with people. We are reporting a common-sense approach to the complexity of the human being. The book contains core information, case studies of real-world application, and developmental exercises to enable you to create a systematic plan for further balance as a means of enhancing your leadership capability. (Personal experiences related in the book were written by Norma Barr; however, the book is entirely drawn from collaborative interplay of Lee and Norma's insights through work in their consulting firm.)

We have worked with thousands of executives, managers, and supervisors. In the continually changing work world, stress is increasing at an alarming rate. Enormous need exists for stable, clear, decisive leadership with the ability to inspire commitment and trust. The need is measurable in terms of accident rates, sick leave, unexplained absences, lost or damaged equipment, damaged client-customer relationships, unmotivated employees, turnover, lawsuits, and employee complaints. The need for world leadership is measurable in terms of serious problems with environmental destruction, drug traffic, illegal arms sales, wars, food shortages, economic chaos, trade imbalance, national debt, and energy manipulation. The need for leadership is measurable in terms of broken relationships, drug abuse, alcoholism, loss of ethics, white collar crime, and physical abuse. LEADERS: The world needs you!

With the demise of the ironclad control of the Soviet Union, nations are desperately seeking leadership that can help them

⅃ infrastructure, change philosophy, and create stability ⅰn chaos. Leaders are greatly needed as countries so long dominated find themselves in the confusing position of self-governance.

Leadership is needed to address problems, to see clearly, to know what needs to be done, and then to motivate people to work on solutions. Many of the problems seem insurmountable, too large to tackle. Yet, problems involve people; so as long as we have life, we have the opportunity to make a difference where we are. We have the opportunity to develop balance that maximizes our capability to respond to what is needed. In the pages that follow, we are laying out a developmental course for achieving balance in communicating (Extroversion-Introversion), in perceiving (Sensing-Intuiting), in judgment (Thinking-Feeling), and in interaction (Judge-controlling/Perceiver-adapting). Although we cannot assume that developing balance in style will produce leadership, we can guarantee that it will increase response capacity.

Genuine leadership involves courage, integrity, intelligence, maturity, and strength — all difficult to measure but easy to recognize.

Since people relationships are the basic component of leadership, we chose a systematic method for increasing your capacity to understand yourself and others as a manageable way to chart leadership development. The actual title of "leader" can only be given by those people who have seen measurable results of your ability and therefore decide to take a chance on you by assuming that you see more clearly, know what has to be done, and will lead the way to achievement.

Chapter 1 introduces a leadership model to help clarify the difference between genuine leadership and pseudo leadership. Stages of development are identified to give you a behavioral map of the terrain.

Chapter 2 addresses critical information for overcoming fear, the major block to developing the balance required for leadership. The leader must confront fears and overcome them. Simultaneously, the leader must guard against getting too comfortable and thereby losing capacity to risk, to dare, and to grow.

Chapter 3 develops the rationale for achieving balance on the lifestyle dimension of Extroversion and Introversion as an important basis for development. Exercises are presented.

Chapter 4 explores developing balance in perception. Knowing the limits of a dominant Sensor or Intuitor preference gives you a map of perceptions that lead to imbalance. Additionally, developmental exercises are included to improve perception by using the assets of both ways of seeing.

Chapter 5 deals with developing balance between thoughts and feelings. You will see the problems of imbalance on Thinker-Feeler preference. Distorted perception and judgment can be lethal to a leader. Developmental exercises are presented to enable work toward balance.

Chapter 6 presents arguments for balancing Judge-controlling and Perceiving-adapting as the leader wrestles with the paradox of being decisive while remaining open to changing situations.

Chapter 7 explores the dynamic nature of leadership and change that requires you to continually grow, test, and then grow some more. Leadership development requires a continual upward spiral of learning, testing, risking, and growing.

Chapter 8 focuses the synergy of Stage IV Leadership and teamwork by building on understanding of personal style, power style, the role of fear and defense mechanisms as we influence the dynamic process of organizational life.

Chapter 9 summarizes basic concepts of leadership, power, and the typical power game.

With this book you can develop your roadmap to systematically cover the distance between where you are now and where your leadership vision propels you to be.

– 1 –

Leadership:
Stage IV Use of Power

Main Ideas of Chapter 1:

1. Genuine leadership requires balance of personal and power style.

2. Personal style and stage of power development provide an axis for reading people.

3. Four stages of power development are:

    A. Stage I   Dependency
                 (1) Terrible Tyrant
                 (2) Helpless Infant

    B. Stage II   Autonomy
                 (1) Abusive Dictator
                 (2) Benevolent Dictator

    C. Stage III Competition
                 (1) Competitive Intimidator
                 (2) Competitive Manipulator

    D. Stage IV Leadership
                 (1) Fearsome Leader
                 (2) Inspirational Leader

4. Only Stage IV fits the criteria for leadership; the other three stages represent immature power use.

5. Stage IV Leaders gain clarity of perception and judgment by confronting and overcoming their fears.

At first glance the power player and the leader look alike, as they both wield considerable influence. However, astute people assessment skills enable you to tell the difference.

Leaders use personal power to empower others, while power players use power to dominate and control others. Power players manipulate and control others for personal gain. Leaders create relationships of trustworthiness, integrity, maturity, and caring that provide a cultural environment for growth and discovery.

LEADERS BUILD RELATIONSHIPS

The young man's face was strained, he was perspiring, and he jumped when L. F. Bass walked in the door. L. F. recognized the anxiety and spoke to the employee. "Hey, how's it going?"

The employee was hastily gathering his transparencies and charts for a presentation to an important client. He said, "I'm just getting ready to make the Doran presentation. I've really been working hard on this." He nervously knocked a stack of papers off the desk. "I'm sorry, sir. I'm just a little nervous, but you can count on me to do my best."

L. F. replied, "I know you will. You have some well-designed graphics there. Let's have a look at them." L. F.'s strategy was to calm the young man down by helping him focus on the tangible parts of the presentation. Together they looked over the transparencies and L. F. casually drew out the main points of the employee's presentation. The interaction was so skillfully handled that the young employee never seemed to realize that he had just reviewed his presentation, received support for his work, and controlled his nervousness. L. F. had helped the employee get focused and ready to make the presentation.

L. F. is a leader. He recognized that the employee was scattered and nervous. The important presentation had obviously stirred concerns about failure or success. As an astute reader of people, L. F. knew that the employee would calm down as he focused on the tangible preparation he had done. The employee's personal style is Extrovert, Sensor, Thinker, and Judge (ESTJ), and L. F. recognized that helping the employee get grounded in the Sensor tangible graphics while reviewing the Thinker logic of the presentation would help the young man get reconnected to his own strength and most natural style. The employee calmed down, became focused, regained the confidence that hard work had provided, and went on to give an excellent presentation that yielded a lucrative contract for the company and expanded potential for the employee.

As L. F. walked down the hall, he was stopped by the personnel officer. He was told that Jane, the recently promoted head of marketing, was already in a harangue with operations. The personnellist thought L. F. should intervene.

Jane Thompson, the head of marketing, is an aggressive, intelligent thirty-year-old, eager to redefine the world in her own image. L. F. knew when Jane was promoted that she was going to need firm guidance. She has the raw material for leadership but not the development. He had worked out a development plan with the senior vice-president to whom Jane reports and this information about her aggression was not unexpected. L. F. thanked the personnel officer and told him to keep him advised.

L. F. knew that Jane was not seasoned enough for the job but with guidance she could grow into it. He began to reflect about Jane and her development plan. She is an Extrovert, Intuitor, Thinker, Judge (ENTJ) with strong preferences. L. F. uses the Myers-Briggs typology to enable his management staff to work out realistic and targeted development programs for managers. He reflected on the challenge of bringing her into a more balanced use of personal style and enabling her to develop mature use of power.

L. F. is also an ENTJ in personal style. He remembers how he struggled to balance his own style, and what it was like to be thirty years old and have the untested assurance that comes with youth and energy. He, too, once believed that success was the only desirable outcome. He bought the American fascination with power and disdain for powerlessness. Thus, he had arrived at age thirty with a love for power and a hatred for powerlessness. Looking back on it all now, he realized the value of powerlessness to learn compassion and genuine understanding of people.

He, too, had become a department head early in his career. He was so full of energy and winning that he had no tolerance for anything else. He marched right through high school and college capturing the leadership positions and getting things done. He shudders now as he recalls how arrogantly he manipulated people. He hated losers and had little understanding of failure. He was thirty-two years old before he experienced any significant failure himself. He was promoted to a more difficult competitive job, went through a divorce, and broke his leg in a skiing accident in one six-month segment of his life. He responded to the challenges by being even more aggressive and controlling. He fought failure with a ferocity that was awful to watch.

His problems worsened until the intervention of a seasoned warrior who had earned his leadership hat years earlier in the corporate wars. He pulled L. F. into his office and gave him the confrontation of his life. In vivid language that it is still etched in memory, L. F. got a clear picture of his own style. He remembers the words with crystal clarity. The leader said, "Are you about ready to quit being an asshole and get on with developing the strength to become a real leader? Or, are you so addicted to throwing your weight around that you are a power junkie for whom there is no redemption? I've watched you ride roughshod over other people, becoming more bloated with self-importance, and so full of personal egotism that you can't see anyone or anything but yourself. Well, boy, you are way overdue for a heavy dose of screw-ups that you have to pay for. I was beginning to think it was going to come too late to do you any good."

L. F. recalls how stunned he was to hear such a description. After the leader stripped him to the bone of his illusions of power and greatness, he found L. F. too scattered to argue. The leader did a thorough job of revealing L. F.'s favorite power games — ones he arrogantly thought no one else knew about. He became more and more defenseless as the games were described with chilling accuracy.

The leader looked straight at L. F. for a long time and then said slowly, "It feels like shit now, but it's damned essential. See, boy, you don't have any tolerance for people going through a hard time. You've had it so easy that you made the mistake of thinking that everyone had it the same way. You haven't learned real toughness. Look at what happens to you when you run up against someone like me who can take your bullshit apart. Where's your strength now? You can't keep your shit together in the face of real problems. You can't win in a straight game . . . you count on the card dealer's con to set it up so you hold the aces without risks. Well, if you want to lead you have to risk when you don't know where the cards are. You have to rely on your inside guts for an accurate reading of the next move. You're so full of arrogance that you can't tell a deuce from a king."

L. F. was stunned. To develop mature leadership ability one must have dealt with the dual sides of the coin. L. F. loved power; he had the charisma to get other people to do what he wanted. He became so accustomed to having his way that he began to lose his tolerance for frustration or opposition to his will. He had not learned the value of powerlessness. He was overdeveloped in wielding power but did not have the counter balancing insights of powerlessness. L. F. began to misread other people because he could not realistically assess the feelings of powerlessness. In fact, he could not read people. He operated solely on a clear picture of what he wanted, which led him to run over people and create roadblocks for the future.

L. F. mused about the painful lessons he had to learn to bring his personal style and power needs into a healthy balance. He chuckled to himself, "If I can do it, anyone can. Jane will make it. I know that it won't be easy, but she'll make it."

As he recalled the experiences that enabled him to balance his style, deal with his fears, develop gut-level experience with power and powerlessness, rejection and acceptance, conflict and harmony, and success as well as failure, he remembered well the painful route to leadership. He knows it is not an easy route. It takes courage, strength, and devotion to something beyond selfish interests to make the journey. He's betting that Jane will make it. She has the right stuff as raw material, and she has some seasoned leaders to help show her the way.

PERSONAL STYLE AND POWER DEVELOPMENT

Leadership requires maturity. L. F. knows there are no shortcuts to leadership. Development occurs by purposefully rising to the challenge. Maturity requires developing potential to a state of usability. L. F. accepted the leader's role in developing raw employee potential. If the leader is more unlimited, more wise, and more courageous than anyone else around, the leader is thereby the most mature for having already walked that pathway and continues to forge new levels of growth for both self and others.

Personal style and power development comprise the two poles around which people patterns align. We present four dimensions of personal style and four stages of power development as the basis for a behavioral map of leadership development:

PERSONAL STYLE	POWER DEVELOPMENT
Extroversion-Introversion	Stage I Power Dependency
Sensor-Intuitor (N)	Stage II Power Autonomy
Thinker-Feeler	Stage III Power Competition
Judge-Perceiver	Stage IV Leadership

In our book *The Leadership Equation,* we presented the premise that a balanced style equals leadership enhancement. Using the Myers-Briggs typology as the basis for systematically organizing human behavior, we assert that genuine long-term leadership requires balance of interpersonal style. Integrating preferred with least preferred personal style to achieve balance enables a person to respond fully to each situation. In this book we add the other critical part of leadership enhancement: *power development.*

Each person has a preferred personal style that is natural. Preferred style is easier and takes less energy. It's comfortable. Skills have to be developed for the least preferred style. Initially it feels awkward and uncomfortable to use the least preferred side. Mastering the skills for that side of preference leads to comfort and less energy expenditure.

Consider the following equations:

Balancing Style	= Leadership Enhancement
Balancing Extroversion and Introversion	= Energy efficiency
Balancing Sensing and Intuiting	= Clearer perception
Balancing Thinking and Feeling	= Clearer judgment
Balancing Judging and Perceiving	= Flexible directionality

People have a preference for Extroversion (outgoing activity and interaction) or Introversion (privacy and introspection), Sensing (realistic and factual) or Intuitive (abstract and imaginative), Thinking (analytical and rational) or Feeling (relationship and value-oriented), and Judging (controlling and influencing) or Perceiving (adapting and responding). Preferences determine habitual ways of seeing, deciding, communicating, and interacting. Least preferred parts of our style require more energy, feel more risky, and may increase our sense of vulnerability. Thus, we have a tendency to use that which is easier and thereby we neglect learning the skills necessary to comfortably use our least preferred side.

A person, for example, whose preferred expression is Extrovert, Sensor, Thinker, and Judge (ESTJ) needs to develop skills for utilizing Introversion, Intuiting, Feeling, and Perceiving in order to develop potential and increase leadership enhancement. Preferred style is usually better developed and more used than the least preferred, thus leaving much potential untapped.

PREFERRED STYLE (inherent tendencies of a person)
- easiest expression
- requires less energy due to familiarity
- less perceived risk
- natural

LEAST PREFERRED (learned expressions of a person)
- more difficult to develop
- requires more energy due to unfamiliarity
- more perceived risk
- unnatural

Objective: To develop potential, first identify your preferred personal style to establish a clear understanding of what is natural for you. Then you can develop a systematic plan for developing the potential of your least preferred expression.

If you have not developed skills to balance your preferred and least preferred expressions, you may be as inefficient as an unbalanced wheel. Balance increases the smoothness of the spin, develops potential, increases ease with any situation, and allows you to be more aware and sensitive to others. Balance improves your ability to get results.

BALANCE TO ENHANCE LEADERSHIP

Balance action-oriented Extroversion with introspective Introversion. Balance practical Sensing with innovative Intuiting. Balance objective analytical Thinking with the warmth of subjective Feeling. Balance Judge-controlling with Perceiving-adapting in personal style as a way of increasing your potency.

When you see someone consistently respond to any situation with clear judgment, clear perception and calm resolve, you are watching a balanced person. You are seeing the smooth flow that comes from a balanced style. Natural preferences that have been counterbalanced with excellent skills produce a center from which actions flow smoothly and effectively.

Genuine leadership is measured by what the leader influences others to do. Leaders *consistently* influence people to go beyond their perceived limits to give energies and talents to accomplish organization or group goals.

How do you recognize leadership? How do you distinguish genuine from pseudo leadership?

Critical Questions for Identifying a Leader

1. Do people grow, increase skills, discover talents, increase in strength and knowledge as a result of working with the person?

2. Do followers noticeably increase their ability to risk?

3. Does the person demonstrate continual clear perception and judgment?

4. Is the person serving something larger than self — an organizational goal, a vision that will benefit many instead of a few, a worthwhile community or national project, a principle or point of ethics, a fight for something because it is right?

If you answer "yes" to the four questions, you are identifying a leader.

Realistically, leaders have a complex set of actions and reactions. You have to observe people over time to clearly identify real leadership. By careful observation you can discern organizing patterns and formulate the answer to the four questions.

For a personal application: Have you ever worked with a genuine leader? The critical questions to ask yourself are: "Did I grow? Did my skills increase? Did I discover talents I didn't know I had? Did I increase in strength and knowledge? Did the leader force me to develop my abilities?" Don't confuse pain and pain-lessness with your judgment of leadership. There is pain in growth and there is pain in being stifled. So pain alone doesn't imply growth. Purposeful discomfort that pushes you to use your potential is the proof. Apply those same questions to the people who work with you. Do they grow and learn and develop as a result of your influence?

If you pass the tests so far, then see how you rate on the criteria for maintaining leadership capability.

Maintaining Leadership Capability

1. Do you do constant, brutal self-examination?
2. Are you on a continual self-growth course?
3. Do you do continual development of followers?
4. Are you continually focused on others and avoiding the distortions of self-focus for personal gain?
5. Are you self-motivated?
6. Do you know how to motivate others to grow, to keep the growth curve ever active?
7. Do you embrace change and welcome it as opportunity?
8. Are you centered in the midst of chaos and confusion?

Next we'll meet Don. Let's see if he passes the tests.

CASE STUDY: BALANCED LEADERSHIP

Don had been chief executive officer of a large corporation for twelve years. During that time he took a failing corporation and turned it into a profitable one. He changed the corporate culture from an abusive "win-at-any-price-no-matter-whose-throat-you-slit" to an innovative, participative, healthily competitive place to work. That was not an easy task and it did not occur overnight. He does not participate in the quick cosmetic fix where a razzle-dazzle executive comes in to do image manipulation rather than genuinely rebuild the company.

Don describes the work atmosphere twelve years ago as being analogous to a combat zone. "I am not minimizing a soldier's
experience in the brutal realities of war," he explained. "I fought
in Vietnam, so I have real experience by which to compare what
I saw. When I interviewed for the job, I noticed that people were
intense and guarded. They spoke and moved cautiously. There
were enough stories of corporate ambush to keep them looking
over their shoulders. People were uptight." Don talked about his
strategy. "I like to learn about a company as quickly as possible. I
read the paper trail and get a picture of the fiscal and physical
reality quickly. The more complex task is to get a clear picture of
the people terrain. I ask questions and I listen intently. The first
month I was here, however, my questions yielded little substantive information. What I got was a heavy dose of defensive rationale. More than telling me what they had done, I heard elaborate
defenses of why they had done what they had done. They were so
afraid of retribution that little focus was given to accomplishment."

Though Don is a leader, the CEO he replaced was a power
abuser. Don found a management group with a habitual reaction
to problems: "Find out who is responsible and make them pay."
The previous CEO had a reputation for abusive behavior. He got
in people's faces, yelling insults. He fired accusative questions at
machine-gun rate, never waiting for answers. His questions contained his judgment. He had already decided his employees were
full of stupidity and error. Meeting with him did not yield discussion; it was a barrage. He used interaction as an opportunity to
reinforce his reign of terror.

Don knew the former CEO who showed many of the characteristics of a bully. He was ingratiating to peers and demeaning to
subordinates. The former CEO used very expensive suits and
shoes as power symbols. He told power stories to impress and
distance people. The former CEO's determined efforts to shape
perception and to control his image were clear indications to
Don of the fear driving the behavior. The damage done by the
former CEO was readily seen in the frightened, defensive, cautious, and guardedly angry people he left behind.

Fear ate up their energy. The creative energy that keeps
companies alive and on the competitive edge had been usurped
by the employees' dogged need to protect their jobs. The high

morale that comes when people like their jobs and know they are doing something worthwhile was missing. The amazing problem-solving capacity of good minds was siphoned off into job-survival thinking. Truth was too expensive. The former CEO had a reputation for hanging a bloody head outside his office door once a week as a reminder to all the rest. The standard question was: "Who will it be this week?" He was so intimidating and insulting that he psychologically tortured and abused people. He literally did not understand anything about people except fear and force. That was what was driving him, although he was too blind to see himself clearly. He frequently spoke of his own fearlessness and took delight in cutting others down. He pictured himself as a giant in an organization of wimps.

Don clearly had his work cut out for him. He found managers deeply entrenched in the siege mentality — "Stay out of my department!! If anyone comes around, it only means trouble." The prevailing mood was bunker mentality, with people digging in and protecting territory. Don did not find a single manager with a reputation or track record for developing people. The energy of the company was flowing like a gusher into CYA (cover your ass) tactics. Employees had that tired, lackluster energy which was easily seen in the way they moved, talked, and interacted. They were not being renewed by the energy that comes with growing, learning new skills, and gaining new understanding. They were not alive with energy to risk. Their perception was clouded over with the negative and abusive work environment. The dominant motivation appeared to be protecting themselves.

One month after Don came to the company, he brought five people in to help him turn the company around. The company was stagnating and fearful. He decided that a crash course was necessary to get things turned around in time to survive fiscally. He infused the company with leadership and teamwork energy.

Don remembers his own leadership transformation. In the eighteen years since Don was tested, taken apart, and reshaped on an almost daily basis in Vietnam, he dedicated himself to understanding people. He became an astute reader of people and a master developer. He personally guided the development of many managers and set the model for leadership aspiration. He could look across the country and see many men and women who would eagerly jump at the chance to work for him again.

They knew that growth and opportunity were involved in working with Don. He selected five of them and set his plan in motion for turning things around.

The five new people brought different talents and skills to the executive team, but they also had some things in common. They were characteristically astute people readers with excellent communication skills. They were tough-minded thinkers with heart, integrity, and commitment to ideas larger than themselves. The key is their capability to think, feel, and act in a manner consonant with Don's managerial philosophy.

Don's market strategy, financial planning, and fiscal decisions were based upon clear, rational thought. His plan for recharging people with the excitement of learning, growing, discovering, and risking is worth looking at in more detail.

Essentially, Don's plan was clear and straightforward. He focused on an immediate, visible starting point and spent no time talking about or revisiting past company cultural norms. He knew the value of focusing energy on his vision for the company. He refused to waste time in revitalizing the past through talk. He led toward a future that he envisioned.

Don's plan for changing the company culture was: (1) demonstrate responsiveness to workers, (2) communicate his managerial philosophy, (3) replace authoritarian dominance with leadership, (4) involve people in the planning process, (5) set the pace for leadership behaviors by executive demonstration, (6) assess people's skills and abilities for better use of people resource, and (7) improve communication with customers, vendors, and community leaders.

Plan to Change the Company Culture

Don outlined his action plan:

(1) Identify worker needs for equipment or space and move quickly to update, fix, or maintain what is needed by workers. He knew the value of action. People want tangible proof of his sensitivity and responsiveness to the backbone of the company — the people who make the products.

(2) Communicate his managerial philosophy to managers immediately. He wanted the tenets of his philosophy known, demonstrated, and communicated. He wanted to change the corporate culture to establish an open, problem-identifying, prob-

lem-solving, cooperative place to work. His managerial philosophy emphasizes people, action, accountability, innovative thinking, and rational judgment. Don's managerial philosophy is:

(A) People are the most important resource we have in this company.

(B) Self-discipline and commitment are expected.

(C) Actions outweigh words and intentions.

(D) Authority should be used sparingly.

(E) Trying doesn't count; doing does.

(F) Trying and failing is acceptable if next efforts show lessons learned.

(G) Think clearly and articulate your rationale.

(H) Productivity without employee growth and development is short-term gain with long-term cost. We are interested in building solid strength for our company's future.

(I) Managers have a priority directive to develop the people resource of this company.

(J) Managers are expected to identify problems and utilize the best people in this company to solve problems. Territoriality must give way to unified and cooperative efforts.

(3) Authority was restructured with five divisions, with each of the new staff in charge of one of the five divisions. They were given one month to assess work in each area and were to involve managers and employees in rethinking the work methods. Don expected each of the five executives to be accurate in their assessments and exemplar in the way they dealt with people. He understood that the environment of distrust would be prevalent during the first six months, with building of trust accelerating during the last eighteen months of the first two years if they succeeded. Don knew that he and his initial team must earn people's trust. He knew employees currently distrusted him and his team by viewing them as outsiders. He knew his team would have to earn the right to lead, and he developed a strategy to overcome the distrust.

(4) At the end of one month, the executive team and managers would hold planning meetings. They would identify the worker-recommended changes and present to Don their addition-

al recommendations. They would present clear statements of problems they were addressing, alternatives they considered, the control variables in the problems, and their recommendations for decision. He expected those planning meetings to take approximately three months.

(5) The five executives would be expected to demonstrate Don's managerial philosophy.

(6) Don expected that he and the executives would have excellent opportunity to assess the problem-solving skills, maturity level, and habitual style of the managers by the end of his first six months. At that point, he would be ready to move or replace people to provide maximum use of people resources.

(7) Don had a plan to actively improve relationships with customers, vendors, and community leaders.

Don intended to rebuild the company with a solid foundation by putting people in jobs that best matched their next level of skill. He believed in keeping people on the growing edge. He demonstrated his talent of accurately assessing people's growing edge. He knew how to make people stretch without killing their incentive. He knew how to take them beyond the lethargy of too much comfort and familiarity without drowning them in ambiguity and fear. The relationship between stretching people for growth and breaking them by destroying their incentive is a judgment call. There is no sure-fire formula. It's an intuitive knowing that Don applies to each individual he assesses. Don's executive team used excellent people assessment skills to provide the clarity necessary for helping people grow into their potential.

The proof of Don's approach comes with the results. Within twelve months the company did not look or feel like the same place. As it turned out, most of the people were so eager to come alive again that they welcomed the change. The team established a general environment of trust sooner than originally expected. Don acted decisively to remove those managers who clung to their fearful CYA tactics. He, likewise, rewarded those who demonstrated people savvy and measurable productivity. Of the 800 people employed when Don came, 52 were fired. The common thread among those fired was their inability or unwillingness to grow. The two types of resistance to Don's managerial philosophy were those who continued to abuse power and those who continued to play it too safe to produce.

Don fired the 52 people within a 48-hour period. He acted quickly. He knew that firing people activated fear in a work force. He did not wish to produce a long period of anxiety during which people wondered about their fate. He held an employee meeting the next morning to reiterate his managerial philosophy and to share his decision rationale. He did not justify his actions. He explained his decision rationale and accepted full responsibility for the dismissals. He identified the challenges ahead and asked people for their best efforts.

By advocating a people-centered managerial philosophy, Don was under constant scrutiny. People watched him carefully to see if he were going to live up to his words. Through lessons learned, he works continually to keep his style balanced. His natural preferences are Extroversion, Intuition, Thinking, and Judging (ENTJ), but early in his career he found that he had problems getting people to work with him. That realization led to his decision to develop balance in his style. He now has a solid foundation for a flexible and genuine personality – the bedrock of leadership.

Let's turn back the pages to look at Don's ENTJ style and his point of development sixteen years earlier. He did not start his career as a seasoned leader. Earlier, as a young Extrovert, Don overwhelmed people with his speed and enthusiasm. His intuitive mind moved so rapidly to connect information that other people frequently couldn't follow what he was saying. He had great ideas but failed to communicate them because of his panoramic view of subjects. He used strong reasoning and overpowering persuasion. He could win arguments handily but in turn lost people's good will. He could overpower them into verbally giving up, but he wasn't gaining their support. When he realized that he was a superstar with no team following him, he decided he had to make some changes.

Don toned down his Extroverted energy and developed his Introverted abilities to concentrate. He worked on putting himself and others at ease. He discovered a balance. He then matched his use of energy to the situation. If the situation needed Extroverted enthusiasm, he could easily respond. If it called for Introverted focus and introspection, he could switch to that set of skills without losing his center. Don developed the skills for his least preferred side without losing his natural style.

He was sharp enough to realize that leadership requires personal stability.

At first Don's preference for Intuitive perception made him impatient with those who preferred Sensor perception. He thought Sensors were slow and tedious. He found it difficult to slow his mind to the pace of the methodical, factual approach so natural to Sensors. Before disciplining his perceptual preference, he frequently missed the other person's point. He was so preoccupied with adding and rearranging ideas that he frequently misinterpreted others. His own preference distorted messages. He had not yet learned the strengths of Sensors; he had not learned how to work well with someone whose style was not like his.

Before Don decided to consciously manage his style, he was such a strong Thinker that he frequently overlooked or discounted the emotional content of messages. His rationale included hard evidence and little emphasis on what he called "personal opinion." He dismissed emotional content as personal opinion and reasoned that it had no place in clear thinking. He overlooked the impact of feelings in his disdain for opinion. He hardly considered feelings as evidence. After years of working on balancing Thinking-Feeling, Don learned to identify behavioral indicators of feelings as inferential evidence that should not be overlooked. He found that logic convinces the head but commitment comes from the heart.

With his Judging preference, Don had to learn to balance his desire to control with learned skills of flexibility. We will review Myers-Briggs typology in later chapters. For now, we will focus on Don's evolution into leadership.

When asked if he thinks he is a leader, Don replied: "I think you will have to ask others that question. You will have to look at my track record. If you don't find evidence of achievement and people development, then I can't claim the title. I think leadership has to be conferred by others. I don't think it's a term I can claim and make it stick. I think I have to earn the title with repeated performance. Ask the people who work with me. They know whether I am a leader or not."

To decide if Don is a leader, ask the critical questions: Do people grow, increase skills, discover talents, gain strength and knowledge as a result of working with him? Do they noticeably increase their ability to risk? Does Don demonstrate clear perception and judgment? Is he serving something larger than himself? You can form your position, but these questions are best answered by those who work for him.

LEADERSHIP

We distinguish between the terms *leadership, management,* and *gamesmanship.* We define *management* as getting work done through others by utilizing planning, organizing, implementing, and evaluation skills — managing basic routines efficiently. We define *gamesmanship* as manipulating people for personal gain. We see *leadership* as a dynamic process of judgment and communication that guides others toward positive personal and organizational achievement. Leadership is the mature use of power to enable others to achieve higher goals.

Over 350 definitions of leadership exist. Notable definitions include Bennis and Nanus' concept in their 1985 book entitled *Leaders:* "Power is the basic energy needed to initiate and sustain action or, to put it another way, the capacity to translate intention into reality and sustain it. Leadership is the wise use of this power: Transformative leadership." (pg. 17) In Kotter's book *The Leadership Factor,* he defines leadership as "the process of moving a group (or groups) in some direction through mostly noncoercive means. Effective leadership is defined as leadership that produces movement in the long-term best interest of the group(s)." (pg. 5) In 1925 the U.S. Military Academy defined leadership as "the art of imposing one's will upon others in such a manner as to command their obedience, their confidence, their respect, and their loyal cooperation." (*The Psychology of Military Leadership,* pg. 102) A more recent military leadership document reads: "Military leadership is a process by which a soldier influences others to accomplish the mission." (pg. 44)

One point of agreement among the definitions is the *dynamic process* of leadership. The nature of leadership is determined by two critical factors: the use of power and personal style. We will continue the discussion of personal style development later and focus now on the use of power.

POWER DEVELOPMENT

David McClelland's work on the power motive provided a framework for our research into leadership. He defined four modalities for classifying power and described power in four stages: dependency, autonomy, assertion, and maturity. We adapted McClelland's four development stages of power. We observed managers' behaviors through rigorous observation and documentation of power in companies and organizations. To describe the four stages of power orientation, we noted the dual nature of power in each stage.

Each stage of power orientation has a more subtle manipulation that is not as negative in appearance as well as a more obvious manipulation that is easily identified as negative use of power.

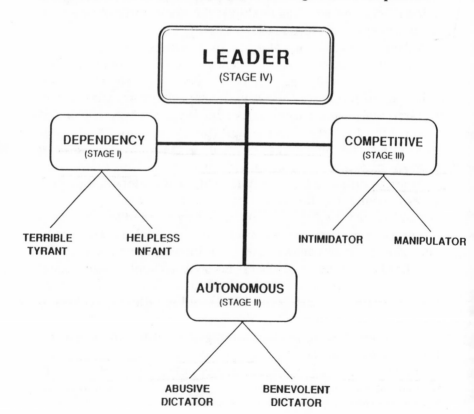

How do you hit the bullseye? How do you maintain balance without slipping off into one of the other stages of power and getting stuck there? How do you recognize when to use various stages of power? We have identified eight roles that capture the behaviors within the four stages.

Stage I power users play the role of Helpless Infant or Terrible Tyrant. The purpose of both roles is to make others responsible for them. As they abdicate responsibility for what happens to them, they become dependent on making other people take care of them. The Helpless Infant manipulates through guilt, helplessness, and passive aggression (term used descriptively and not as a clinical diagnosis). The Terrible Tyrant intimidates through emotional tantrums, threats, and insults. Stage I power users switch roles if they don't get what they want, but they are more habituated to one or the other role.

Stage II power users play the roles of Benevolent or Abusive Dictator. Driven by a desire to be independent and in control, they do whatever it takes to force people to let them have their way. The Benevolent Dictator acts like a generous parent when others (the children) do what they want. When thwarted, however, they can easily become Abusive Dictators who feel fully justified in dumping their wrath on others. They defend their abuse by asserting "You made me do this." They hold others responsible for failure, but quickly grab the praise for themselves.

The Benevolent Dictator role is not as personally expensive as the abusive role. The Benevolent Dictator takes on the "nice person" role. Since it is more difficult to detect the selfish interest driving that role, clear perception is critical. The Abusive Dictator role is easier to recognize, though more costly. The American sense of fair play is easily aroused by openly aggressive or hostile acts. Therefore we see more Benevolent Dictators than Abusive ones. The cost of subtle manipulation does not appear to be as great as open attack.

Stage III power users play the role of Competitive Manipulator or Competitive Intimidator. They are driven by a need to make themselves look good at other people's expense. The Competitive Manipulator is harder to detect than the Intimidator. The Manipulator competes to win but likes to take a magnanimous view by pretending to win graciously. Having no such inhibitions, Competitive Intimidators like to win and humiliate simultaneously. Winning ceases to be enough to satisfy their bloated egos; they like to humiliate or destroy the competition. Again, it is a more easily identified role, thereby carrying a higher cost.

Stage IV power users play whatever role works. At times they will play the Inspirational Leader role and at other times they will be the Fearsome Leader. Mature use of power is only acquired after tremendous testing and self-discovery. To maintain mature use of power, continual brutal self-examination must be done. Power is seductive. The ability to rationalize our actions is a potent trap.

STAGE IV LEADERSHIP

Stage IV is the power orientation that we call leadership. Strength and courage characterize Stage IV. It can take the form of Inspirational Leader or Fearsome Leader. Either form is a force to be reckoned with. The Inspirational Leader role draws best effort from followers through a combination of inspiration, guidance, and trust. The Fearsome Leader forces risk and growth by becoming more dreaded than the followers' internal fears that block development of potential.

The leader has the vision to see what needs to be done and the toughness to stand alone when necessary. Stage IV Leaders have inner direction and do not need others' approval. They are willing and able to endure followers' anger and resistance for the growth period when the followers are not clear enough to see that the struggle produces growth. Leaders frequently lead people in directions they do not want to go. The force of the leader's personal style provides incentive for risk and the attendant opportunity for growth.

Many people confuse leadership with comfort. However, leaders cause people to stretch and risk – a condition that is rarely comfortable.

Stage IV Leaders have paid dues by confronting themselves. They know their strengths and weaknesses, their fears and hopes. They have reached a mature use of power by arduous growth and testing. They have personally evolved to the point that working for something beyond themselves is the only worthwhile use of power. They have evolved past the ego-centered use of power.

Stage III power users are hooked on competing and beating someone. Winning is the only acceptable outcome. Stage II power users want autonomy and control and do not value teamwork or cooperation. Stage I power users are stuck in dependency and manipulating others to take care of them. Stage IV is the only stage of power use that qualifies as the *foundation* for leadership.

Stage IV Leaders are motivated by helping others develop and focus energy to achieve organizational goals. Leaders drive for goals that supersede personal interests. Potency exponentially increases when individuals join together in a shared effort to do a worthwhile mission. Stage IVs truly understand synergy. They know that sharing power increases the potential to achieve more. They know that empowerment works.

Understanding both the challenge and potency of teams, leaders help people develop teamwork. Cooperation is the theme, with healthy competition as the spur toward excellence. They keep the focus on growth, productivity, and high standards.

Inspirational Leaders stir followers to reach toward excellence and superior achievement. Using a mixture of challenge, acceptance, esprit de corps and shared vision, Inspirational Leaders inspire followers to creatively and continually develop greater capacity to give. Through giving to something larger and more worthwhile than selfish self-focus, followers grow and move toward Stage IV development.

Fearsome Leaders use whatever methods necessary to get people to develop potential. Because Stage IVs have explored their own fears and limits, they are free to play any role required to push a subordinate to develop. They are free to use coercion, force, threat, challenge, or reward. They develop followers by applying either negative or positive forces — whatever it takes to urge the subordinate off the fence of mediocrity and on to the road of superior performance.

If you were expecting a simple formula for one of the highest levels of development, you won't find it here. Are you questioning whether a Fearsome Leader is showing genuine leadership? Does the Fearsome Leader look and sound too much like an abusive power player?

If balanced style allows a person to appropriately respond to the situation, then we must consider that a Fearsome Leader approach may be situationally appropriate. Genuine leaders find themselves responding in all eight of the power roles at one time or another. Sometimes their behavior looks abusive, mismatched with the situation, excessive. Infrequent observers will have trouble reading the long-term effect of the leader's behavior. Remember the test: Are people strengthened, toughened, supported, developed? Without clear perception, it is difficult to see beneath the appearance and discover the process at work. Without genuine internal balance, it is too easy to get caught up in one of the roles and begin using it inappropriately.

Think about a painful experience from the past. Examine it carefully to see what you learned. What did you discover about yourself? Are you stronger and more knowledgeable for having gone through the experience? People have to pay for excellence. We admire athletes who strenuously adhere to rigid work regimens to bring their bodies and minds into harmony. Is it not reasonable to assume, then, that leadership as one of the most important development processes would also be strenuous, difficult, rewarding, and painful? Why should developing mature use of power be excluded from this pattern?

Only those who have walked the difficult pathway of self-knowledge and risk-taking understand how to bring someone else through it.

Stage IV Leaders are cooperative out of strength and free choice. They do not cooperate because they are afraid of the consequences of not cooperating. They are strong enough to do what is necessary. Inspirational Leaders choose cooperation out of strength but are willing and capable of meeting others in whatever style is demanded. They approach an interaction with a preference for cooperation — not a *need* for it. If the leader needs to slip into Fearsome Leader, it is done without loss of internal balance or clarity. The leader can intimidate or inspire — whatever style is needed.

A genuine leader does not throw power around. S/He has no need to display power for egotistical, self-serving reasons. Leaders frequently use cooperative methods. People who are stuck in one of the other uses of power (Stage III Competitor, Stage II Dictator, or Stage I Dependent) frequently underestimate the Stage IV Leader, since most people see power as aggressive and intimidating. Sometimes other stages miss the genuine strength because of too much familiarity with force and manipulation as expressions of power. They may be unaccustomed to seeing the potency of cooperative, clear, direct leadership.

Stage IV Leaders accept complete responsibility for what they do, think, feel, and are. They see themselves as responsible and as models for accepting responsibility for achieving goals. Self-respect, personal integrity, dynamic energy, and the ability to both envision and execute the vision characterize leaders. They see beyond appearance, beyond obstacles, beyond selfishness, and beyond today's pain to achieve the vision. They use whatever communication style conveys the meaning in the way most appropriate to the goal. They might be charismatic and persuasive, blunt and forceful, inspirational and fearsome. They project presence, possibility, and achievement. Balancing interpersonal style and developing mature use of power are the foundation for Stage IV Leadership.

PSEUDO LEADERSHIP – POWER PLAYERS

Pseudo leadership is based on an egoic need to feel good and maintain control. The pseudo leader demands compliance, agreement, and personal egoic bathing. Only "yes" people are allowed into the inner sanctum of the pseudo leader's presence. The pseudo leader becomes enamored with the praise and agreement and loses realistic perception. No longer will bad or disagreeable news be tolerated. The pseudo leader begins to believe in his/her own invincibility, specialness, and superiority to such an extent that reality is blocked and no longer is perception accurate. Hitler could not recognize the factual evidence that he was losing the war. He believed that the force of his personal will could alter the facts. He distorted the facts and blamed people for upsetting him. Mussolini ignored the facts and lost his ability to assess the real situation.

The real test: Can the leader keep it together when all hell breaks loose? Can the leader see clearly amidst the panic? Can the leader judge accurately when issues and events are in disarray? Can the leader think clearly in chaos, threat, and uncertainty? If you are observing a Stage IV Leader, you could answer yes to all of those questions.

Leaders are distinguished from power players by observation of their intention, influence methods, ethics, and effect on people. Power players are consumed with self-interest, self-importance, domination, and control. The way they operate reveals them. Their own interests are put above the organization. Their self-importance comes out as superiority of always being right and tolerating no criticism. They dominate by overriding opposition by any means required. They control by single-minded determination to get their way. They do not listen nor do they seek clear input; they demand compliance.

Clear thinking is required as we question intention, influence methods, ethics, and effect on others:

Intention: What is the person's intent? Are the actions, attitudes, and motives to get something for themselves, for personal aggrandizement, and to promote self-interest at others' expense? Leaders intend to achieve the greatest benefit for people, mission, and the organization.

Power players are supreme egotists, driven by their intention to gain personally. Leaders are mature enough to demonstrate intense personal discipline of their own egoic nature in order to repeatedly act in the best interests of others.

Influence methods: How does the person influence others? Do you observe intimidation, discounting, and domination? Does the person use force, ridicule, humiliation, or insincere ego-stroking to manipulate outcome? Leaders involve others, get their commitment, stimulate them to perform and contribute their best. Leaders use challenge, wisdom, opportunity, confrontation of real issues, and clear feedback.

Power players do whatever it takes to get their way. They run right over people who resist with either the force of humiliation or the force of flattery — whatever it takes.

Power players at their most private level do not feel restricted by rigid ethical codes. They fool themselves into believing that what they want *is* what's best for the organization. Leaders understand people, different styles, and individual motivations. Leaders draw from people their own best efforts by providing clear challenges, candid feedback, purposeful action, and clearly understood vision.

Ethics: Is the person consistent in ethical standards? Are professional standards applied? Are people's concerns and values fairly considered? Does the person operate within acceptable limits of honesty, candor, integrity, competency, and trustworthiness? OR, are ethics situational, purely dependent upon what is wanted?

Power players frame ethics in terms of personal desires and frequently rearrange standards to get them what they want. They reframe the ethics framework easily. Leaders operate from dependable, consistent ethics of clear perception and sound judgment while demonstrating a wide range of behavior.

Effect on others: Does the person control and dominate? Does the person cause others to do bare minimum work? Does the person demand mindless compliance? Is the person surrounded with dependent people who are programmed to agree with the power player? Leaders cause others to want to give best efforts. Leaders are continually drawing people toward them and helping them experience growth that sets them free from their own limitations, thus creating greater strength and maturity.

Power players cause others to be dependent upon them for supplies, information, direction, and approval. They do not encourage free thinking nor independent, innovative effort. Leaders cause people to do their best in thought, action, and response. Leaders help people discover significant lessons from their failed efforts while encouraging them to continue growing and risking. People discover talents and abilities that they were unaware of until the leader framed the challenge, supported them as they struggled, provided the opportunity, and led the way.

Stage IV Leaders have developed skills to balance their preferred style and have developed mature use of power that comes only through rigorous confrontation of fears and vulnerability of growth.

To increase your ability to accurately read people and to recognize patterns of power use, we offer the developmental exercises for Chapter 1.

DEVELOPMENTAL EXERCISES

Exercise 1:   Stage IV Organizational Culture

"The test of a leader lies in the reaction and response of his followers." — General Omar N. Bradley

Select an organization or a work group with which you are quite familiar. Examine it to see if it has the organizational culture that results when leadership is present. Identify the organizational culture by the behaviors of people who work there. Check *yes* or *no* in the appropriate column to evaluate the organizational culture.

PEOPLE: THE LIVING ORGANIZATION

Yes No

___ ___ People are continually challenged by the leader and the insistence on excellence.

___ ___ Leader understands human behavior — reads people, matches people, develops people, and motivates or inspires people for the overall result of excellent achievement of both individual and group goals.

___ ___ Leader demonstrates "others first" behavior by putting the mission and team development ahead of personal interests.

___ ___ Leader consistently demonstrates responsible use of power and does not rely heavily on formal authority to command.

___ ___ Leader consistently demonstrates the right to lead through clear perception, clear judgment, and pace-setting behavior.

___ ___ Leader intuitively reads future demands and leads the organization/group on a readiness course to meet the demands.

___ ___ Participation and cooperation are the norm (expected).

___ ___ Conflict and competition are seen as normal outcomes of motivated people working together. Positive confrontation is used to deal with conflict. Full force competition is focused on problems and market competitors, not on others in the organization.

___ ___ Mature acceptance of responsibility is expected; no

"passing the buck" is tolerated — only a clear statement of the situational factors and commitment to action is acceptable.

_____ _____ High expectations are the norm.

_____ _____ Followers feel free to identify problems.

_____ _____ Decisions include assessment of impact on other parts of the organization. Organizational mission supersedes territoriality.

_____ _____ Inappropriate behavior is confronted immediately, clear appropriate behaviors are identified, improved behavior is contracted either formally or informally, measurable performance objectives are set, and behavioral change is assessed periodically. Irresponsible or counterproductive behavior is not tolerated.

_____ _____ Followers show ownership of the mission by continuous innovation for improved productivity.

_____ _____ People like working there.

_____ _____ People know they are valued and respected. They know that the living organization is the foundation for the technical, formal, structural organization. They know that the leader demonstrates that people are more important than the buildings, machines, and paper.

SUMMARIZE: Identify the strengths and weaknesses of the organizational culture and what can be done to focus on continuous improvement:

YES Topics (Strengths)

NO Topics (Weaknesses)

SUGGESTIONS FOR CONTINUOUS IMPROVEMENT:

Exercise 2: Stage IV Leadership Behaviors

Leaders are involved in a dynamic process of influencing people to give their energies to accomplish organization or group goals while simultaneously developing their potential. A leader is a person who

- attracts people
- understands human behavior
- motivates and inspires
- communicates effectively
- sees the vision

- expresses winning attitudes
- projects presence/confidence
- sets the example of excellence
- does what is needed
- maintains integrity

Evaluate yourself against the behavioral indicators for Stage IV Leaders. Rate the extent to which you believe the behaviors are true for you. Use a scale of 1 (low) to 9 (high) to rate the extent to which each of the following behaviors characterizes you.

____ Read people accurately. Rarely fooled in assessment of people.

____ Actively involved in helping people develop skills.

____ Continually finding growth opportunities for employees.

____ Effective in building strong team relationships.

____ Action-oriented with enough strength to do what has to be done without letting personal egotism push others around.

___ Confident enough to ask for help when you need it.

____ Give clear, accurate, adequate information.

____ Able to sell ideas and win commitment.

____ Refuse to be intimidated. Step right up to a problem and confront it.

____ Confront issues and negotiate effectively.

____ Behave rationally and compassionately in handling conflict.

____ Confront dysfunctional behavior so clearly that people know what specific behaviors have to be changed, then you systematically assess the behavior change required.

____ Encourage and anticipate questions, opposite viewpoints, and open discussion.

____ Give others clear, descriptive, useful feedback.

____ Support people . . . back people . . . enable them to risk and learn.

____ Hold people fully responsible for their commitments.

____ Listen actively and ask probing, clarifying, reflective questions.

____ Help others solve problems through tough, mind-expanding discussion.

____ Require rational problem-solving behavior when appropriate; require intuitive, risk-taking behavior when appropriate.

____ Accept responsibility and expect others to do the same.

____ Admit mistakes and openly examine reasons and thought processes involved.

____ Demand growth and excellence for self and others.

____ Know clearly your strengths and weaknesses.

____ Do continual brutal, honest self-examination to keep clear perception and judgment.

____ Work continually on balancing natural preferences with learned skills.

____ Accept change as natural phenomena and set the pace and direction.

____ Continually discard obsolete methods, ideas, or behaviors.

____ Find continual ways to learn, adapt, and expand.

____ Feel comfortable with power and authority.

____ Know powerlessness as well as powerfulness and demonstrate wisdom that comes from being well developed in both sides of power. Demonstrate fearlessness of both power and powerlessness.

____ Demonstrate preference for cooperation without demonstrating a *need* for it. Cooperation is a preference, not a weakness due to a fear of confrontation.

____ Develop innovation and creativity in self and others.

Add up your scores to assess your Stage IV behaviors:

Scores 224–288 indicate perception of *superior* Stage IV behaviors

Scores 160–223 indicate perception of *average* Stage IV behaviors

Scores 96-159 indicate perception of *lack of adequate* Stage IV behaviors

Scores 32-95 indicate perception of *absence* of enough Stage IV behaviors

Ask someone who knows you well to assess you on these behaviors.

Exercise 3:   Stage III Competitive Intimidator Behaviors

Stage III power players are propelled by competition as a driving force. Impulsive aggressive actions or carefully planned moves against others dominate Stage III behaviors.

Stage III players need to defeat others or put others down in order to maximize their feelings of power. They see their boss and other people as competitors to be beaten or controlled. They see themselves as the source of power, and their endeavors must be measured on a win-lose continuum.

Select someone you believe is a Competitive Intimidator and check the following behaviors of Stage III players to see if your inference is accurate.

COMPETITIVE INTIMIDATORS . . .

_____ Own numerous "status" possessions and use their possessions as evidence of superiority.

_____ Sprinkle conversation with names of powerful people and imply personal relationships to give them more implied status.

_____ Take pride in having "insider" networks, implying advance information, special privilege, and exclusive membership.

_____ Make themselves look important by sending someone else to "fetch" things . . . sending "minions" to do the unimportant.

_____ Ask penetrating questions designed to put others down, or make personal remarks to throw others off balance and into reactionary states.

_____ Use subtle insult through innuendo that challenges the credibility of someone else's idea.

_____ Use humor viciously to insult and embarrass.

_____ Use cruel insult by probing sensitive areas.

____ Find an area of weakness or lack of knowledge in someone and then take the person apart mercilessly.

____ Assign menial tasks for revenge.

____ Try to scare people into complying.

____ Willing and able to do emotional violence by using temper as a weapon.

____ Attack a person's pride, hoping to stir up anger and fear, then attack credibility.

____ Grab others' territory and resources and fight brutally to protect own turf.

____ Are up-to-date on rules and regulations in order to catch violators and expose them.

____ Play Eric Berne's game of confrontation (NIGYSOB — Now I Got You, You SOB) by finding slightest slip-up and tearing the person to pieces; good at "gotchas" and guilt.

____ Tell numerous "power" stories about how tough or right they are.

____ Develop a surveillance network for information by getting people indebted and then coercing them into revealing information.

____ Will not accept responsibility for error — "It's someone else's fault." They pass the buck.

____ Try to keep others off balance through unpredictable behavior by alternating sociability with cutthroat attack and insults, compliments with sarcasm, and cooperation with attack.

____ Try to win the favor of powerful people who can help them advance.

____ Try to sabotage others who are rising to positions of power similar to or below their status level.

____ Like to intimidate with intellectual reasoning.

____ Are on continual guard against retaliation or usurpation. "Keep your guard up at all times" is the motto.

Review the Competitive Intimidator checklist a second time to identify those behaviors that you use frequently. Stage III power orientation is one that every person uses at one time or another, even if it is only used during a loss of temper or an expression of anger. Leaders must be very aware of these behaviors in self and others.

Exercise 4:   Stage III Competitive Manipulator Behaviors

Stage III power players using the Competitive Manipulator role are not as easy to spot as Competitive Intimidators. Manipulators use a blend of charm, challenge, and befriending to get what they want from others. They are driven by a need to win and be liked and admired for winning. Their internal drive is usually monitored by the command thoughts: "I will defeat you and show you the model of winning behavior. I am the essence of good sportsmanship. I will beat you, but be magnanimous about it." When Competitive Manipulators lose, they usually grandly accept responsibility for the loss, while subtly implying that someone else really failed but they are noble enough to cover up and accept the undeserved blame. They thereby elevate themselves to a heroic model of good sportsmanship.

Identify someone whom you believe to be a Competitive Manipulator and check the following behaviors. Another alternative is to see how many of the following behaviors you manifest regularly.

COMPETITIVE MANIPULATORS . . .

_____ Tell power stories and exaggerate their sportsmanlike role in the victory.

_____ Practice image control by using carefully placed rumor and power stories to promote the winning image.

_____ Try to disarm others with friendliness in order to get information that they may subtly use to hurt someone with later. They frequently use happy hour or some informal social occasion to create a friendly arena to get people to talk.

_____ When leaving a job or committee, Manipulators try to split their job into several duties so no one can effectively take their place — thus enhancing their reputation for having "shoes that no one can fill."

_____ Have a tremendous need to be right . . . to win.

_____ Use charm, humor, salesmanship, flattery, looks, power dressing, and appearance of cooperation to set up positive reactions in others.

_____ Try to challenge, then befriend their opponents.

_____ See boss as a prime object to manipulate.

_____ Use status symbols to promote themselves as winners — very conscious of living in the right spot in town, driving the right car, and owning the right status "toys" designed to promote the Manipulator's right to win . . . "I deserve it."

_____ Appear to be good-natured about winning to defray the interpersonal cost.

_____ Appeal to a person's sense of pride and flatter outrageously at times.

_____ Get people to commit to do tasks by withholding critical information about the difficulty of the task. After getting the other person to commit and generously flattering and thanking the person, the manipulator abandons the task. By the time the person realizes the set-up, the mechanism of doubt is in place. "Surely s/he didn't know that this was going to turn into such a hard job."

_____ Carefully project the notion that the positive regard of the Manipulator will yield profitable connections and career opportunities.

_____ Project that style more than knowledge wins the argument.

_____ Set others up to look bad in front of the boss. The Manipulator finds out an adversary is under time or schedule pressure, then asks the person to accept additional tasks in front of others — making the person look less committed.

Exercise 5: Dealing with Stage III Behavior

Habitual Stage III power players are gamesmen who capitalize on surprise, control, and manipulation to get what they want. They either consciously or unconsciously try to incite some form of fearful reaction in their adversaries. To prepare to deal with Stage IIIs, you begin with a thorough awareness of your own fears that manipulators and intimidators try to use against you.

Ironically, they, too, are driven by fears, though they project themselves as fearless. They cover their fears by causing other people to react defensively. The power high they get from beating others helps to cover up their own insecurities and fear-driven behavior.

Step 1 Make a list of the projections that bother you the most. Identify the kinds of statements, attitudes, or nonverbal behaviors that are likely to cause a disquieting emotional reaction in you. For example:

"You're too stupid to understand."

"You're not good enough."

"I can't believe someone with your background could have done that."

"Why do you buy such cheap stuff?"

"I need to give this project to someone with more experience and dedication than you."

"You're too old . . . out of touch."

"You're too young to have sound judgment."

Tell how you respond to attitudes and behaviors
   . . . that reject your contribution or worth
   . . . that treat you like a failure, a klutz, or inadequate
   . . . that ignore you
   . . . that threaten your reputation, your physical or mental
         well-being
   . . . that threaten your ability to produce
   . . . that judge you to be incompetent

Think of someone who easily makes you angry or irritated. What are the projections that push your reactionary buttons? List them. It annoys me when people . . .

Step 2 Examine the fears that drive a person's need to win to unhealthy proportions:

Fear of failure ("You can't cut it; you'll be humiliated.")

Fear of powerlessness ("There's nothing you can do.")

Fear of ridicule ("What a stupid thing to do!")

Fear of inadequacy ("You really aren't smart enough.")
Fear of impotence ("You're a wimp, a pushover, an ass.")
Fear of rejection ("I hate you! Get out!")

Step 3 Confront your own fears through carefully reviewing an interaction you have had with a Competitive Manipulator and with a Competitive Intimidator. Note the way you felt, what you thought, how you acted. Become very familiar with your own fears. Confront them.

Step 4 Recall a time when you were a Competitive Manipulator or Intimidator. Remember how you felt and how you treated your adversary. You can gain rich insights into the roles.

Step 5 Balance your style by examining your weaknesses thoroughly.

Exercise 6:   Stage II Abusive Dictators

Stage II power roles use autonomy as a control mechanism. They keep others at a distance by intimidation or parental roles. They demand independence but are unaware that their insistence on autonomy actually creates the dependency they profess to disdain. They try to avoid involvement as a way of keeping others from getting close enough to make demands. Dictators want to be in control while being unemotionally involved. Dictators try to increase their own power by *withholding information, energy, people, and resources.* By withholding they try to ensure their ability to say "No" or their ability to have information that no one else has.

Dictators use coercive and reward power as their main sources of power. They coerce through withholding until their desires are met and reward through dispensing when they are getting what they want. They seldom admit fault but like to catch others in error.

Recall someone whom you would describe as a Stage II Dictator. Check the following behaviors that describe the person.

ABUSIVE DICTATORS . . .

_____ Refuse to delegate. Have everyone report directly to them to maximize control.

_____ Close off lines of communication between subordinates and other parts of the organization.

_____ "Forget" to have staff meetings so information won't be shared.

_____ Act as critical parents and punish bad children (employees).

_____ See their bosses as critical, bad parents . . . continually ridicule their bosses as not knowing what's going on.

_____ Demand to be left alone by other departments . . . tolerate no interference in their domain.

_____ Find a way to resist following orders, while demanding that subordinates be absolutely obedient.

_____ Use anger to intimidate others into compliance . . . threaten to get upset or to make others miserable.

_____ Attack subordinates by pointing out failures and criticizing them in front of others as "bad children" for being so stupid.

_____ Try to control through projecting aloof superiority.

_____ Make self look good by making others look bad.

_____ Play perpetual Monday Morning Quarterback by readily criticizing other people's efforts with remarks such as "I knew that wouldn't work," "If you'd asked me, I could have kept you from messing up, but you didn't ask," and "I told you so."

_____ When a subordinate messes up, the Dictator "rubs the person's nose in it," and ridicules the subordinate frequently about the painful incident, while projecting their own superiority in judging the inferiority of the subordinate's actions.

_____ Have a "know-it-all-attitude" – not open to opposite views.

_____ Manage to guilt by helping people who are in trouble as a means of creating indebtedness so the Dictator can increase power over them.

_____ Can be cruel and humorless.

_____ Make assignments in small increments so subordinates cannot see clearly how their work fits with others. Give assignments out of any recognizable context to give the Dictator more control.

_____ Use employee dependency to create frustrated high activity level. The frantic nature of the chaotic activity can fool others into thinking the Dictator's people are overworked.

Exercise 7: Stage II Benevolent Dictators

Benevolent Dictators play the good parent role and they protect the "children" who work for them in much the same way as a controlling, doting parent does. In turn, Benevolent Dictators see their boss as a good parent to please, thereby trying to placate and manipulate authority into treating them with the special status of "good child."

Benevolent Dictators see themselves as the all-powerful person who knows what's best for others. They usually avoid open conflict and rely heavily on passive aggression, avoidance, and guilting techniques to get what they want.

Identify someone whom you believe to be a Benevolent Dictator. Check the behaviors you have observed that person exhibit.

BENEVOLENT DICTATORS . . .

_____ Do not like to delegate . . . like to have subordinates report directly . . . may use supervisors but don't allow them the decision-making authority to do the job . . . keep people dependent.

_____ Manage by confusion through withholding information.

_____ Give each subordinate a slightly different impression of company goals or objectives of projects to keep the Dictator controlling the information.

_____ Give assignments to more than one subordinate without telling them, in order to keep subordinates distrusting each other.

_____ Pour on the work without giving authority to organize or prioritize the work . . . create a state of perpetual dependency.

_____ Give assignments in such a way that no one but the Dictator has an overview of where the pieces fit.

_____ Try to assign all work, maintain schedules, set deadlines.

_____ Tend to overcommit staff so they will be over budget, behind schedule and generally dispirited — setting the condition for the Benevolent Dictator to dispense mercy or forgiveness.

_____ Don't define work well so employees don't have enough information to judge how things are going; thus, they are dependent upon the Benevolent Dictator for evaluation and guidance.

_____ Keep information coming from other departments separate and disorganized.

_____ Discourage intercommunication — especially anything of a planning nature.

_____ Use attitude or behaviors such as "Just take care of your work and let me worry about the rest."

_____ Choose the "nice person" approach to get more positive acceptance, thereby creating less resistance to their control.

_____ Don't admit fault . . . make excuses . . . find someone to blame.

Remember: Dictators are driven by dual fears of commitment and rejection. They prefer kingdoms to managerial responsibility. They play their roles in order to keep people from getting close enough to steal power or make demands. They are terrified of being out of control; thus, they rely on rigid parental roles with employees. They use some form of bribery (dispensing or denying privilege) to avoid employee resistance to their projected right to parent and dominate. They don't want mutiny.

Dictators are afraid of the balanced openness of genuine leadership. Dictators rely on rigidity to keep their fear suppressed. They have rules of the way they must be treated and how "good" employees will act. The most effective strategy for dealing with Dictators is balanced openness which allows a Leader *to respond situationally.* Dictators spend much energy trying *to control situations.*

Exercise 8: Stage I Terrible Tyrants

Stage I power players use dependency as a control mechanism, thus manipulating others into taking care of the difficult parts of a job. This tactic could be called the "ball and chain" method of dependency. You can sometimes identify this use of power more easily in relationships such as husband-wife, parent-child, expert-novice, older-younger. However, some Stage I power users, unfortunately, have management jobs. We have found Stage I players in every organization.

Stage I players increase power by getting more powerful others to accept responsibility for them. They are usually clever at selecting and attaching themselves to powerful others. Dependent persons see others as powerful, so they concentrate on manipulating powerful others for protection. Stage I players project "Take care of me and I will reward you with compliments and excellent public relations. I will tell others how wonderful you are." The potential damage they can do to your reputation is inherent in the projected reward. The moment you disappoint Stage I types, they bring incredible guilting techniques to bear while feeling they have the right to do so.

Identify someone whom you believe to be stuck in a Stage I Terrible Tyrant role. A telling behavior is the threat to throw an emotional display of displeasure if not appeased. When you see that behavior, you are dealing with a Terrible Tyrant — one who will issue an immature, childlike threat to have a temper tantrum if s/he doesn't get appeasement.

Terrible Tyrants . . .

____ Use emotional blackmail by threatening to throw emotional tantrums if not mollified; willing to scream, curse, or insult to get their way.

____ Condition others to placate so they won't *have* to throw tantrums, thus making others responsible for keeping them "nice."

____ Use anger like a weapon, promoting their tough reputation.

____ Are afraid of conflict unless they are causing it.

____ Are afraid of failure so they won't take responsibility for error. They like to punish others for wrongdoing.

_____ Use surprise attack and personal insult to promote reputations for vengeance, thus manipulating people to try to "stay on my good side . . . don't make me mad or you'll really be sorry."

_____ Use clever irrationality to frustrate others who rely on rationality for the basis of a comfortable interaction.

Remember: Terrible Tyrants count on other people being embarrassed at emotional tantrums. They capitalize on the fact that civilized societies take pride in controlling emotions; therefore Tyrants can tyrannize an office just by their willingness to yell and rage. They become office bullies and frequently amass lots of privileges just because people have been conditioned not to make them angry, thus letting them have their way. When you confront an office bully, be prepared for word or task ambush, frontal verbal attack, vicious use of the rumor mill, and remarkably accurate probe of your sensitive issues. And don't forget that Terrible Tyrants specialize in emotional intimidation.

Tyrants can be confronted. Prepare yourself for emotional intimidation and the attendant pain and discomfort that always comes as part of the price for challenging a bully.

Exercise 9:   Stage I Helpless Infants

Stage I Helpless Infant types are terrified of open conflict. They have enormous need to please others. They choose the "nice" approach to dependency hoping to get more potential guilting power, which results in more control of others while pretending to be helpless. They see the "nice" approach as a useful way to please others and get what they want simultaneously.

Helpless Infant types refuse to take responsibility for error. They use denial, blame, or martyr-like acceptance of blame. They seek peace at any cost, smooth potential conflict, hide their anger and then punish through passive aggression. They can "nice you to nausea." Being nice while getting even is the passive aggressive cover that protects Helpless Infants from negativity usually associated with Terrible Tyrant tantrums. When disagreement occurs, Helpless Infants withdraw, avoid, and smooth over signs of conflict. They bury their anger but don't forget it — they get even in passive-aggressive ways.

Helpless Infants operate from a hidden sense of superiority. They perceive that their niceness gives them a "purity" point of view. On the surface Helpless Infants appear to be nice, cooperative, and complimentary; yet, internally they judge harshly and find fault. The surface niceness camouflages the internal harsh judgment, so little evidence shows on the surface of the demanding manipulation underneath. Helpless Infants continually get others to take care of them, while expertly guilting them for not caretaking perfectly. They are quite skillful in making other people feel guilt by blaming them for even letting the problem occur.

Helpless Infant types play roles superbly. They frequently play best the Christian caricature — projecting that they are "too saintly" to hurt others, offend others, curse, display anger, or in any way be anything other than nice. By carefully controlling their image of "nice person" they make it expensive for anyone to confront them. They manipulate the crowd to feel sorry for them; therefore, anyone who hurts them has to pay the cost of being seen as picking on a "nice person" who is good to everyone, thus setting up the bully image. Helpless Infants make it risky to displease them. They can poison the rumor mill with their "caring concerns."

HELPLESS INFANTS . . .

_____ Control others while pretending to be helpless.

_____ Insult you while pretending to be interested in your welfare.

_____ Use blame, denial, or martyr-like acceptance of blame.

_____ Manipulate sympathy to get reassuring warm fuzzies by using such phrases as "I can't do anything right," "I always mess up," "I try so hard, but I just can't please you," "I tried, but you wouldn't let me."

_____ Avoid people who give upsetting information.

_____ Blame others for their own emotional state.

_____ Avoid open conflict.

_____ Are afraid of open discussion.

_____ See open conflict as dangerous and negative; therefore, at first signal they try to withdraw, avoid, or smooth over.

_____ Get even no matter how long it takes.

_____ Bring up old hurts that happened months or even years ago.

_____ Project superiority to conflict and patronizingly dismiss displays of aggression as childish . . . projecting "I'm too nice to act like that."

_____ Are afraid of confrontation, rejection, failure, and anger.

_____ Give lavish compliments as a means of guilting others into taking better care of them . . . and doing it *right.*

_____ Are ready with excuses and may generate lots of memos as a means of protecting themselves.

_____ Arouse guilt in others by appearing defenseless, making others feel like bullies if they take advantage of nice, dependent ones.

_____ Are emotionally immature, since they have practiced expressing positive emotions but avoid the other half of the emotional range that they see as inappropriate, thus avoiding what they term as negative emotions.

Remember: Stage I players are afraid of others. They try to manipulate and control other people's reactions to them. They use emotional blackmail to get their way. Helpless Infants use "feel good" emotions that come from compliments and praise, while Terrible Tyrants use "feel bad" emotions generated by attack and embarrassment.

LEADERSHIP DEVELOPMENT

If leaders accept the job of helping people develop potential, recognizing power stages and personality styles is the axis upon which people development moves. The goal is balanced style and Stage IV power use.

PERSONAL STYLE	POWER DEVELOPMENT
Balanced style	Stage IV Leadership

RATIONALE

Premise: Balance of personal style is a way to work toward Stage IV Leadership.

Premise: Imbalance of personal style is more likely to show Stage III, II or I behavior.

Premise: Balance of personal style does not automatically produce Stage IV Leadership.

Premise: Balance is, however, a basic principle of Stage IV Leaders.

Premise: Stage IV Leadership style develops people.

Premise: The Myers-Briggs is a typology for understanding people.

Conclusion: Stage IV Leadership can effectively use Myers-Briggs typology for developing people.

– 2 –

Confronting Fear:
Direct Route to Development

Main Ideas of Chapter 2:

1. Fear is defined.
2. The Pain-Pleasure Principle is the framework within which fear flourishes.
3. Fear distorts perception and judgment.
   A. Four fears that are principal blockers of potential are:
      (1) Fear of powerlessness
      (2) Fear of failure
      (3) Fear of rejection
      (4) Fear of conflict
   B. Defense shields cued by fear distort perception and judgment.
4. Personal egotism prevents Stage IV Leadership development.
5. Maturity is demonstration of seven capabilities.

Two primary assumptions are: (1) Stage IV power develop-

44

ment is essential for genuine leadership and (2) balancing pre-ferred style strengths with acquired skills in the least preferred functions is essential for Stage IV Leadership.

FEAR

"If I can make him feel, I can take him out of the game!" This statement was made by a banker, and the game was the futures market. The same message stated by a drug dealer had just one minor change: "If I can make him hurt bad enough, I can take him out of the game!" Both men were involved in the power game — one legitimate and the other illegitimate — but power games nonetheless.

Manipulation of fear is one of the oldest power games in history. The threat of pain is used to attempt to change attitudes, behavior, and ownership of possessions. Fear is used to demoral-ize people, to cause them to give up, to stimulate enough confu-sion and fear to make them predictably controllable.

Fear can be defined as anxiety and agitation caused by the presence of danger, pain, or evil as perceived by the individual. Fear is a feeling of uneasiness, concern, or frustration. We expe-rience different degrees of fear, from high to moderate to low intensity. Most people are aware of the times when they have high intense fear but may let moderate or low intensity fear go unnoticed.

Self-awareness feeds self-development and requires a greater recognition of motives behind reactions. Urges are not random. Examining urges leads to a deeper understanding of ourselves and our intentions. Leaders do not act on unexamined urges.

Fear is a controlling force. Unless we confront our own fear, we cannot be free from its numbing surprise. We begin our jour-ney toward freedom by first recognizing our own fear and then learning to manage it wisely. Knowing and managing our own fear enables us to act purposefully rather than in "knee-jerk" fash-ion. Stage IV Leaders must know fear so well that it cannot fool them nor blackmail them into avoidance or inaction. They must know their own fears and the way they work. Fear steals personal will and dilutes resolve. Fear can sap the energy away from doing what is really needed. The best defense is clear-headed assess-ment of fear.

Fear is the fuel that supports Stage I, II, and III power players. Stage IV Leaders must understand the relationship between fear and the use of power. Leaders recognize and confront their own fears. They must be able to think clearly despite being the focus of power games that feed on fear. Leadership requires clear thought in the presence of fear-driven emotions. Fear drives the first three power stages. Power players try to stimulate fear in others but seek to avoid their own fears. Manipulating others to give them what they want is the object of Stage I, II, and III power players. They try to cause such perceptual distortion in others that there is too much confusion to recognize the power play . . . much less confront it.

PEOPLE AND THE PAIN-PLEASURE PRINCIPLE

People have a basic tendency to seek pleasure and avoid pain. Is it any wonder, then, that we prefer to use the style and power stage that is easiest?

The pain-pleasure principle is the overarching framework for understanding fear and the way we cloud and distort our own perception. Note your response to words that connote pain: discomfort, distress, suffering, anguish, woe, ache, misery, sorrow, dissatisfaction, uneasiness, vexation, worry, grievance, tribulation, anxiety, adversity, trouble, unhappiness, uncertainty, vulnerability. There is a natural tendency to see those words unilaterally as negative.

What about your response to words that connote pleasure: enjoyment, well-being, joy, gladness, felicity, delight, happiness, comfort, ease, contentment, peace, relief, solace, gratification, indulgence, preference, will, favor, inclination, fulfillment, confidence? Do you experience these words as positive?

People tend to see pain as bad and pleasure as good. Yet, developing potential is difficult work. It requires risk, discomfort, and vulnerability until potential becomes actual habit. Does it therefore follow that people tend to see change and growth as bad because of its attendant discomfort?

In today's business world we are bombarded with words about building teams, activating potential, increasing productivity, improving quality, achieving excellence, using process action teams, and managing change. Behind the words the actual task of personal development requires discomfort and pain by continually confronting fear and systematically overcoming it. Leaders have to get down to the real work of helping people confront their own fear-generated blindspots. We are talking about developing individual potential — not the perceptual game of developing image clones.

When anxiety is aroused by remarks, physical threats, or challenging cues, people are motivated to try to rid themselves of the unpleasant emotional states that ensue. If the discomfort does not disappear, people tend to avoid hurtful stimuli, get angry, and erect shields to defend themselves.

Threat to well-being activates the fight-or-flight mechanism. Danger evokes fear that produces physiological response. Faces become flushed, bodies become cooler or hotter, fists and jaws clench, breathing rates increase, etc. Unfortunately, the discipline to think clearly despite the rush of physiologically disturbing sensations is difficult to master. Those who have not systematically confronted fear use defensive shields to avoid emotional anxiety caused when cues arouse unpleasant emotional states. Each time a shield is successfully used to distance us from pain, the habit is *strengthened*. Each time the pain is successfully avoided, the escape mechanism becomes more automatic. Therefore, personal growth requires knowledgeable dismantling of our protective devices that distort judgment and perception. Personal growth also requires us to know when to use defense shields purposefully.

Imagine trying to receive information through a three-foot-thick protective shield. If we are terrified of pain and keep strong barriers and shields in place, how can we do the work necessary to see clearly?

How could a rational person assume that this life can be lived painlessly? Have you ever known anyone who lived without pain? Can you recall a single life that did not have pain as well as relief from pain? Those who pursue the painless life do not find it. It is hardly possible to get drunk enough, drugged enough, active enough, or endlessly happy enough to forestall the painful side of life.

We cannot get through this life without pain. Pain is part of our life experience. The choice is not whether or not we want pain; the choice is how we deal with pain. Out of pain, character can grow. This idea of pain is not a philosophical matter. Pain is reality!

Without pain, compassion cannot be genuinely developed. Without pain, strength cannot be bedrock deep. Without experience of pain, understanding is shallow. We may talk of pain, but we can only know its effects by having experienced it. Wisdom brings appreciation of pain's strengthening capability. After enormous pain, appreciation of its cessation adds lustre to moments of peace.

Physical fitness coaches tell us to work until we feel the burn. If we only exercise to a level of comfort, we can't truly get into good physical condition. Have you ever achieved anything of excellence without a great deal of effort — without a great deal of discomfort?

Think about physical pain: the aches and pains of daily living, the discomforts of physical exhaustion, the need for work that stresses muscles and joints and causes gastrointestinal flare-ups. What about all those sprains, strains, and pains? Can you get through life without toothaches, headaches, backaches? Can you get through life without skinned knees, splinters, mosquito bites, and insect invasions?

Similarly, can you get through life without mental and emotional pain? What about relationship disappointments, hurts, or betrayals with friend, spouse, lover, father, mother, brother, sister, employer, employee, son, daughter, or colleague? Who is exempt from disease, death, and diminished capability? Can you avoid the aging process — the gradual diminishment of eyesight, hearing, muscle tone, physical strength, virility, boundless energy, unlimited enthusiasm for life?

No! We cannot avoid pain. Pain is one side of a two-sided coin. Both sides are equally valuable. Both the eagle and the man on the quarter have value — they combine for the total 25-cent value. You can't spend one without the other.

Why do we deceive ourselves? Run from emotional pain and it increases — for we carry it inside us. We take it with us wherever we go. We can distract ourselves, but we cannot dissolve it by running from it. We must turn and face it in order to grow from the experience of pain.

We are not celebrating pain. We are attempting to bring reality to unbalanced images promoted in the American culture.

Media bombards us continuously with images of painless existence, flawless skin, perfect bodies, more and more possessions. We are subtly seduced into believing that possessions will bring the elusive "satisfied state."

We *do* have experiences of painlessness, pleasure, power, and satisfaction. But we do not experience them continuously, as advertising and happiness gurus would have us believe. Tell people what makes them "feel good" is a centuries-old formula for get-rich schemes — but has yet to prove truly able to sustain the good feelings.

We *do* have experiences of enjoyment, fun, pleasure. We even have some mountain-top experiences when our bodies, minds, and emotions tell us that anything is possible. We experience the joy of relationships that connect us with others of shared values, shared risks, and shared successes. We do have those experiences of excellence. We experience joy, happiness, excitement, pleasure, peace, insight, and discovery.

Only when we have truly experienced powerlessness can we come to maturely understand the responsibility of power.

Can we truly experience higher evolution of giving and service if we have not admitted the effect of our selfish-taking natures that must be constantly disciplined? By owning both we stand a chance of evolving to clear-headed and appropriate use of each experience. There's a time for taking — taking away a privilege can get the attention of a self-focused individual. There's a time for giving — giving to those who truly deserve can bring attention to the joy and value of caring relationships.

Is health actually valued, without comparing it to health problems? Can we truly value happiness if we have not experienced unhappiness?

We cannot avoid pain. We cannot avoid pleasure. Maturity comes when we recognize and accept the value of both.

Stage IV Leadership requires realistic understanding of duality. Reality on this planet is fashioned by comparison of dual nature. Defining one-half of duality imposes the definition on the other half. Define good and its opposite is illuminated. As pain is defined it illuminates its opposite — painlessness, which traditionally carries a good-bad value (pain is bad and painlessness is good). Stage IV Leaders move beyond this view to the holistic reality that pain and painlessness are two routes to learning that produce growth. They themselves were developed through both pleasurable and painful experiences. They know the value of both kinds of situations.

CASE STUDY: LEARNING FROM PAIN AND PAINLESSNESS

Tom explained his path to leadership this way: "I went through school taking all of the leadership positions that I wanted. I graduated from college and was immediately hired into a fast-track management program at a Fortune 500 company. The recruiter took a look at my leadership positions in school and signed me up. Success came easy and I loved it. What I hated was failure. I hated anyone who smelled of it. I ridiculed failure and worshiped winning. I figured that failure was based upon stupidity, and I hated stupidity. You would have pegged me easily as a Stage III Intimidator. What an asshole I was!"

He continued, "I was sailing along from promotion to promotion, feeling full of myself and impervious to others. The only people who received my attention were other power jocks who were essential to my own plans. Reality struck in the form of a merger. One day I was the rising young star who could do no wrong and the next day I was that dangerous egotist who needed to be purged along with the original management group. I was out on the street looking for a job. I figured that my track record would open the door of my choice. But it didn't work that way."

The first month of looking for a job was not alarming, since Tom rather enjoyed the free time. But as the first month turned into three months, he began to struggle. He pictured himself as a confident winner. The experience of being rejected continuously on job interviews began to erode that confidence. Tom is an ESTJ (Extrovert, Sensor, Thinker, Judge) and his self-picture was at that time highly dependent upon how his environment treated him. Former contacts refused to take his phone calls, former buddies didn't have time for him anymore, and his inquiry letters about job positions received delayed or no response. His cash began to dry up, and Tom's self-confidence began to shatter.

He began to doubt his abilities. He found it harder and harder to get out of bed in the morning. He was irritable and confused, restless and apathetic, worried and angry. In short, he began to wonder if he were going crazy. He remembered the biting sarcasm he usually used when anyone showed signs of inner turmoil. In the past he condemned confusion as a sign of weakness. He remembered interviewing people for jobs and enjoying their discomfort as he probed to find out how desperately they needed the job. If he found signs of desperate need, then he refused to hire them. He remembered too much these days. He seemed to have endless hours for such uncomfortable reflection now that he had to find a job.

As he went to interview after interview, he hated being in the position of having to ask for a job; he much preferred being in the position of telling and demanding. He was quite uncomfortable with asking and accepting.

Tom said, "It was seven months before I found another job. I fought overwhelming fear when I found myself without authority, power or position. And for the first time in my life I had a prolonged experience with the dark side of my own nature. I hated every minute of it and I began to hate what I was becoming. At the time I was wrestling that agony, I had no idea the benefits I was gaining. I learned some important lessons: failure may come as a result of circumstances beyond your control, so now I no longer arrogantly condemn a failing person as stupid; failure makes you aware of your vulnerability, so now I no longer see myself as invincible; being a displaced person without a job or a place to belong puts you outside the social norm, so now I no longer ridicule people just for being different; failure provided a link to a part of the human experience that I had looked down on and hated, so now I know the value of both sides of the coin. I will never again forget the dark side of my own nature, and that makes it much harder for me to blatantly condemn it in others. Failure is a reality stabilizer when I am experiencing great success. It provides a healthy balance. I learned valuable but costly lessons. I paid dearly, mentally, emotionally and physically — besides the financial beating."

During the many months of waiting for interview appointments, making the rounds at corporate personnel offices, working with head hunters, Tom found himself talking and relating to other people who were also out of work. He developed a sense of shared experience with people whom he would not even have noticed prior to the joblessness experience. He would have ignored them as being outside the winner's circle where he and the other elite resided. Now he shared the struggle to reestablish a sense of identity, self-esteem, and reordering of his life. He now knows what it feels like to be excluded from the winner's circle.

Tom said, "That seven-month period was pure hell, but without it I would have continued on the quickest road to asshole fame and become the flaming asshole among assholes. I still have that capacity alive and well inside me, but during that period I began to develop compassion, connection to the suffering side of life, and the dawning of reality. I came to understand that without compassion, I could never understand another person's position. If I couldn't understand them, then I couldn't effectively reach them. I came to understand that pain gives opportunity for growth. Without it, self-importance and too much comfort make me soft and stagnant. I don't seek pain, but I can now recognize its potential value. In my case, I needed to fail in order to succeed."

LEARNING TO APPRECIATE DUALITY

In 1986 a concern of Japanese companies grabbed American attention. Fearing softness that too frequently comes with success, Japanese companies were sending some of their top executives through a rigorous training camp which they nicknamed "Hell Camp." The training was designed to stretch them physically, mentally, and emotionally. The executives were told to expect pain and discomfort to return them to the growing edge. It was their antidote to success softness.

We are not recommending "Hell Camps." The point of focus here is a successfully competing nation recognizing the danger of success and the importance of risk and discomfort as necessary parts of strength and readiness. We are not suggesting that Japan's recognition of the pain-pleasure principle is a mark of leadership, but it is a statement of reality.

A realistic understanding of the pain-pleasure principle is critical to Stage IV Leadership. Leaders maintain compassion while having the wisdom to guide the painful struggle that can produce strength and insight. In other words, real leaders are not spooked by pain. They have the warrior's insight into the nature of duality. They have the warrior's wisdom of the pleasure-pain principle. They don't stand idly by while pain is purposelessly inflicted, nor do they play the rescuer just because someone is experiencing pain. Stage IV Leaders are wise managers of pain. They manage pain in themselves and others based upon the bedrock of their own experiences with pain and painlessness, power and powerlessness, love and rejection, success and failure. They know that most valuable growth has a price, and their experience teaches them that the price is usually pain. Pleasure at paying the price comes later as strength and wisdom result from the struggle.

Both halves of duality have equal value. This understanding is essential for Stage IV Leadership. How else will the Stage IV know how to lead employees through the struggle to the pleasure of expanded potential? Pain can teach sensitivity and compassion. It prepares people for the reality of life. Real leaders must be prepared to deal with pain.

Mature users of power and influence learn to avoid self-deception. Through continual work they learn to balance opposing forces. The desire to perpetuate and protect our self-image is strong.

To the undisciplined, one of the dual forces is far more attractive than the other one. We are rarely instinctively drawn to powerlessness, pain, and criticism. Fortunately, human beings have the power of choice. We are distinguished from animals by our ability to think, to choose, and to conceptualize. If we choose the difficult path of discipline required for clear perception and sound judgment, we must master dual forces. We can learn, evolve, and achieve greater understanding by realizing the necessity to accept opposite forces. Our thoughts and judgments determine appropriateness of each.

Some of the potent forces that create both intrapersonal and interpersonal struggle are listed below.

Power *or* Powerlessness
Giving *or* Taking
Thankfulness *or* Wanting
Criticism *or* Praise
Service *or* Privilege
Wholeness *or* Dividedness
Others *or* Self

Easy *or* Hard

Open *or* Closed

Amidst the pull of opposing forces, leaders must be able to think clearly. People wrestle with power players and they also wrestle with themselves. A person may struggle with a desire to possess something while feeling guilty for not being grateful for what s/he has. Internal struggles with ourselves can often be more fierce than struggles with others.

Fear distorts perception and tends to prompt us to find ways to avoid the pain of that which we fear.

CASE STUDY: THE FEARFUL SALESMAN

"You'll never sell me anything. You don't give a damn about service. You just want to make your profit and run. Well, you can kiss this deal goodbye. I don't want to ever see you in my company again. In fact, I'll do my best to see that you are kicked out of the industry." The harsh, angry words hurled at Frank seemed to hit him right in the chest. He felt his own anger explode and add force to the wildly gyrating thoughts and feelings inside him. He and his customer had been working out the details of a service contract. He thought the negotiations were proceeding amicably; then, out of nowhere, the other person was angry at Frank for being hard to deal with and too aggressive.

Frank was really counting on that sale. He and his family had already put up earnest money for a new home and he needed that sale to enable him to carry through. When the customer began shouting at him, Frank felt a rush of such intense anger that he shouted back and escalated the disagreement. At the moment he had no idea the amount of fear that was causing his actions.

Driving back to his hotel, he was plagued with questions. "What went wrong? Why didn't I see that coming? Was he looking for a way to back out? Did he see me as easy to goad into a shouting match? Did I fall right into the trap? The boss is going to have my hide for blowing this deal!"

Frank's mind raced with thoughts. "The wife and kids loved that house. I'm still on probation on this new job. The boss ridiculed a guy at the last sales meeting. He'll probably get me next. The guys are going to think I don't know what I'm doing. They're going to think that SOB outsmarted me. They probably knew that guy was impossible and they set me up."

Unacknowledged fear can pack a knockout punch when activated by angry outburst. Frank's own fears overwhelmed him and he temporarily blanked out the techniques he had learned to overcome customer objections. When Frank angrily fired back at the customer, the sale was lost.

Frank replayed the scene over and over in his head, looking for ways to justify his reaction. He searched his memory for evidence that the customer was an SOB. He blamed the whole incident on the customer. He wanted relief from his feelings, so he began to see the customer as totally wrong and himself as totally right — innocent of contributing to the disagreement. Frank, unaware of his polarized thinking, was also unaware of the fear driving the distortion. In short, he didn't really know what was happening to him. He didn't understand, so he just used the typical human response of perceptual distortion to handle emotional distress.

Frank is not yet skilled at reading the signals of power roles, set-ups, nonverbal cues, and interaction dynamics. He knows sales techniques, but he doesn't know himself very well. He is unclear about the parts of his style that irritate others. He was so surprised at the angry outburst that his automatic reaction was typical: to meet force with force. He responded to threat with counterthreat.

People frequently respond to perceived danger with anger. It can be directed toward others or oneself, suppressed or managed, focused or unfocused. Anger is frequently a response to vulnerability, a feeling which is triggered when fear is aroused.

Frank was not ready to acknowledge that he was afraid. He thought he was an excellent salesman. He likes to sell. He has been pretty successful in the self-talk techniques for sales. He pretends he isn't afraid. Because he has been successful in the past, he thought his confidence was a dependable commodity that was his forever. He was unaware of how anxious he has been lately. He hasn't taken time to look at the changes in his life that are activating his deeper fears, thus eroding his confidence and increasing his unacknowledged feelings of vulnerability.

If Frank's boss were a leader, he would see the teachable opportunity presenting itself. He could help Frank learn to replace undisciplined reaction with conscious action. Experiencing the disturbing feelings and chaotic thoughts of failure opens possibilities for Frank to confront his fears. He can acknowledge them and start to manage them instead of letting them manage him through subconscious reactions. As long as he is denying the source of the reaction, he is losing his opportunity to take conscious control of his actions. A leader would see Frank's condition as an opportunity to confront his deeper fears, rather than let the teachable opportunity disintegrate into perceptual distortion. Frank is no longer acting out the role of confident salesman. His comfortable self-picture has been attacked.

KEY TO SELF-DEVELOPMENT: CONFRONT YOUR FEAR

Of all the possible psychological cues to help us find the surest route to substantive development of potential, we selected confrontation of fear. Fear represents the largest stumbling block to growth and change, thereby offering the most direct route to significant development.

Fear of discomfort, fear of failure, fear of losing what we have, and fear of the unknown are foundational fears for maintaining the status quo. Fear of appearing ridiculous, unskilled, unaware, or unintelligent are stumbling blocks to developing potential. Since fear is a principal blocker of self-development, confronting fear is the most direct route for maximum growth. Any serious consideration of developing leadership capacity or employee potential requires a look at the role fear plays in resistance to change.

We will look at peeling off successive layers of fear. We'll discuss mechanisms for strengthening confrontation skills in the arduous task of confronting our own fears. It is a process that takes common sense.

We are going to deal with the kind of fear that has a knowable cause. It is subject/object specific. Abnormal or neurotic fears will not be addressed. We are working with regular people wanting a direct route to balancing and improving their own style as a means of helping others. Leaders must first have confronted their own fears to gain the experience to help someone else.

Most of us do not have the time nor do we want to spend $100 an hour deciphering the complexity of human personality.

Managers and leaders need a common-sense approach that is readily identifiable and useful. We believe that *confrontation of fear is the master key to unlock potential.*

Fear causes us to use a power role that is situationally inappropriate, since fear drives Stages I, II, and III. Fear drives the Terrible Tyrant and the Helpless Infant to manipulate and control as ways to manage their fear. Fear drives the Benevolent or Abusive Dictator to bind people into rigid roles so that predictable control can insulate them from unexpected events. Fear drives the Manipulative or Intimidating Competitor who sees beating others as the protective wall that insulates.

Fear causes us to get stuck in our preferred communication style. It feels safer, more natural, less vulnerable. If we are comfortable in Extroversion, why risk the discomfort of developing Introverted skills?

Genuine strength is needed to lead. Strength comes from successfully confronting fears that limit. For when confronted and managed, our imagined limits get pushed further out and potential is turned into force for action. The more potential we claim, the more strength we claim. The more potential we claim, the more potential we find to claim. People have vast stores of untapped potential.

CONFRONTING PERSONAL EGOTISM

Any discussion of development of potential requires discussion of personal egotism. We are not talking about the academic use of the term "ego." For the purposes of our work in the real world of organizations and daily life, we define *egotism* as *selfish focus, committing actions for personal gain irrespective of the cost to others.* We use the term "egotism" to refer to that part of us that is strong-willed, selfish in nature, and willing to do whatever it takes to get our way. Egotism can be called the lower nature, our animal nature. When left unchecked, egotism seeks to dominate and control our lives. In the absence of self-discipline and confrontation of fears, we can be trapped by our lower nature in selfish focus.

Leadership requires clear perception, clear judgment, and selflessness. You cannot lead with undisciplined egotism. You can manipulate, dominate, coerce, fool, and seduce; but you cannot measure up to the definition of the leader as the wisest, most fearless, clearest, and ablest developer of people if you have an egotistical self-focus. It costs to lead. Leaders have to put others' needs before their own. Mission and people come first and self comes last; thus, it requires maturity to truly give. Only after discovering, acknowledging, confronting, and mastering one's own ego can true maturity occur. Genuine compassion and understanding occurs from truly disciplining one's own ego. We lose our tendency for quick condemnation of others when we recognize and accept our own weaknesses. Real acceptance of our own egotism forms the basis of compassion and understanding — two required characteristics for leaders.

Personal egotism is constantly on guard for anything that is uncomfortable or painful. Our egotistical nature watches carefully for any sign of attack on its prized self-picture. It employs mechanisms to defend itself, its will, its desires. Egotism employs defenses that seriously distort reality. We can develop selective perception if we do not confront our fears more directly. Many fears are stimulated by our lower nature's desire to avoid anything that is painful or uncomfortable. . . thus contributing to laziness, apathy, and indulgence.

A bloated self-concept provides a fertile ground for egoic fears. An exaggerated idea of our own specialness makes us unusually alert for any external signals that question our superiority. A bloated self-image causes us an imagined vulnerability that produces exaggerated perception of threat, thus activating our defense patterns. After we confront fear and discover our increased capacity to deal with it, we change our notion of what is truly threatening.

Selfish people have tremendous fear of information or situations that challenge their self-worship. They do *not* have the capacity for brutal self-examination since they are completely focused on protecting their false self-image. The energy used for perceptual distortion makes less energy available for helping others. Fear of being revealed keeps people focused on themselves. The greater our fearlessness, the greater our capacity for selflessness.

We distinguish clearly between coping with fear and confronting it. Coping with fear usually means using defense shields. Confronting fear uses direct recognition and action.

FEAR BLOCKS CLARITY

Coping with fear tends to entrench our habitual use of defensive reactions; whereby, confronting fear tends to strengthen us and diminish the potency of fear.

Successfully confronting fear leads to increased ability to maintain clarity of perception and judgment in times of extreme stress. Confronting fear enables us to decrease fear of failure by increasing our ability to accept the possibility of it. Confronting fear increases our ability to risk and to fight for what we believe. It increases our ability to know what needs to be done and to do it without bowing to difficulties and potential blocks. Confronting fear increases our capacity for heroic action. Heroes typically experience enormous fear but have the ability to overcome it and answer the higher call by responding to what is genuinely needed. We learn to confront fears that could otherwise cripple us and keep us from achieving a higher expression of ourselves. We lose our fear of doing the unpopular thing when our best judgment points us in that direction.

We are in no way saying that you will never again feel fear. We are saying that you will have the ability to overcome fear and act decisively while feeling enormous fear and emotion. You don't lose fear; you overcome it and learn to respond clearly despite its presence.

Years of participant observation in organizations have enabled us to identify the four most common fears that tend to trap people in the status quo, causing them to resist change as if it were a destructive enemy.

FOUR FEARS THAT ARE PRINCIPAL BLOCKERS

Stages I, II, and III are driven primarily by four fears: powerlessness, failure, rejection, and conflict. They also try to provoke the four fears in others. A Stage IV Leadership orientation must not contribute to manipulation of fear by succumbing to it. Leaders must resist being manipulated by fear. They need the power of understanding to manage fear while never retreating from their original vision.

Dysfunctional power users are so afraid of powerlessness that they will rearrange truth to whatever degree necessary to avoid the feelings of powerlessness which in turn trigger the fears of rejection, failure, and conflict. They are afraid of conflict, unless they instigate it. They are afraid of rejection, unless they do the rejecting. They are afraid of failure and therefore will do almost anything to avoid it, while being quick to advertise other people's failure.

It is easy to get people to agree with the *need* to develop potential, but hard to know what action to take. Look for the problems that keep us from our potential. When you look at the complexity of a human being, it is easy to get lost in a psychological maze. Do you work with beliefs, attitudes, habits, patterns, thoughts, feelings, or behaviors? Strong arguments are made for each of these approaches. Of all possibilities we believe that fear leads to the most direct identification of those obstacles that prevent us from achieving our full potential. By identifying fears, we discover avoidance patterns that tend to keep us locked in the safe comfort zone of the familiar.

Fear acts like a parasite with a voracious appetite for distorting perception and skewing judgment. It gobbles up the true reality and spits out an altered version designed to smooth over the disturbance. Fear grows in direct proportion to our unwillingness to experience pain. Fear drives self-deception. Fear causes us to deliberately blind ourselves to reality if we perceive the threat of too much painful awareness. The truth is often painful. Rather than see things as they really are, we humans try to rearrange perception in such a way as to protect our image of ourselves.

Conscious or unconscious fear affects our physical system. It affects our thoughts, activates feelings, and causes reactions in our body. Fear has a systemic effect on us. It causes us to feel uncomfortable, uneasy, and uncentered. Our physical systems are incredible information processing systems. Unfortunately, we are so dedicated to ease and comfort that we frequently blind ourselves to credible internal signals because we do not want to deal with the possibilities of pain. Learning to read our own internal signals, having the courage to follow the thread of discomfort to its origin, and confronting the fear producing the discomfort is the fastest route to developing potential.

In one organization an alcoholic had been smelling of alcohol, slurring his words, and failing at his job for thirteen years.

The new boss identified the dysfunctional behaviors immediately. Investigation showed, however, that the behavior had gone on for years. It was common knowledge; yet, the alcoholic had all adequate performance appraisals in his file. The former director was afraid to confront the problem, so he chose to distort his own perception and excuse the behavior by saying, "He's given us some good years. We can't overlook that." Because the director was unwilling to confront his own fear of becoming entangled in a justifiable personnel action, he abused himself and all employees who were working hard and disciplining themselves. It took the new director nine months to get the true condition documented and get legitimate help for the alcoholic.

The alcoholic's former manager ignored the problem and admitted his unwillingness to deal with the problem. The manager was removed from management and placed in a staff position. He was put in an employee development program. In working with him I discovered that he was so uncomfortable with the alcoholic employee that he did not want to become entangled in the web of problems. Later, he told me that he had an alcoholic father and the employee reminded him of painful times that he wanted to forget. It slowly dawned on him that his decision to avoid those memories also marked his demise as an effective manager.

He sadly remembered his early aspirations of leadership as he began to see that the death of his leadership vision occurred with the hundreds of small decisions he made to avoid conflict because of its discomfort. He said, "I didn't realize I had become so comfortable with things going smoothly that I started avoiding anything that upset me. We had so much work to do and we were getting it done, so I thought I was a great manager. How can you start out with such noble ideas and wind up so far off track? It all happened so gradually . . . I didn't even notice."

We could have looked at his beliefs, attitudes, habits, patterns, thoughts, feelings and behaviors and we would have wasted a lot of time in the search. The real indicator of the distortion was his discomfort with the truth. By tracing the discomfort he found the fear that was fueling the distortion. He began to deal with the cause rather than tinker with the symptoms. He said, "I went to numerous management courses where we studied motivation, performance evaluation and the usual stuff.

Those were not the answer. It's ironic that the answer was in me the whole time. I am painfully discovering how many things in my life I don't see clearly because I am unwilling to feel the sadness. I can see why people would rather fool themselves than deal with the real problems." Follow the discomfort and you find the parasitic fear. This man had willingly rearranged beliefs, attitudes, thoughts, and feelings as the price for conscious relief from the real situation.

Emotional upset of any kind tends to interfere with attention, perception, thinking, planning, and judging. If the emotion is fear-based, it can lead to loss of mental efficiency and irrational activity. People recognize intense fear since its physiological effect is so strong. Much harder to detect are moderate to low levels of fear that affect our perception and judgment. Fear can cause a temporary impairment of our mental efficiency. It is therefore imperative for Stage IV Leaders to confront fear consciously rather than be controlled subconsciously.

One cannot reach nor maintain Stage IV Leadership without the development that comes from gut-level experiences with both sides of duality. Stage IVs can only maintain their balanced use of power through the wisdom that comes when they have been so tested with and without power that they no longer fear either experience.

The character test comes at the extreme ends of the duality dimension. What happens to ethics and clarity during successes that bring power and privilege? What happens when failure brings powerlessness and loss of privilege? The Stage IV Leader has fought through the egotism and self-importance of success and has humbly learned through the doubts and depression of failure. The Stage IV knows the value of both power and powerlessness; for power offers the ultimate opportunity for personal egotism and self-aggrandizement while powerlessness gives opportunity to learn humility and acceptance.

Maintaining personal clarity and realistic self-assessment in the face of success is a seductive test. Powerlessness provides the hard test of our confidence and self-worth. Through the tests of powerlessness, genuine compassion and empathy become possible. Through the tests of powerfulness, mature acceptance of responsibility and rigorous self-examination become possible. Leadership requires genuine compassion and empathy to clearly touch and lead others. It requires the maturity to carry the cross of responsibility and the discomfort of rigorous self-examination. Personal egotism stands ever ready to feast on power.

Stage IV Leaders must continually confront their own fear as an antidote for personal egotism. They must continually confront other people's fear to remove the barriers to development of potential.

Advantages of confronting fear:

1. We become aware of our real limits rather than our imagined ones.
2. We reduce the likelihood of being manipulated by fear.
3. We increase our ability to maintain clarity of perception and judgment.
4. We increase our ability to risk for worthwhile endeavors.
5. We increase our ability to do what needs doing without bowing to blocks and difficulties.
6. We increase our capability to stand up and do what's right.
7. We increase our capacity for heroic action.

Heroes are not superhuman. They are people who are able to overcome their fears, focus their energy, and answer a higher calling to respond to what is genuinely needed. Overcoming fears to act decisively is a basic tenet of Stage IV Leadership. Leaders must both overcome their own fears and help other people overcome theirs.

Fear can distort our judgment and drive us to reaction instead of action. Fear drives our alert system, causing us to continually scan our environment for signs of danger. When we pick up high-intensity signals, we feel vulnerable and immediately search the environment for information to decide how to respond. The undisciplined and thereby typical way people deal with fear is to use defense shields instead of confronting fear directly, for confronting fear tends to diffuse it. When we feel uncomfortable arousal cues in our physical system, we tend to throw up a shield to block the pain.

MOST COMMON FEARS THAT BLOCK GROWTH: FEAR OF POWERLESSNESS, FAILURE, REJECTION, CONFLICT

Fear of powerlessness: In a culture that spends billions of dollars in pursuit of power, powerlessness is seen as an evil condition to be avoided at all costs. Losers are avoided and winners are worshiped. Public adoration of overnight media personalities demonstrates the easy manipulation of perception to award hero status in image making stories. The stories of losers tend to repel, while winners tend to attract.

Powerlessness is the inability to control outcomes. We are falsely taught that powerlessness is bad and power is good.

Fear of powerlessness takes various forms. *Loss of authority* can activate old forms of insecurity and self-doubt. Just the threat of *loss of control, access, opportunity, or influence* can activate chest-tightening fear. The *fear of boredom, mediocrity, or obsolescence* can absorb conscious attention and subconscious defenses. Human *fear of being controlled* by some overwhelming force, dominant person, or tumultuous situation tends to clog our thought channels. The *fear of physical impairment* due to accidents or disease can result in physical, mental, and emotional powerlessness. With countless millions spent to ward off *aging, the fear of reduced potency* makes people easy prey to suggestions that we can be eternally young. People still chase the alchemist's dream of finding the secret to reversing the aging process.

Irrational fear of powerlessness blocks growth toward balance. Leaders must know powerlessness equally as well as powerfulness. Knowing one well does not lead to balance until the other side is just as familiar. Strength comes from not being afraid of power or powerlessness.

Patrice is an executive with a recurring dream that she refers to as "a disturbing event." She awakens with her heart racing, her palms sweaty, and her body in a high state of alert. She dreams that she is in charge of a meeting and people will not pay attention. They grow increasingly more unruly and finally they walk out. She tries desperately to stop them, but she cannot persuade them to stay. As we began to talk about her dream, Patrice discovered that the dream was an enactment of her fear that she could lose her executive influence. She decided that the dream was an "inexpensive" lesson since she experienced it in the privacy of her own home. She decided to try to get comfortable with the idea of losing control of a meeting, accepting loss of influence, and accepting loss of authority. She even practiced consciously reliving the dream in order to become more familiar with the effects of fear.

Eighteen months later, we were attending the same meeting. Attendees were distracted and engaged in side conversations. In the past Patrice would get so upset at the behavior that she became stern, domineering, and controlling. This time, Patrice said, "It appears that you are quite distracted. Let's do a process check to see what we need to do to make our time more productive." She facilitated an interesting discussion about a merger rumor that was the big distractor. After twenty minutes of letting people discuss their concerns, she refocused the meeting. She was no longer afraid of losing control. She confronted her fear of powerlessness and was able to see clearly that the group needed to talk about something other than what was on the agenda. The meeting still ended on time with the task accomplished.

In a hierarchical society, powerlessness is too often measured on the dominance-submission continuum. Blind acceptance of this notion will block clear assessment since the mind would be cued to automatically reject powerlessness.

John wanted to learn to fish for catfish. He met a seventy-two-year-old with the reputation of being the most sure-fire fisherman in the area. As they talked, John acknowledged that he didn't know anything about catfish. He accepted the powerless role and demonstrated his willingness to learn. He did not try to control, impress, or struggle with the older fisherman. He acknowledged the difference in their understanding. He endured the kidding by two of his friends, who asserted that anybody could catch a catfish. No boasting for John! He admitted he didn't know, and became a willing learner. The older fisherman shared his years of knowledge about the effects of weather on the water depth in which catfish lay. He shared tips about bait, hooks, line, and years of honed technique. John accepted powerlessness and was accepted as a student by the old pro. Genuine friendship resulted . . . to say nothing of the successful fishing duo.

Fear of failure: Doubts about the ability to succeed can keep people from trying. Some would rather not risk than bear the discomfort of failure, thus the power of the status quo. One man said, "I may not have what I want, but at least I know what to expect." He preferred status quo numbness rather than face his fear to try and then risk possible failure.

Fear of failure takes many forms. *Fear of public speaking* affects approximately sixty percent of all Americans. Getting up in front of people who could *ridicule, humiliate,* or have plenty of time to *judge and criticize* causes trepidation in many. *Loss of self-esteem, fear of damaged reputation, loss of respect, or loss of status* keeps many people from going beyond their comfort zones to risk. Some people are afraid to risk because they *fear losing material possessions;* they would rather guard and hoard what they have. Fear of failure activates thoughts, feelings, and body reactions that distort and block self-development if not confronted.

Consider the situation of a woman who stays in a difficult marriage because of fear that she cannot make it on her own. A man stays in a job that bores him and has bored him for the past fifteen years, but he is afraid to try something else. A little boy pretends that he is a great baseball player but won't even play Little League baseball because he is afraid of missing the ball or striking out. When prodded by an older brother, the child replied, "I don't want people yelling at me and thinking I'm a nerd."

Fear of failure restricts people and causes them to do that which is known and familiar and to avoid the new and challenging. Failure can teach valuable lessons for those who have the courage to sift through their own pain to find the lessons provided. People erect walls to protect themselves from hurtful relationships. They wall others out but, ironically, they wall themselves in — safe from others inside their bunker of loneliness.

Fear of rejection: People try to avoid the pain of being told or shown that they are undesirable, unwanted, or unworthy. We feel rejected when we are excluded from an admired group, ignored by important decision-makers, ridiculed by colleagues, or treated as inanimate objects. Rejection attacks self-worth. It hits an invasive blow to our desire for approval and acceptance by worthwhile others.

Fear of rejection takes various forms. *Fear of hatred, retaliation, and fear of being misunderstood* is seen in organizational dynamics. People don't say what they are really thinking and feeling and too often try to avoid risking rejection. For every outspoken person in an organization, there are likely to be a hundred others who keep their thoughts to themselves or express them carefully to trusted others.

Fear of losing support, losing access, or losing approval shapes behavior and causes laundering of overt responses. People *fear losing esteem* and therefore *losing trust.* One plumber enjoyed his reputation for being able to do any job he was given. He was so afraid of messing up that he began to do just that. He was so afraid that he began to try too hard. He began to misdiagnose problems, thereby applying wrong solutions. He was still working hard, but his fear of losing esteem so clouded his judgment that he lost his dependability reputation and was referred to as a "klutz."

Americans have a cultural heritage of idealizing fair play. The cultural value simultaneously feeds *fear of unfair treatment.* Our cultural value of adoring winners feeds the *fear of inadequacy.*

A fast-track young lawyer appeared to be a sure bet to make partner. Others treated him as if he already had the coveted position. When he was passed over for partner, he found people distancing themselves from him. He said, "One day I'm okay and the next thing I know, people don't even have time for a cup of coffee with me. It's as if they don't want to catch whatever they think I have." He was quite upset about people's reactions. As long as they believed he would soon have increased power as a partner, he was treated with deference. When the partnership was given to someone else, he picked up the contamination of failure and people rejected him. He was stunned.

One of the lawyer's colleagues remarked, "I don't know why the partners didn't give him a partnership. Until I know what their reasons were, I don't want to be seen with him too much. I don't want to be guilty by association and ruin my own chances."

The *fear of betrayal* was strong in the rejected lawyer. "I have played it right by the rules – maximum hours charged, working on weekends, dressing right, belonging to the right clubs, and working my butt off. Why the hell wasn't that enough?"

People's fear of powerlessness, failure, and rejection influenced their reactions as they avoided the passed-over lawyer. They didn't want to be "guilty by association."

Fear of rejection can override fundamental values and cause

people to behave in ways they don't even approve of themselves. Too much fear of rejection robs people of individuality and binds them to dependence on others for identity and approval. Leaders often enable followers to confront fear to begin development of potential.

Fear of conflict: People tend to fear conflict. They do not want to risk the explosion of their own unconfronted fears if they get too close to someone else's fear. Since they see emotional expression as dangerously contagious, they tend to avoid open conflict. Most conflict in American organizations is expressed in passive-aggressive forms — getting even in subtle ways while overtly denying aggression. Managers in America tend to avoid confronting people problems. They would rather avoid them than "stir up a pot of trouble." Intimidators and bullies count on people's fear of conflict. They literally use emotional blackmail to get what they want. They grab power by threatening to make others pay emotionally and mentally for challenging them.

Fear of conflict takes many dual forms since it raises fear that conflict may bring out the worst in us as well, causing us to respond in a manner that we later disparage.

Conflict triggers a potent pack of fears: *fear of being emotionally out-of-control, fear of anger, fear of verbal attack, fear of physical attack, fear of the cost of damaged relationships, fear of entrapment, fear of sabotage, fear of escalation of conflict, fear of group reprisal,* and *fear of vindictiveness.* If fear of conflict leads to perpetual avoidance, personal power erodes. Leaders must confront, must step up to problems, must risk personal attack, must willingly pay emotional costs to confront and solve people problems as well as problem situations.

We were asked to work with a department that was embroiled in conflict. We interviewed each person in the department, asking each one the same set of questions. We were told that the employees had vowed not to talk to us. When they actually came in for a private discussion, the issues came rolling out. We assured each interviewee that they would not be quoted. We summarized the issues and brought them to the all-staff conflict resolution meeting. Although 24 of the 30 people were extremely vocal about their anger at a manager and "his favorite," they were unwilling to express their concerns openly.

We utilized an organizational culture questionnaire plus the interview information to introduce the issues and outline the facts. People were afraid to confront the issues openly. As the consultants, we assumed the role of confronting the issues. Even those who were angry became uncomfortable with open discussion. Although the discussion was conducted within careful interaction rules, people were still afraid of conflict. They wanted the problem fixed, but did not think they should feel discomfort. The prevailing attitude was for someone else to fix it.

The four categories of fear that block responsible interaction are *fear of powerlessness, fear of failure, fear of rejection,* and *fear of conflict.* Leaders must continually confront those four fears in themselves and in those whom they lead.

Stages I, II, and III use of power are fear locked. Only the Stage IV use of power demonstrates effective management of fear for long-term personal growth and productivity. The key to an effective organization is, of course, productive, motivated people whose talents are utilized and whose potential is tapped. How does a leader bring about that process and create a culture of responsible action?

MATURE USE OF POWER

Giving in to fear leads to immature responses. Maturity requires us to manage our fear instead of letting fear manage us. Fear arises from a pool of beliefs, desires, experiences, and primitive urges. To confront fear, we must go within. Going inside one's own cave to dive into the dark pool of experience, memory, feelings, and fears can be a frightening experience. We uncover aspects of ourselves that have been well hidden from consciousness.

Leaders must work continuously to bring more and more of their unconscious into awareness. Most people are largely unaware, since it is such hard work to become fully conscious. Estimates of percentage of consciousness and unconsciousness predict about 10% conscious and 90% unconsconscious processing.

Awareness is fundamental to clear perception and sound judgment. Awareness is focused attention that engages central nervous system readiness to respond to stimuli. Attention spotlights awareness of some aspect of our inner and outer environment.

We receive far more information than we consciously recognize. In Zimbardo's work on the nature of consciousness, he refers to Broadbent's work on attention. "Broadbent conceived of attention as a *selective filter* which handled the large amount of sensory information constantly arriving by (a) *blocking* out most unwanted input while (b) *relaying* specific desired information — admitting it to consciousness. Such a filter acted a little like a tuning dial on a radio or TV, which lets us receive certain of the many available messages, but not others." (Zimbardo, pg. 26)

One executive shared an experience of filtered perception. Diane said, "I can share with you a painful experience of selectively filtering information. After I discovered that my protégé tried to damage my reputation with a client, I remembered flashes of uneasiness that should have warned me. I denied them and focused on his charm and his potential. He really does have great potential. I wanted to see him develop and become a real contributor to the company. Looking back, I had plenty of warning that his character was too flawed to handle power wisely . . . I had flashes of his taking credit for things he didn't do, his subtle use of innuendo to create doubt, his saying he was willing to work hard but his failure to follow through. He always had such plausible excuses. I had plenty of warning messages which I filtered out. I wanted to see him succeed and I wanted him to be grateful to me for helping him. What a fool I was!"

As we listened and asked thought-provoking questions, Diane made some amazing discoveries. She explored factors that contribute to selective filtering. She uncovered fear of powerlessness and fear of rejection that seriously affected her perception. She was very afraid of being rejected by someone whom she thought was powerful. Diane blocked slightly ridiculing messages from her protégé, although she recalls a twinge of discomfort that tried to get into consciousness to warn her. She blocked the protégé's self-aggrandizing messages and excused the messages that were relayed to consciousness as youthfulness and lack of experience.

While talking to us, Diane was amazed to hear herself say that she wanted her protégé to be obligated to her. She was sure that he would amass more and more influence in the company. Through discussion she discovered what was going on in her subconscious. Her startled response indicated that she had not known what was really driving her distorted perception. Even worse, she had not known that she had distorted perception! She was amazed to discover that she was afraid of the way the protégé uses power. Her unconscious strategy was to placate him, mentor him, and thereby hope to prevent his aggression toward her.

Few people have the courage to seek the truth about themselves. It is far more satisfying to imagine ourselves as capable, noble, courageous, and wise than to do the gut-wrenching work of confronting our own delusion. Our own fear of emotional discomfort can keep us from doing the brutally honest self-assessment needed for clear perception. Diane much preferred to think of herself as perceptive, powerful, confident, and right. She was saddened and upset by the true situation. She struggled, made excuses, blamed her protégé and then finally accepted her own errors. She said, "It really hurts to realize that I was fooled, afraid, and denying what was really going on. I don't like the way this makes me feel." We discussed what she could do to continue to clear up her peception. She wants to cut down the odds of being duped again.

A strong self-concept provides the foundation of Stage IV Leadership development. Self-concept, however, must be based upon a candid assessment of both strengths *and* weaknesses. Fear goes unchecked if we pretend that we have no weaknesses while pursuing the comfort of focusing only on our strengths.

MATURITY AND SELF-UNDERSTANDING

Does the leader have to be a psychology expert? We don't think so. We think a person who has consciously and actively taken risks, confronted personal fear, discovered internal resources, used clear thinking to uncover the process, and continues to actively learn and stretch can capitalize on commonsense, personal experience, clear communication, and a few process tools for the wisdom to guide and the compassion to help others develop their potential.

If the leader is going to maintain clearer perception and clearer judgment than those who follow, the leader must know the self-development pathway well. The leader must have personally walked the jungle of internal distortion so many times that the pitfalls are well known, the feelings are familiar distortions, the thoughts are old foes, the perceptual tricks are worn strategies, and the fears are known war zones. In short, leaders can't lead followers on the self-development pathway, if they have not personally experienced and mastered the process.

Self-deception sets us up for easy manipulation. We can fool ourselves, but we cannot fool a wise, perceptive leader. S/he will see right through us. Ironically, so will a power player!

Maturity requires awareness and whole person integration. A mature person integrates mind, body, values, and soul functions to provide a balanced approach to internal forces. A mature person also demonstrates balance in several areas: reality testing; sound judgment; thought processes; drives, emotions and urges; defense mechanisms; interpersonal relationships; and relationship with external environment.

Maturity for Leadership — Seven Capabilities

(1) *Reality testing* — The mature person distinguishes clearly between inner and outer stimuli.

   (a) Accurate perception includes awareness of time, place, and external events (Outer Reality Testing).

   (b) Accurate perception of internal state (Inner Reality Testing).

(2) *Sound judgment* — The mature person's judgment is free from error, fallacy, or misapprehension.

   (a) Accurate assessment of likely consequences of intentional behavior (accurate assessment of probable effects, dangers, legal implications, social censure, appropriateness, or disapproval).

   (b) Behavior reflects awareness of likely consequences.

(3) *A well-developed thought process*

   (a) Focuses attention

   (b) Sustains concentration

   (c) Anticipates accurately

   (d) Accesses memory

   (e) Forms concepts skillfully

   (f) Commands language

(g) Utilizes symbology

(h) Interprets meaning accurately

(4) *Discipline and control of drives, emotions, and urges*

(a) Self-control of strong internal forces so that actions are deliberate rather than defensive.

(b) No action caused by unexamined urges.

(c) Delay and frustration control is exercised.

(d) Distinguishes between urge and intuition.

(e) Can act on clear intuitive message without conscious factual evidence.

(5) *Management of defensive mechanisms*

(a) Manages defensive mechanisms so they do not inhibit ideation.

(b) Manages defenses adaptively, not maladaptively so they do not unconsciously interfere with needed action.

(6) *Healthy interpersonal relationships*

(a) Demonstrates a readiness and willingness to invest in relationships.

(b) Accepts full responsibility for own state of being.

(c) Sees others as having separate identities and right to choose.

(d) Can sustain worthwhile relationships despite challenges, phases of frustration, and varying priorities.

(7) *Mastery of interaction with the environment and culture*

(a) Demonstrates competence in interacting with surroundings.

(b) Demonstrates success in integrating attitudes, values, beliefs, actions, and self-representation.

(c) Demonstrates comfort, harmony, and relaxed awareness.

Immature people have difficulty distinguishing between inner and outer stimuli. They see others as extensions of themselves and their values, or as enemies, or as unworthy of attention. Immature people want others to think like they do. Immature people see things as black or white without gradation.

They depend on routine and easy categorization in order to avoid the uncomfortable process of seeking the truth.

Families, work groups, and organizations have shared illusions. An unwritten agreement forms about what will receive attention and what will be ignored. Occasionally, someone sees an obvious wrong and goes to the authorities to report the violation. They are commonly referred to as "whistle blowers." They shatter the shared illusion. They violate group agreement not to notice.

Both individuals and groups have selective attention that filters information. It blocks unwanted information by dumping it into unconscious processing, while relaying desirable information to consciousness. We have *mind guards* that sort information. Mind guards appear to be primarily triggered by a desire to avoid pain . . . No upsetting information, *please!*

We were dining at a nice restaurant when a family of five were seated at the table next to us. The children appeared to range in ages from about two to ten. The two-year-old immediately crawled onto the table and stood up. The parents continued to carry on their conversation while the child weaved back and forth in their visual range. The six-year-old began to pour salt on the table, while the ten-year-old discovered that his chair rolled, so he began a race course around the table. As the waiter approached their table with a disdainful look, the mother made a remark that indirectly warned the waiter. She said to her husband with strong intentionality, "I am so happy that our children are expressive and individualistic. I don't want them to be inhibited little conformists." Her husband looked directly at the waiter while replying to his wife, "Yes, I absolutely agree. They must be allowed to express their individuality."

The parents of those children decided to emotionally censor the waiter and other diners' reactions to their children. The parents saw their children's behavior as expressive of a value they were encouraging — individuality. We saw the behavior as unruly, inappropriate, and invasive. The waiter nonverbally tried to show his disapproval, while holding his words in check. Later, as the waiter brought our check, he murmured his apologies for the noise, the chair that ran into our table, and the occasional spray of food particles. Two other groups who had not received food yet asked to be seated elsewhere. Each of us interpreted the children's behavior through our own filters. We interpreted by assessing their behavior against our own attitudes, values, beliefs, and social norms.

Why do lousy supervisors usually get promoted? Why is inferior work tolerated? Why do we eat too much sugar and fat and then wonder why our clothes fit uncomfortably? What drives our ability to rearrange our perception rather than confront issues?

When a stimulus occurs, the information goes through a filtering and coding mechanism for interpretation. As the stimulus moves through the filtering system, several factors are brought to bear. The stimulus is interpreted for routing. It is relayed to consciousness or blocked and sent to the subconscious. If it is potentially anxiety-producing, it will likely be blocked from consciousness. Sometimes people respond with unconscious reactions. Nonverbal responses tend to reveal unconscious reactions as well as conscious intentions. Paul Ekman, an expert on nonverbal communication, calls the face our least leaky nonverbal channel by explaining the face as having the greatest capacity for deceit. The rest of nonverbal reactions are usually much harder to control from unconscious reactions. If we are unaware of our unconscious fears and attitudes, we will not consciously know to try to control our nonverbal behavior. A tone of voice, a stiffened spine, a change in skin tone, a head movement, a sudden movement all can reveal deeper messages.

Truth is frequently uncomfortable. The human tendency to screen out anxiety-producing signals can be overridden with personal will and determined exploration of fears, attitudes, and beliefs.

The brain produces pain-management chemicals resulting in urges that help us bear physical and emotional pain. When ill, the body automatically signals the need to withdraw, rest, and restore vital energies. Our body signals the need for rest and recuperation. This slowing down of metabolic rate, the reduced energy for activity, and the general numbing is helpful in the healing process. Yet the natural process to avoid physical, mental, and emotional pain tends to interfere with perception. Just as the body has natural pain-avoidance warning systems for the physical body, the mind and emotions also have a numbing capability for pain management — called *selective perception.* The problem with the pain-avoidance process is that reduced awareness results.

The brain produces a type of morphine called opioids which reduce the conscious experience of pain but also dims our attention. Our brains have a limited capacity for awareness. The natural tendency to avoid pain has to be managed and disciplined in order to achieve clear perception. If we avoid painful awarenesses, deceive ourselves, filter anxiety-producing messages, allow our mind to guard against disturbances, and allow avoidance of disturbance, then we cannot hope to see clearly enough to make accurate judgments.

Human beings have perceptual defenses that protect us from unpleasant, taboo, or other threatening messages. The capacity to protect ourselves from disturbance has many positive uses, but when unmanaged, leaves us to be controlled by our fears and personal egotism.

BLOCKED PERCEPTION

Sometimes blocked perception gets people through seemingly unbearable circumstances. In the midst of a personal executive development planning session, a woman shared with us a painfully guarded family secret. To protect her identity we will refer to her as Linda.

As the oldest daughter in a ten-person family, Linda was sexually molested by her father. The abuse began when she was five. When she was twelve she tried to tell her mother but was told to stop her filthy imagination. Dad was a respected businessman, as well as a community and church leader. She tried to tell her priest, and he ordered her to do penance for her imagination and angry attitude.

With the authority figures in her world telling her that she was wrong, Linda began to accept that she was bad. She tried to bury the hurt. She wanted to sleep with her light on but was soundly ridiculed by her father and the ridicule was quickly echoed by her brothers and sisters. She finally decided that she was bad and was going to hell anyway so she should just go ahead. She decided to die and face the consequences. She got some rat poison in granule form and ingested it. She was found, rushed to the hospital, and was very sick for six weeks.

The incident apparently frightened the father enough that he left her alone after the attempted suicide. She hoped that her father had been frightened into changing his ways. She developed a blind spot that kept her from noticing her father's behavior with her sisters.

Later, while the five sisters waited in a hospital waiting room to deal with a tragic family accident, the sisters seemed to drop their guard as they struggled to cope with their fear. Linda tentatively broached the subject of her abuse with her four sisters. She was startled to discover that they, too, had been abused. For about fifteen minutes the sisters haltingly shared the truth and Linda hoped for healing and shared grieving. They were interrupted by news from the emergency room and did not have further opportunity to talk until two days later. Linda tried to bring up the subject, but all four sisters turned on her angrily and told her to stop hurting them. They accused her of being jealous and spiteful. In just two days the old family-shared illusion was back in place. Dad was protected. The sisters apparently unconsciously agreed to resurrect the illusion rather than work through the pain.

Linda recounted her rocky road in trying to override her pain enough to work through it and accept the truth of the situation. She talked of confronting first her fear of sleeping in the dark. Next came her realization that she was terrified of relationships. She could not bring herself to trust anyone. She could not let down her guard with men or women. Initially, she could not make herself seek psychological help.

Getting a puppy seemed safe. Linda hoped she could start trying to develop a relationship with a puppy, who could not betray her emotionally. She was rewarded by her effort. She was amazed at the healing effect of unreservedly expressing affection, even if it was to an animal. Later she decided that she had to try to develop a friendship with a human being. It became too comfortable to pour her affection into her dog. She also gave herself to worthwhile causes . . . but not to human beings.

One step at a time, she confronted the hidden terrors that blocked her professionally and interpersonally. She has achieved hard-won awareness. She said, "If people could only know the freedom that comes from facing the fear, they would be willing to do whatever it takes. I was imprisoned by my fear. Don't misunderstand me. I know that I am emotionally and mentally scarred. I just decided to remove as much of the scar tissue as I could. I will be confronting fear the rest of my life, but I still say, *It's worth it!*"

Linda prepared several copies of the seven maturity capabilities we identified. She talks openly about her terrible fears and her attempts to avoid pain. She does reality testing to sort out inner and outer stimuli. She values sound judgment in herself and in others. She demonstrates well-developed thought processes and inspires others to use their thinking potential also. Her behavior is disciplined and controlled, and she rarely acts on an urge without knowing what is driving the urge. She is becoming more aware of defense mechanisms. Linda has three satisfying, close interpersonal relationships and has developed some relaxation with people in general. She is more confident at work and in her personal life. Yes! We see that she means it when she says that it is tough work, but *it's worth it.*

CASE STUDY: FEAR-LOCKED MANAGER, STAGE II BENEVOLENT DICTATOR, AND STAGE III COMPETITIVE INTIMIDATOR

Ken Adams is described by most people as a nice guy – a pleasant, likable man. He had been gradually promoted during a twenty-year career with an engineering firm until he became area manager. The company had a reputation for promoting from within the company. Ken had been area manager for six years. During the last fourteen months, however, his area experienced a 50% increase in projects. He was responsible for $780 million worth of projects. His staff grew from a 24- to a 48-person staff to manage the additional subcontractors and clients. His area experienced fast growth and all the changes that are inherent in expansion.

When it became apparent that problems were increasing in Ken's area, his boss was eager to help, since he felt personally responsible if any of his employees failed.

Ken's personal style and his power style contributed to his fear-induced stuck position. On the Myers-Briggs Type Indicator, Ken had a clear preference for Introversion, Sensing, and Judge-controlling (ISTJ). He had a slight preference for Thinking. His civil engineer degree reinforced his notion that he should be a Thinker. He had not really resolved the Feeler values that seemed to continually challenge him internally. He used a Stage II Benevolent Dictator approach to management. He took pride in seeing himself as an employee advocate.

We received a call from the CEO asking if we would work with Ken and his manager. Several problems were verified as a result of internal audits. When the problems were identified, Ken had his staff develop a reorganization plan and investigate a new computer system. Although the problems indicated managerial style problems, Ken responded with organizational system solutions only.

The problems identified were: (1) of the 112 client projects, 71 were behind schedule, (2) phone calls were not being returned in a timely fashion, (3) letters took approximately six weeks to get through the in-house system before responses were mailed, (4) modifications of blueprints for minor revisions were taking two to four months to get through the internal bureaucracy, (5) lack of cooperation was identified between planning branch and technical support branch, (6) problem behavior was not confronted, (7) Ken was perceived as attempting to micromanage the complex operations, (8) five department heads were described as territorial and uncooperative, (9) decisions were bottlenecked in Ken's office, and (10) information was also bottlenecked waiting for Ken's personal review.

When Ken received the first internal audit report naming the ten problems, he was shocked. As he discussed his reaction to the report, he said: "I can't believe the internal auditors are so harsh, accusative, and vindictive." I noted the value-laden words he used to describe his reactions to the report. He continued, "In the audit exit interview, they ignored all of the things I've put in place since last year." Ken talked at length about systems he had put in place but did not discuss outcomes. He was clearly in a defensive posture.

Years ago Ken's first supervisory job left an unfortunate imprint on him. His boss was a Stage III Competitive Intimidator, who ridiculed employees in front of others and controlled people with a mixture of shouting and kidding. His Extroverted style gave him the reputation of having the "fastest lip in the West" in delivering sarcastic, stinging reprimands. Ken felt so victimized by that style that he still talks about its effect on him. He resolved to be kind to his employees. Unfortunately, that reaction resulted in his unwillingness to confront problems. He did not realize that avoiding problems is one of the unkindest acts of all.

Ken's experience with the Stage III Intimidator deepened the four fears that cause people to resist change. On a daily basis for the two years Ken worked for the Stage III boss, Ken experienced powerlessness, failure, rejection, and conflict. He did not learn to stand up to the Stage III. He developed defensive reactions instead. He developed habits of withdrawal, denial, avoidance, rationalization, and intellectualization. Each time he employed a defensive reaction to deal with the pain activated by his fears, the patterns became stronger. They turned into habitual responses. Now, eighteen years later, he has an enormous task. He has to confront his fears or be unable to marshall enough energy to change his managerial approach in time to save his job.

Withdrawal from problems is a natural fit with Ken's Introversion. When someone or something upsets Ken, he withdraws in order to avoid the emotional pain and discomfort. When an employee caused problems, Ken withdrew from the employee, hoping that the employee would recognize the cause for the withdrawal and correct the problem.

Steve is one of Ken's department heads who knows how to manipulate him. Steve's power style is Stage III Competitive Intimidator. He scores as an ESTJ (Extrovert, Sensor, Thinker, and Judge) with very clear preferences in each catagory. He manipulates Ken's unresolved feelings about his first boss. Steve carefully treats Ken as an adored parent when he is with him and then ridicules him behind his back. Steve uses obsequious behavior with Ken in order to manipulate him easily. The rest of the staff observe Steve's hanging around Ken's office and running to him with "juicy tidbits" of information, or seeking advice on something Steve has already done. Steve knows that Ken likes to feel needed by his employees and likes the feeling of being a kind, responsive boss. Staff is clearly offended that Ken does not recognize the manipulation.

As a clever power player, Steve figured out quickly that Ken is easily upset by conflict. Just a subtle threat that conflict is a possibility sends Ken into his Stage II "good daddy" routine with immediate attempts to guilt the "children" into behaving in a way that won't upset daddy.

Steve is clever in giving Ken second-hand reports of his own treatment of staff, subcontractors, and clients. Steve tells power stories that don't quite offend Ken but keep driving the message home that Steve is not someone to cross. Each of Steve's power stories sends a subtle message to Ken's fears that Steve won't attack Ken as long as he is a nice guy. That game allows Steve to virtually run amuck with his power abuse. Other staff members attempted to go to Ken to deal with problems that Steve was causing. Ken became agitated and gave his famous "We're supposed to conduct ourselves like family" speech. The staff could give the speech in its entirety, with just the right accents. I heard the speech three times from Ken while observing management meetings. It was astonishing how well staff could mimic him.

Ken denied people problems. He acknowledged system problems and seemed to enjoy working out wire diagrams or designing system charts that he thought would address the problems. However, he avoided dealing with the people problems. Even when he redesigned the organization chart and implemented a new computer system, he did not provide the leadership to get people to buy-in and support the changes. He seemed perplexed that putting designs on paper didn't bring about the desired changes.

Though Ken had evidence from the internal audit that problems existed, he firmly denied them. He frequently said to staff, "I wish the home office would leave us alone and let us get on with business." He communicated consistently that anyone outside his area office was an outsider and interfered with work.

As I sat down with Ken to discuss the problems, he used a consistent pattern of avoidance, denial, and intellectualization. As I stated a specific problem, Ken would jump up from the work table and rush over to his desk to get something, or leave the room to look for a file, or move over to the computer to call up some inconsequential piece of information. I could not tell whether his reaction was a conscious or unconscious attempt to avoid frank discussion, but the pattern continued each time we worked. He simply would not sit down and focus on the discussion. He used interruption, redirection, avoidance, and focusing on technical details as means to control his fear of open discussion of issues. He seemed unable or unwilling to grasp the larger issue. He repeatedly demonstrated behavior indicating that he was overwhelmed by problems. He avoided them by focusing on some technical detail that was more manageable and less threatening.

He repeated that pattern in management meetings both in his area and at the head office. The patterns were deeply ingrained defensive responses that he used whenever cues stirred his fears.

Ken is a bright man. His patterns of avoidance were so strong, however, that he simply did not make the changes necessary. Ken, his boss, and we worked out a detailed plan of actions needed to correct the ten problems verified in the internal audit report. We set a specific plan in clear Sensor, Thinker, Judge terms (STJ) — specific actions, specific deadlines, measurable indicators of progress, and measurable outcomes.

Ken looked at the management plan for addressing the problems, signed it, and gave strong lip service to his commitment. Every time we visited him his words were strong, but his behaviors did not match. He became even more preoccupied with manipulating diagrams and paper and clearly avoided carrying out the plan.

Three months later, the projects were still behind schedule, and he was not following through on the specific plans to resolve issues and get them moving. He still was not returning phone calls and had not implemented a plan to get the rest of his staff to respond immediately. He was still insisting on personally signing all correspondence that left the office. The bottleneck was worsening, since he was spending even more time out on the jobs, attending to minor details, instead of working on the overall plan to get things moving. The more time he spent out of the office, the more information stagnated. The more frightened he became, the more he wanted to control. The more he tried to control, the less he was able to manage.

When employees disagreed about something, Ken had a predictable method of taking the responsibility away from them and managing it himself. He didn't trust anyone but himself to get the job done. He was perceptually blind to the fact that he was using a losing strategy. He would not delegate and consequently became further and further behind. His Judge-controlling preference began to work against him. The more his job overwhelmed him, the less work he was able to do; yet, the more desperate he became to control the work. Once deadlines passed, they became like a personal enemy to him. Even items that would take less than ten minutes for him to complete and get out of the way would get shoved further and further to the bottom of the stack. He talked about the anger he felt every time he looked at the stack of overdue items. "They are like an accusing jury. Sometimes I just want to use a match and watch them go," he remarked as his hand rested on a large stack of work.

The more his boss demanded benchmarks and proof of how things were going, the more Ken attempted to micromanage. He would visit the job sites and give orders on the spot that caused problems for department heads, clients, subcontractors, and staff. He seemed desperate to find something that he could manage.

He said the right words whenever you cornered him, but observing his actions showed the stuck behavior. The more he feared failing, the more he employed failure methods. The more he attempted to control power by micromanaging, the more powerless he became. The more he feared rejection, the more rejection he received. The more he tried to avoid conflict, the more conflict he created.

Ken was given tangible evidence that problems existed. He denied the evidence and therefore denied the problems. He was given help to resolve the problems. The home office made some of its best talent available to him and he would not use it. They sent him to an expensive leadership course at a prestigious university, yet nothing substantially changed. They funded a new computer system, gave him additional staff, and hired consultants to help him. In short, the company did everything possible to help him succeed. Yet, Ken never moved past his denial of the problem. When his boss was on site, Ken would talk as if he understood the problem and was committed to taking action. Yet, the moment the visible pressure went back to the home office, Ken returned to the old habitual responses.

Ken even lost the capacity to articulate problems clearly. He did not demonstrate the ability to grasp a problem and plan action for resolution. The more fearful he became, the more he focused on designing paper systems and correcting details. While business worsened, he spent much of his time correcting wording on letters, checking personal expense vouchers to see if people were buying expensive meals or staying at luxury hotels, personally testing cement consistency, designing elaborate systems for correcting minor problems, etc. In short, his perception and judgment were so distorted that he became immobilized.

The company was unwilling to fire him, so he was removed from his job. His boss felt that the company had some responsibility for the expansion that put him in a position that he could not handle, and they should have noted that fact earlier. The job just grew out from under him. They put him on a special project as project manager where he had one project to manage and could use his natural preference for supervising details and building on his engineering experience.

Ken's slight preference for thinking reinforced by his engineering training made it difficult for him to recognize the amount of dissonance he felt between his rational cause/effect process and his rational value-oriented process. He frequently felt torn. His overreaction to the Stage III Competitive Intimidator perpetuated his lock on blind insistence of kindness to employees. By holding that principle clearly in mind, he blinded himself to the problems that needed addressing. In his reactionary state he locked himself also into the Stage II Benevolent Dictator use of power.

Ken indulged his Introverted tendency to withdraw into privacy when something disturbed him. He indulged his Sensor preference for detail and refused to discipline himself to work with the issues and implications. He indulged his Judge-controlling by suppressing problems and trying to control tangible systems rather than managing or leading people. Even when given clear evidence of his dysfunctional patterns, he could not stay focused long enough to act. He showed temporary understanding of a problem, but seemed unable or unwilling to act. The moment the person left who was helping him focus, perceptual distortion was immediate.

We observed an interaction with his boss in which Ken agreed to do a specific action. The boss left and in thirty minutes Ken was giving an order that was completely contradictory to what he had agreed to do. He showed no behavioral evidence of recognition of the contradiction. He appeared relieved to have ended the stressful interaction, and the relief seemed to blot out the substance of their transaction.

No matter how clearly the actions were identified, Ken could not or would not focus the energy to carry them out. Unless someone was standing right beside him, spoon feeding the actions, he dropped right back into absorption with extraneous details while ignoring the real problems. The company offered him as much support as they could and then felt they could no longer afford to wait for corrective action. Unable to provide therapy for managers, the company provided managerial feedback to give Ken the identified behaviors that were contributing to the management problems. Fortunately, Ken's boss clearly distinguished between documented behaviors affecting performance and therapy to confront deeper issues.

After the reassignment, Ken became so aware of overwhelming feelings about his experience that he did in fact seek therapy on his own. With the behavioral information about Ken's response patterns in management situations and the help of the therapist, Ken developed a long-range plan for systematically confronting the fears that drove him into dysfunctional management behaviors. He is realistic about the amount of work it will take to do it. He says, "I was really depressed the first six weeks after my reassignment, then I slowly began to feel relief. I am lucky that my boss remembered the many years of hard work I've given the company and is giving me a job with an opportunity to work through some of this. I know it is going to take a long time. Looking back, the most prominent feeling of the last five years is a low-level feeling of panic . . . as if some part of me was expecting it all to come apart. I guess I was relieved at some level when it did. I am not sure I ever want that kind of load again. I guess time will tell."

DEFENSE SHIELDS THAT DISTORT

Defense shields are attempts to avoid unpleasant emotions. As defense shields are dual in nature, they provide positive functions also. Most people use them, but many may be unaware of doing so. Watch the way people handle criticism or problems to see if they accept or deny responsibility. Do they use defense shields to protect themselves from acknowledging the unpleasant emotions aroused by the possibility of powerlessness, failure, rejection, or conflict? Do they blame others as a means of restoring their sense of self-esteem, thus avoiding the pain of failure? Sometimes we need time to absorb the information and the defense shields provide us with that opportunity. Sometimes we need to focus our attention on the immediate situation, and defense shields allow us to delay the interruption.

Reviewing commonly used defense shields gives leaders a conscious capability to recognize readily the complex defense process. We will name the major defensive games, describe and identify the process, and discuss strategies whereby leaders may help followers find more productive ways to deal with discomfort, challenge, and change.

Defenses are responses partially learned by imitating other people's responses to uncomfortable situations. Unless they are specifically dismantled through conscious effort, they operate automatically outside of awareness. Egotistical defense against anything that questions self-worth operates from the subconscious in automatic barricade against hurt. If a person has not learned to consciously deal with defense mechanisms, perception and judgment can easily be distorted by discomfiting cues. Clarity comes through conscious choice and awareness, which requires us to know when we are employing defensive distortions.

In the last case study, Ken had such deeply patterned defense shields of withdrawal, avoidance, denial, rationalization, and intellectualization that even when he acknowledged the patterns intellectually, he was still unable to confront his fears directly enough to enable him to drop the defenses and deal with the problems.

Defense mechanisms are one of the ways we defuse anxiety in order to avoid pain. We are willing to reduce our awareness, reshape reality, and do whatever it takes to avoid the painful truth.

The most commonly observed defensive games in work environments are: withdrawal, projection, rationalization, denial, intellectualization, repression, blaming, and attack. A working definition of each pattern enables us to identify and manage the process more efficiently. When cues alert people to discomfort, unpleasantness, or intense pain, they tend to use these defense shields to distance themselves from the pain:

Withdrawal — leave the painful stimuli by withdrawing physically, mentally, or psychologically; shut down, tune out, withdraw attention.

Avoidance — keep away from people or issues that cause

discomfort by taking a different path and avoiding interaction; avoid people, thoughts, feelings, and situations that arouse discomfort.

Projection — protect against painfully buried and repressed feelings by attributing those feelings or actions to someone else; criticize others instead of own actions; condemn in others what is buried inside in order to feel morally superior as a way of avoiding pain.

Rationalization — create excuses for behavior for the purpose of self-justification, thus allowing the person to avoid accepting the painful responsibility for actions; explain with excuses rather than accepting responsibility for behavior.

Denial — refuse to accept the truth by insisting on substituting pleasant for unpleasant perceptions of external stimuli; refuse to pay attention; use self-imposed censorship of words, thoughts, feelings, actions, or images that are upsetting; deny frustration, anger, or rejection.

Intellectualization — place exaggerated emphasis on thought as a way to avoid feelings involved in the situation; use excessive discussion of ideas devoid of emotional content; talk away the feelings by analyzing and thus moving from the uncomfortable feelings into a sanitized version that is carefully stripped of its hurtful feeling content.

Repression — push emotional responses deep into the subconscious and refuse to look at the feelings or own them; push pain and discomfort so deep into the subconscious as to program mind guards to avoid becoming aware of any stimulus with the potential to jerk the feelings into consciousness.

Blaming — refusing to accept responsibility for own actions by implying that someone or something else caused them to act that way; blaming others, blaming circumstances, and seeing someone or something else as the cause of the problem.

Attack — physically, emotionally, or mentally discredit the perceived source of the discomfort; either actively or passively project anger at someone else; criticize, belittle, humiliate, or angrily blast others for own discomfort.

Ken used withdrawal, avoidance, rationalization, denial, and intellectualization as ways to avoid the pain of his failure.

Withdrawal behaviors were exhibited as Ken continually got up from the table or desk to retrieve some item of information or small, tangible object whenever he became uncomfortable with discussion. The key element here is the pattern noted over countless observations. In midsentence he would become silent and stare off into space. During discussion his expression would become bland and his words would lose tone. These signals were subtle, quickly followed by his redirecting the focus away from the original issue. He tried to leave the painful stimuli by withdrawing physically, mentally, or psychologically.

Avoidance behaviors were also exhibited. Ken had not visited the planning or technical engineering branches in one year. He had physically avoided going there after the internal audit report cited conflict between the branches. I noted an interaction between Ken and a computer operator with whom he enjoyed lighthearted banter. The computer operator asked Ken to resolve a disparity between information given him by two department heads. Ken became observably uncomfortable and returned to his office. For the next ten days, Ken did not speak to the computer operator, even though he had to walk past his desk several times a day. Ken would deliberately look the other way or appear to be preoccupied. The computer operator mentioned that he shouldn't have upset Ken with the problem.

Rationalization caused Ken to find excuses for each of the ten identified problems. He excused the long delay in letters as his holding the line on quality. He explained his refusal to return phone calls as putting the needs of his employees first and outsiders second. He refused to confront problem behavior by insisting that "they didn't really mean it." He refused to acknowledge micromanagement by insisting that he was "not above rolling up his sleeves and pitching in." He rationalized being behind on schedules by citing shipment delays and clients' unreasonable demands. He used rationalization to avoid the problems with his personal and power style, thus avoiding the painful responsibility for his actions.

Denial caused Ken to refuse to accept the internal audit report, although plenty of evidence occurred on a daily basis. He insisted on talking about the work group as a family and their loyalty to the organization. He ignored the tangible reality while clinging to more pleasant perceptions.

Intellectualization was used when anyone became too direct about the low morale and the conflict in the office. He would launch a detailed explanation of motivational theory and then move on to explain some aspect of engineering. Eventually, he would touch on the idea of low morale, but by then it would be devoid of emotional content. He talked about the idea of morale as an impersonal element to be examined.

Ken could talk easily about his managerial philosophy. He used phrases like "win-win, teamwork, include people in the family feeling of the company, make this a pleasant place to work, promote harmony and cooperation." Indirectly, one could see that he valued success, empowerment, acceptance, and harmony, which are all worthwhile values — unless driven by the fear of powerlessness, failure, rejection, and conflict.

CHANGE AND FEAR OF THE UNKNOWN

Since corporate America does not acknowledge fear, few managers are trained to deal with its reality. In the corporate power game, bluff and confidence are the guidelines. Dealing realistically with fear is not part of the usual managerial training. Yet, fear is one of the realities of organizational life that is difficult to measure.

The enormous rate of change experienced by today's companies fosters a climate of fear. People wonder about the security of their jobs, about the management of their careers. Remembering to define fear as anxiety, uneasiness, concern, expecting with misgiving, we get a more realistic picture of fear. We rarely see the palm-sweating, goosebump-producing intense fear in the corporate setting. Most of the fear that managers deal with is moderate or low-level fear — the kind that is easy to misperceive, easy to deny or call by a less startling name. People would rather refer to frustration, stress, overwork, worry, concern, or irritation. Look behind most of those terms and you will probably run right into fear. Look at the term "low morale" in the work force and consider what may be happening to individuals in the face of uncertainty.

The rate of change is so fast that it is hard to predict. Unpredictability and change raise uncertainty that tends to foster fear.

Carolyn Corbin in *Strategies 2000* states, "Rapid innovation rushing out of a period of calm stability has profound effect on the American people. Growth and change are accelerating at exponential rates. For example: One-half of the energy consumed in the past 2,000 years has been used in the last 200 years. One-half of all products on supermarket shelves were not there a decade ago and will likely not be there a decade from now. For a child who is ten years old today, there will be four times as much knowledge available to that child when he goes to college as is available to him now. When that ten-year-old becomes fifty years of age, knowledge will have increased by thirty-two times today's level. People who are seventy years of age or older today have seen most of the technological innovation that has taken place in the United States. It is almost staggering to the mind to believe that most of the people living today have actually seen and experienced a total technological revolution in America." (pg. 25-26)

Change affects people differently. Change can be exciting, frightening, and stressful. In changing conditions, people must deal with how they will fare. Will they be as successful as they were in the past? Will their expertise be enough? Are they still relevant? Have they learned enough to handle it? Is their bag of experience deep enough to help them survive?

In a newspaper article entitled "In Defense of a Nation," the focus on change was well depicted: "The changes that are sweeping the world these days are stunning . . . economic warfare seems to be on the rise. From Asia, the economic challenge to the United States from Japan and a half-dozen mini-Japans seems to grow daily. Meanwhile, Western Europe is organizing itself into a trading bloc that may prove as tough and unyielding a competitor as Japan. Indeed, some analysts worry that by the end of the century, the free world may be divided into three great trading blocs — Europe, the Americas and a Japan-dominated Asia — battling for the same limited markets." *(Austin-American-Statesman)*

Identifying a major assumption about the next five years, Michael Kami in his book *Trigger Points* states: "The only thing we can depend on is unpredictability." He supports his assertion: "Consider what has happened just in the space of a few years: Inflation soared from 3 percent to 18 percent and descended to 3 percent again. The prime rate jumped from 6 percent to 22 percent and then fell to 7.5 percent . . . Oil went from $3 a barrel to $36, then down to $10 and back up to $18. (Within a few months in 1986, oil fluctuated between $32 and $10.) Gold soared from $40 to $800 and experts predicted it would top $1,000. It went below $300 . . . In 1986, copper was selling at 1932 prices. Are these just aberrations — exceptions to the norm? No, they indicate a major fundamental change in the world's economic structure." Kami explains that the era of predictability ended in 1973, and since then change has been accelerating rapidly.

One executive remarked, "It's getting harder and harder to know what to expect. It keeps me on edge trying to call it." His sentiment is echoed in many corporate suites in America.

Resistance to change is frequently fueled by fear of the unknown. Even unpleasant "knowns" are frequently more tolerable than the unknown, for some anxiety is reduced by knowing what to expect. That is hard to do today. In 1993, more than 2,000 mergers occurred in America. Such rapid change creates an uncertain climate for many workers. "Unknowns" represent the possibility of loss and powerlessness, rejection and job loss or job change, new power alliances, and perhaps failure. Fear of the consequences of change stimulates fear of losing resources such as money, supplies, contact persons, authority channels, privileges. Change can stimulate threat to territory, loss of authority, loss of control, loss of expertise and competence. Change can mean new rules, changing reward and punishment systems, changing evaluation systems, new values.

Before you think we are overlooking the positive side of change, please consider that a Stage IV Leader must realistically know how to see and predict the effect of fear due to continual change. Managing the positive effects does not present the same kind of challenge as leading people by helping them move through their fear to adapt, innovate, and produce despite rapidly changing situations.

STRATEGY FOR CONFRONTING FEAR

Recognition of fear is bringing unconscious fear-induced reactions into consciousness. When a person is unaware of the underlying fear, unconscious defense shields move automatically into place. Acknowledging fear and becoming fully aware is crucial to actively confronting it. We recommend two primary ways of confronting fear: the *subtle internal process* or the *tangible external experiential process.*

The subtle process involves mentally imagining the fear until you become comfortable with the images. Open yourself to the feelings of those images. Get comfortable. *Fear grows through avoidance and diminishes through confrontation.* The second way of confronting fear is to go out and find real-world circumstances and make yourself confront the fear. Unfortunately, this is not always possible, but you can approximate a situation to force yourself to the brink of realistically confronting fears. You are the best one to determine which of the two ways of confronting fear works best for you.

The developmental exercises that follow are designed to help confront fear.

DEVELOPMENTAL EXERCISES

Exercise 10: Confronting Fear: Subtle Internal Confrontation

This exercise is not a comfortable one. If you truly are not prepared to allow the disquieting thoughts and feelings to enter your consciousness, skip this exercise. The exercise is designed to bring unconscious thoughts and feelings into consciousness. As long as they are unconscious, fear feeds on them and can produce deep responses in you that may even surprise you. Becoming conscious of thoughts and feelings allows you more control instead of having unconscious reaction when you experience them at work. Find a quiet place where you will not be disturbed. Close your eyes and do this work internally. (You may want to make notes of your insights.) See Exercise 11 if you have difficulty doing this exercise.

Step 1: Recognize fear. Become aware of it. Think of an experience where you felt fear.

Step 2: Become comfortable with the images evoked by the fear.

Step 3: Open yourself to the feelings of those images.

Step 4: Relax. Then, imagine your worst case scenario.

Step 5: Note how consciously working with images and feelings begins to expand your tolerance for them.

Step 6: Relax. Do a comfortable amount of deep, diaphragmatic breathing to increase your comfort with the thoughts and feelings.

Step 7: Affirm that you can remain clear despite intense thoughts and feelings.

Step 8: Relax. Do more comfortable deep, diaphragmatic breathing and experience expanded awareness of your own thoughts and feelings.

Exercise 11:   Case Study of Subtle Internal Confrontation

John was working on a proposal for a presentation to a large company. If he could win the account, he would gain instant recognition and career enhancement.

As he walked into his office one morning, he felt uneasy. He looked around and noticed that the upper right-hand drawer of his desk was not quite closed. He scanned the credenza and noted that his usually neatly stacked work was slightly disarrayed. He became instantly angry, making a hasty search to see if anything was missing. He then raced out to his secretary's desk and asked her if she had been going through his papers. She was startled by his question and told him that she knew how he felt about privacy and assured him that she had not been in his office.

He was red-faced and angry. As I walked up, he was making wild assertions about people going through his things. He asked me if I had time to come in his office. We sat down to talk. He said he was really surprised at the way he was feeling.

John's secretary brought a letter for him to sign. He reached for his pen and was startled to find that the handsome pen and pencil set in the carved holder was gone. He sat back in his chair in disbelief. "Why would someone take my pen and pencil set? That was a special gift."

John was perplexed by his feelings. "I'm overreacting. This is ridiculous." We discussed the irrationality of feelings. He was surprised to acknowledge that he was reacting much stronger than the value of the lost pen and pencil set. "They didn't cost that much. It's the principle of the thing. Why am I so angry? Is this what you were talking about last week in executive development? I guess this is a good time to find out what's going on here.

You said that anger was usually driven by fear." John sat down, became quiet, closed his eyes, and began the internal search that he had practiced the week before. Here's the description of what he experienced in using the subtle internal process of confronting fear.

Step 1: John closed his eyes to help him focus on the anger he felt. He noted that he was breathing fast, he felt warmer than usual, he felt a bit queasy, and he felt the energy building to take some action. He noted the thoughts that were running through his consciousness. "I'll get whoever did this and make them pay. They had no right to take my things or go through my papers. I'll start locking my office. I'll catch whoever did this." (Note the effort to reclaim a sense of power and control.)

Step 2: Images of powerlessness began to flood his mind. Images of someone taking his high school letter jacket from his locker. The sadness and injustice of that loss years ago came back with astonishing clarity. Images of guarding possessions, a stronger lock on his locker, a friend stealing his Tonka toys out of his sand pile, his girlfriend going out with another guy the night he stayed home to study for a test, losing his favorite pocket knife. John just let the images roll through his mind. One image seemed to cue another one as they came tumbling into consciousness.

Step 3: Feelings of sadness, betrayal, loss, vulnerability, and anger at the injustice moved through him. Instead of blocking or controlling the feelings, he allowed himself to become increasingly aware of them. He was surprised that someone going through his things and stealing his pen and pencil set could evoke images and feelings from as long ago as when he was four years old.

Step 4: John took several deep breaths as he deliberately practiced diaphragmatic breathing. When he felt that he was not fighting or resisting the images or feelings that had been activated, he began to imagine a worst case scenario.

He began to imagine that someone was trying to steal his work for the client presentation. Memories emerged of long hours of research, designing and redesigning ways to present information, the acclaim and rewards that would come with successfully landing the account. Then, he deliberately imagined a competitor gaining entry into the building late one night, going straight to John's office, locking the door behind him, and lesiurely going through John's things. He imagined seeing his notes and his private papers being exposed to the ridicule and control of his most aggressive competitor for the account. He forced himself to imagine that he was watching and knowing the thoughts as the man judged John's work and controlled the outcome. He made himself watch as the competitor took parts of the presentation. He watched as the competitor then systematically destroyed John's office. As he experienced the pain of watching the man tear up papers, destroy files that took John twelve years to compile, reduce his information base to shreds, steal the floppy discs that represented his professional career, and then take the picture of his wife and children and smash the glass, John slowly opened his eyes.

Step 5: He took a few more minutes to get consciously in touch with the rich information that he experienced. He took time to notice that he had been carrying those concerns in his subconscious but had no idea they were so strong. He took time to expand his tolerance for awareness of the concerns. He then identified his fear of powerlessness as driving his anger at the person who "violated" his office.

Step 6: We discussed the effect of powerlessness and the potent emotions evoked. John talked about the weblike thoughts and feelings that seemed to unravel when he allowed them to become conscious. He talked about the release he felt inside from the experience.

Step 7: John closed his eyes again and revisited the worst case scenario in his imagination. He did not interfere with the competitor's destruction of his property. He focused instead on allowing the thoughts and feelings to flow through him while he reaffirmed that he would remain clear. His personal power was not in his papers but in himself. His fear of the powerlessness of losing his possessions had irrationally affected him. He reaffirmed that his ability to remain clear despite the unsettling thoughts and feelings was the real victory.

Step 8: John then did some more deep breathing and enjoyed his expanded tolerance for remaining clear in the face of intensity.

If you are unfamiliar with the potency of the mind, mental rehearsal, and truth replacing unconscious fabrication, you may question the validity of John's experience. Nevertheless, he claimed expansion and learning. Examine the eight-step process of John's experience to reinforce the method of recognition, comfort with images, opening to feelings, imagining worst case scenario, expanding tolerance, affirming reality and truth.

Exercise 12:   Fear of Powerlessness

Power is identified as the potential to influence. Powerlessness then implies the inability to influence or control outcomes. Powerlessness evokes thoughts and feelings that are uncomfortable for most people. This exercise allows you to increase your recognition of expressions of irritation or anger that may be fueled by the fear of powerlessness.

Match the expressions with the type of powerlessness expressed. (One type of powerlessness may apply to more than one expression.)

EXPRESSION OR THOUGHT

1___"I can't tolerate sick people."
2___"I didn't want to go anyway."
3___"He always challenges my order."
4___"She only includes people who are her age."
5___"It makes me mad when he interrupts."
6___"If the boss finds out, I'm finished."
7___"She probably won't buy my ideas. She acts like they are old hat."
8___"I can't stand to be kept waiting."
9___"Don't repeat what I said: he doesn't take prisoners."
10___"She never compliments my work."
11___"I dread that new computer system. I like the way we are doing it now."
12___"I just can't keep the hours I once did."
13___"Those meetings are so dull that I can hardly stand them."

FEAR OF POWERLESSNESS

a. fear lack of authority
b. fear lack of control
c. fear lack of access
d. fear lack of approval
e. fear mediocrity
f. fear loss of health
g. fear loss of opportunity
h. fear obsolescence
i. fear boredom
j. fear retaliation

14__"I used to be the only one who could run that program."
15__"That's my job. That's my decision!"
16__"I should have been asked to join the management team for that meeting."
17__"Don't tell my employees what to do."
18__"I hate doing the same things daily."
19__"Don't include his work with mine; he is too careless."
20__"I can't stand last minute changes."
21__"That announcement wasn't sent to my office. I wonder why not."
22__"I probably won't get a chance to try my luck."
23__"This fast pace takes lots of energy; heaven help anyone who gets sick!"
24__"He sabotaged Tom for opposing his idea."
25__"I don't want my office to be hard for people to find."

Have you improved your ability to recognize discomfort signals?

Answers:

1. f	6. j	11. b	16. c	21. c
2. c	7. e	12. f	17. b	22. g
3. a	8. b	13. i	18. i	23. f
4. h	9. j	14. g	19. e	24. j
5. b	10. d	15. a	20. b	25. c

Exercise 13:   Fear of Failure

Fear of failure involves our unwillingness to risk because of the possibilities of failure. It keeps us from trying. When we doubt our ability to succeed, we are less likely to try. The comfort of playing it safe outweighs the discomfort of failure — thus the status quo provides potent resistance to change. Fear of failure activates thoughts, feelings, and body reactions that distort and block self-development if not confronted.

Prioritize the following forms of fear of failure. Rank order the concerns using 1 to represent the highest concern and 10 the lowest concern in trying something that is professionally risky.

FEAR OF FAILURE

____ Getting up in front of a group to present information.

____ Challenging a power person's argument.

____ Doubting if you are being as persuasive as you should be.

_____ Concern about coming on too strong and turning people off.

_____ Getting fired or demoted.

_____ Concern about adequately responding to challenges or questions.

_____ Not wanting to be put down in front of others.

_____ Not wanting to appear stupid.

_____ Not wanting to appear unprepared.

_____ Concern about your performance and your reputation.

Exercise 14:   Fear of Rejection

Self-picture is the collection of images that we hold to be true about ourselves. If we see ourselves as intelligent, hard-working, successful, and innovative, then we tend to try to avoid information that contradicts our preferred image. We guard against rejection messages that suggest we are undesirable, unwanted, unworthy or dysfunctional. We don't want to be excluded by those whom we like. Rejection attacks self-worth. We vary in the degree of approval and acceptance we want, depending upon our personal style and power development.

Rate the degree to which the following situations would bother you:

1 = Not at all 3 = It would bother me 5 = It would upset me

_____ Being told you didn't get the promotion.

_____ An important client refuses to work with you.

_____ You are taken off an important project and a very ambitious person takes over.

_____ Your favorite employee asks to be transferred to another section, stating that s/he wants exposure to other management styles.

_____ You were one of three people who didn't get invited to the boss' party.

_____ You took an hour to help an employee, then she did not follow your advice.

_____ You overhear two employees talking about how strongly an upper-level executive dislikes you.

_____ You just stated your point of view and the boss says, "That's quite enough. I know where you stand. Let some others have a chance to speak."

Exercise 15: Fear of Rejection

Rate the following according to the intensity you think you would feel:

1 = Unconcerned 2 = Some Concern 3 = Concerned
4 = Upset 5 = Very Upset

_____ Someone at work hating you

_____ Power person planning to get even with you for a perceived offense

_____ Being misunderstood

_____ Being treated unfairly

_____ Being seen as inadequate

_____ Losing approval of someone whom you respect and like

_____ Losing support of someone with whom you work frequently

_____ Being excluded from referent groups that help you achieve

_____ Being treated as untrustworthy

_____ Being lonely and unsupported

_____ Being betrayed by trusted colleagues

_____ Being fired

_____ Being demoted

_____ Losing your base of expertise

_____ Losing recognition and esteem

Exercise 16: Fear of Conflict

People tend to avoid conflict. Only a small minority of people go around seeking conflict; the rest tend to avoid it. Most people remember a minor disagreement that escalated into a major conflict. Reluctant to repeat that kind of experience, people tend to smooth, avoid, or passively aggressively get even to avoid the possible explosion of overt conflict. People who avoid their own fears rather than confronting them cannot adequately predict the force of their own feelings. Rather than take a chance on conflict bringing out their worst behavior, they tend to avoid it.

When you recognize conflict and consider the need to address it, which of the following expressions of fear of conflict will you have to deal with in order to act? Put a check mark by the ones with which you would have to deal in order to confront the situation.

____ Fear emotional escalation that could get out of control

____ Fear the expression of anger

____ Fear the verbal attack on you that might result

____ Fear the conflict ending in physical attack

____ Fear vindictiveness of people involved

____ Fear later sabotage as a result of the confrontation

____ Fear group reprisal from referent groups of people involved

____ Fear the cost of damaged relationships that may not be rebuildable as a result of the confrontation

____ Fear the litigation that might result

____ Fear embarrassing the organization with your actions

____ Fear the impact on productivity

____ Fear your boss won't back you

____ Fear entrapment in a nasty situation

____ Fear the additional paperwork required to defend your action

____ Doubt that justice will be upheld

____ Fear that rational thought may not be enough to counter the politics involved

____ Fear gaining the reputation of a trouble-maker

____ Fear gaining the reputation of being difficult with which to deal

____ Fear losing people's good will; they may not understand or accept your position

____ Fear getting involved in something that could consume too much time

Now take time to review the concerns that you checked and identify the pattern of your concerns. Find experiences in your past when you chose not to confront a problem for the reason you checked. Replay it in your mind in order to get in touch with how strong your fear of conflict was in each situation. From that search of your own reactions and experience base you can then set a realistic plan for increasing your ability to confront problems when necessary. Losing the fear of conflict is essential for increasing leadership capacity.

Exercise 17:   Defense Shields

If defense shields automatically go up without conscious awareness, the likelihood increases of distorted perception and judgment without your knowing it. If you are not aware of your defensive state, you have more trouble seeing information or a situation clearly. Defense shields play an important role when they are employed consciously. There are times when using a shield is situationally important. The key is to know what you are doing at a conscious level, for that is where we take up-front responsibility for our actions. Identify the shields you employ most often by rank ordering them from 1 to 9, with 1 representing the most frequently used and 9 the least used. *Remember:* Most of us will acknowledge that we are wrong when we are presented with enough proof. The defense shields go up, however, at the first disturbance cues. They move into place quickly and perhaps unconsciously.

Rank order defense shields that you use when you feel threatened:

____ **Withdrawal** – leave, get away from the painful stimuli by withdrawing physically, mentally, and/or psychologically.

____ **Avoidance** – keep away from people or issues that cause discomfort by taking a different path and avoiding interaction; evasion of discomfort or pain by purposively avoiding it.

____ **Projection** – protect against painfully buried experiences and feelings by attributing the feelings to someone else and/or by judging them mercilessly in others. To avoid the pain of self-reproach, attack the behaviors in others as a form of self-protectiveness.

____ **Rationalization** – hold the perception of self as above reproach, thereby creating excuses for personal behavior for the purpose of self-justification. This allows one to avoid accepting the painful responsibility for actions that did not succeed, thus allowing credit for good intentions while avoiding responsibility for the actual outcome.

____ **Denial** – refuse to acknowledge the truth by refusing to look at reality that is uncomfortable; refuse to accept the truth by insisting on substituting pleasant for unpleasant perceptions of external stimuli – or rearrange perception.

____ **Intellectualization** – using an intellectual smoke screen by stripping situations and issues of emotional content and using cold logic only to analyze the situation; putting an exaggerated emphasis on thought as a way to avoid feelings in the situation by using excessive discussion of ideas devoid of value content.

____ **Repression** – pushing emotional responses deeply into the subconscious and refusing to look at them or own the feelings.

____ **Blaming** – refusing to accept responsibility for own actions by implying that someone or something else caused the action.

____ **Attack** – Use anger and attack to beat back the feelings of frustration; physically, emotionally, or mentally discredit perceived source of the discomfort.

Note: Defense shields are not labeled as bad. We are identifying them as perceptual and judgmental distortions if they are happening to you and you are unaware of them. A Stage IV Leader must be capable of responding situationally appropriately. The Leader must be able to spot defense shields in self and others in order to read people and situations accurately.

Exercise 18:   Case Study: Stage II
Benevolent Dictator and Stage III Competitive Manipulator

The leader's task is to read people clearly and help develop their potential. Tom Thompson is an electrical engineer whose ambitious goals call for his making it to department head within ten years after graduation. He's been with the company nine years and is assistant to the department head, just one position away from his goal. His boss, Alan, is content being department head and does not intend to give up the position.

Tom found Alan's Stage II Benevolent Dictator role an easy one to manipulate. He charms and befriends Alan. He consistently identifies the parts of the job that are distasteful to Alan and volunteers to relieve him of the tasks. Tom put himself in charge of a number of crucial reports to give himself high visibility with upper management. He gradually increased his span of control until he absorbed much of Alan's job. The CEO sees Tom as a tougher power player than his boss. He has been watching Tom to see if he can grow into the higher quality executive the CEO demands at the top.

Tom is a Competitive Manipulator who spends more time controlling his image and oiling his information network than in actually working on tasks. He skillfully exaggerates his own role in important events and increases his importance in the retelling. He focuses on winning the favor of powerful people who can advance his career, while manipulating less powerful people to give him what he wants. Fortunately, the CEO recognizes Tom's unchecked ambition and identifies him as questionable upper-level material. The next rung above department head is vice-presidency. The CEO continually scans for management potential for that upper level.

Tom attends a management meeting in Alan's place. An important issue is raised concerning maintenance and the electricians. He says, "Just let me handle this. Alan has his hands full. One more crisis is not what he needs right now. I'll take care of it."

The CEO asked Tom about the improved productivity records for the past month. Tom said, "Yes, I put in lots of extra hours with our people but it paid off." The CEO noted the eagerness with which Tom claimed all the credit for himself. The CEO decided to test him further. "Productivity output was up, but so were maintenance costs. Why were they so high?" he asked.

Tom responded, "Yeah, I noticed that too and talked to Alan about it. He said for me not to worry about it. Some months are like that."

"I thought you personally authorized the overtime on the Kaiser equipment. Wasn't that your signature I saw on the permit?"

"Oh, yeah, but I was just signing for Alan because he was out of pocket. I would have handled it differently if it had been my call. Let me tell you how I handled that storage problem on the large equipment. I had to design a whole new tracking system but I was glad to work extra to get it into operation."

The CEO interrupted the self-adulation and refocused the discussion on the original problem. When the group reached resolution on the problem, the CEO told Tom to advise Alan about the situation, the solution, and the action dates.

What would you predict Tom would do with the situation?

A. Go back and give his boss Alan an accurate account of the interaction.

B. Go back and take care of the situation himself in order to get credit for solving a problem that had executive council attention.

C. Go back and tell Alan about the situation while under-representing its importance so Alan won't interpret it as executive request for specific action.

The first prediction is the most unlikely. Tom is committed to the Competitive Manipulator power style. He is predictable to a large degree.

Tom did not realize that the CEO could read his game so easily. Tom fell right into the trap. He went back to his office and devoted maximum time to controlling the problem. He ignored other things and focused instead on the grandstand performance of the situation he thought would reveal his boss' failure and put himself center stage. He did not understand that he was dealing with a savvy CEO — a Stage IV Leader who understands people.

If it is your task to help Tom deal with his stuck position in a Stage III Competitive power orientation, what would you do? There is not a textbook answer, but here's what the real CEO did:

1. Moved Tom for a six-month job rotation.
2. Put Tom under a more mature manager.
3. Described to Tom the power behaviors that he wanted corrected.
4. Described clearly the kind of consistent behaviors required for movement into the executive level of the company.
5. Described clearly the power games he had personally observed Tom playing, spelled out their consequences, and reiterated that Tom had the intelligence and ambition to make it to the top but his personal style and use of power would block him.
6. Told Tom that he would have to stop playing games and commit himself to the difficult task of developing real strength and experience instead of manipulating perception.
7. Assured Tom of the executive attention he had been trying so hard to manipulate, so he can now prove or disprove his capability.

The outcome of this case is that Tom's game was so thoroughly described by the CEO that he could no longer use the defense shields of projection, blaming, denial, and rationalization in dealing with the executive group. They held him accountable for what he actually did and said; they helped him with a leadership development plan that he pursued.

– 3 –

Extrovert-Introvert: Finding the Balance

Main Ideas of Chapter 3:

1. Balance of natural and acquired skills of Extroversion and Introversion is needed for Stage IV Leadership development.
2. Dominant function in personal style should lead in developing the other three functions.
3. Most effective development of potential uses natural preferences to develop least preferred functions.
4. Systematic development of potential is needed; habits are deeply embedded, thus requiring consistent attention.
5. Confronting fears produced by preference for Extroversion or Introversion aids development of potential.

DEVELOPING EXTROVERT-INTROVERT BALANCE

Activating potential is crucial to Stage IV Leadership. Using the organizing principles of the Myers-Briggs, personal style can be readily identified. Using the behavioral principles of the power model, the stage of power development is also identifiable. With these two frameworks, a behavioral inventory of a person's personal style and power stage can be used to design a systematic development plan.

PERSONAL STYLE	GOAL
Extrovert-Introvert	Balance of natural and
Sensor-Intuitor (N)	acquired skills
Thinker-Feeler	
Judge-Perceiver	

POWER STAGE	GOAL
Stage 1 — *Dependency*	Stage IV Leadership
Terrible Tyrant	development
Helpless Infant	
Stage 2 — *Autonomy*	
Benevolent Dictator	
Abusive Dictator	
Stage 3 — *Competition*	
Competitive Manipulator	
Competitive Intimidator	
Stage 4 — *Leadership*	
Inspirational Leader	
Fearsome Leader	

In Chapter 1 we developed the leadership model for Stage IV use of power. We define a leader as one who sees clearly, decides wisely, and acts in the best interests of others. That raises a practical question: How does one get to the point of clarity, wisdom, and selflessness?

In Chapter 2 we presented a rationale for a route to development. Our premises are:

(1) Fear distorts perception and judgment:
    A. Four fears are principal blockers of potential: fear of powerlessness, failure, rejection, and conflict.
    B. Defense shields cued by fear distort perception and judgment.
(2) Confronting fear is the most direct route to developing potential.
(3) Personal egotism prevents Stage IV Leadership development.

We make two primary assumptions: (1) Stage IV power development is necessary for sustainable leadership and (2) balancing style preferences with acquired skills from your least preferred style is essential.

In this chapter we focus on development of potential by looking at Extroversion/Introversion as the key to setting a realistic development plan. The Extrovert's most natural style is action and experience in the external world; whereas, the Introvert's most natural style is ideation and understanding in the internal world. They obviously have different keys to developing potential. The Extrovert wants to try it; the Introvert wants to understand it. In the worst case, the Extrovert could spend a lifetime trying things that didn't systematically develop potential, thus squandering energy by sampling life without an overall direction. Similarly, the Introvert could spend a lifetime pondering life without getting around to acting on it. Thus, Extroverts' key to potential lies in finding a systematic way into their inner world to order and focus. Introverts' key lies in finding a systematic way to turn internal focus into external action.

Stage IV Leaders manifest the characteristics of both Extroversion and Introversion. Their natural preference will be balanced with excellent skills developed for the least preferred side. They use the strengths of both Extroversion and Introversion so smoothly that the average person would be unable to detect preference. Stage IV Leaders have a wholeness and a balance that communicates their genuine ability to utilize the best of both halves of style preference.

The following chart reviews the basic differences between the Extroverted and Introverted preferences.

EXTROVERT-INTROVERT CHARACTERISTICS

EXTROVERT	INTROVERT
Outside world	Inner world
People, action, things	Ideas, thoughts, meanings
Prefers interaction — Active	Prefers reflection — Reflective
Sociable — External events	Territorial — Internal reactions
Usually talkative and outgoing	Usually quiet and reserved

Sociable with many friends — refers to many people as friends	Introspective with a few close friends, discriminating carefully between acquaintance and friend
Tends to like meeting new people	Tends to postpone meeting new people
Tends to seek new experiences	Tends to avoid new experiences
Tends to expand rather than conserve — Expansive	Tends to consolidate, defend and protect — Contractive
Reacts to stress primarily by increasing activity	Reacts to stress primarily by decreasing activity
Energized by activity	Energized by privacy and intimacy

Isabel Myers, describing Introverts, said they "can be thought of as silent, reserved, slow to unbend, and inclined to mind their own business and leave others to do the same." (pg. 28, *Gifts Differing*) Introverts are much more focused on their inner world than they are the outer world. The private cave of the Introvert is a cozy world of ideas that offers a warm sanctuary from the demands of the external world. When uninvited, uncomfortable situations or messages intrude into the cave from the outer world, the Introvert focuses laser-like energy to restore idea harmony and integration.

Introverts' central world is inside the privacy of their own caves. Development of potential requires action which will involve them in the external world. One young supervisor with ISTJ (Introvert, Sensor, Thinker, Judge) typology slowly progresses in her job. She has the same problem at every major growth juncture — she wants to arrange the growth by reading and thinking about it. She postpones actually acting on it. For six years she has stubbornly held to her Introverted pattern. When her boss insists that she learn something new or improve her communication skills, she looks for books to read on the subject. She always designs a plan to follow that invariably includes reading, thinking, and meditating. She stops short of developing a plan to act on the challenge externally. She tries to control the challenge by keeping it safely contained in her internal cave.

Myers described Extroverts as "being more open, accessible, communicative and friendly." (pg. 28, *Gifts Differing*) Extroverts prefer to do their growth and development in external activity. In contrast to the Introvert's home base in the internal cave, the

Extrovert's home base is right out in the middle of the playing field. The key to developing Extrovert's potential lies in getting a clear and comfortable path into the internal cave of reflection and introspection.

Bill is an Extroverted banker who has difficulty spending enough time alone to reflect on where his life is going. He stays in perpetual action mode. Even when something is seriously bothering him that he needs to carefully consider, he always postpones it in favor of a tennis game or some external activity. He is now fifty-four years of age and has so many issues stacked up in the cave that need sorting, that he avoids his Introverted world with intensity. He fills every day and night with activity so that when he does have to be alone, he can go to the cave for sleep rather than reflection. Bill avoids personal growth by staying so active that he doesn't have time to think. "Doing" replaces reflective thinking.

Introverts need to show up on the playing field to stretch potential into reality. They have to give up hanging out in their cave too much and spend more time trying out their internal discoveries. Introverts can fool themselves easily. An idea they have been excitedly exploring internally can be so provocative that they can become engrossed in looking for applications in the external world. Introverts can become so involved in watching others that they feel no need to act themselves. By observing someone else's activity, they can falsely conclude that they gain the same value from watching the experience that others get from acting out the experience. Watching others allows the Introvert to become familiar with the activity. Observing others is a safe way to test ideas. By observing someone else take a risk, Introverts do not have to feel the sensations and vulnerability involved in doing it themselves. Thus, Introverts have ideas with lots of external world observation, many of which they have not actually tried out. Thus, they can have well-developed ideas that lack the wisdom of tested experience.

Extroverts, conversely, can collect lots of experience without taking the time to examine it. They seek experiential exposure. Unless they take Introverted time to organize the significance of their experience, they can travel lots of miles and wind up someplace they never wanted to go. Extroverts can race from activity to activity without a clear destination; whereas, Introverts can have well-developed maps for their destination but never actually start the car.

If you compared the problem of developing potential to an automobile, Extrovert machines need to work on braking and guidance systems and Introvert machines need to work on ignition switch and action gears.

Stage IV Leaders are deeply involved in both their inner and outer worlds. Becoming too involved in one world at the expense of the other causes distortion. At some point in maturing toward Stage IV, self-reliance replaces inner or outer world dependency. Thus, freedom to respond situationally is won.

DOMINANT FUNCTION

Four functions are used to provide perception and judgment for the individual (Sensing, Intuiting, Thinking, Feeling). One of those functions operates as a dominant function — the one that is in charge of the rest. The dominant function is used in the favorite world of the individual. Healthy Extroverts use their dominant function in the external world and Introverts use their dominant function in the internal world. This may sound confusing, but the point is useful in developing potential.

Dominant function is determined by whether a person is primarily a Judge-controller or Perceiver-adapter. The fourth dimension of the Myers-Briggs addresses the way individuals deal with the external world. Therefore, a person who scores as a Judge will use the judging function of either Thinking or Feeling as the main communication channel with the external world. A person scoring as a Perceiver-adapter will use the perceiving function of either Sensing or Intuiting as the external channel. So far, that is easy to follow.

The complexity occurs in trying to understand Introversion. Remember the principle that Extroverts and Introverts use their dominant function in their favorite world. It therefore follows that Extroverts use their dominant function in the external world and Introverts use their favorite function in the internal world. The secondary function is called the *auxiliary function*. Introverts use their auxiliary function in the external world and save their dominant function for their private world, thus contributing to the greater difficulty of understanding Introverts. "What you see is not necessarily the one in charge."

An ISFP manager will appear to the external world to be primarily a Sensor. Anyone who makes a presentation to him for a decision and uses facts only will probably not get the expected decision. The ISFP's controlling Feeler function operates in the ISFP's private world. Listening to the Sensor aide doing the talking can lead to the wrong assumption that one is dealing with a dominant Sensor. Though the words sound Sensor, the private Feeler control function is continually evaluating decisions for the people impact and values involved.

Don't despair with the complexity. There are clues that you learn to recognize that help you unravel the mystery (see Exercise 31). First clue is to note whether you are dealing with an Extrovert or Introvert. When dealing with Extroverts, listen to the way they word ideas and interests. When dealing with Introverts, listen to the subtle clues hidden within the main thrust of the expression.

For example, the ISFP manager listening to a request to try a new program used a pattern of questions that sounded like fact questions but had a subtle people-impact pattern. He asked, "How much will it cost? Will the employee assistance program be affected? From whose department will you be taking the materials? How will you coordinate the tasks with the holiday pressures?" Careless interpretation of the questions would assume that the manager is just checking the facts. Careful analysis shows the underlying concern for the impact on people. The Sensor aide gathering the facts is easy to see, but the subtle concern from the controlling function in the cave is probing for his primary Feeler interest of impact on people.

Using organizational terms, we call the dominant function the CEO (chief executive officer) and the auxiliary function the administrative aide. In dealing with Extroverts, you can more readily identify the CEO; however, when dealing with Introverts you may have difficulty realizing that the externalized expression is really the aide and you may not be accurately reading the decision-maker CEO. In the following illustration, you see the sixteen Myers-Briggs types that show who deals with the external world and who is in charge of the internal world. The CEO operates in the favorite world and sends the aide to deal with the other world.

Extroverts use dominant process in the external world, while

Introverts use dominant process in the internal world. The following chart shows dominant function for each of the sixteen types. (Large bold letter indicates the CEO in charge.)

ISTJ	INTJ	ISTP	INTP	ESTJ	ENTJ	ESTP	ENTP
ISFJ	INFJ	ISFP	INFP	ESFJ	ENFJ	ESFP	ENFP

Research indicates that we are likely to develop the two middle letters (the functions of Sensing or Intuiting, Thinking or Feeling) first. The other two functions are likely to be less developed initially. We refer to the four functions in the way they are used in communicating and processing information. We refer to the functions as first, second, third, and fourth channel in their likely use in verbal communication. We will indicate the dominant function for each of the sixteen types, keeping in mind that Extroverts use their dominant channel in the external world as first channel while Introverts use their dominant internally. Introverts use their auxiliary channel to meet the world while reserving their dominant channel for their private world.

Communication Channels

	ESTJ	ENTJ	ISTJ	INTJ
First channel	Thinking	Thinking	Thinking	Thinking
Second channel	Sensing	Intuiting	Sensing	Intuiting
Third channel	Intuiting	Sensing	Feeling	Feeling
Fourth channel	Feeling	Feeling	Intuiting	Sensing

	ESFJ	ENFJ	ISFJ	INFJ
First channel	Feeling	Feeling	Feeling	Feeling
Second channel	Sensing	Intuiting	Sensing	Intuiting
Third channel	Intuiting	Sensing	Thinking	Thinking
Fourth channel	Thinking	Thinking	Intuiting	Sensing

	ENTP	ENFP	INTP	INFP
First channel	Intuiting	Intuiting	Intuiting	Intuiting
Second channel	Thinking	Feeling	Thinking	Feeling
Third channel	Feeling	Thinking	Sensing	Sensing
Fourth channel	Sensing	Sensing	Feeling	Thinking

	ESTP	ESFP	ISTP	ISFP
First channel	Sensing	Sensing	Sensing	Sensing
Second channel	Thinking	Feeling	Thinking	Feeling
Third channel	Feeling	Thinking	Intuiting	Intuiting
Fourth channel	Intuiting	Intuiting	Feeling	Thinking

Instead of trying to understand the way dominant and auxiliary works in sixteen different types, just zero in on your own type. As you come to understand the complexities of the way the process works in you, the foundation for understanding others is laid. Find your style in the chart to understand the way the process works in you. We will continue the analogy of the CEO being your dominant function, the aide being the auxiliary function, and the other two functions operating as workers. Apply the actual relationships between CEO, administrative aide, and workers for your interpretation. The CEO has the most power and authority, while the administrative aide has primarily a support role. Workers usually receive more orders than opportunity for input into decisions. In most healthy people, the four functions operate similarly. The dominant function is primarily in charge of the other three functions. In Stage IV Leadership each of the functions has clear input.

The greatest untapped potential usually lies in the least preferred functions. It therefore follows that systematic development of least preferred style should greatly increase personal potency.

BALANCED TYPE DEVELOPMENT

We use perception to see and judgment to decide about what we see. The preferred functions are likely to be the two skilled processes in a person's Myers-Briggs style. An ISTJ prefers the dominant Sensing perception and auxiliary Thinking judgment. In healthy type development, these two skilled processes work well together. The auxiliary does not fight the dominant for control, but rather works to support it.

We are dependent upon a well-developed auxiliary function to bring balance between the messages of the Extrovert and Introvert worlds. An Introvert with an undeveloped auxiliary function would be somewhat trapped in the internal world without the confident auxiliary to take care of the external demands. An Extrovert with an undeveloped auxiliary would be somewhat locked out of the internal world. Without good development of the dominant and auxiliary functions, balance cannot be achieved between the inner and outer worlds of an individual.

"The supremacy of one process, unchallenged by the others, is essential to the stability of the individual." (Myers, *Gifts Differing*, pg. 183) For the Extrovert the auxiliary is the way-shower into the internal world; while for the Introvert the auxiliary is the doorway to the external world — the main communication channel with the outside world. Development of potential becomes more precise when you work with your natural personality style. Most people, however, take random approaches to development and do not know how to tailor information nor techniques for maximum utilization. We spend billions of dollars on training courses in this country with little awareness of the way individuals absorb and process the training. Knowing who takes charge of the information (your CEO), to whom it is dispensed for action (your administrative aide), and to whom it is given for integration and exploration into the whole response system (least preferred functions) allows more precision in developing your own potential.

For example, an ISTJ manager listening to an employee request for authorization to purchase a new computer program processes the request according to his preferences. The Thinker administrative aide takes over the external questioning by checking the logic of the request.

Thinker Administrative Aide begins asking questions:
What's wrong with our current program?
What evidence do you have that we need to change?
What is our analysis response time now?
What do you expect to achieve with the new program?

The **Sensor CEO,** sitting silently in the cave, is waiting for the employee to give him the critical Sensor data, such as assurance of workability, field test results, other companies who have used the program, reliability of results, anticipated implementation problems, names, dates, costs and numbers.

If the ISTJ manager has mature style development, then his Feeler worker will provide accurate assessment of the importance of the request to the employee. His Feeler will assess the impact on others, the customer service gain, and other value-added possibilities. His Feeler will force him to go beyond the facts. The Intuitor worker will produce additional possibilities of uses and impacts.

An ISTJ manager without excellent type development will focus primarily on the facts and logic and overlook people impact, value-added, meaning, and importance since the CEO Sensor and the Thinker AA dominate the thinking process.

Extroverts comprise approximately 75% of the American population; therefore, they usually set the norms. The smaller percentage of Introverts are forced to develop their auxiliary functions if they are to successfully deal with the demands of the external world. There is a much more identifiable penalty for Introverts who have not developed balance in their style. They are seen as strange, uncommunicative recluses. Introverts with effective type development have acquired skills to handle external demands and can function comfortably in the inner and outer worlds, as do Extroverts with good type development.

The dominant process tends to become quite absorbed in the world of greatest interest to them. Their favorite world (internal or external) is the most interesting, most important, easiest place of focus where they function best. "If the dominant process becomes deeply involved in less important matters, the main business of life will suffer. In general, therefore, the less important matters are left to the auxiliary process." (Myers, *Gifts Differing*, pg. 13) In other words, the CEO focuses primarily on the favorite world and the administrative aide deals with the least favorite world.

To develop the necessary strength for Stage IV Leadership, balance must occur between the inner and outer worlds and among the four functions. Myers clearly points out that balance among the dimensions does not imply equality. Rather, balance implies proper relationships of the functions. Balanced leadership requires an individual to have a dominant CEO function that utilizes and develops the administrative aide's auxiliary function, while paying close attention to the information of the other two functions. Thus, a leader's balance comes from integrating Thinking, Feeling, Sensing, and Intuiting to provide perceptual clarity and good judgment.

The following case study shows the problems that occur with inadequate balance between the outer and inner worlds.

CASE STUDY: THE ISTP INTELLECTUAL INSIDE THE INTROVERT'S CAVE

Bob is an intelligent man earning a living as an electrical engineer. He is a family man, respected in his community and known for his stability. People most often characterize him as "a nice man." Bob, however, is stuck. He does not even come close to living up to his potential. He has been at the same level for the past ten years, working at a lethargic pace and paying little attention to the deadening of his creativity and the death of his personal ambition. Referring to Bob's stability is an innocuous way of describing his boringly predictable behavior.

Bob is an ISTP (Introvert, Sensor, Thinker, Perceiver-adapter) in personal style and a Stage II Benevolent Dictator in power style. We've known Bob for many years but have only recently begun to work with him on developing his potential.

With clear preference for Introversion, Bob is reluctant to draw attention to himself. He does not cause waves nor verbalize unpopular views. He goes along to get along, while holding a far different reality about himself internally.

Using organizational terms, Bob's personal style CEO is his Thinker, with his administrative aide as Sensor. According to good type development his Sensor would have the job of interacting with the external world and representing reality to the CEO Thinker in the cave. Sensor function is best at accurately reporting reality as it exists in the physical world. Even though Bob's Introversion makes his favorite world internal, he has an able servant in the Sensor aide to keep him reality based. That, however, is not true in Bob's case.

Since we depend upon the auxiliary service of the administrative aide to provide access to our least favorite world, it needs to be well developed and clearly integrated. Bob needed his Sensor aide to keep him reality based, while his Thinker CEO analyzed consequences.

Bob spent much of his time as a child preoccupied inside his own head. He loved to be alone in his room. By the time he was eight he was reading advanced books and was well on the way to developing intellectual capability. His Thinker CEO loved idea formulation and understanding. More and more he forced the Sensor aide to interrupt him less and less. He developed a deep habit of rejecting realistic information from his external world, while increasing his internal interest and enjoyment. He developed strong defense shields that protected his Thinker world. His inner world allowed him to block irrational information that challenged the orderly logic of his world. He disliked the chaotic irrationality of the outer world. He liked to be in charge of his cave, where he could reign as king. He simply beheaded the bearer of messy news.

When the Sensor aide brought information that disturbed him, he discounted through denial, repression, blaming, and intellectualization. More and more he internally stripped messages of emotional content, putting exaggerated emphasis on thoughts in order to avoid feelings. If provoked and forced to engage in "disruptive" communication with others in the external world, he attacked. He lost the balance between his inner and outer worlds. He really wanted to be left alone to read and think. His inner world was safe and interesting. It was in the outer world that he felt uncertain, disconnected, and unsure of himself.

He became more and more fearful of external demands and interruptions. He restricted the Sensor function to monitoring for useful facts in order to defend his privacy. He did not use it for reliable data about his interaction in the outer world. He lost touch with reality by failing to adequately use his auxiliary function.

He dismissed Feeler information as irrational and ignored Intuitive input about the implications of his patterns. He was content to allow his Thinker to be authoritarian in controlling his perception and judgment. If you looked at the organization of his personal style you could easily identify his Thinker as a Stage II power style. His Thinker was the authoritarian dictator who tolerated no dissenting or uncomfortable information. He used defense shields to monitor realism (Sensor), screen out value-based information (Feeler), ignore process impact information (Intuitor). He blocked anything that could disturb the pristine world of logical thought (Thinker). He controlled information to keep himself comfortable. He was comfortable, but at considerable cost. He self-induced perceptual blindness.

Bob's boss had tried multiple strategies to get him motivated and inspired to develop his latent talent. Nothing worked. Bob plodded along, steadfastly defending his internal world against intrusion.

Finally, the day arrived when Bob got a less-than-satisfactory performance evaluation. His boss wanted to get his full attention. Bob listened to the evaluation while anger flooded through him, though he was careful not to let it show on his face. He told us that he ignored much of what was said and internally focused on two descriptors used in his evaluation: "irresponsible and unresponsive." Those two "insults" directly affected his self-concept.

In the privacy of his internal world, he saw himself as intellectually superior, high above the emotionalism of the average person, and dispensing his wisdom from the unquestioned superiority of an advanced Christian position. ("How dare anyone criticize me!") To be told in a performance appraisal that he was irresponsible made him instantly angry. He began using the appraisal to gather factual evidence of the boss' inferior perception and judgment. At the time, he did not even consider the possibility that the description could be true.

The moment he felt the emotional response in his body from the negative feedback, he became instantly defensive. But with the well-practiced art of Introverted Thinking, he did not betray his position with careless verbal or nonverbal disclosure. He appeared to passively receive the information while he was internally seething.

While his boss was discussing his patterns of irresponsible behavior, Bob was internally denying the possibility. He was mentally listing all the ways that he was responsible. He recalled a barrage of defensive facts to counter the irresponsible charge: "I teach Sunday school. I have three children. I don't cheat on my wife. I show up for work. I am a Bible scholar. I am absolutely responsible." His boss, however, was citing evidence about Bob's doing just enough to get by, but nothing extra. He did not initiate, he did not innovate, and he had to be guided from task to task. He was irresponsible in not managing his work well. He was behaving as if he were a workman requiring constant supervision. If the boss didn't say to do it, he didn't. He didn't accept the responsibility to keep clients informed nor apprise his boss of possible problems. He put in his day and let the work stack up as he kept his slow, methodical pace. He removed himself from any responsibility to notice or solve problems.

When Bob received information that countered his self-picture, the following pattern occurred:

1. He became internally defensive.
2. He maintained a passive external role to mask his inner anger.
3. He used vigorous internal dialogue to list facts to deny the validity of the charge.
4. He mentally, psychologically and, as soon as possible, physically withdrew.
5. He used the privacy of inner thoughts to destroy the "accuser's" credibility. A favorite strategy was to list the faults of the "accuser," which allowed him to ignore the feedback and increase his Thinker notions of power as he destroyed the credibility of his perceived attacker. He drained off the development potential by reinforcing his defense shield and further indulging his Thinker habits.
6. He subsequently avoided the person making the charges.
7. He reported that for several days afterward, he became absorbed with looking for proof to reinforce his picture of himself.

The charge of unresponsiveness in the performance appraisal triggered other memories also. His boss sounded vaguely like his wife's description of his being cold and distant. His boss was citing instances of ignoring people, failing to provide information that clients needed, being uncommunicative, unfriendly, and too reserved. His wife used more explicit descriptions, but the messages sounded nauseatingly familiar. They really disturbed Bob. He saw himself as a superior, wise sage above the vagaries of daily life. He saw himself as the epitome of Christian steadfastness. The image of being cold and unresponsive just didn't fit. Armed with his intellect and his defense shields, he focused maximum energy to destroy the credibility of the charges. He ignored the growth opportunity. Acceptance of the realistic feedback would have allowed him to start growing again.

Bob saw his wife as emotionally needy and intellectually inferior. He saw his boss as an arrogant snob who couldn't possibly understand.

Looking back on the self-delusion, Bob realizes that he developed an elaborate game to prove that he was a good man. His rationale was that a good man would have to be responsible, responsive, and caring. While resisting the requests of his wife and children for affectionate attention, he volunteered for community projects which he could then use as Sensor proof that he was good. His fear of admitting that he was cold set him up for easy manipulation. People in the community learned quickly that they could get him to help with projects where he could use his electrical expertise. He would agree to help them in order to get the egotistical bathing that comes from others recognizing his talent. When it came time to act, however, he secretly resented the demand on his time.

At home he projected constantly that he was too busy to be bothered. When his children wanted to talk to him, wanted a hug, or wanted him to play, he got irritated. He scowled at them for interrupting and disdainfully projected annoyance. He internally judged their emotional needs to be signs of weakness. He looked down on their demands to play as frivolous. Occasionally, he dropped into a parent-child role so he could play superior adult correcting their foolish thoughts or incorrect actions. But he did not commit to actually working with the children. He just judged them and withdrew. If the children were emotionally upset, he sent them to their mother to get their emotional needs met. He didn't want to be bothered.

If either his wife or children made emotional demands on him, he made them pay by withdrawing his attention and ignoring them. When he felt they had been properly punished, he casually responded with an attitude of bored condescension as he begrudged the time and energy taken away from the "real" work inside his own head. It was rare for him to set himself aside and open up to others and their needs. He was virtually a stranger to his family since he didn't allow them into his privacy cave.

At this point you may be disagreeing with the earlier description of Bob as an intelligent man. Recall the rationale presented in Chapter 2 and you can readily see how intelligence can become overgrown with personal egotism. The premises state that fear distorts perception and judgment, personal egotism prevents Stage IV development, four fears are main blockers, and defense shields distort perception and judgment.

Bob was driven by fear. As he allowed his personal egotism to grow unchecked, his judgment became more distorted. At age 38, this intelligent man was on the verge of losing his job and his home. He had a huge personal debt, he was emotionally estranged from his wife and children, and felt trapped in a personal style that was dysfunctional.

By indulging in his inner world of thought while ignoring facts, feelings, and implications, Bob became filled with personal egotism. Gradually, he began to allow no personal criticism, no real internal invasion, no reality testing, fewer and fewer personal demands. He built a well-defended wall at the entrance to his Introverted cave. At age 38 he had an overdeveloped intellect, an underdeveloped auxiliary function, and malnourished and immature Feeler and Intuitive functions. As he became more and more fearful of disturbing information, he became more entrenched behind defense shields.

Bob gave up his personal ambition as he bowed to his fear of failure. He tried to avoid failure by withdrawing from the external world where he perceived the most threatening form of failure. He became so addicted to the power of his Thinker intellect that he would do anything to avoid the powerlessness of confused thought, including blinding himself to reality. He became so afraid of the feelings engendered by rejection that he didn't venture out of his cave with affection that might open the door to pain. He kept his affection restricted to his fantasy world, where there was no recognized risk. He was so afraid of entanglement in the outer world that he became passive to avoid any possibility of conflict. He gave up his ambition and withdrew from as much active involvement with the external world as he could control.

Bob's wife, Betty, is an ESFJ (Extrovert, Sensor, Feeler, Judge). She learned early in their relationship how to manipulate him. As an active Extrovert she wanted to go out frequently. To combat her Introverted husband, who wanted to be left alone to read and think, she learned to project subtle messages at him that he was boring. He defended against that projection by withdrawing into his private world of superiority where he did not have to indulge in the "childish worldly entertainment of the less evolved." Thus she could project the image that he was boring, he would withdraw, and then she was free to go out and entertain herself and spend money which they could not afford. She wasn't interested in studying life; she wanted to live it without too much examination. She considered talk about the meaning or direction of life to be a waste of time.

When the debts became too large, Bob played the head-of-the-family role and gave dire warning. Then he returned to his inner world and let the family go ahead and spend without further challenge. He credited himself for the cautionary words about debt and ignored his responsibility when they went ahead and raised the family debt. He could then blame them for not heeding his advice. This game allowed him to avoid the conflict that would occur if they dealt with the problem realistically. He could then retreat to his cave, rationalizing his responsibility by claiming that he tried but the family just wouldn't cooperate.

As an expressive Feeler, Betty constantly criticized Bob for not being responsive to what he called an insatiable need for affection. To keep her from making too many emotion-laden demands on him, he developed a variety of subtle games: criticizing her, ridiculing her through hurtful humor, withdrawing from her, locking her out of his inner world, looking down on her as being intellectually inferior, privately listing her faults as a means of reducing the credibility of her criticism, and withholding affection and acting bored and uninterested when others were around whom she wanted to impress. This kind of relating between married people is all too common.

Before you write Bob off and decide he is too far gone to help, consider that the job of a leader is to help people wherever they are. We don't get ideal cases. Stage IV Leadership requires astute observation of behavior and keen understanding of people. It also requires long-term commitment to draw out the potential. Rarely does potential turn into actuality overnight; it is a time-bound process. Most people don't want the entanglement that Stage IV Leadership demands. Leaders demonstrate genuine interest in helping people overcome obstacles and move systematically to activate potential.

How would you help Bob? We are not talking about therapy. We are talking about helping a person realistically assess the distortions that block growth. Managers are obligated to give feedback on behaviors they observe, if the behaviors interfere with mission accomplishment. In this case Bob's intelligence was used to develop elaborate defense shields so artfully constructed that he fooled himself. He had no idea how the distorted perceptions happened. When enough pain and problems finally penetrated his inner world, he became immobilized by apathy.

A clear understanding of the helping process allows you to evaluate the outcome. As we helped him unravel his personal style and identify his deluding mechanisms, we hoped he would actively implement a personal development plan. He was reluctant, so progress was much slower than we anticipated.

The first step was to get Bob to accept that he had problems. We had to give Bob behavioral evidence of the problems resulting from his personal style. We knew that his Thinker process was still filtering and controlling information. We had to repeatedly identify Sensor facts that could not be refuted. This process had to be repeated frequently since he was still using his habitual way of judging, i.e., looking at evidence to refute the disturbing information instead of looking at evidence objectively. We urged him to develop a specific, measurable plan. He resisted. He wanted to keep control of the plan safely inside his own head.

After five weeks of Sensor factual evidence, we gained enough credibility with him to start inferring the patterns of his own behavior in a tentative move toward getting him to develop his Intuitive function. Still we are working with his dominant Thinker control. He would not trust the Intuitively recognized patterns. He had to be led methodically through Sensor evidence in a logical set of inferences to ultimately recognize the patterns. He was shocked to realize how off-course his life had become. As he became more comfortable with the acceptance phase of development, he focused his logic on what to do about it. The Thinker function is a natural problem-solving mechanism, so he began to use the natural strengths to work on solution.

The second phase of development includes confronting fears that fueled distortions. This phase involved Bob's deciding on two or three tangible things he could do to start confronting his fear. He was stuck here for eight weeks. He finally decided that he would begin work on a four-point plan: (1) he would be more responsive to clients and colleagues at work, (2) he would get a second job to help deal with their huge debt, (3) he and Betty would make a budget and stick to it, and (4) he would become more emotionally involved with his wife and children by reading less and spending more time listening and sharing his thoughts. As we urged him to be more specific in the plan, he resisted. Again, he didn't want to make too strong an external commitment. He wanted to retain control of the plan. We had to wait and hope that his desire to improve was genuine enough that he would risk more when the four-point plan failed.

It sounded like a workable plan, but the lethargy of old habits gradually drew him back to the status quo, as we knew it would. The first week he made himself talk more and be more responsive at work and at home. The second week he got a second job and worked four hours before he judged the job to be making unethical demands, and he quit. The third week, when the family surpassed the budget, he made a few critical remarks and did nothing further. By the fourth week, he was reading books about professional growth, family relationships and communication, and he had effectively withdrawn again from an active role in the outer world. He half-heartedly filled out two applications for part-time jobs but did nothing to actively pursue them.

Bob's boss worked with him to set up specific, tangible, measurable goals for improving his work. The real possibility of his being fired from his job kept him partially focused on the improvement program at work, but something more was needed. His good intentions gradually became diluted with the old habitual ways of processing and judging.

With Thinking and Sensing as his two main functions, he needed a much more specific development plan. He needed something to measure against. The task of developing his potential seemed so overwhelming that he found himself avoiding it as much as possible. He made half-hearted efforts to improve at work but indulged his old habits at home.

Ultimately, Bob is responsible for developing his potential. We again urged him to develop a specific plan that covered life at work and at home to give him a better chance to change those deeply ingrained habits.

He began to see the terribly confusing jumble of thoughts, feelings, facts and patterns that contributed to his stuck position. He is now empowered with the knowledge of how his system works and the way it should work in order to develop potential and get out of his apathetic rut. We knew that we had to engage his Thinker and Sensor functions to lead the charge against the habitual responses.

Finally, he agreed to write down his goal and his objectives:

GOAL: "I want to free myself of my perceptual prison and become the man I want to be: perceptive, wise, caring, principled, competent and contributing to a better world."

OBJECTIVES:

1. Become more comfortable in Extroverted activity.

*2. Pay my debts and balance my budget by getting a second job and actively working with Betty to manage our budget.

3. Improve my engineering skills by taking a night class.

*4. Do at least three Extroverted activities every day that make me uncomfortable and make me experience risk.

*5. Give at least an hour a day and a minimum of one-half day on the weekend to my family to do what they want to do.

*6. Verbalize appreciation and affection every day.

7. Seek feedback instead of blocking it.

8. Use emotional discomfort as the signal to watch out for my defense shields.

9. Increase my tolerance for discomfort, confusion, and risk.

*10. At the end of every day, review my day to see if I see patterns occurring, old habits reappearing and simply checking up on what I thought and how I reacted.

11. Confront my fear of failure by trying things I have wanted to do but was afraid to try.

12. Confront my fear of conflict by speaking up when I disagree.

*13. Make a life line that starts with my earliest memories and identify choices I made that contribute to my Benevolent Dictator style. I'm going to identify the experiences that led to my dominant or withdrawal style.

14. Picture the type of leader I want to be.

*15. Develop the skills and characteristics to lead.

* Indicate specific, measurable activities that required Bob to take action. (*Remember:* He indulged in his Introverted preference for contemplating instead of doing.)

Bob's objectives address his need to develop balance between his inner and outer worlds through reality testing, feedback, and action. He is trying to discipline his runaway Thinker function by legitimizing feelings as an important function to balance his judgment. He's learning to express more feelings as a tangible way to increase his respect for and development of the Feeler function. He is developing his Sensor ability to more accurately observe his external environment and is trying to develop the ability to see the patterns in the data to further develop his Intuitive function. He is developing a picture of the leader he wants to become.

The task of changing dysfunctional habits and replacing them with a balanced style isn't easy and is not for the faint-hearted. It is tough, uncomfortable, and frequently depressing to move out of comfortable ruts and begin to live life more fully. It is painful, but can you think of anything more worthwhile? Developing your own potential is an adventure into the ultimate frontier. It takes courage and the ability to risk.

Bob began to make progress as soon as he had a more measurable route through the complex patterns that were blocking his growth. Based upon behavioral evidence, he logically constructed his improvement plan with enough specificity in it to satisfy his Sensor auxiliary function. He included development for Intuitive and Feeling functions. Using the strengths of the Thinker and Sensor functions, he found renewed energy to act.

EXTROVERT-INTROVERT FEARS

If balance is not achieved between the inner and outer worlds, fear can build up to prevent integration. Introverts naturally conserve energy while Extroverts naturally spend it. Introverts primitively see the world as a hostile place that is continually trying to drag them out of their cozy caves into public action. They are afraid their environment will make too many demands upon them. They are afraid of becoming too involved in activity that could drain their energy and time. Unless Introverts have adequately developed Extroverted skills, they may fear their external environment controlling them; thus, they stay constantly on guard. One man said, "You must study the world around you carefully to keep it from surprising you or dragging you into something you don't want to be involved in." He probably expressed a rather common Introvert attitude.

Extroverts basically see the world as a friendly place that rewards them. They can easily develop an unhealthy fear of their environment rejecting them if they do not interact with it continually. An Extrovert said, "I'm afraid if I don't go, I will really miss something." He admitted that he was afraid of being bored, of being left out, or missing out on activity.

Extroverts must deal with their fears of rejection. If they are left out of an activity they can easily blow the omission out of proportion. Their focus on the outer world causes them to be more aware of activities and events. Introverts may be much less aware of activities since they want to select carefully the activities they attend. When Introverts' privacy is invaded without consent, they must deal with feelings of conflict and perhaps powerlessness.

Careful discrimination is required to distinguish between a healthy preference and a fear-driven attitude. Look at the following summary of statements by Introverts and look at the possibility of fear driving the attitude.

"I am reluctant to delegate. I would rather do it myself; it's easier."

(*Possibility:* Fear of powerlessness that Introverts experience with too much interdependency, meaning they guard against unwanted involvement?)

"I don't want to talk until I get my thoughts together."

(*Possibility:* Fear of failure and public ridicule if the idea isn't thoroughly developed and defensible?)

"I hate to be put on the spot."

(*Possibility:* Fear of failure, powerlessness, and rejection in intense situations?)

Consider some Extrovert responses for the possibility of fear-driven attitudes.

"I hate to be in my office hour after hour. I'd rather be out and about."

(*Possibility:* Fear of rejection that comes with feelings of being left out? Fear of powerlessness that comes with being too long in Introverted activity?)

"I don't really like meetings where you have to sit and listen, but at least I get to find out what's going on." (*Possibility:* Fear of internal conflict produced by feeling separated from environmental data and action/or conflict from being inactive instead of active?)

"I wouldn't miss that meeting. If a showdown comes I want to be in on the action." (*Possibility:* Fear of powerlessness of not participating in major action?)

The following lists of weaknesses are summarized from 112 interactive workshops. They represent common perceptions about Extroverts and Introverts. The perceived weaknesses of Extroversion and Introversion indicate attitudes and judgments about the E/I preference. These represent ordinary perceptions and do not represent laboratory research of correlation between the perceptions and actual characteristics of Extroversion and Introversion. *The work world is a world of perception* rather than rigorous academic research in human behavior. The important thing to note from these lists is the commonality of perception among those people who are not accustomed to thinking in strictly psychological terms. They stated what they thought and consequently what they acted upon. We used participants' wording of the ideas to capture the practical application of their attitudes. The lists represent those perceptions that surfaced in at least 75% of the sessions. Geographic sections across America were included.

EXTROVERTS' WEAKNESSES IF THEY DO NOT BALANCE

1. Somewhat poor at listening.
2. Lack focus . . . tendency to ramble with lots of "B.S."
3. Tendency to waste time in aimless conversation.
4. Tendency to dominate conversations and come on too strong.
5. Tendency to influence decisions and opinions by filibuster rather than well-reasoned dialogue; thereby inordinately and inappropriately influencing outcomes.
6. Confuse situations by failing to discipline their thoughts, talk, or approach.

7. Tend to lose focus and go off in too many directions.

8. Tend to use a decision process not carefully thought out.

9. Seem to have such a great need for people that they often pay too high a price to avoid being alone (i.e., spending time with people they don't particularly like or value).

10. Assume that everyone feels or should feel the same way they do.

11. Don't take the time to check out other people's ideas; they too frequently assume that if you are not verbally disagreeing, then you are agreeing with them.

12. Don't seem to read subtle cues; they seem to need words as the main indicators of a person's position. Seem to pay little attention to nonverbal cues of doubt, disagreement, or resistance (particularly applicable to Extroverted Thinkers).

13. Tend to be nonstop talkers; seem to get uncomfortable with a lull in the conversation.

14. Sometimes appear inconsistent by stating vigorous position at one time and then later in a different group say the opposite.

15. Sometimes can't be pinned down to give an in-depth explanation about an idea.

16. Indulge in too much energetic, random, nonpurposeful activity.

17. Talk too much and don't skillfully draw others into the conversation.

18. Tend to bring up emotionally explosive issues without real commitment to patiently work through them.

19. Are in continual launch mode.

INTROVERTS' WEAKNESSES IF THEY DO NOT BALANCE

1. Expect others to know what they are thinking without their having to say it.

2. Seem to have difficulty fielding questions that interrupt their train of thought.

3. Tend to expect the information network to take care of itself, while Extroverts tend to oil the information network.

4. Seem to be unduly frustrated by unscheduled calls or visits.
5. Seem to be unfriendly or uncommunicative.
6. Seem to be reluctant to delegate; seem like they just don't want to be involved with others so they would rather do it themselves.
7. Tend to deliberate so long that the optimum opportunity to express passes them by; don't always seem to have a smooth sense of timing.
8. Tend to lose the richness of thought in meetings because they withhold ideas and information.
9. Seem to have to be treated carefully to keep them from withdrawing.
10. Tend to take discussion of ideas as disagreement; seem to be too touchy and defensive about their ideas and opinions.
11. Show subtle impatience with others without taking the responsibility to speak up to clear up the interaction.
12. Cannot or will not handle multiple subjects at once.
13. Cannot or will not be spontaneous and let the ideas flow verbally.
14. Take things too seriously and tend to expect others to do the same.
15. Too hard to persuade to try new things.
16. Don't appear to take risks . . . seem to play it safe and pre-planned.
17. Seem to know how to use silence like a weapon; they expect others to be so uncomfortable with silence that they will respond.
18. Not easy to work with when they won't express opinions or give information about whether they agree or disagree with the approach.
19. Seem to take a long time to thaw out and warm up.

CLAIMING THE STRENGTH OF BOTH

Most of what goes on in the brain involves perception and judgment. Without balance and development, we run the risk of unconscious reactions that may or may not yield accurate information. We may be seeing the world through prejudiced, distorted lenses, but it is the basis of our action.

Accepting the natural style of Extroversion or Introversion is essential to developing balance. Then you can systematically develop the skills for the other side of the continuum. Be your natural self and develop skills for your alternate expression and you should achieve balance. You will then have at your command the strengths of both.

Extroversion offers natural interaction with the environment, stimulation of activity and ideas, energizing of group activity, broad span of interests, natural attention to people networking, and ability to switch gears easily. Introversion offers natural concentration in the inner world, ability to focus on issues in-depth, high level of discretion with information, longer attention span, serious and thorough consideration of issues, and calming energies.

We are not suggesting that you give up your natural style. You maximize your natural style and develop skills for the other half.

Extroverts have an affinity with the external world and therefore may have more comfortable social skills. Introverts develop social skills as a result of conscious decision to do so or at the insistence of a strong influencer like a parent, role model, or boss.

Introverts have an affinity for concentration and focus. Extroverts have to develop concentration skills. You simply find what is natural and easy for you and then develop the skills for those requirements that don't feel so natural.

Extroverts are naturally drawn to activity and people, so balance on this dimension comes through adequate skills for quiet time, reflection, and concentration. Introverts are naturally drawn to quiet and thought, so balance comes through adequate social and group skills for activity and interaction.

Extroverts' attention naturally flows outward to people, objects and situations, so balance requires skills to keep from becoming so affected by the immediate environment that energy is siphoned off from goals and tasks. Researchers report that conformity is usually consistent with the Extrovert's lifestyle and inconsistent with the Introvert's lifestyle. (Cooper and Scalise) Balance in the Extrovert's lifestyle comes with Introverted skills to maintain individuality and focus in an active environment. Whereas, with the Introvert's natural resistance to conformity, Extroverted skills are the antidote to isolation.

Researchers also report that the cognitive inconsistency that occurs when expressed attitudes differ from actual beliefs is almost intolerable for an Introvert. Since the internal world of thought is most real for the Introvert, such inconsistency upsets the order of the internal cave.

Extroverts show greater tolerance for expressing attitudes contrary to their actual beliefs. (Cooper and Scalise) In the workshops we frequently heard perceptions that suggest the truth of these assertions. Some of the comments were: "Introverts state well-thought-out opinions." "They don't say much, but when they do you can count on it." "They are precise when they do tell you what they think. It tracks with what they do." "Introverts are definite in their answers. You can believe they mean it."

Every individual has both Introvert and Extrovert capacity. One of those is natural and the other has to be developed.

STRENGTHS OF INTROVERSION

Strengths to be gained from Introvert capacity are:

- Concentrated energy
- Well thought-out decisions, ideas, and opinions
- Focus on a subject in-depth
- High level of discretion with information
- Longer attention span
- Tenacious and serious
- Calming energies
- Energized by the flow of ideas and feelings internally ordered; energized by privacy and intimacy
- Internally directed . . . scans and probes inwardly for stimulation
- Focus on ideas, concepts, inner impressions; reflective
- Time and space to process life experience internally and present thoughts selectively to external world
- Consolidation, defense, moderation, and control of personal disclosure and interaction
- Comfort with one-to-one or small group situations

STRENGTHS OF EXTROVERSION

Strengths to be gained from Extrovert capacity are:

- Brainstorming readily
- Gathering information quickly
- Speaking and acting in straightforward manner
- Stimulating communication — inviting talk
- Stimulating new ideas or unexplored thoughts
- Not easily upset by interruptions
- Capacity for spontaneous response
- Ability to switch gears easily
- Usually comfortable in social interaction
- Ability to use humor to lighten tense situations
- Energizing and energized by people, activities and the environment
- Scanning the environment for stimulation
- Active and interactive
- Expansive rather than conservative
- Talking in order to sort out experience — as a method of figuring out thinking, thus others have more access to the Extrovert's thought process

STAGE IV LEADERSHIP E/I BALANCE

A Stage IV Leader takes full responsibility for Extroversion or Introversion preference but does not indulge in the preference. The Stage IV responds situationally with what is best. Understanding the natural flow of energy is useful in communicating, motivating, and team-building.

Specific Stage IV leadership behaviors that benefit from clear understanding of the Extrovert-Introvert dimension are: (1) reading people accurately, (2) helping people develop skills, (3) finding growth opportunities for employees, (4) building strong team relationships, (5) giving descriptive feedback, (6) enabling people to risk and learn, (7) helping others solve problems, (8) knowing strengths and weaknesses, and (9) taking full responsibility for own actions while expecting others to do the same.

The Extrovert-Introvert preference can inordinately influence perception and judgment if fear-induced reactions go unchecked. Introverts must confront and manage their natural tendency to withdraw and reflect to insure that their behavior is not skewed by fear of involvement and loss of privacy. Extroverts must confront their natural tendency to interact to make sure that their behavior is not skewed by fear of loneliness and exclusion. Seeing and judging clearly is essential. Balance of natural preferences and learned skills provides the richness that both Extroversion and Introversion offer.

Remember: The leader continually develops personal potential.

1. Leaders systematically and continually develop their own potential.
2. Personal growth keeps the leader freshly aware of the way the growth experience evolves.
3. Self-examination helps the leader recognize "stuck positions" in self and others.
4. Leaders give assignments that challenge people to move out of their "stuck positions."
5. Acute behavioral awareness is necessary to identify strengths and weaknesses.
6. Leaders remind individuals of the responsibility to develop their own potential.
7. The leader's job is to guide, motivate, inspire, encourage, and give feedback about development.

DEVELOPMENTAL EXERCISES
Exercise 19: For Extroverts

Estimate the amount of time you spend in the positive or negative aspects of Extroversion or Introversion. You can also use these continua to estimate the positive or negative expression you observe in someone else. Assign 100% value on each line.

For example:

Friendly . . . . 30% . . . . . . 0 . . . . . . 70% . . . . . Distant

This example indicates approximately 30% of the time is spent in friendly expression and 70% of the time the person is distant.

If you are an Extrovert, estimate the percentage of time spent in positive or negative expression:.

POSITIVE POSSIBILITIES		NEGATIVE POSSIBILITIES
Active	0	Too Active
Talkative	0	Too Talkative
Outgoing	0	Too Demanding
Sociable	0	Too Sociable
Charming	0	Too Manipulative
Readable	0	Too Readable
Open	0	Too Open
Broad Scope	0	Too Shallow
Energetic	0	Scattered
Gregarious	0	Too boisterous
Enthusiastic	0	Overwhelming

Exercise 20: For Introverts

If you are an Introvert, estimate percentage of time spent in positive or negative expression:

POSITIVE POSSIBILITIES		NEGATIVE POSSIBILITIES
Private	0	Inaccessible
Quiet	0	Too Quiet
Internally Focused	0	Withdrawn
Reflective	0	Too Serious
Prudent	0	Too Careful
Territorial	0	Too Protective
Reserved	0	Impenetrable
Concentrative	0	Too Intense
Calm	0	Boring
Discreet	0	Too Subtle
Contemplative	0	Too Slow

You can now figure the overall estimate of effective use of Extroversion or Introversion by adding up the percentages on the positive possibility side of zero and dividing by 11. If you do not get the percentage that you think best represents where you want to be, you can isolate the characteristics that are giving you the most trouble and set a very clear plan to work on them.

Exercise 21:   Development of Extroversion and Introversion

Extroverts naturally prefer . . .

1. To interact with their environment.
2. To stimulate activities and ideas.
3. To energize group activity.
4. To have broad interests.
5. To have many friends and acquaintances.
6. To be active people networkers.
7. To be spontaneous.
8. To focus on things quickly with short attention span.

Which of these characteristics do you want to develop further?

Introverts naturally prefer:

1. To maintain privacy and interact selectively with their environment.
2. To maintain maximum concentration and order in their internal world.
3. To focus on issues in depth.
4. To be very discreet with information and actions.
5. To have a few friends and many acquaintances.
6. To have longer attention spans.
7. To seriously and thoroughly consider issues and decisions.
8. To calm and quieten people.

Which of these characteristics do you want to develop further?

Remember: Extroverts are naturally drawn to activity and people; therefore, balance comes through adequate skills for quiet time, reflection, and concentration. Introverts are naturally drawn to quiet and thought, so balance comes through adequate social and group skills for activity and interaction.

Extroverts risk being too captivated by activity, objects, and people in their immediate environment and can become easily distracted from goal-orientation. Introverts naturally resist being captured by activity, objects, or people in their immediate environment and can easily develop negative resistance to external demands.

Exercise 22:   Stage IV Leadership Balance on E/I

Select someone whom you believe to be a Stage IV Leader. How does that person compare on the following dimensions?

Remember: A Stage IV Leader is comfortable with developed skills as well as natural preference, enabling the leader to respond situationally appropriately.

STAGE IV IS ABLE TO:

Interact	and	Maintain privacy
Stimulate the environment	and	Stimulate the person
Energize group activity	and	Calm group activity
Utilize broad scope	and	Utilize narrow scope
Inspire group trust and loyalty	and	Inspire personal trust and loyalty
Actively maintain information network	and	Actively maintain inner order
Communicate openly	and	Communicate discreetly
Be spontaneous	and	Be selective
Focus quickly	and	Focus thoroughly
Maintain friends in loyal, trustworthy relationships	and	Maintain individuality; focus on own vision
To act quickly and decisively	and	To wait and consider
To take risks	and	To be prudent
To respond to the environment	and	To ignore the environment

Exercise 23: Introvert Development of Extrovert Potential

Introverts like to understand things before they try them. Consider the following rationale for an Introvert who is seeking to develop his/her Extrovert potential:

1. Develop the potential in "the cave" first, in utmost privacy.

2. Mentally rehearse the Extroverted behavior you want to develop. Imagine yourself in Extrovert situations. Actually assume an Extroverted role, practicing the dialogue and action that you imagine you want to use. The more energy you put into the mental rehearsal, the better you will be prepared to try the behavior in the external world. Imagine yourself talking to people easily, moving with confidence and grace. Feel it, imagine it, experience the dialogue internally, for that is important to behavioral change. Feeling and experiencing body sensations are important aspects of changing behavior.

3. Mentally examine the reasons for developing more comfortable Extroverted expression. Convince yourself of the benefits you can gain from developing your potential.

4. Get clear about where the Extroverted potential fits in your lifestyle, your profession, your job, your goals, and your relationships.

5. Practice the Extroverted behavior in the privacy of your own room or in front of a mirror, if you wish.

6. Set a definite deadline to make yourself try out the Extroverted behavior in the external world.

7. Select a low-risk situation where you do not have much to lose. Find a low-threat environment to test your behavior. For example, try Extroverting in a shopping mall, to a stranger in a safe but impersonal setting.

8. Note the feelings, thoughts, and body responses you experience in trying the Extroverted behaviors.

9. Set an action deadline to confront your discomfort by making yourself try the Extroverted behaviors with people who know you. In other words, increase the risk as you increase your ability to risk.

10. Take time to understand how your Extroverted behavior affects others.

11. Note the fears you confronted when you explored the potential of your Extrovert expression.
12. Set a realistic goal for full integration of the chosen Extrovert behaviors into a comfortable expression of yourself.

Exercise 24:   Extrovert Development of Introvert Potential

Extroverts like to try new behavior before they take too much time to understand, analyze, or interpret it. Extroverts' propensity for talking and action should be utilized in developing potential.

1. Talk about qualities that you admire about Introverts.
2. Talk about actions you see Introverts taking that you admire.
3. Talk about behaviors that you have seen Introverts use that brought them desirable results.
4. Ask an Introvert to describe for you what it is like to be an Introvert in an Extroverted world.
5. Attend a meeting where you do not have a major role to play. Observe people, noting what you see as Extroverted and Introverted behaviors. Teach yourself to look for indicators that tell you which expression is most natural for each person. Notice the subtle clues for Introversion: changes in skin tone right before speaking up in a new group, nervous body movements, careful wording and phrasing of ideas, quick eye contact and release, reluctance to interrupt, etc. Notice the more obvious clues for Extroversion: more talk, more movement, more brainstorming, more discussion, more impatience when someone uses more than three or four sentences.
6. Attend another meeting where you do not have an important role to play and pay particular attention to your internal response to the people speaking. Note your feelings, body reactions, and thoughts. Note the response each one elicits from you. Stay focused on your internal reactions. Don't get distracted and pulled into the conversation or interaction.
7. Select an Introverted behavior that you want to master. Observe an Introvert who demonstrates the behavior well.

Practice the Introverted behavior in at least three different settings, paying particular attention to the way your environment responds to you.

8. Withdraw from the external world. Go into your internal cave and concentrate on what you experienced until you thoroughly understand it.

9. Practice the Introverted behavior every day for seven days.

10. Notice other people expressing a similar behavior to what you are practicing. By doing this, you are increasing your awareness of the behavior in your external environment and thus are anchoring it in your favorite world.

11. Set four benchmarks in the next four weeks where you will stop and evaluate how you are doing in integrating the behavior into your style. Set both time and behavior measures that will indicate when you are succeeding.

Remember: You tend to like to try new behaviors but fail to practice them enough to make them your own usable expression. Your key is to focus and use the developmental behavior often enough to integrate it into your regular expression.

Exercise 25:   For Extroverts to Develop Their Introversion

Find an Introvert whom you admire — someone who has the Introverted talent already working in a way that appeals to you. Talk to them, watch them, try to match your energy level to the Introvert by pacing your communication with theirs. If they are talking softly, soften your voice. If they are speaking slowly, slow your rate. Get really in touch with the comfortable pacing of the Introvert's approach to speech and thought. *Remember:* You get energized by talking and activity.

Now, make notes about your reactions and discoveries as you try to get in touch with your Introverted side. Tracking your insights is useful to reinforce your learning.

A.   What was most difficult for you?

B. What was easiest?

C. Specifically note your reactions in the following
    categories:

(1) Body movement

(2) Breathing

(3) Rate of speaking

(4) Volume of speaking

(5) Pacing of thoughts

(6) Interest level

(7) Kinds of things that distracted you

(8) Kinds of things that irritated you

Check out your impressions by discussing them with an Introvert.

Exercise 26:   For Introverts to Develop Their Extroversion

Select an Extrovert whom you admire — someone who has
the Extroverted talent already working in a way that appeals to
you. Observe the Extrovert at three different times, being careful

to observe the way s/he interacts with others. Observe and note the Extrovert's use of:

1. Body language

2. Space (how close the Extrovert gets to others physically and emotionally)

3. Rate of speaking

4. Variety of topics discussed

5. Volume at which the Extrovert speaks

6. Body movement (how often the Extrovert repositions)

7. Energy level (enthusiasm and animation)

8. Image and appearance

After three observations, take time to organize what you observed in each of the eight categories. *Remember:* You want to understand first and experience second.

Next, you are ready to experience. Talk to the Extrovert and try to match energy levels. Demonstrate more energetic response, more enthusiasm and animation. Pace your voice volume, rate, and delivery to the Extrovert's pattern. You can process later. Concentrate on experiencing the Extrovert pace and pattern.

When you are alone, note your reactions:

1. What was easiest for you to do?

2. What was most difficult?

3. What kind of things distracted you?

4. What kind of things irritated you?

5. What patterns did you note in yourself, such as wanting to control, rearrange, or withdraw?

6. How much tolerance did you have for Extroverted expression? In other words, at what point did you start to tire?

After you have time to process your experience in emulating the Extrovert's patterns and pacing, discuss your insights with the Extrovert.

Now, try developing your own expression of Extroversion by going beyond the person you admire. Go from admiring someone else's Extroversion, to emulating their Extroversion, to finding your own individual expression. Extroverts can use the same process to find a way to express their individualized Introversion.

Note: It is too easy for Introverts to get stuck in observation and fail to experience and integrate their understanding into actual behavior. It is too easy for an Extrovert to dabble and sample behavior without taking the time to reflect about it and integrate it into regular behavioral repertoire through clear understanding. Extroverts tend to squeeze experience dry for the action thrill without anchoring the learning in their "cave" so it is readily usable when they want it. Introverts tend to squeeze observation dry for the understanding thrill without anchoring it in external world experience in order to make it readily usable when they want it.

Exercise 27: Behavioral Challenges for Extroverts

If you are an Extrovert, read the following list of behaviors that Extroverts have to develop. They do not come naturally. Put a check mark by the behaviors you think you need to work on. Check every one that you want to list on your long-term development plan.

1. ___Increase awareness of another person's need for privacy.

2. ___Improve listening abilities.

3. ___Reduce interruption of others.

4. ___Discipline the tendency to dominate interactions, conversations, and time.

5. ___Draw Introverts into the conversation gently. Don't overwhelm them by throwing the spotlight on them to perform according to expectations that you place upon them.

6. ___Increase your tolerance for long or thorough explanations, despite your preference for short exchanges in a tennis-match conversational pace.

7. ___Don't verbalize carelessly just to entertain − you may seem insincere or phony. Explore your internal store of memories and ideas to add substantive information to the conversation.

8. ___Extend concentration skills by learning to use deep breathing techniques to focus your energy at the top of your head. Then hold the topic in your thought, gently but firmly ignoring interfering images. Bring your attention back to the topic as many times as needed in order to continue concentration. The mind can be as unruly as an undisciplined child unless you take charge of focusing your attention and ignoring distractions.

9. ___Continually assess the other person's interest in the interaction.

10. ___Notice when seriousness is more appropriate than playfulness.

11. ___Establish a comfortable conversational pace.

12. ___Let others talk too − just because they may not want to fight for center stage doesn't mean they have nothing to say.

13. ___Take time to ask for and listen to feedback.

14. ___Increase integrity by discriminating more carefully that which a person intends to be confidential.

15. ___Tone down your energy when you note other people's discomfort.

16. ___Be more selective in what you say in order to avoid the impression of having "verbal diarrhea."

17. ___Increase patience and tolerance with others who may not talk as fast as you.

18. ___Try not to finish other people's sentences or ideas by assuming that you know exactly what they mean.

19. ___Calm down and get quiet when you become too scattered.

With which behavior do you want to begin systematic development of your potential? Select one behavior that you want to master first. You need to select one, rather than trying to work on them all at once. *Remember:* Focus and concentration are challenges for the Extrovert who has not developed Introverted skills.

Exercise 28:   Behavioral Challenges for Introverts

If you are an Introvert, read the following list of behaviors that Introverts need to develop because they do not come naturally. Put a check mark by behavior you think you need to develop. Check each one that you want to list on your long-term development plan.

1. ___Increase your tolerance for small talk by recognizing its role in oiling the social fabric of our world.

2. ___Increase your tolerance for social events by expanding your understanding of the role they play in organizational life.

3. ___Share more personal information in your conversation.

4. ___Enliven your expression with facial animation and body gestures.

5. ___Reduce seriousness as your standard expression.

6. ___Don't habitually reject new experiences — develop more spontaneity.

7. ___Share more of your internal rich identity rather than re-lying on a few well-developed roles for the outer world.

8. ___Be more playful at times and don't worry about what others think of your behavior.

9. ___Learn how to skillfully disagree without having to resort to forceful denouncement or rejection of another's point of view.

10. ___Increase your openness by discriminating carefully if you are judging something to be confidential when it isn't.

11. ___Speak up when your opinion would offer a much needed perspective, even if you have to push yourself forward.

12. ___Force yourself to join a conversational group, even though it makes you uncomfortable.

13. ___Learn to think aloud occasionally, even if you do not have your thoughts already ordered. Temporarily set aside your desire to work it all out inside before you speak. Increase your tolerance for exploring ideas ver-bally.

14. ___Practice speeding up your delivery and/or hitting the main ideas when you notice that others are losing inter-est.

15. ___Give feedback. Show interest, emotion, and involve-ment so that others have a better understanding of your response.

16. ___Learn to initiate conversations.

17. ___Ask someone out to lunch whom you do not know well but would like to know better.

18. ___Decrease your need to explain fully without interrup-tion, increase your tolerance for interruption by smoothly following the interaction.

19. ___Don't talk too long at one time; increase your ability to dialogue instead of indulging in monologue.

20. ___Develop ways to join interaction that has already begun.

21. ___Monitor your tendency to filter out sensory input from the external environment while exploring exclusively your internal store of memories, ideas, and impressions.

With which behavior do you want to begin systematic development of your potential? Select one behavior you want to master first. You need to select one, instead of trying to think about all of them. *Remember:* The challenge for the Introvert is to act and experience in the external world, so don't become overwhelmed by trying to focus on too many.

Exercise 29:   Professional Development Roadmap

It is not possible to pick up a golf club for the first time in your life and become a professional golfer in three easy lessons. Neither is it possible to develop potential in three easy lessons. Developing potential demands that we change something that is habitually and unconsciously our easiest way of behaving. A specific plan for change uses focused concentration, a plan, action, and measurement. Much of our behavior is habitual, thus to develop potential we must develop the desired behavior until it, too, becomes comfortable.

The following development plan helps prepare for behavioral change. It addresses the behavior to change, thoughts that facilitate and impede, feelings involved, actions to take, and success indicators that let you know you are achieving the behavioral change you want. Sample plans are given in Exercises 30 and 31.

BEHAVIOR:

I want to _____

_____

_____

Instead of _____

_____

_____

_____

THOUGHT:

To keep my efforts focused on my goal, I will use the command thought of _____

_____

_____

_____

Instead of thoughts like _____

_____

_____

_____

FEELINGS:
I will expand my tolerance for feelings of_____

_____

Instead of indulging in feelings of _____

_____

ACTION:
I will start

_____

_____

_____

SUCCESS MEASURES:
I will know I am succeeding when _____

_____

_____

_____

_____

_____

_____

_____

Making a clear map of the inner terrain is useful in bringing about systematic development of potential. To expand, alter, or radically change a habitual way of responding takes conscious, disciplined effort.

Exercise 30: Sample Introvert Development Plan

The following development plan was used by Sharon, who had a strong preference for Introversion. She was assigned to a ten-person work group that was given a critically important company assignment. She knew she was much quieter than the others. After the work group completed the Myers-Briggs Type Indicator (MBTI) as a means of developing teamwork, Sharon discovered that eight of the group were Extroverted. The other Introvert had a slight preference for Introversion and found little difficulty matching group energy level and work culture. The members learned about each other's preferences. They seemed truly surprised that legitimate differences do exist. None of them knew how to see differences nor use the strengths of both Extroversion and Introversion. Sharon developed the following plan for herself.

BEHAVIOR:

I want to speak up more often and give people more information about what I think and feel. Instead of keeping my thoughts to myself and being upset when they go in a direction where I see problems that they don't seem to realize . . . Instead of having team members wonder if I agree, I am going to declare my opinion either by saying so or letting my body signal my position.

THOUGHT:

To keep my effort focused on my goal, I will use the command thought: "I want to play on this team as a useful dependable member, so I must help with open communication. I will speak up when I can contribute."

Instead of giving in to thoughts like: "They probably don't want to hear what I have to say." "They would probably laugh at my ideas." "They never ask for my opinion so I'm sure they don't want it." "I don't want to get into a hassle over this." "I don't want the responsibility if it fails for someone saying it was my idea."

FEELINGS:

I will expand my tolerance for feelings of discomfort, fear, and vulnerability. I will confront my fear of being ridiculed, humiliated or attacked. I will confront my fear of powerlessness that comes when others make too many demands on me. I will confront my fear of being seen as inadequate or misunderstood. I will confront my fear of being caught in heated discussion where someone attacks my ideas. Instead of indulging in feelings of comfort, safety, and independence, I will speak up.

ACTION:

1. I will speak up when I see that my opinion has not been voiced. 2. I will speak up when I think the group is overlooking something important. 3. I will speak up when I disagree with a person or a procedure. 4. I will use gestures to signal my approval when I am supporting something someone else is saying or doing. 5. When I am listening carefully to someone, I will use more facial and head gestures to let people know that I am following. 6. I will say "good morning" to each member of the group 7. I will increase my tolerance for small talk since team members like friendly banter.

SUCCESS MEASURES:

I will know I am succeeding when (1) I review my interactions at the end of the day and I can't think of a single idea that I wished I had said but didn't. (2) When I bring up something that the group is overlooking, every time I see something. (3) When I bring up the idea at the time the group is discussing it, instead of waiting to think it over more carefully when I am alone. (4) When I regularly respond verbally or with easily readable actions when someone is talking to me. (5) When I give feedback that lets the others know where I stand on ideas and issues. (6) When I say "good morning" as an automatic habit, instead of having to carefully remember to do it. (7) When I can participate in small talk without feeling that it is shallow or superficial . . . I'll know when I am comfortable with conversation for the purpose of friendliness instead of serious content. I always admired my sister's social skills and wondered why I am not as charming as she is. Now, I know that I'm an Introvert and I am relieved. I do want to develop my own way of Extroverting so I can be more comfortable around other people.

Sharon understood the internal things with which she had to deal in order to develop her Extroverted potential of speaking up and letting people have more information about her thoughts and feelings. She became much more realistic about what she expected of herself in Extroverted expression.

Exercise 31:   Sample Extrovert Development Plan

Paul was told that he must improve his people skills if he wanted to advance further in the organization. He is an Extrovert with a strong preference. At Paul's performance appraisal, his boss told him that he talks too much and runs over people in meetings. As they discussed his impact on others, Paul realized that what he thought was fun and enthusiasm, other people experienced as pushy and steamrolling. He decided to do something about it. He developed the following plan.

BEHAVIOR:

> I want to improve my interaction skills by listening more, talking less, and putting people at ease. I want to quit talking too much, coming on too strong, and turning people off.

THOUGHT:

> To keep my effort focused on my goal, I will use the command thought: "Slow down, listen more, discover other people's thoughts and feelings and let them move at their own pace." Instead of going with thoughts like, "I already know what they think, so I'll get on to something that I'm more interested in." "That reminds me of what I did last night." "They better speak up now, or forever hold their peace." "How long do I have to stand here and listen to this drone?" "I'll just cut in and finish the thought for him 'cause it takes him forever." "What I have to say is much more interesting. They'll love this."

FEELINGS:

> I will expand my tolerance for feelings of boredom, impatience, and irritation. I will confront my fear of missing something more important, of being left out, and of losing a more valuable opportunity. I will confront the powerlessness I feel when I get stuck in something boring. I will confront my fear of being controlled by something that keeps me from being free to chase the hottest action. I will confront my fear of boredom.

Instead of indulging in the fun feelings of being entertained and stimulated, I will accept the feelings of irritation. Instead of indulging in being the center of attention and feeling warmth, satisfaction, and interest, I will accept the feelings of boredom. Instead of constantly getting other people to play my game and respond to me, I will accept the feelings of impatience while I try to put others first.

ACTION:

1. I will start using no more than three sentences at a time in conversation, to allow others to have the floor. 2. I will try to draw others out by asking questions to allow them to respond in their own way. 3. I will let someone else direct the interaction in group activity. I will make myself listen carefully to others by (a) not interrupting, (b) not using the mental time to figure out what I'm going to say next, (c) using more non-verbal messages and less talk to encourage others to talk more, and (d) making myself listen to what others are saying by noting their thoughts, feelings, and attitudes by making the interaction a detective discovery game to keep my mind actively focused on the speaker . . . otherwise my mind tends to wander off easily. 4. I am going to slow myself down so others will not be uncomfortable with me. 5. I am going to match my energy, volume, and tone to others as a way of making them more comfortable with me 6. I am going to relax more and reduce the wild movements that I use when I am letting me all hang out.

SUCCESS MEASURES:

I will know I am succeeding when: (1) I can go three days in a row without dominating interactions, (2) be comfortable using no more than three sentences and smoothly and willingly hand the conversational ball to someone else, (3) I go three days in a row without interrupting someone else or finishing their thoughts for them, (4) I can stay focused on what the other person is saying without mentally rehearsing what I am going to say next or when I stop listening for the best place for me to butt in and take over, (5) I can feel as satisfied with nonverbal supportive messages to others as I currently do when I am talking, (6) I can walk away from six interactions in a row where I actively paid attention to others' ideas,

feelings, and attitudes, (7) I ask a question that draws information out with positivity and I see the person warm up to
the conversation instead of shutting down, (8) when I see
Alice, Fred, George and Ann stop avoiding me or getting
away from me as fast as they can, and (9) when people relax,
breathe calmly, and talk easily with me, I'll know I've done it.
I'll know I have a good start on developing my Introverted
potential for concentration, depth, and understanding. I
want the best of Extroversion and Introversion. I'll need it all
to get me where I want to be.

Exercise 32:   Administrative Aide:
The Key to Developing Potential

The chief executive officer (CEO) of the Extrovert is used in
the favorite world of the external environment. The Introvert's
CEO is used in the favorite internal world. Thus, the key to developing potential lies in the auxiliary or administrative aide (AA).
The CEO and AA are chosen from among the four functions
(Thinker, Feeler, Sensor, or Intuitor). It is useful to actively engage your auxiliary function to develop potential.

The following material is intended for reference only and
does not require mastery of sixteen types. It is useful in planning
for systematic development of potential. Just look for the style
you are considering.

Remember the letter designations:

E = Extrovert	I = Introvert
S = Sensor	N = Intuitor
T = Thinker	F = Feeler
J = Judge-controller	P = Perceiver-adapter

SENSOR ADMINISTRATIVE AIDE

Sensor serves as the administrative aide for four types: ESTJ,
ESFJ, ISTP, and ISFP. For ESTJs and ESFJs to gain successful
entry into their inner worlds, their Sensor AA provides the key.
ISTPs and ISFPs use their Sensor AA to provide access to the
external world.

The Sensor function provides immediate, practical, realistic facts for the CEO's consideration. ESTJ and ESFJ's Sensor AA abstracts sensory impressions and presents data that are most important to the individual CEO. The AA sorts data carefully for intense effects of pleasant or unpleasant stimuli. ESTJs and ESFJs usually have strong sensory preferences and are usually quite clear about what they dislike. Thus they must get their AA to provide strong sensory data to support development of their Introversion. Unless there is specific evidence in the environment that suggests the need to develop more Introversion, the CEO will not support the internal development.

The Sensor AA of the ISTP and ISFP observes the sensory data that appears to be important in the external world, and pays much less attention to the CEO's individual preference. Since the Sensor AA is presenting information gleaned from the external world to the internal CEO, it is presented more impersonally without the personalized intense judgment used by the Sensor AAs of the ESTJ and ESFJ. Thus, if the Sensor AA is to be of help in developing the ISTP and ISFP's Extroversion, sensory data must be sorted and prioritized for data that best matches the personal preference of the private CEO. Since the CEO has little interest in the external world that does not directly affect the inner world, Sensor AAs need to select data that motivates the CEO to develop in the external world.

ESTJs and ESFJs use their Sensor AAs as the doorway to their Introverted world. ISTPs and ISFPs use their Sensor AAs as the doorway to the Extroverted world.

THINKER ADMINISTRATIVE AIDE

Thinker administrative aide serves ESTP, ENTP, ISTJ, and INTJ. Thus, development of potential is done through developing clear rationale to prove the necessity of development in the least favorite world. ESTPs and ENTPs use their Thinker AAs to access their inner world, while ISTJs and INTJs use their aides to access their outer world.

Thinker AAs are trained to analyze for cause and effect and to organize information according to logical conclusions. They analyze actions for possible outcomes.

Thinker AAs serve the CEOs of the ESTP and ENTP primarily by trying to make logical interpretation of events. To develop Introvert potential, the CEO has to assign the Thinker AA to spend private time ordering and analyzing the internal condition, rather than spending so much time serving the Extroverted CEO in the external world. The Thinker AA has to be given introspection time to establish clear internal cause and effect order in the cave. ESTPs and ENTPs have to take time to think about their actions, outcomes, and directions. They have to take time to concentrate, focus, and thoroughly consider their development. Otherwise, their Thinker AAs will be preoccupied with organizing cause and effect data to show the CEO how to maximize their impact in the external world.

ISTJ and INTJ CEOs remain in the cave while sending their Thinker AAs out to interact with the external world. Since the CEOs are much more internally focused, their Thinker AAs work under strict orders to objectively organize externally gathered data into objective cause and effect information with very little personal involvement. The CEO wants the information arranged to conform to the logic inside the cave and rarely wants to be drug into the sorting process with conscious attention. The Thinker AAs can best serve Extrovert development when they show the CEO in the cave that internal dissonance will disturb the peace of the cave if potential for dealing with the external world is not developed.

FEELER ADMINISTRATIVE AIDE

Feeler administrative aides serve ENFP, ESFP, ISFJ, and INFJ. Feeler AAs monitor for feelings of comfort or discomfort. The key to the internal world of the ENFP and ESFP is through feelings and personal values. ISFJs and INFJs relate to the outer world through feelings and values.

For ENFPs and ESFPs to effectively develop their internal worlds, their Feeler AAs must prove the value to the Extroverted CEO. They must prove that internal development, concentration, and focus will have value in their people relationships in the external world. They are more likely to develop Introverted balance if their external relationships demand it.

ISFJs and INFJs utilize their Feeler AAs to do the primary interacting with others so the CEO can remain somewhat undisturbed in the cave. The Feeler AA scans the environment for cause-effect data that interprets what others feel and particularly feelings about them. Though they appear to be very sensitive to other people's data, they are usually under the control of the CEO in the cave determining what the information really means in relation to their private world.

INTUITOR ADMINISTRATIVE AIDE

Intuitor AAs serve ENTJ, ENFJ, INTP, and INFP. ENTJs and ENFJs use their Intuitor AAs primarily to internally organize external experience into ideas, concepts, and theories so that the Extroverted CEO has the big picture from which to work. Adequate Introverted development requires the CEO to allow the Intuitor AA to take time to see the relationships, possibilities, and meanings of the CEO's experiences in the external world. If the Intuitor AA is continually employed to assess the external world, it will be difficult for the ENTJ and ENFJ to balance Extroversion and Introversion. The Intuitor AA is critical to their internal development.

INTPs and INFPs use their Intuitor AAs to gather external data and organize it according to potential, possibilities, and implications. The Intuitor AAs are particularly assigned to look for possibilities and therefore may not bring their CEOs realistic assessments of the external world. The Intuitor AAs need specific permission from the CEO in the cave to allow them to show that external development fits neatly into the internally held self-picture. When the conceptual bridge is laid and clearly connected to the CEO's self-picture, development of Extroversion has more energy and support assigned to it.

SUMMARY:

Sensor administrative aide is best used to perceive visible, immediate, realistic, practical facts taken from experience.

- Sensor provides access to the inner world for ESTJs and ESFJs.
- Sensor provides access to the outer world for ISTPs and ISFPs.

Thinker administrative aide is best used to provide objective analysis of cause and effect with rationale and consequences to prove the viability of a course of action.

- Thinker provides access to the inner world for ESTPs and ENTPs.

- Thinker provides access to the outer world for ISTJs and INTJs.

Feeler administrative aide is best used to provide personal value judgments and interpretations that provide subjective analysis of cause and effect with rationale to prove why that approach feels best.

- Feeler provides access to the inner world of ENFPs and ESFPs.
- Feeler provides access to the outer world of ISFJs and INFJs.

Intuitor administrative aide is best used to provide insights into possibilities, implications, relationships, patterns, and meanings in order to organize the overall concept.

- Intuitor provides access to the inner world of ENTJs and ENFJs.
- Intuitor provides access to the outer world of INFPs and INTPs.

Therefore, to stimulate and motivate development in the least favorite world the administrative aide needs to be enlisted to make the connections between the inner and outer worlds.

Sensor finds facts and sensory evidence to connect the two worlds and provide a pathway for development.

Intuitor finds theories, explanations, relationships, patterns, and meanings to connect the two worlds and provide the picture for development.

Thinker finds a logical rationale with clear cause-effect inferences to connect the two worlds and provide logical reasons for development.

Feeler finds personal values and motivational feelings that help connect the two worlds and provide commitment and energy for development.

– 4 –

Sensor-Intuitor:
The Way We See The World

Main Ideas of Chapter 4:

1. Sensing or Intuiting as a primary perceptual process fundamentally affects the way we see the world.

2. Sensing or Intuiting is critical to the way we construct reality.

3. STJs (Sensor, Thinker, Judge) way of approaching change management basically differs from NTJs.

4. Knowing strengths and weaknesses of each preference is useful to leaders.

5. Sensors and Intuitors have different preferences for determining criteria for a best-boss profile or best-employee profile.

6. Much of the power game is played in the arena of perception.

7. Stage IV Leaders must be alert to perceptual games.

"Get the facts and check the rules," said the Sensor manager. The Intuitive manager said, "We can't wait. Let's give it our best

159

shot. Take a leap beyond what you see." The two have very different dominant processes for perceiving. It is easier for the Intuitor to see possibilities than to slow down and exercise the discipline to see the factual reality; whereas, it is easier for the Sensor to zero in on the facts than to see patterns and possibilities.

All human beings use both Sensing and Intuiting processes, but one of those is more trusted and tends to dominate perception. Sometimes people get stuck in overreliance on one type of perceiving, thus severely limiting the ability to respond situationally.

Sensors attend to details and prefer step-by-step processing; although the process may be rapid, it is still linear. They focus most easily on what is happening in the present, paying close heed to what is said and done. They trust practical, factual information most readily. With their direct, down-to-earth approach, they tend to be action-oriented, hard-driving doers. They prefer tangible, immediate feedback that they can readily verify for themselves.

Intuitors see possibilities, outcomes, and patterns among facts without too much focus on individual details. Intuitors read between lines, identify inferred meanings, and attend to implications. Details require more concentration. Intuitors prefer the "big picture," emphasizing concepts, systems, theories, and relationships. They enjoy developing strategies for long-term impact and preparing for future eventualities.

With change occurring ever more rapidly in organizations, clear recognition of these two perceptual differences is useful in management of change.

CASE STUDY: THE INTUITIVE LEADER AND THE SENSOR ORGANIZATION

A highly intuitive commanding military general, responsible for a seasoned group of civil service professionals, recognizes that the structure of the huge government organization is obsolete for the changes they are experiencing. Due to congressional legislation, decreasing funds, and increasing competition from the private sector, the organization has to change the way it does business. It is not meeting the changing conditions; it moves too slowly, has too much red tape, and is too rule-bound.

The general is an idealistic, innovative, improvement-driven, outcome-focused leader with exceptional ability to articulate his vision. He sees the need for a more efficient and innovative organization. He recognizes that changing an organization means changing perceptions and behaviors. The term "organizatonal culture" is a usable concept to the general, but to many managers it holds little importance. They focus on projects, budgets, and suspense dates which are far more real to them.

We define organizational culture as the way people behave — the norms, rules, traditions, tolerances, intolerances, customs, habits, and patterns of interaction. Obviously, we are talking about the *process* of work, not the *product* of work. Trying to prove to senior management that people dynamics are the key to organizational effectiveness is a tough task. They prefer scientific method and mathematical certainty. Their actual culture is a duty-oriented, rules and regulation, project-producing organization. Senior management tends to believe that people process is just too unpredictable and imprecise. They tend, instead, to manage by power and precedent by focusing on "taskings" and compliance.

The challenge is to prove that people have strongly repetitive ways of thinking, reacting, and interacting that can be predicted. People need to learn that most behavior is somewhat predictable once you learn how to organize what you see. Being able to read and predict behavior is an important leadership skill in today's rapidly changing environment. Clear people assessment is essential to developing a strategy for change. Using the four-dimensional Myers-Briggs, a behavior profile of senior management can be identified to provide the foundation for developing a change strategy.

A sample of senior managers in the organization showed a dominant profile of ISTJ (Introvert, Sensor, Thinker, Judge). Using interview and observation techniques, a clear pattern of senior managers emerges that shows resistance to change. Although most people tend to resist change, ISTJs have a particularly difficult time embracing change readily. It is, however, usually annoying to them to be considered resistant to change.

A meeting was held at the local level rather than in Washington, D.C. The local managers had a reputation for being very difficult to manage. Their reputation with employees and outside agencies is clearly characterized by the local group's resistance to outside influence, rigid interpretation of rules, avoidance of problem resolution through dogmatic rejection of alternate viewpoints, and their intellectual arrogance of asserting their "scientific approach" as superior to anyone else's.

In response to the request that they become more process-oriented, they became instantly defensive. They asked for a definition of process. The general sent a high-ranking civil service person to discuss the situation. He defined *process* as "methods by which you approach a problem." The group wanted it defined further. He explained, "Methods are judgment, conflict management skills, communication skills, facilitation skills, and interaction skills." (Sensor-Thinkers tend to want clear definitions and rules stated right up front.) The answer was a set of processes, i.e., dynamic interactive actions, behaviors, and perceptions. (Intuitor-Thinkers tend to expect that the definitions are implicit and don't need explaining.) The predominately STJ group were annoyed at the "vague" description.

The managers are primarily action-oriented Sensor-Thinker-Judges. They like specific tasks, verifiable and measurable with specific time frames and outcomes. Also, they like taskings and the reporting chain to be identified. They are frustrated about being asked to improve their interaction and problem-solving process. They have no great respect for the term "interpersonal relations." Their frustration increases as they are asked to improve the process of the way they do business. The mounting irritation puts a strain on organizational connections between the local group and the next management level. Tempers are short, and tightly controlled anger undergirds most remarks.

How do you prove that the way people treat each other on a day-to-day basis is the culture carrier and not written policy, rules, and regulations?

The rationale for change included significant trend data to show the rate of change and the need for organizational flexibility. The general's vision included the need to respond to changing needs and environments by changing traditional ways of doing business. He talked about the need to innovate and find new and better ways to work.

In the work session, the local managers stated angrily that they saw no reason to change. They spent several hours defend-

ing their resistance to becoming process-focused. Their responses were:

> "We have an outstanding record for doing excellent projects.
> So why should we change?" (Sensor preference for citing
> proof of task-accomplishment)

> "By following the rules and regulations and attending care-
> fully to details we have an excellent record of not losing cases
> in court or arbitration. We have a record of being right."
> (Sensor-Thinker preference for framing the issue around
> past experience, i.e., track record, as certainty of proof)

> "I have seen several new regulations in the last six months
> and they have said nothing about process. So how do we
> know that Washington really intends to move on that?" (Sen-
> sor-Thinker preference to value action more than words and
> the tendency to wait for the authorized version in writing,
> duly signed)

> "I don't get evaluated on how nice I am. I get my butt chewed
> if I miss a suspense date, go over budget, or mess-up on a
> project. I am product-oriented. I don't get anything for im-
> proving process. Why should I? What's in it for me?" (Sensor-
> Thinker preference for verifiable tasks tied to job descriptions
> and performance reviews than for hard-to-verify processes)

> "I don't see why there's such an emphasis on process. I am
> very careful about rules and regulations. I use good judg-
> ment. It's too bad if other people don't like the way I treat
> them. I would rather be right than liked."

> "There's nothing in my performance standards that shows me
> I'm going to be evaluated on process. So, until there is, I'm
> going to do things the way I always have." (Sensor-Thinker
> reliance on official authority for evidence of real intention)

> "What do we care if other agencies think we interpret rules
> too rigidly? They don't pay our salaries." (Sensor, Thinker,
> Judge preference for title and entitlement according to chain
> of command)

> "How can you interpret rules too rigidly? They are absolute."
> (Sensor, Thinker, Judge preference for clear rules)

> "There are no gray areas in our work. We're dealing with the
> courts. We have no choice but to be precise in our interpreta-

tion. We put a great deal of thought into our decisions." (Sensor, Thinker, Judge preference for verifiable proof to justify certainty of position)

The managers spent much energy explaining why they didn't have to change. They argued over definitions of words and individual scenarios instead of discussing issues and processes.

We facilitated their discussion by continually using their own words and behaviors as evidence of the need to work on process. By establishing the process fact base using words just spoken, behavior just demonstrated, and examination of their thinking processes, the Sensor-Thinkers began to consider the viability of using behavior as factual evidence.

Sensor preference for tangible evidence was engaged as they remembered the words and behavior just expressed or witnessed. Their Thinker preference was unaccustomed to the validity of behavioral evidence, but their bodies and minds retained the memory and sensation of the words and behaviors. Thus, two of the more stuck people continued to argue vehemently, while the others began to disengage from their defense to watch the process unfolding. Those with less ego involvement got in touch with their Sensor body memory and their intellect by seeing the behavioral evidence.

One important step in the process occurred. The more vehement managers became so irrational in their assertions of their own perfect thinking and superiority that the other managers started to disengage from them. As I watched the group, I saw body language that indicated the shift. At that point most of the group were looking for a way to disassociate from the obnoxious arrogance of self-proclaimed intellectual superiority.

One of the opinion setters in the group made the disaffection clear. He said, "Well, I don't agree with all of the things people say about us, but I guess the fact that our employees, other agencies, and central office say that about us does have to be considered. We can't change overnight, but it is becoming clear to me that we are going to have to work on this."

He was quickly joined by another important opinion setter, and the group process finally jumped the hurdle of denial. It took approximately five hours of venting their frustration to guide them to a climate where they could more readily decide to do something about it.

The local culture as well as the overall organization across the country is an STJ culture. It demonstrates the following characteristics:

- Enforces hierarchy of chain of command
- Uses power of authority much more often than power of positive interpersonal relationships
- Is rule-oriented and legalistic in interpretation
- Driven by schedules and regulations
- Critical and opinionated about the way rules and procedures should work
- Excellent on tasks and details
- Skeptical of group process
- Skeptical of change

The kind of organization needed is one that is leadership-driven through excellent process skills, rather than product-driven through rigid rules and procedures. Their organization needs to . . .

1. Have a quick response capability
   - Cut red tape everywhere possible
   - Move resources to meet priority problems
   - Be mission- and leadership-oriented instead of turf warriors
2. Innovate continually
   - Continue doing quality work with ongoing improvement of techniques and methods
   - Streamline paperwork wherever possible
   - Continually examine procedures and process for obsolescence
3. Develop flexible systems for quick reconfiguration to meet changing needs
4. Develop people for continual readiness of management, technical, and support staff
5. Demonstrate positive people-orientation with emphasis on action

6. Demonstrate superior process skills and pace-setting leadership

7. Reinforce common vision that integrates different styles without destroying them (unity through excellent leadership of different styles for maximum quality)

The change strategy has to meet the group where it is. Unless a life-threatening situation demands immediate change, people start with their current reality. Let's look at the advice the STJs (Sensor, Thinker, Judge-controllers) gave for management of organization or policy change.

STJ'S Preference for Change Management:

1. Gather information carefully before making the change. (Notice that "change" is referred to as something tangible rather than a dynamic process.)

2. Explain why we have to change the way we currently do things. Don't give us theory. Give us facts. Show us what's wrong with the way things are. (Before you can focus on change, you must start with the present and show evidence that current practices will not meet the changing priorities.)

3. Explain what we can expect. (Prefer tangible reality.)

4. Set standards for the change — when it's going to happen and what rules apply during the transition. (Rules and regulation conscious.)

5. Identify what results you expect to get from the change. Who will benefit and how will you measure it to know if it is better?

6. Describe the change verbally and in writing. (Clear directions.)

7. Get input from the people most affected. (Honor task savvy.)

8. Coordinate the change between management and personnel who have to carry it out. (Clear authority lines.)

9. Plan carefully the execution of change and let us know who's going to do it, how they are going to do it, and when. (Tangible, measurable results.)

10. Give us time to learn to live with it, before you do it. (Time to adjust reality base.)

Some STJ managers can move through their resistance to change rapidly and move quickly to embrace needed changes. The ones who are stuck, however, will take more time to respond favorably, if they ever do.

The general's strategy for change involves (a) clear articulation of his vision to include both visionary images and concrete examples, (b) assessment of the organizational culture including the Myers-Briggs style of key personnel, (c) assessment of past changes and their impact, (d) selection of critical opinion setters to lead the changes at various levels of the organization, (e) policy revisions or deletions, (f) selection of proven results-getters to lead the change process on a full-time basis, (g) establishing guidelines for the transition, (h) establishing measurable benchmarks to show where they are in the process, (i) encouraging managers at all levels to establish performance standards for effectively responding to changing needs, (j) encouraging managers to establish performance standards for the process skills of judgment, communication effectiveness, negotiation and teamwork, (k) selecting leaders who will actively and visibly demonstrate the process behavior that will eventually dominate the organizational structure.

The leadership results-getting group selected by the general to spearhead the organizational change had to design their communication campaign from the inside out. They had a five-day retreat during which they used creative problem-solving techniques to discover the best way to communicate the vision, the outcomes, the benchmarks. They were urged to continue to keep it simple, easy to repeat, and easy to remember. One-hundred-page change strategies are rarely read and certainly cannot be repeated easily. The general knew the value of brilliant and memorable images, clear direction, and precise language. He wanted it so clearly worked out that people could easily repeat it during casual conversations.

The process has been under way for six months. Only time will tell the effectiveness of the plan. The general's selection of leaders and opinion setters to accelerate the change of focus is critical to success. He selected Stage IV Leaders and encouraged them to select opinion setters from all over the organization to persuade people to support the vision. Leaders know the potency of the power games that can be imposed to stop or impede the process. Therefore, they plan in advance to counter the opposition.

Effective leadership of change is dependent upon excellent communication skills, interpersonal trust, and focused management of group process.

TWO FORMS OF PROCESSING INFORMATION

Power could be described as control of perception. In Stages I, II, and III, perception is used to manipulate, intimidate, and control.

A clear understanding of the way your own perception works helps you to diffuse power games. Your perceptual preference is not only your antidote for manipulation, it paradoxically sets you up for it. Perceptual strength can become your weakness, if it is not adequately balanced by skills for your least preferred style. To remain clear, you must have groundedness in physical reality and insight into implication, relationships, and possibilities.

From the moment of birth, human beings use perception to gather information. Some use Sensing as the main perceptual process, thereby focusing on tangible reality, while others use Intuiting to focus on intangible reality and possibility. Two people hearing the same words may not get the same message. A Sensor hears what was said and treats words as facts; the Intuitor hears what was meant and treats perceived intentions as facts.

Perception is the process by which we gather information from the outer world about what is going on around us and from our internal world to see what our reactions are. Sensors and Intuitors rely on different primary ways of obtaining information.

The perceptual processes of Sensing and Intuiting provide information and interpretation of what we see, while the judging processes of Thinking and Feeling provide judgment and decision about what we see.

Those who use Sensing as their primary perceptual process gather information and interpret it primarily with their body senses — sight, smell, taste, touch, and pain-pleasure sensitivity.

Primary Sensors interpret information by using their experience to help them name and categorize information. For instance, when looking at a profit-and-loss statement, they compare what they see to the rules of what a PandL should look like. Sensors prefer to deal with concrete things that can easily be named and categorized according to the norms. Past experience with the norms defines the reality of the new information; thus, the incoming information is compared with previously defined sensory data.

Sensors like information that is dependably verifiable and provable with their senses. The tangibility of rules makes Sensors more rule-bound than Intuitors in interpreting information. Sensors interpret information by comparing it with what it should be, what it has been in the past, and what they count on it being in the future. They like the predictability of the world as their senses interpret and test it. Sensors use their body senses to establish reality. They want to show or be shown in a tangible way what is happening, a result of their focus on the material world.

Sensors perceive information in sequential, step-by-step procedures which require verbal identification skills of categorizing and naming. Sensors sort and categorize information according to *their* learned and accepted definitions and believe that the analytical, verbal, linear way of interpreting is the "correct" way to perceive. Sensors can sort information very quickly due to their careful storing of prior experiences. They have readily formed categories of experiential data. If what they are processing is similar to something they have already experienced, they are more likely to sort and integrate very quickly.

Intuitors report the Sensor way of seeing as laborious and tedious for them. Intuitives process information as holistic impressions of the relationships and possibilities in the data. Where Sensors say, "Let me see it with my own eyes and verify it with my senses," Intuitors say, "I see it in my mind's eye." When the flash of insight occurs in the Intuitor's mind, it is verified as real at that very second. Sensors verify reality by sensorily/physically seeing, while Intuitors verify reality as soon as they have the intuitive flash of insight. Intuitors frequently have little need to verify their flash of insight in the external world. Sensors verify through the body senses and want external proof; Intuitors verify in their mind's eye and trust their insight despite lack of external provability.

The primary Intuitive perceptual process is a fast integration that does not involve figuring things out in logical order. The Intuitive person visualizes, symbolizes, and understands through a complex process of integrating the information and seeing the patterns, possibilities, relationships, and implications in information. Intuitors get a hunch, an insight, a general impression, an overview in an instant flash — rather than through rational, analytical means.

Hunches do not imply insight without empirical data. Hunches are frequently based upon Intuitive scanning. This scanning process produces insights abstracted from an amazingly swift assimilation of experiences, ideas, and probabilities. Intuitive hunches are not pulled mysteriously out of the air. They are better explained by comparing hunches to the result of a powerful computer that sorts thousands of bits of data at lightning speed to yield insight, i.e., the hunch. Intuitive hunches go from stimulus to insight in an unidentifiable way.

STRENGTHS AND WEAKNESSES OF PREFERENCES

For the most part, we perceive only those aspects of the environment to which we attend. Attending is a readiness to perceive, a pre-perceptive set of expectancy, based on one's interests and motivations, as well as the nature of the stimuli which impinge upon us. (Munn, Fernald, Fernald)

Our natural preference for perception affects the information to which we attend. Sensors attend primarily to factual information, while Intuitors attend naturally to the possibilities. Sensors categorize information according to experience and principles they have come to accept as true. Intuitors clump stimuli together, looking for similarities, connections, proximity, or paradoxical associations. Intuitors may group sounds, objects, people, ideas together due to some similarity of shape, feeling, intensity, or image. They have a tendency to sort through information looking for stimuli that belong together or connect in some way.

Dr. Carl Jung discussed the difference in Intuiting and Sensing:

The primary function of intuition is simply to transmit images, or perceptions of relations between things, which could not be transmitted by the other functions or only in a very round-about way. These images have the validity of specific in-sights which have a decisive influence on action whenever intuition is given priority . . . sensation as the conscious function offers the greatest obstacle to intuition. Sensation is a hinderance to clear, unbiassed, naive perception; its intrusive sensory stimuli direct attention to the physical surface, to the very things round and beyond which intuition tries to peer. (*Psychological Types,* pg. 366–367)

Dr. Jung suggests that the best Intuitive functioning depends on suppressing sensation so that larger implications can emerge. The "simple and immediate sense-impression" must give way to the bigger picture. Intuition focuses on the widest range of possibilities, while sensing "strives to reach the highest pitch of actuality." Dr. Jung further describes:

The intuitive is never to be found in the world of accepted reality-values, but has a keen nose for anything new and in the making. Because (the intuitive) is always seeking out new possibilities, stable conditions suffocate him. He seizes on new objects or situations with great intensity, sometimes with extraordinary enthusiasm, only to abandon them cold-bloodedly without any compunction as soon as their range is known and no further developments can be divined. (*Psychological Types,* pg. 368)

Sensors look for details, names, language, actions, and events for sequencing because they process information primarily as a detailed recognition of events in moment-to-moment progression. They are notorious for accurate details of the event, but may fail to note background, intent, implication, and relationship to future events.

Though we have carefully documented Sensors' description of the way they process information, Roy Woene's description is a clear self-portrait. His article entitled "What It Is Really Like To Be An ISTJ" carries a description that is worth sharing. Keep in mind that he is a Sensor Judge:

How do I describe my memory bank? I have no experiential way to do this. All I can do is describe a four dimensional grid . . . Think of a rectilinear set of boxes going across, up and down and into the distance with no limit on the size of the boxes or how many. Each of these boxes may again be divided in a 3-dimensional GRID; now add time as the fourth dimension. As I go through life most of the external impressions picked up by the five senses and impressions generated by the inner world are sifted, cataloged and filed away in this Grid with a time function added when necessary; similar things are filed in the same box or adjacent boxes. From this GRID many "truths," "absolutes" or "blocks of knowledge" are generated and filed for future use. Also, habits of thought are stored so that a consistent pattern of analyzing, judging and critiquing is used. New boxes are being added constantly and old boxes are discarded (forgotten). This part of the GRID is involuntarily used, it is ON all the time and controls the thought process including the use of the memory . . . When preparing for a task or for a problem that needs solving, I will, by way of the GRID, review all possible operating options at my command and select the one that seems most efficient or most applicable for use on that particular problem. If, down the road, I find that things are not going right I merely apply one of the other options, or part of it, as a "fall back" position . . . no time is lost in muddling around trying to find a way to get the job done. Getting to the goal is all important. No time is lost "smelling the roses" unless the goal is to find the most fragrant rose.

Although Woene writes about his ISTJ style, he articulates the acknowledged process of many of the Sensor managers with whom we work. The Sensor preference for ordering the tangible into practical categories of experience tends to be true across different Sensor styles. Sensors tend to sort information according to previous experience and actions.

Sensors' storage of information based upon experience usually gives them a sense of mastery once they understand something. Since Sensors tend to store information sensorily, their information tends to be more systematically organized — thus, supporting a thoroughness that feels like mastery. The Sensor-Thinker tends to store tasks, actions, and outcomes as the important data, while Sensor-Feelers tend to organize according to positive or negative associations involved in the tasks, actions, and outcomes. Sensors tend to store memories with sights, sounds, smells, locations, dates, and times. Such memory storage gives them much more detail and specificity when recalling events. Some Sensors talk about organizing memory around particular houses in which they lived, jobs they held or parts of the country where the incident occurred. Sensors tend to store more specific information than Intuitors do.

Intuitors do not usually have the certainty of mastery. Intuitors clump and group stimuli in a continually changing pattern of associations. Therefore, to recall what they know about something, they have to rely on scanning to recall multiple associations rather than recalling a clearly marked category. Intuitors who do not know how the process works may have trouble recalling with certainty what they know about issues. Information is in a continually unfinished form in the mind of an Intuitor, due to the continual search for improvement and insight. This may lead to a feeling of not quite mastering many areas of information in which the Intuitor, in fact, has ample understanding. One ENTP (Extrovert, Intuitor, Thinker, Perceiver) said, "You don't know how much it helps me to understand how my Intuition works. I thought I had Alzheimer's. I just can't remember detail. It's good to know that I can remember if I see a real use for it. I felt crazy . . . at times I felt brilliant and other times I felt stupid. I wish I had known this years ago. I could have saved myself some real anxiety."

Let's review some Intuitors' descriptions of their insight process. The process links information accumulatively.

> "It's an inner impression, that's all. It throws light on a problem in a secure and reassuring way. A person will get an impression or idea or gut feeling, but won't always listen to them. In the past, I've been hurt because I didn't pay attention to these feelings." — Louis Golden, president of Commodity Steel and Processing, Inc.

> R. Buckminster Fuller called Intuition "cosmic fishing." He warned, "Once you feel a nibble, you've got to hook the fish. Too many people get a hunch, then light up a cigarette and forget about it." (Roy Rowan, pg. 11)

> "Intuition works in proportion to need. All that high voltage down there in the subconscious has to be invoked." — Joseph McKinney, chairman of the Tyler Corporation (Rowan, pg. 12)

> "It seems that a massive accumulation of experiences and judgments is brought to bear, but at some point the person is confronted with the unknown and takes a chance, and makes his career on an intuitive choice. I would therefore add the

quality of courage or guts as a necessary component." — Chief executive of large Chicago corporation (Dean and Mihalasky, pg. 36)

A former vice-president of Bethlehem Steel was asked if intuition played a part in his job. He replied: "Intuition is nine out of ten in my job. In my company we have over a hundred specialists. If I need any information, I go to the specialist and get it. But I mustn't spend too much time with him, or else I'd become a specialist too. And that's the thing I must guard against in every way I know how. If I can remain the generalist, intuition will keep on flowing through me and I'll make the right decisions for my company and my shareholders — even though I don't really know how I do it." (Dean and Mihalasky, pg. 56)

"I've been accused more than once of playing hunches . . . I further believe most people have them, whether they follow them or not." Conrad Hilton says the key to intuition is listening for a response. (Dean and Mihalasky, pg. 67)

"An idea begins playing around the edges of my mind, just out of mental sight. I know my intuition is working on something but I can't quite drag the topic into consciousness. I begin to note a slight quickening, almost like excitement but much more subtle, as my intuition notes a bit of information from a movie, a conversation, a situation or a book. I feel a subtle anticipation of insight and discovery, though as yet my conscious mind is unaware of what my intuition is working on. Then, suddenly, the darkness of my subconscious mind comes alive with a maze of lightning flashes that connect the whole thing together and an insight is hurled into my consciousness. The insight excites my whole system. I feel energized, excited, inspired, relieved and unconquerable. The wonder of the insight can energize me for days." — A corporate executive

Compare the specificity of Roy Woene's Sensor description and the abstractness of Intuitors' descriptions. Sensors describe in primarily realistic detail, while Intuitors use concept, impression, and metaphor more frequently.

Successful interaction of Sensing and Intuiting information brings the fullest understanding. Intuitive insights come through a process that cannot easily be explained. Albert Einstein said, "There are no logical paths to these (natural) laws. Only intuition resting on sympathetic understanding of experience can reach them." "He called the theory of relativity 'the happiest thought of my life.' " (Rowan, pg. 4)

Both Sensors and Intuitors have strengths and weaknesses. The following lists were developed by executives and managers in management seminars, conflict resolution sessions, executive transition conferences, and team-building sessions conducted by Barr and Barr Consultants during the past sixteen years. The strengths and weaknesses represent both observed behaviors systematically recorded and operating perceptions of professionals in the business of managing. Too much of a good thing becomes a bad thing. Positive aspects can become troublesome to clear perception if taken too far.

SENSOR

TROUBLESOME POSSIBILITIES	POSITIVE POSSIBILITIES
Attention	
Too much step-by-step analysis and overlook the guiding principle	Orderly in using step-by-approach
Demand for proof may cause missed opportunity while waiting for proof	Linear in organizing data
Can be too focused on why things won't work, resulting in pessimism	Cautious examination of data
	Ground ideas in reality by comparing new ideas to accepted way of doing things
Action	
May be so task-driven as to become intolerate of people relationships by putting work before people	Task-driven . . . gets the job done
May fail to coordinate due to action-orientation . . . would rather get things done than talk about them	Works at a steady pace
Too practical . . . may reject new ideas	Sensible

Reduction

Too detailed . . . may be a nitpicker	Focuses on details and facts
Too factual and literal; may overlook implications	Values the tangible
Too rule-oriented. . . tends to argue for narrow interpretation of rules	Likes to play by the rules
Reduces issues too narrowly	Examines issues thoroughly

Status Quo

Too resistant to change . . . prefers the tried and tested way	Realistic
Prefers experience-based methods; may use obsolete methods	Experience-based
So focused on short term that future demands aren't seen in time to prepare	Dependable

Sensors and Intuitors worked on the positive and troublesome possibilities. Sensors readily acknowledged tendencies for too much step-by-step analysis, too much focus on why things won't work, so much practicality that they may reject new ideas, becoming too detailed, and nitpicking. Intuitors expressed the most frustration, however, with Sensors (1) being too resistant to change, (2) refusing to try something new, (3) being too rule-oriented, (4) interpreting rules too narrowly, and (5) being too focused on the short term.

Both Sensors and Intuitors agreed on Sensor strengths as being sensible, dependable, task-driven, getting the job done, and realistic.

INTUITOR

TROUBLESOME POSSIBILITIES	POSITIVE POSSIBILITIES

Attention

Places too much value on possibility, thus overlooking realistic problems that could block the action	Is visionary
Scans too quickly and misses essential details	Scans for fast understanding

May give secondary variables too much weight and distort the picture	Sees possibilities
Goes beyond the meaning to look for symbolic or figurative meanings	Sees the overall picture

Innovation

May be so innovative that others do not relate . . . they are too far out!	Is improvement-driven
Easily gets too broad and scattered	Is imaginative
Creates so many possibilities that starting becomes hard . . . immobilized finding a place to start	Is innovative

Expansion

Tends to think in convoluted web of ideas and may get caught in the web	Uses divergent thinking
Tends to expand ideas to an unmanageable complexity	Does not respect restrictions
Tends to overgeneralize	Does relationship thinking
So improvement-driven that satisfaction for performance eludes	Does possibility thinking

Communication

Forgets to use transitions to help others follow thoughts — Ideas just pop out	Thinks quickly
Gets bored easily and tunes others out	Trusts hunches

Troublesome possibilities of the Intuitor style that tend to cause the most irritation are: (1) scanning too quickly and missing essential details, (2) creating so many possibilities that starting becomes hard, and (3) so improvement-driven that satisfaction is elusive. Sensors talk heatedly about how impossible Intuitors are to please. An often heard comment is, "No matter what you do, they (Intuitors) always have to change it, even if it's just a little. You can't really satisfy them."

Intuitors quickly note that they forget to use transitions to help others follow thoughts. Ideas just pop out and they see the look of confusion and annoyance when other people wonder where that idea came from. They also cite getting bored easily and tuning others out as very troublesome habits. Interestingly enough, Sensors never select those two descriptors as trouble-some. Note that the two things selected (no transitions and tuning others out) are more abstract processes that are much harder to detect; they are not readily identifiable by Sensors.

Perception is a complicated process. The following analogy explains perception's vital role in leadership development. Let's compare perception to the operations of a marvelously equipped room we'll call the Data Center. The main components are multiple high-speed receptors, a synthesizer, a huge screen, a powerful projector, a potent beam of light, and a large library of information storage. There are two operators of the Data Center: one is the conscious operator and the other is the subconscious operator.

The functions are:

Data Center is designed to process both internal and external stimuli to interpret what is happening. The Data Center is run by your favorite and most trusted perceptual process: Sensing or Intuiting.

Receptors receive multiple stimuli such as visual images, verbal sounds, body sensations, smells, tactile messages, impressions, instinctual responses, feelings, thoughts, and insights. Your favorite perceptual process affects the sorting of stimuli.

Synthesizer integrates and sorts stimuli for conscious operator to use in the beam of light called attention, and for the unconscious operator to use in the unlit, unaware background. The Sensing process prefers attending to real-world stimuli, while the Intuiting process attends more readily to possibility and meaning of the stimuli.

A huge screen is used for organizing, connecting, comparing, and discarding stimuli for perceptual use.

The powerful projector of attention is used to amplify, enlarge, and project perception.

The conscious operator selects a small portion of the information reaching the receptors to translate into conscious recognition, while the unconscious operator receives the rest of the information and sorts, reacts, and integrates below the level of consciousness.

The Data Center managed by a Sensor general manager tends to sort stimuli with a preference for concreteness over abstractness. Greater concreteness makes more extreme distinctions between stimuli, such as good-bad, right-wrong, real-unreal, and black-white. Sensor tends to see fewer shades of gray and fewer levels of meaning in stimuli. Secord and Backman in their book *Social Psychology* suggest that those who prefer greater concreteness "depend more on authority, precedent, and other extrapersonal sources as guidelines for actions; are intolerant of ambiguous situations, and have a low capacity to act 'as if' to take the role of the other person." (pg. 74)

Sensors sort data based upon experiences and organize it accumulatively to determine current reality. They tend to recall specific facts, events, and sensorily acute memories. Intuitors, however, store information in larger idea or conceptual categories. They respond to a stimulus by quick scans of their data banks and flash onto the perceptual screen relationships that make sense to them. They tend to link parts that comprise an information framework that can conceptually tie the disparate bits of data into an understandable picture.

The Data Center managed by an Intuitive general manager tends to prefer the abstract for concept formation. The Intuitor relates diverse behavior and multiple stimuli to integrate meaning and understanding.

The Sensor and Intuitor vary markedly in the complexity or simplicity of their perceptual integrations. Sensors tend to categorize stimuli as positive or negative, with little tolerance for integrating complex opposites. Intuitors tend to integrate more diverse concepts under a single broad insight or concept, thereby enabling them to see and integrate more complexity.

Sensors sort people information according to learned expectations associated with roles, status, and norms. In sorting people information, they apply appropriate role expectations of the behaviors, privileges, and responsibilities that "should" go with that role. Sensors, therefore, process much of their information according to learned role expectations. They have certain regularities of their feelings, thoughts, and predispositions to interpret various aspects of their environment.

Intuitors sort people information according to concept and meaning with much less emphasis on roles, status, and norms.

They emphasize ideas, concepts, and relationships for their perceptual process.

PREFERENCES FOR BOSSES

Sensors and Intuitors were asked to identify the best bosses they knew. Their descriptors indicate different types of information processing also.

Sensors describe the Best Boss as one who:

1. Is consistent.
2. Is punctual.
3. Is honest.
4. Gives well defined objectives.
5. Communicates clear expectations.
6. Is methodical with attention to detail.
7. Has job expertise and experience.
8. Can solve technical problems.
9. Is available and accessible when needed.
10. Sticks up for employees.
11. Gives recognition and reward for jobs well done . . . gives us credit.
12. Gives feedback and fair evaluation on our work.

Intuitors describe the Best Boss as one who:

1. Challenges us without being directive.
2. Is innovative . . . not stuck in status quo.
3. Let's us do it our way . . . respects individuality.
4. Encourages us to take risks.
5. Offers little structure, only general guidelines . . . no guideposts please!
6. Has high standards.
7. Judges us on results instead of the way we arranged the tasks.
8. Gives us the freedom to develop our own projects . . . We know the overall mission, so trust us to know how to come up with projects that will support the mission.

9. Facilitates the talents of diverse people.
10. Is non-authoritarian.
11. Gives us the authority to come up with our own solutions and then holds us responsibile for the outcome.

Sensors' descriptors are based on tangible, experiential behavior that clearly establishes parameters, whereas Intuitors' descriptors are based on process, individual freedom, and removal of constraints. Sensors note that they have difficulty respecting a boss who cannot demonstrate technical expertise. Intuitors have trouble respecting a boss who is not intelligent and innovative. This does not imply that Sensors do not also want intelligent, innovative bosses; it is just secondary to technical expertise.

When managers were asked to list the characteristics they liked best for employees, Sensors and Intuitors showed different preferences.

PREFERENCES FOR EMPLOYEES

Sensor Preference	*Intuitor Preference*
1. Punctual	1. Creative
2. Task-oriented	2. Open-minded
3. Reliable	3. Self-starter
4. Common sense	4. Independent
5. Straightforward	5. Follow-through
6. Competent	6. Likes challenge
7. Loyal	
8. Conscientious	
9. Honest	

Whether describing best bosses or best employees, Sensors value behaviors that can be observed for consistent indication of reliability and predictability. Intuitors value processes, attitudes, and behaviors, thus their high tolerance for complexity and intangible processes.

When asked to describe the way they respond to rules and regulations, Sensors and Intuitors again responded quite differently, with Sensors respecting rules and Intuitors seeing rules as creative opportunities.

Sensors' responses about rules and regulations:

1. There's a need for rules . . . they help decide what you can and cannot do.
2. We think rules, regulations, and laws represent group norms to order the way way we interact.
3. If you need to challenge rules or bend them, then do it properly by going through the chain of command.
4. You must take responsibility for them; you cannot disregard them.
5. Abide by them, follow them, and research to see if you can get around them by looking for precedents that hold up under serious challenge.
6. Seek out reliable sources for interpretation.
7. Question them, bend them, but don't break them, because that would be too confusing.

Intuitors' responses about rules and regulations:

1. Use them only as a guide.
2. Do interpretive reading of them.
3. See how they are situationally appropriate.
4. Rules should enable instead of inhibit.
5. Get rid of them — they are too frustrating and impose too many limits to creative response.
6. They are written by uptight people who have not the slightest idea about our jobs or challenges.
7. They are general indicators . . . not concrete forms of action.

Much conflict in organizations results from Sensors carefully interpreting the rules while Intuitors tend to interpret rules more loosely. Sensors argue, "The rules don't say you can," and Intuitors respond, "They don't say you can't."

In a study of retail store managers employed by a national mass merchandiser, ESTJ (Extrovert, Sensor, Thinker, Judge) and ISTJ (Introvert, Sensor, Thinker, Judge) did best. Nine characteristics/tasks were emphasized by the companies: (1) planning, organizing according to company policies, (2) knowing/

applying merchandising concepts, (3) maximizing sales and profits, (4) ability to work through others to achieve company policies, (5) analytical thinking and decision making, (6) following orders that may be unpopular, (7) leadership skills, (8) having good relationships with employees and customers, and (9) emphasis on people-orientation. The sample of managers involved 65% Extrovert, 83% Sensing, 93% Thinking, and 92% Judging. (*Journal of Psychology Type*, Vol. 7, 1984, pg. 19–24)

TRADITIONAL STUCK ORGANIZATIONS

Traditional organizations have many of the troublesome Sensor characteristics that are present when a balance between Sensing/Intuiting has not been achieved.
Characteristics of stuck organizations are:

1. Rule and regulation bound – rigid interpretation.
2. Little discretionary use of resources.
3. No incentive to innovate . . . new ideas are met with disapproval.
4. Too many kingdoms . . . too much segmentation . . . large number of components sealed off from one another.
5. Restricted communication.
6. Information is guarded and secretive.
7. Hierarchy reigns . . . not teams, but tall hierarchies.
8. Vertical relationships dominate interaction.
9. Demand honor of chain of command.
10. Protocol is more important than results.
11. Virtual absence of lateral communication or cooperation.
12. Conflict escalates easily.
13. Tools, support, and assistance are hard to get.

(The thirteen characteristics were abstracted from Dr. Rosabeth Kantor's book *Change Masters*.)

TODAY'S HEALTHIEST ORGANIZATIONS

Characteristics of today's healthiest organizations show a need for Intuition and Sensing:

1. Innovate continually.
2. Improve continually based upon creativity and originality.
3. Immediate response capability.
4. Teamwork abounds with mission being more important than turf.
5. Flexible systems.
6. Continual readiness and development of managerial and technical pool of candidates.
7. Leadership.

A better educated work force and people's expectation of meaningful work are requiring more of managers and organizations. The classical assumptions are being challenged. Employees no longer placidly accept the assumption that people at the top have a virtual monopoly on vision and knowledge while people at the bottom have the bodies and muscle to carry out the vision. Recent estimates of the work force suggest *only* 42% of the U.S. work force is now motivated by the work ethic of hard work in exchange for security and responsibility. Today we see achievement, advancement, recognition, responsibility, and interesting work as the values. The social climate of work is increasingly important.

Stage IV Leaders with balanced style and mature use of power are the best fit for the higher demands of today's work force.

STAGE IV LEADERSHIP AND PERCEPTION

Perception is a continual process of interpreting what is happening. It is our way of seeing and processing what is going on around us and inside us. Perception is an essential process in communicating and leading.

Tremendous forces are battling for control of perception. Billions of dollars are spent on advertising to create a desire for products where no real need exists. "Spin control" is an accepted practice where the most potent perceptual projectors take charge of information to put the perceptual spin on the information for maximum control and greatest influence. "Disinformation" has replaced "We lied." Reshaping facts and situations in order to obtain the most benefit is as ancient as the beginning of intelligent life on this planet. So, what's new about the fight for control of perception?

The explosion of the information age provides sophisticated systems for shaping perception. We are bombarded mentally, emotionally, and physically with strong projections to shape what we see, value, accept, and buy. How does a leader compete with these bombarding demands for followers' perception? How does a leader keep others clearly focused and committed during intensely aggressive demands on followers' perception?

Most leadership books today extol the necessity of the leader not only having a vision but also having the essential talent to project that vision into the hearts, minds, and actions of others. We are told that the leader inspires, shapes, and communicates the vision that propels people forward to accomplish the goal. But, the question remains . . . How does the leader maintain clear perception and clear judgment?

Today's leader not only has the responsibility for articulating and selling the vision, but has an additional and more difficult job — helping people resist perceptual manipulation, distortion, and control.

A genuine leader tries to demonstrate clear perception by accurate assessment of factual data, including meaning and implication. Genuine leaders continually discipline their own use of perception while simultaneously helping others clear their perception. Since genuine leaders know that achieving worthwhile goals utilizes the richness of human nature, they understand the long-term wealth of helping people to increase their clarity of perception and judgment. Stage IV Leaders believe in investing in people as the company's richest asset.

Can you envision the resources of a company composed of people who could see clearly and judge wisely? Can you imagine what it would be like to have a group of people who were difficult to fool, accurate in their assessment of situations and people, clear in their ability to react and interact, and confident enough to take the intuitive leap? Can you imagine trying to compete with that kind of savvy company in the open market or work with that kind of department in a government organization?

The pseudo leader would be out of business if clear perception were true on a grand scale. The pseudo leader uses perception for manipulation, control, distortion, and power advantage. Pseudo leaders count on people's inability to spot lies and distortions. They thrive on misleading information and people manipulation. Unfortunately, more power abusers abound than Stage IV Leaders with the savvy and strength to confront them. Therefore, Stage IV Leaders, though few in number, not only confront pseudo leaders but also teach others to recognize perceptual distortion. Becoming aware of perceptual distortion is the first step to becoming free from manipulation.

We were asked if we were teaching the power game. It is a tough question and is one that we continually wrestle with. Learning to recognize perceptual distortion is critical to resisting it. Genuine leaders must work continually to keep their perception free, and they must guide others to freedom from manipulation. Therefore, we do teach the recognition of power manipulations of Stages I, II, and III in an effort to teach recognition as a means to freedom. We can only hope that the understandings are not used to advance the power game. We hope that revealing the manipulative behaviors is tantamount to being able to free ourselves from them.

"What you focus on tends to become your reality" is one of the profound truisms of perception. It is a basic tenet of the way perception functions in our system. When an idea comes into consciousness, we begin to energize it with our attention. As we think about it and give attention to it, subtle energy flows into that idea. When enough attention is brought to bear on the idea, it tends to become our reality.

Try this example. As you are sitting here reading, think about something that you would really like to eat. Remember when you tasted it last. Recall the texture, the flavor, the feel of it in your mouth. Remember the satisfaction that comes from eating it. Is it possible that sometime in the near future you will find yourself energizing your thought of that food and acting on it? That's a simple example, but find more suitable ones from your own experience.

Goals are just ideas until you energize them with your

thought and action. Making an investment was once an idea that may have become your reality. Think of all the many things you have thought about that you later acted upon. The best business deal you ever made began with an idea that turned into an opportunity that turned into an action. What you focus on tends to become your reality.

Because of the potency of this truism of perception, we urge great caution in identifying the appropriate moral, ethical, and spiritual guidelines for utilizing it. Teaching people to access the potency of mind, personal will, and projection has become big business today. Such power can be as readily used for evil as for good.

Leaders select ideas, energize them, and inspire others to help bring them into reality. Leadership is the art of persuasion and activation. The leaders' potency is directly related to their ability to help others realize goals and personal growth. Unfortunately, the power pool of perception is available to both the pseudo and genuine leader.

Identifying appropriate ways to use perception is therefore advisable, with emphasis on healthy, ethical uses. Perception is a continuous process taking place on both conscious and unconscious levels. We can use the principle of focusing energy on a desired idea to bring about powerful change. Perception is a potent force. Hence, genuine leadership demands some understanding of the ways people perceive. Understanding allows more targeted and principled use of perception.

Immature power players use perception as a major weapon. Stage I dependency types project responsibility for their lives onto others. If they can project potently enough, others respond. Helpless Infants and Terrible Tyrants use guilt as one of their most potent perceptual games. They project such strong guilt messages that others frequently placate them to avoid wrestling with their guilting games. Stage II Dictators project aloofness and unresponsiveness in order to keep others out of their business. Stage III Competitors use projections of superiority or ridicule to overpower opponents.

The power game is primarily a game of perception — played in the mind, and felt in the emotions and the body.

Perception plays an important role in games. People describe golf as a mental game where emotion must be controlled, boxing as a psychic game where you control the mind and dissolve opponent's concentration, and poker as a game of bluff and manipulation.

Politics, too, is a perception game where you control information and create image. Hedrick Smith describes the changing nature of the game in Washington in his book *The Power Game:*

> Altogether, it's a new ball game, with new sets of rules, new ways of getting power leverage, new types of players, new game plans, and new tactics that affect winning and losing. It is a much looser power game now, more wide open, harder to manage and manipulate than it was a quarter of a century ago . . .

The game is more fluid and more open for perceptual manipulation. For those who cannot see clearly, the image of leadership too often substitutes for substantive leadership.

Genuine Stage IV Leaders are well aware of the importance of image. They know it must be managed effectively while simultaneously self-monitoring for substance. For a public that does not bother to work at clear perception, image tends to be enough. Thus, the temptation exists to play to image and forego the painful work of disciplined thought and substantive performance.

In his cogent explanation of the image game, Hedrick Smith uses Lesley Stahl's experience to demonstrate the importance of visual image manipulation. He states, "In the image game, the essence is not words, but pictures . . . The visual wins over the verbal; the eye predominates over the ear; sight beats sound." Lesley Stahl, a CBS network reporter, did a very tough commentary on the 1984 campaign in which she presented the factual difference between Reagan's words and his political record. "Her piece was so blunt about Reagan's technique . . . that she braced for a violent reaction from Reagan's video managers." Stahl carefully explained the techniques used to create image that substance did not bear out. She created a series of vignettes showing Reagan attending various functions that his political actions did not support: such as his appearance at nursing homes, meeting with handicapped athletes, and being photographed with inner-city children of color. She then discussed the way his policies were different from the images created.

"I thought it was the single toughest piece I had ever done on Reagan," Stahl said, recalling her apprehension about the White House reaction. Shortly after the piece aired, Stahl received a call from a senior White House official congratulating her. She asked: "Did you listen to what I said?"

He responded, "Lesley, when you're showing four and a half minutes of great pictures of Ronald Reagan, no one listens to what you say. Don't you know that the pictures are overriding your message because they conflict with your message? The public sees those pictures and they block your message. They didn't even hear what you said. So, in our minds, it was a four-and-a-half-minute free ad for the Ronald Reagan campaign for reelection."

Stahl's intent to do tough, independent reporting of the truth was overridden by the greater potency of the visual, which involves a different perceptual process than the analytical. Political strategists have long known that people criticize politicians on issues, but vote on feelings. Marketing experts have long known that you sell products to the heart through artful manipulation of visual images rather than to the head with weighty evidence and reasoned discourse.

Image strategists know that the average person has little interest in clear perception and adequate information. Few people know how to reconcile the variety of information bombarding their perception. The competing messages of sound, vision, emotion, action, innuendo, context, and manipulative intent create a complex and powerful set of perceptions. External projections mix with the individual's internal messages and the task of clear perception and clear judgment seems almost impossible. Yet, control of perception is a leadership challenge. Perception is the battleground.

CLEAR PERCEPTION – DESIRABLE OR UNDESIRABLE?

One must not assume that people want to see clearly. If truth upsets goals, dreams or profit, people will frequently choose distortion above truth. People tend to want to avoid pain, and if it requires blinding themselves to the painful reality of a situation they frequently choose distortion rather than verifiable evidence of the true situation. A notable example is community reaction to evidence of volcanic danger that threatened investments in Mammoth Lakes, California.

A panel of scientists from the US Geological Survey (USGS) group met with the outraged community of Mammoth Lakes.

"The reality was, quite simply, that these people (the community) did not want to believe the facts. Their town was literally sitting on a volcano that might be ready to erupt, but the residents were refusing to accept the truth." (pg. 261, *On Shaky Ground*) The USGS issued a Notice of Potential Volcanic Hazard which had the people in an uproar. The scientific justifications of the notice were overshadowed by people's anger at the potential loss of business. The notice was issued six days before the resort's biggest weekend of the year.

Scientific evidence showed the buildup of tectonic forces. Even more specific evidence showed something quite alarming: "The area was bulging, rising slowly like a mound of dough in an oven. The rise was very small — a matter of some ten inches since 1979 — but it was very significant, because it was centered over the preexisting magma chamber . . . The logical explanation for the bulge, then, would be magma pressure coming from within the magma chamber below. Additional evidence showed the seismograph tracings of Mammoth aftershocks from a series of small earthquakes bore a chilling resemblance to the seismographs of continuing volcanic activity beneath Mount St. Helens. What that suggested was the movement of magma somewhere beneath the street level of Mammoth Lakes, California." (pg. 265)

The community was able to bring enough pressure to bear on the USGS that they eventually reduced their three-tiered warning of danger to a simple notice to finally no notice at all. Though the scientific evidence continued to mount that Mammoth Lakes is built in the crater of a volcano with evidence of increasing activity, financial interests and denial controlled the outcome. Perception is affected by personal interests.

DANGEROUS PERCEPTUAL GAMES

Attention shapes reality. When we give our attention to something, subtle energy flows into that idea. When enough attention is brought to bear on an idea, it becomes our reality. Perception affects our beliefs, awareness, and behaviors. Let's suppose that you get an investment idea. Every time the idea comes into your consciousness, it grabs your attention. The more you attend to the idea, the more momentum it gathers. As the idea becomes more provocative, it drives out other ideas and you begin to focus more on the investment. You may find yourself considering the idea several times a day and you gather information about the investment. The more you consider it, the more possible it becomes. Carry the process further and you may find yourself with a new investment.

Perception is the foundation for persuasion. Perception is involved in grand visions and in grand schemes. Personal integrity, or lack of it, shapes the direction.

Mind games have become quite popular. Mankind has developed some very sophisticated forms of perceptual manipulation. Awareness of some of the games is useful in knowing how to protect yourself from them.

Several provocative news stories have verified the dangers of mind games. Charles Manson's ability to select followers with weak self-images and reshape them by renaming them, changing their value systems, and redefining their norms is a shuddering example of perceptual manipulation. Manson's ability to reduce followers' individuality with a potent combination of ego stripping and sensual indulgence is testament to the potency of projection. He orchestrated group functions that combined indulgence, obeisance, thrilling disregard for society's rules, and an impassioned vision of specialness and superiority. The havoc he wreaked still startles.

People still analyze the process by which Jim Jones talked hundreds of followers into committing mass murder and suicide at his command. Jones' powerful combination of religious fervor, fear, and control of perception resulted in blind obedience and dependency of over 800 victims. When people give the responsibility for clear perception and clear judgment to someone else, they agree to be victims.

The world watched the dramatic stand-off at the Branch Davidian compound near Waco, Texas. We watched the soap-opera-styled but real-world drama unfold during the 51-day siege. The stand-off occurred between the Bureau of Alcohol, Tobacco, and Firearms, along with the FBI, and the religious group called the Branch Davidians.

Through the safety of our own living rooms we could observe the tragic situation. We watched and perceived and probably judged. Viewers had 51 days of media information that raised serious moral and ethical questions. Most of us were not there to see for ourselves, so what shaped our interpretation of the tragic situation? Was it the media, the facts, the values, our own preconceived biases?

David Koresh apparently controlled perception and judgment of his followers. He named his compound Ranch Apocalypse. He controlled followers through personal charisma, isolation, intense religious fervor, a sense of specialness, and control of thinking/valuing processes. He influenced followers to sever family ties and attach themselves to him. When people willingly give up responsibility to see and think and interpret for themselves, they give perceptual control away. David Koresh was able to keep as many as eighty-six people with him right to the fiery end as the compound went up in flames.

So the question arises: Was David Koresh a leader or a power player?

Mind control occurs in other ways than group control. More sophisticated mind games are being taught today that use subtle forms of hypnotism to control other people. People learn how to access another person's subconscious without their knowing. Thus they don't alarm defense mechanisms or conscious resistance. Through such seemingly innocent techniques as pacing of movement, breathing techniques, touch, and carefully worded sentences the subconscious can be accessed without the person's awareness. Sending the signals to the other person visually and physically while verbally sounding quite innocent is a manipulation technique that can seriously affect behavior. People are learning and using techniques to bypass consciousness to deal directly with the subconscious. Subtle trance induction can be used to control others, sell ideas, dominate thought, and manipulate actions.

Subliminal programming is very popular today. It sounds so easy. That should be the first warning. Subliminal programming is used to place ideas in the subconscious in such a way as to create desire to act in the programmed way. Initially, that sounds innocent enough when you think about losing weight, stopping smoking, or getting organized. You see and hear converts attest to the wonderful results it brings. They attest to the power of the subconscious, with very little understanding of the potent forces at work.

CASE STUDY: TAKING AN EXPENSIVE SHORTCUT

A young supervisor with a number of personal problems responded to an advertisement for subliminal tapes advertised "to help you activate potential." She was married to a man unwilling to work at a steady job. In the seven years of their marriage, he had been out of work more often than he had worked. Julie was working two jobs in order to maintain their lifestyle. She was twenty pounds overweight and was continually plagued with the feeling that she could do more if she were just better organized. She did not take the time to identify the real problems. She just grabbed the handy perception that the problems would be solved if she just worked harder, more efficiently, and could lose weight.

Julie ordered the subliminal tapes on getting organized, losing weight, and winning. She listened to them frequently. Since she was consciously only hearing soothing ocean sounds on one, restful music on another, and nature sounds of birds on the other one, she had no idea what messages were entering her subconscious. She knew what outcomes she was supposed to expect, but didn't know what programming was being used.

Julie came to a management meeting six weeks after beginning the subliminal programming. She had lost fifteen pounds and was excited about the effortless way it had happened. A close look at her showed continually dilated pupils, restless bursts of energy followed by physiological stupor that left her unable to follow ideas. Her eyes had dark circles under them. She said she had been unable to sleep. The moment she tried, she thought of something that needed to be organized and found herself getting out of bed to work. She had completely altered her diet and had developed a rash that her doctor attributed to eating too much citrus fruit — yet she continued to crave it and compulsively ate it.

Julie became ill and found herself unable to work both jobs. She tried to program weight loss, organization, and success subconsciously without dealing consciously with the causative problems. She treated symptoms — not problems — and ended up causing more complications than she could handle. Julie had to seek professional help to try to regain her balance. The physical, mental, emotional, and spiritual systems are intricately linked. Artificially programming the subconscious without regard for the effect on the other systems is dangerous.

THE POWER OF PERCEPTION

Perception is a powerful mechanism. Genuine leaders know and respect its potency. Management of perception should be done knowledgeably, ethically, and responsibly. Leaders must understand both the positive and negative use of perception. They must be able to recognize games in order to know how to remain clear of them.

Highly publicized brainwashing episodes such as that reported to have been used on Patty Hearst have much in common with brainwashing techniques used by the Chinese during the cultural revolution. Elements of brainwashing are: identification of victims' fears, ridicule of values, humiliation, deprivation, alternating roles of victim-villian-valuable-vile, powerlessness, unpredictability, pain, relief, and thought reform. With the destruction of perceptual reality, reshaping becomes possible.

Hitler's manipulation of perception is one of the most studied of the gruesome outcomes of perceptual control that leads to physical acceptance. Hitler used six forms of misperception:

1. A diabolical enemy-image
2. A virile self-image
3. A moral self-image
4. Selective inattention
5. Absence of empathy
6. Military overconfidence

In Ralph K. White's article "Misperception as a Cause of Two World Wars," he clearly explains Hitler's approach. "It is now fairly well established that in Hitler's mind the diabolical character of the enemy, especially the Jewish enemy was extreme and unmitigated . . . the central role played by these delusions of persecution in his justification of his more outrageous aggressive acts" is one of Hitler's most deadly distortions. He saw himself as both virile and morally superior. In a speech delivered September 1, 1939, as he was declaring war on Poland, Hitler said, "I will not war against women and children. I have ordered my air force to restrict itself to attacks on military objectives." Hitler proved the discrepancy between his words and his actions.

Hitler had the ability to project messages powerfully into people's hearts and minds. His selective inattention armed him with "an exceptional capacity for 'double-think.' " Hitler introduced in 1930 his peace propaganda, which he continually projected for almost ten years. His impact was described as: "Inexplicable and incredible, it moved men by this very fact, but also by an undeniable breath of passion. With the same passion Hitler had said the exact opposite. He apparently had a knack of working up a noble passion that he could 'sincerely' feel at the time of making a speech, though it would not necessarily remain salient in his mind at a moment of hard decision-making." (White, pg. 236–237)

Hitler's military overconfidence was seen "in his assumption that after the Nazi-Soviet Pact, Britain and France would not dare to fight, and his suicidal attack on Russia. . . . [Hitler] showed to an extreme degree not only the typical paranoid delusions of persecution but also the typical paranoid delusions of grandeur. Overconfidence is a form of wishful thinking, and it leaves strict realism to be overtaken by perceptual distortion." (pg. 239)

Although these examples are extreme, they identify the outer boundary of perceptual manipulation. Let's look at a more ordinary use of perceptual domination in an office setting.

CASE STUDY: PERCEPTUAL PUT-DOWN

Twenty-three-year-old Cynthia's personal ambition is to be a senior vice-president by the time she is thirty. Her goal is clear. She graduated magna cum laude from a prestigious business school with double majors in finance and economics. She is a smart, hard worker brimming with confidence. Her attractiveness and brains have served her well. She can outthink or outcharm most people her age. She is Intuitive with speedy assimilation of information. She didn't know that her confidence came from successful manipulation of situations where she continually had the advantage.

The morning came, however, when her intelligence and charm were not enough. Her Intuition was not adequately developed to process clearly when her feelings were too strong. She was so controlling that she had little experience with being overpowered. She was like a lamb ready for the Intimidator's slaughter.

Cynthia was to present an investment plan she had prepared for a client. To her surprise Les, a senior vice-president, from corporate office was sitting with her client. She had not met Les, but recognized him from his picture in the board room. She walked over to him to introduce herself. She stuck out her hand, gave him a big smile, and said, "Hi, I'm Cynthia Williams."

Les responded, "I'm not here to meet the hired help. I'm here to see that my good friend gets the best talent we have to offer." He turned to the client: "You know, Ed, I won't let just anyone take care of you." With a wave of his hand he ordered, "Well, young lady, show us what you have. If it isn't what it should be, I'll find Ed someone else. Well, don't stand there. Get started. I don't have time to waste."

Cynthia's face turned very red, her hands started to shake, and she felt so mentally scattered that she began to stammer. As she began her presentation, Les interrupted with pre-emptive questions that put negative twists to her information. He refused to let her develop her investment rationale but instead continued his attack with judgmental questions. Les' interruptive questions caused disjointed answers for which he quickly blamed Cynthia. He overrode the reality that he was controlling her presentation and was playing her professionalism against the power of his role and his right to question. He projected that she was inept, unprepared, stupid, and incapable.

Cynthia was awash with feelings of anger, fear, uncertainty, and confusion. She felt powerless to regain the initiative. She had trouble remembering her presentation. Finally, Les reached over and took the report from her and said, "Here, just leave these beginnings of an investment report with me. It's clear that you aren't prepared to deal in this league. I suppose it's not really your fault. Someone mistook looks for brains. You go on back to work. I'll take care of this."

Cynthia protested that she hadn't gotten to present her work well. Les responded: "Well, go practice somewhere else. We have business to take care of. Just admit that you did shoddy work and don't try to blame it on someone else."

Cynthia didn't know that Les is a Stage III Intimidator. She had never dealt with one before and was quite unprepared for the uncertainty and confusion that she felt. As an Intuitor she usually operates from an internal picture of the end result she wants. She doesn't focus on details as her guiding mechanism during presentation. She relies, instead, on a clear internal picture of the outcome. When Les attacked, she became so internally scattered that her guiding picture disappeared.

I saw her three weeks after the interaction. As she told me about it, her face reddened, tears came into her eyes, and she began to shake slightly. She was still trying to figure out what happened. She knew that she had prepared well and that the investment report was a good one. Even her manager had complimented her on it before she met with the client.

Her anger and humiliation at being unable to hold her clarity during the perceptual onslaught was taking its toll. The memory of the powerlessness she felt at being unable to stop him stirred real fear in her. She said, "I never want to go through anything like that again. I don't need it."

We walked down the hall to a management meeting. I sat down and Cynthia went to speak to someone. A few moments later, Les walked into the room. I looked at Cynthia and saw the bright red flush start creeping up her neck. Her body stiffened and she raised her chin as if to defy the put-down that she feared was coming. The old Intimidator knew victims' predictable responses and as always he intended to remain in charge of the game. He spoke to several other people as he worked his way around the room. Cynthia appeared to grow more tense and her face was now bright red. He walked past her as if he didn't see her. A mixed look of relief and disappointment passed across her face. Just as she unlocked her stiffened posture and prepared to move toward a chair, Les with a surprise animal smoothness intercepted her and said, "Well, if it isn't pretty little Sally. Nice to see you." Then with an abrupt turn, he moved quickly away. The extra emphasis he put on the name "Sally" gave me the impression that he was deliberately using the wrong name. He watched intently to see if she corrected him in order to try to establish her name identity, forcing her into the role of seeking acknowledgment. If she did not correct him, he would know that he got away with his game of devaluing her.

It took several months for Cynthia to work through the fear and anger that surrounded that initial incident. She was so accustomed to being the one who projected the dominant image that she was quite unprepared to be on the receiving end. Every time anyone mentioned Les, she had that disturbing scattered feeling. The battle for control of perception was clearly going on in Cynthia long after the incident occurred. Occasionally, she saw him and the same feelings of uncertainty and fear of being put-down raced through her. Before you write her altercation with Les off as an incident of the young, think about power abusers' ability to shake you up.

Though it was a brief incident in Cynthia's life, it was one of those challenging incidents that question self-image, confidence, perception, and judgment. That fifteen-minute interaction became a significant, emotional event to Cynthia as she began to understand the kind of strength and clarity it would take for her to achieve her goal. She was quite sure that she did not want Les' projection to become her reality. She was determined to dig into the deeper aspects of the incident. She intended to arrive at her senior vice-president's chair with clarity and integrity intact. She was smart enough to realize that she had better understand the game to know how to neutralize its effect on her.

We worked out a development plan for Cynthia. It involved ten steps.

1. Identify Cynthia's communication style (as strong preferences for Extroversion, Intuition, Thinking, and Judge-controlling ENTJ).
2. Identify the strengths and weaknesses for each preference.
3. Use a tape recorder to capture impressions of significant interactions.
4. Process the interactions for thoughts, feelings, and actions as a way of becoming aware of her reactions and then recording them in a development workbook.
5. Use development exercises to increase her familiarity and confidence in using Sensing and Feeling.
6. Study the behaviors of the power stages for ways to recognize the behaviors in daily interactions.
7. Develop a clear picture of her Stage IV Leadership image.
8. Confront fears that interfere with the Stage IV image.
9. Develop plans for periodic testing of her perception and judgment.
10. Commit to leadership development as a way of life for the rest of her life.

CASE STUDY: EVOLUTION OF A STAGE IV LEADER

Sam retired as a veteran of the CEO wars in the volatile and competitive computer industry. At seventy-two years of age he had lived through the industrial revolution and had helped lead the information revolution. He is an endless source of wisdom. He is active on corporate boards, manages his own investment portfolio, and still works actively with young managers and former colleagues seeking his guidance.

He laughingly recalls his first twenty years as a power-oriented egotist. Sam says, "I came out of college with a degree in business, thinking I knew it all. I even picked up an MBA along the way that further supported my bloated opinion of myself. I figured making deals, controlling the budget, and producing bottom-line results was all there was to it. I guess it was the mid-life woolies that got my attention. At forty-two I looked around with a sickening feeling that there wasn't much more . . . and I sure wasn't satisfied. Then my personal life hit me full force and that made my career concerns seem like pennies by comparison."

Sam is a natural ENTJ (Extrovert, Intuitor, Thinker, Judge). He used his style to charm, manipulate, and drive people. One of his former managers from the early years described him as "the most fun-loving con man to ever take over a corporation . . . only his idea of fun was damn hard on the rest of us. He thought fun was outrunning and outgunning everything that moved. Winning was not as great a pay off as making the losers pay homage to his superiority. Oh, he was smooth; he could gut you and you would walk away thanking him. It would be much later that you figured out what he had done to you. He really was a smooth bastard!"

As we repeated that description to Sam, he agreed that it was a fair description of him early in his career. He sighed as he acknowledged that it took him too long to learn about leadership.

Sam said, "I got my big six-figure job when I was forty. I loved the wheeling and dealing. I had always avoided looking at the consequences of the way I treated people. It took a serious accident involving my teenage son, a close call with alcoholism, and my father's suicide to stop me cold in my tracks. I'll use your language to make it clear. At that time I didn't have clear enough understanding to describe it adequately. Now, I see it in terms of my style.

"With the high energy of my Extroversion, the fast thinking of my Intuitive mind, the lawyer-like logic and my drive, I just rolled over opposition without giving it much thought. I was living the charmed life. I could persuade just about anything that had a brain. I didn't call it controlling perception; I called it life in the fast lane. When I got close to a challenge or a deal, I just knew what to do to get my way. I didn't know how I knew; I just knew that I could do it. I didn't spend any time trying to figure it out. It was too much fun doing it. The personal crises in my life were the levellers. The crises stopped my fast drive and slam-dunked me through the experience and I crashed into the floor. My fast talk and deal-making were of no use to me as I watched my son cling to life. I was too late to talk to my dad; I could only bury him."

Sam is quite articulate about the way he relied on his Extroverted enthusiastic charm to persuade and sometimes con others into letting him have his way. He judged others to be stupid because they could not keep up with the speed of his Intuitive-Thinker mind. He could assess situations and see remote possibilities much faster than others. Then, with his Extroverted, Judge-controlling, he could persuade others to support his moves. He said, "It was too easy. I could pull out the old snake oil and sell them before they knew what hit them. I graduated from college full of ethics, but they gradually gave way to the expediency of cutting a deal. I could rationalize any play I wanted to make. You see, I was so good at the old snake oil sell that I failed to realize that I was buying it too."

His son's accident, his father's suicide, and the reality of becoming an alcoholic ripped open Sam's feelings and turned the taste of snake oil to acid. It began to eat up his rationalization, his energy, and his health.

We met Sam sixteen years after the reality-dealing significant emotional events of his forty-second year. He was the head of his own computer company. He was one of the most effective men we have met. You can imagine our surprise when he openly shared the changes that had taken place in his management style.

As he described the way he once dealt with people, we could easily identify the Stage III Competitive Manipulator. He told the power stories, wielded the power symbols, poured on the charm, hustled in the competitive winner-take-all style, and was oblivious to his impact on people.

Sam said, "Can you believe that I hadn't really listened to anyone for twenty years? I found my own ideas so fascinating that I literally tuned out other people and dominated my environment. I had no respect for the people who got stuck on facts and mindless routine activity (Sam's idea of Sensor preference). I saw anyone with sensitivity as someone whom I could easily take out of the game (his idea of Feeler preference). I still feel regret as I admit the way I really was. I am a recovering power addict, and just like the recovering alcoholic, I always will be. I have to do daily reality checks to keep my natural inclinations from overpowering the way I really want to be."

By the time we met him, Sam was a pleasure to watch. In the first four weeks of our work for him, we noted consistent Stage IV Leadership behavior in Sam and saw the effects it had on his organization. We found a positive working environment where people were motivated to do their best. We saw Sam work ten-hour days with constant interruption, and we saw him work quietly alone for two or three hours at a time. He was charismatic and genuine. He was an active listener and a thought-provoking questioner. We recognized his ability to respond situationally without getting consumed by adaptability. He retained his ability to focus quickly, while also demonstrating tolerance and appreciation for those whose minds moved at a slower pace. He demonstrated his ability to balance his natural preferences with his learned skills. He put others at ease through his own comfort with himself and acceptance of others.

Sam's acceptance of others did not mean that he condoned all behavior. His acceptance of differences meant that he gave excellent description when he saw problems. He called behavior in such clear terms that people knew what they needed to work on to improve their professional and interpersonal skills. He continually caused people to strive more and develop their strengths. He was a hard man to fool. He knew the power game inside and out. He knew the games and the pitfalls of distorted perception and skewed judgment. He not only recognized power-abusive actions, he taught other people to spot them also. He exposed the abusive power game every time he saw it. He was amazing. Having been "a real bastard," he could smell power-abusive intent even before it manifested in behavior. In short, Sam knew and understood the potency of perception. He knew its use and its abuse.

Sam used perception irresponsibly during the first part of his career as he manipulated and controlled others for his own benefit. During the last part of his career he worked hard to use perception for the benefit of others — a much more responsible approach.

CHANGE MANAGEMENT

With the rapid rate of technological innovation comes an accelerating need for change; yet, people cling to the familiar and the habitual. The human need to stabilize during the midst of ever changing conditions is fundamental to understanding the stress in today's work force.

The shift from the work ethic to the consumer ethic challenges the old authoritarian style of management, the "all-in-the-numbers" approach to work life, and tacit acceptance of boring work.

Leadership requires the Sensor capability to routinize and standardize work procedures while applying the Intuitor capacity for continually updating and improving the way work is done. Leaders have to balance the practical Sensor task focus with the Intuitor improvement focus.

With only 42% of today's work force operating with the work ethic, much of upper-level management is out of step with the consumer ethic which drives the bulk of the work force. Seeing clearly what those different work ethics do to manager-employee relationships is tantamount to being able to bridge the gap and effectively lead.

The distinguished psychologist Carl R. Rogers said: ". . . in a time when knowledge, constructive and destructive, is advancing by the most incredible leaps and bounds . . . genuinely creative adaptation seems to represent the only possibility that man can keep abreast of the kaleidoscopic change in the world."

Survivability in the face of enormous change requires fresh thinking. Managers need to capitalize on both their experience and creative insights. The most readily recognized creativity is the spontaneous origination of an idea. However, another type of creativity involves linking seemingly unrelated pieces together for fresh insights. Creativity that collects an array of facts, circumstances, ideas, and details and sees heretofore unrecognized relationships is critical to seeing what to do in the kaleidoscopic change. Survivability requires Sensor grounding in reality and Intuitor fresh thinking to see current reality and future probability.

The linear, sequential Sensing process must be yoked to the multidimensional insight process of the Intuitor to provide leaders with a clear perceptual base to respond to future change situations.

Compare yesterday's manager with a today-oriented manager to note more specifically the demand to integrate Sensing and Intuiting focus.

YESTERDAY'S MANAGER	TODAY-ORIENTED MANAGER
Boss-centered	Quality Management
Company-policy	Stakeholder input
Short-term, bottom-line	Strategies for long-term positioning as well as bottom-line profitability
Focus on tasks, budgets, and systems with obedience	Focus on leading people with candor and trust
Delegate responsibility but jerk authority at will	Empower and build an environment of freedom to contribute
Accepted practice of making decisions unilaterally and announcing them	Makes decisions with input from stakeholders (interested parties)
Values roles and titles	Values teamwork and talents
Manages by rules and regulations as principal point of reference	Manages by clear perception and explainable judgment
Plays it safe, with risks taken incrementally if at all	Uses bold, fresh thinking for significant gains
Tends to control through SOPs (Standard Operating Procedures)	Sets reasonable boundaries and expects use of good judgment
Focuses primarily on department goals	Focuses primarily on customer, company, and employee needs

Today's work force demands more flexibility, the right to challenge and question, and a higher quality of work life. Employees are less willing to do boring work than the work-ethic work force, who tended to be more obedient, willing to do boring work, and were more compliant with managerial wishes. It is a challenging time to manage and lead.

DEVELOPMENTAL EXERCISES
Exercise 33: Sensor Development of Intuitive Potential

Sensors need to develop potential by expanding their willinginess to . . .

A. Scan instead of noting details.

B. Develop imagination and free the mind from reality-focus.

C. Be playful with ideas.

D. Make Intuitive leaps by allowing the mind to link seemingly unrelated facts (like Columbo in action).

E. Allow general impression of a situation (a process of unfocusing, zooming above the situation or away from it for the whole picture to form).

F. Allow reflective conceptualizing where a situation is observed and the general notions come into consciousness.

G. Deliberately look at a person, situation, or task and see possibilities, outcomes, and patterns.

H. Listen to dialogue to receive whole messages (implications from feeling, verbal, and nonverbal messages).

I. Allow spatial mapping of the environment for the purpose of synthesizing parts into a whole.

J. Discipline the drive to limit, reduce, and install limitations.

K. Confront the fear of intangible reality, the fear of that part of reality that isn't touchable and therefore unconscious.

L. Develop tolerance for spending the time to order and discover the intangible in a situation or task or relationship.

M. Expand tolerance for starting in the middle — learn to forego the demand to start at the beginning.

N. Remember that stressed Sensing can result in loss of groundedness.

WORK PLAN

Identify one of the ideas and design a plan for further development:

1. Pay attention to the way you react to the ideas selected.
2. Identify your propensity.
3. Decide what you will do to discipline the tendency.

4. Visualize clearly what you want to do instead.
5. Develop a way of practicing.
6. Develop a way to measure your success.

Exercise 34: Intuitor Development of Sensor Potential

Intuitors need to develop potential by learning to . . .

A. Live in the present.
B. Enjoy things as they are, instead of agonizing over they way they should be.
C. Observe and note details purposefully.
D. Remember names as well as faces.
E. Integrate innovation with experience.
F. Provide others with transitions for leaps of thought.
G. Break thoughts, designs, and ideas into manageable chunks.
H. Note when to limit and focus conversation instead of expanding and generalizing.
I. Discipline the Intuitive tendency to generalize too far.
J. Accept that Intuitive recall is often impressionistic, fluid, and not bound by logic, coding, classifying or ordinary sequence of time as is the Sensor recall mechanism.
K. Recognize when Intuitive preference for possibilities, expansion, exploration, and discovery needs transition into translatable, communicable messages with concrete application and real-world grounding.
L. Control the need for expansion and freedom from factual limits.
M. Discipline the fear of being dominated by fact, detail, and boredom.
N. Look at three rules or regulations and apply them precisely as they are written and note the Intuitor irritation with limits. Watch your mind examine the rules for possibility and flexible interpretation.

Identify one of the areas and design a plan for further development:

1. Pay attention to the way you react to the idea.
2. Identify your propensity.
3. Decide what you will do to discipline the tendency to resist.
4. Visualize clearly what you want to do instead of your usual habit.
5. Develop ways of practicing.
6. Develop a way to measure your success.

Exercise 35:   Balancing Opposites

Find ways to incorporate Intuitive process into Sensor approach. Sensor preferences are numbered; Intuitive potential is in brackets.

1. Make things practical, workable, tangible.

    [Select a task, think about it idealistically, imagine multiple applications of the ideal.]

2. Find tasks with immediate feedback or results.

    [Identify trends. Imagine yourself five years from today. Do something to prepare for five years from now.]

3. Plan action in terms of direct, measurable experience — Who, What, When, Desired Outcomes in terms of Measurables, and Immediate Steps.

    [Discuss an action that you are going to take in a month. Discuss the ideas involved, the outcomes expected, the possibilities, but deny yourself the pleasure of planning specifics.]

4. Use action to relieve anxiety . . . making something happen immediately satisfies the results-oriented Sensor approach.

    [Force yourself to sit down and identify the relationships, the ideas involved, the stakeholders, the possibilities while disciplining the urge to jump right in and get started.]

5. Note intense, fast-paced, competitive action.

    [Do an exercise in strategic planning, using long-term rather than short-term needs.]

6. Note structure, specific methods, standard operating procedures so natural to experience-based Sensors preferring the tried and tested.

   [Try something new that is unlike anything you have tried before.]

7. Take things apart to analyze the details to build an inductive understanding of exactly the way things work.

   [Start with a notion. Initially accept it as real. Find facts and proof of the notion . . . extend comfort with deductive approach.]

8. Operate from reality-testing position, to see learning for practical use.

   [Learn something that has no immediate practical value to you.]

9. Be observant of the external environment, observant of nonverbal.

   [Listen to a group interaction. Focus on the meanings, the relationships of people and ideas, note the intentions, note the feelings, identify your internal sensations while observing the group.]

10. Live in the present and tend to enjoy it rather than foregoing today's enjoyment for possible future achievement.

    [Withhold doing some pleasurable task and instead plan for some future event. Identify one of your skills and examine it carefully for improvement . . . deliberately extend satisfaction into that future state.]

Exercise 36: Sensory-Intuitive Perception

Sensory perception appreciates physical reality of the immediate situation. Focusing on physical sensations of sights, sounds, smells, flavors, shapes, and a variety of environmental details is natural to Sensors, but has to be more consciously developed in Intuitors. Sensors focus on experiencing life, while Intuitors tend to focus on interpreting life.

Sensory perception involves more than the five body senses that bring stimuli from the external world. Also included is internal Sensory response to stimuli, as well as experiential memory of Sensory response to events. Sensory perception is primarily attentiveness to stimuli. Practicing improved Sensory perception requires alert attentiveness to physical sensation.

SENSORY DATA

1. Look around the room. Look consciously, attentively at each item in the room. (Pay alert attention to each object.)
2. Attend carefully to the color of each object in the room. (Focus attention primarily on color data in the room.)
3. Attend carefully to the shape of each object in the room. (Focus attention primarily on shape data in the room.)
4. Attend to the tactile quality of each object as if you were touching it. (Focus attention primarily on texture data in the room.)

Remember: Sensor perceptual preference focuses on physical reality and notes primarily the facts of a situation, while being much less comfortable with generalizing beyond the facts, making risky Intuitive leaps to connect disparate data.

Sensors need practice in generalizing data and in seeing the connections between seemingly unrelated facts. Now, switch to Intuitive focus.

INTUITIVE DATA

Sensory perception prefers quantitative, sequential, procedural, structural, and controlled reception of data. Intuitive perception uses visual, conceptual, simultaneous, relational, spontaneous reception of data. Intuitor prefers idea-generation while Sensor prefers idea-testing.

Continue looking at the room around you. Practice using the scanning nature of your Intuition to uncover visual, relational, and spontaneous reactions to the room.

5. Focus on the entire room now by scanning across the room quickly for a general impression of the room and describe it. (Focus on the overview — the overall visual aspect, not the details.)
6. Imagine the room decorated in shades of green with only the furniture remaining in natural wood colors. (Focus on

changing the room.) Note your reaction to the room done in green. Do you like it? Do you like it better than the way it is now? Did you dislike it before you visualized it because you dislike the color green?

7. Plan three different functions in this room. (Example: a board meeting, a luncheon, a concert.) Note your struggle or ease at seeing the room for different usage.

8. Give yourself permission to be playful. Let your mind play with images of the room.

• The room is like:

• The room reminds me of:

• A song that matches the mood in this room is:

• The kind of people who would be most comfortable in this room are:

• Five things I would do to improve this room are:

Exercise 37:   Creative Tension Between S&N

Within each of us is a Play-it-safe voice and a Go-ahead-and-leap voice. The two voices give us different points of view. Compare some of the opposing messages that create dissonance within an individual and conflict among people with different preferences on Sensing and Intuiting.

Select a specific situation at work. Look at the two lists, noting one line at a time for examination. Identify your tendencies and examine your preferences in a real-world situation. Practice the creative balance between the two perceptual demands.

PLAY-IT-SAFE (REAL-WORLD) SENSOR	GO-AHEAD-AND-LEAP (POSSIBILITY) INTUITOR
Wants to know	Willing to guess
Wants it to fit	Tolerates loose ends
Values the known	Values the unknown as a challenge
Realistic	Wishful
Intellectualizes	Imagines
Relies on experience for reassurance	Relies on insight and concept for reassurance
Makes rules for responding to situations (oughts and shoulds)	Bends rules to make them fit the situations (coulds and mights)
Analyzes the pieces	Searches for patterns and links
Dislikes confusion	Tolerates confusion to search for meaning
Demands clear and orderly work	Tolerates muddling through the chaos for thrill of discovery

Exercise 38:   Sensor/Intuitor Conflict

An ISTJ vice-president of operations was angry with an INTP vice-president of information management. Examine the following exchange for proof of the Sensor/Intuitor conflict.

ISTJ: (Talking about the INTP VP) "He came to me to get some information. The purpose he stated initially was not what he actually did with it. When he actually worked with the information, he just went off on a tangent."

INTP: (Talking about getting the information from the ISTJ) "He talks about such basic, day-to-day stuff that I had to connect it to the overall needs of the company. He gave me a lot of information to explore. I came up with some great ideas."

1. Sensor expects the information to be used according to the stated purpose (seeing the purpose as static and specific).

2. Intuitor states the purpose as a beginning point with unexplored and therefore unknown possibilities (seeing the stated purpose as directional and dynamic).

3. Sensor judged the divergence as negative ("off on a tangent") while the Intuitor sees divergence as natural to find

the greatest potential in the information ("came up with some great ideas").

4. Sensor interpreted the information as it related to operations, while the Intuitor related to the overall company.

ISTJ: "He called me and asked if I would send a couple of managers to sit down with his computer programmers for about an hour to discuss what our business units need. I agreed. Then a week later I received a memo that outlined three eight-hour sessions. He also asked for my guys to prepare a large amount of business unit information for the meeting. He set me up with that innocuous request for an hour and tried to trap me into a huge planning process that would easily eat up 65–70 hours of my guy's time."

INTP: "It occurred to me when he was supportive of a planning session for business unit needs that this was the opportunity to do long-range planning . . . Something we've been needing to do for a long time. I was delighted that he was ready to do this."

1. Sensor agreed to the specific request ("a couple of managers for about an hour").

2. Intuitor extrapolated from the agreement support of the planning process (Sensor agreed to an hour meeting, which the Intuitor generalized to mean support for a long-term planning process).

3. Intuitor saw a possibility to get a long-term need met (saw possibility rather than the Sensor's real position) and played the situation from a short-term discussion of immediate needs of the business unit to a long-term planning session of company's future.

4. Sensor agreed to two managers to participate in a one-hour discussion (figured a total of a two-hour cost to operations) while the Intuitor focused on the general acceptance of the idea. Sensor multiplied three 8-hour sessions X 2 managers + research time and figured the reality at between 65–70 hours of operations time.

5. Sensor VP thinks of time as money and therefore thought the Intuitor had deviously set him up to get the VP's staff to do the data collection, thus saving the Intuitor's depart-

ment money as he got Operations to pay. The Intuitor was focusing on the idea and didn't even consider time or money. He did not see the problem.

ISTJ: (concluded) "He's untrustworthy, incompetent, unreliable, vague, and a fuzzy communicator. I don't trust his motive." (Notice the Sensor judging the Intuitor for not playing by Sensor rules.)

INTP: (concluded) "He agreed to this but now that it is time to set up the meetings he's resisting. He doesn't like anything unless it's his idea. He's so tunnel visioned that he can't see beyond today's quota in operations." (Notice the Intuitor is judging the Sensor for not playing by Intuitor rules.)

Summary: Review the basic differences between Sensors and Intuitors.

SENSOR	INTUITOR
Strong expectations	General impressions
Cautious agreement and testing	Intuitive leaps and acceptance
Dislikes ambiguity	Dislikes concretized limits
Dislikes long-range plans	Dislikes short-term mentality
Dislikes unplanned change	Dislikes too much structure
Prefers incremental improvements	Prefers variety and change of systems or methods

Strategy: How would you propose that these two vice-presidents who have equal authority in the formal system work out their differences? Use your best judgment, then check the keys on the following three pages.

Exercise 39:   Keys for Communicating with Sensors

Outline an idea using the following keys for messages for Sensors. Intuitors need to use the following keys in communicating with Sensors:

1. Work on specificity and establish a logical progression of agreement with clear parameters of the work.
2. Be factual — thoroughly work out details in advance.
3. Show why your idea makes sense — emphasize the practical application.

4. Be brief and specific.

5. Show respect for those who get the job done.

6. Use some phrases that usually appeal to the Sensor practical preference for action and forthrightness:

   "Suppose I skip the details for now and tell you the *specific result* I'm looking for."

   "I'll *get* right *to the point.*"

   "This will have an *immediate payoff.*"

   "We'll *get right on it!*"

7. Some phrases or messages that Sensors are likely to use:

   "Make it *quick!* I've got work to do."

   "*Get going* on that. We'll worry about exceptions later."

   "What *steps* are involved?"

   "What do we do *first?*"

Exercise 40:   Keys for Communicating with Intuitors

Outline a presentation to an Intuitor using the following keys:

1. Give the global scheme showing the system relationships by verbally painting clear pictures of the connecting elements.

2. Be conceptual and link outcomes with goals.

3. Describe the outcome as it relates to the overall company.

4. Identify the issues or concepts involved.

5. Discuss possibilities, then probabilities.

6. Indicate the challenge and emphasize future value.

7. Allow ample time to explore ideas.

8. Use phrases likely to appeal to Intuitors:

   "It's a rather *unique* approach."

   "This will pay-off even more in the *future.*"

   "Let me begin by giving you an *overview,* then the basic *ideas.*"

   "This approach fits well with your *concept* of . . ."

"Most people are afraid to try an *innovative* approach."
9. Some phrases or messages Intuitors are likely to use:
"That could cause problems *next year.*"
"That *might be* good *when* we get into the budget process."
"What's *different* about that? Does that fit the *philosophy?*"

Exercise 41:   Imbalance of Styles

Develop a strategy for managing a group of Sensors and Intuitors who are stuck in the rigid application of their own preferences:

SENSORS	INTUITORS
Too detailed	Too broad
Too literal	Too loose in interpretation
Too rules-oriented	Too rules-aversive
Too unimaginative	Too imaginative
Too structured in step-by-step approach	Too improvement-driven, resulting in continual rearrangement
Too focused on the present	Too focused on the future
Too task-focused, thereby overlooking process and strategy	Too strategy-focused, thereby overlooking necessary tasks
Too reluctant to change by clinging to past experience	Too ready to change to avoid boredom
Too traditional	Too innovative

Remember: The goal is to minimize these weaknesses and guide both Sensors and Intuitors into balanced interaction.

Exercise 42:   Sensing-Intuiting Situations

Recall previously experienced situations that will help you use your own information in exploring the following situations to integrate both Sensing and Intuiting information.

1. You are walking toward your car parked on a dark street. Your fight-flight mechanism fires and you are suddenly alarmed. The hair follicles on your neck stand up, your heart starts to race, and you become very alert.

    a. Do you move quickly to protect yourself?

    b. Do you stop to look around carefully?

    c. If you see no evidence of danger, are you more likely to assume that something is wrong with you and you are overreacting, or are you more likely to trust the unsubstantiated threat and accept that you really are in a threatening situation?

    d. How much factual verification do you need to accept that you are reading the situation accurately?

2. You are at a meeting. You propose a solution to a problem. You receive verbal agreement but you experience wariness instead of satisfaction. People say they agree to your solution but you don't feel confident that they intend to follow through. Recall an actual situation where this occurred.

    a. What were the identifiable facts (words, actions, body language) that caused you to doubt the sincerity of the agreement?

    b. What were the facts, behaviors, or insights that you linked together to verify the lack of commitment? (If you are having difficulty, read the next case study.)

Exercise 43:   Confusing Messages

Paula is a dedicated nurse specializing in pediatrics. She is acutely aware of patients and their needs. She observed that a commonly accepted practice in treating a particular obstetrics problem caused much pain and anguish in the patient. The practice of administering a large shot of medicine every four hours in the hip area caused pain, dread, and bruising. She thought of a way to administer the dosage through intravaneous injection using the tubes that were already in place in the patient's arm. She asked to be placed on the physicians' meeting agenda to propose the change of procedure.

The five physicians at the meeting listened carefully as Paula began with a vivid description of patient anxiety and discomfort over the painful shots. As she talked, two of the physicians exchanged looks and their eyes widened slightly as if in acknowledgment of shared outlook. One of them moved his chair away from the table a bit, folded his hands, and looked out the window. The other physician reached for a file of papers and began looking at them while Paula talked.

She carefully explained the method for administering the medicine, shared the research she had done to explore the effect and safety of the procedure, and again argued that patients were suffering needlessly. She offered a better way.

A third physician asked her what gave her the right to practice medicine. She sidestepped the "put-down" tone of the message and responded with more data about the procedure. He listened carefully, asked specific questions, and then said, "We'll consider your idea carefully, though the procedure you are trying to change has been used for years."

The physician who had been reading a report looked up and addressed the other physicians. "Can we move on? We agreed to consider the nurse's recommendation. I commend you for your concern."

Paula left the meeting dispirited. Identify the facts, the verbal messages, the messages in the nonverbal responses, and the inferences to suggest that the physicians are not going to accept Paula's idea.

Exercise 44:   Sensor Creativity

Sensors frequently think of themselves as not creative. When they define creativity as originative, they may feel overshadowed by Intuitors (the natural idea generators). If, however, they focus on the adaptive or applicable creativity, Sensors can set the pace.

Sensors frequently need a fact or a real situation to stimulate their adaptive creativity. Sensors are creative about making things work in the "here and now." Since they are grounded in reality, that's where they most comfortably start. Sensors usually don't move into adaptive creative mode until they see a real-world need.

1.   Relax. Give yourself permission to explore your own creativity. Suspend premature criticism. Experience the internal sensations.
2.   Take seven deep breaths of air while consciously noticing the body sensations involved.

3. Drop your hands loosely at your sides. Notice the sensations in your fingers and hands. Enjoy the relaxing sensations.

4. Recall a specific place you have been where you felt deeply relaxed and aware of enjoyable sensations. Play back the internal videotape in your mind of the sensory experience.

5. Now, using the sensation of relaxed awareness, imagine the same set of sensations in a very different setting.

6. Move the same set of sensations into your office setting.

7. Create the ideal setting where you can easily feel and identify your own abilities and talents.

8. Now, see yourself five years from today in your future office. Note carefully the details of what you are doing, where you are, what you are wearing, people with whom you interface most frequently, and the career moves you made in the five years. Are you using the same abilities that you now have? Any new ones?

9. Project even further into the future. Recall the sensations of relaxed awareness and imagine yourself ten years from today in your future location. What are you doing? With whom are you interacting? What skills and talents do you have that build on what you currently do?

10. Create your own future. Take the limits off. You have unlimited potential, resources, and opportunities. Create your own future experience.

The preceding sequence of activities addresses Sensor preferences. The exercise is designed around the following premises:

A. Start with a known experience and incrementally leap into the unknown of the turbulent world of creativity.

B. Sensors are apt to stop with current reality without resisting it or pushing beyond it; thus, by using progressive grounding, the Sensor can carry preferred skills of body awareness of breathing to the abstract challenge of creating their own future.

C. Sensors may need aid to break out of the present.

D. Sensors can more readily move from experiencing concrete objects or remembered sensations into an adaptive application.

E.   Start with a realistic beginning grounded in real-world sensation and build toward abstraction and application.

F.   Creativity is enhanced by suspending premature criticism of why the exercise is useless or won't work. Criticism tends to kill creativity.

G.   Increase tolerance for ambiguity and lack of insight in the early stages.

Exercise 45:   Intuitor Creativity

The Intuitor is more accustomed to perceptual ambiguity during information intake and incubation than the Sensor. Before the insight flashes into consciousness, bits and pieces of thoughts, impressions, and facts occur but have not yet arranged themselves into an integrated picture. The Intuitor has more tolerance for the unfocused period where a broad number of unrelated pieces of information have not yet come together to produce understanding.

The Intuitor notes experiences, facts, and slivers of understanding and waits for them to come into clear focus, producing what some call the "Aha!" experience — the excitement and relief that comes with insight.

Sometimes an idea smoulders just outside of conscious awareness. The process is like having an idea in the back of the mind but not quite focused or reachable. The formulated idea can occur quite suddenly after a period of little progress. It seems as if the fragments are quickly arranged and flood rapidly into the conscious awareness.

To access the Intuitive part of mind, one frequently has to slough off acceptable practices and traditional approaches. Try some of the following techniques to access your Intuitive approach to creativity:

1.   Find a quiet place. Sit up straight in a comfortable chair. Take several deep breaths of air and let your thoughts drift.

2.   Imagine that you are sitting in a leisurely time zone, where you are unhurried. As you relax, assume the role of an indulgent parent watching the demanding antics of your thoughts. As thoughts come into consciousness and demand your attention, just leisurely observe them but don't

grab them and hang on. Watch your thoughts try to get you to grab them and concentrate on them. Don't get caught up in your thought process. Just relax and watch the thoughts as if they were children demanding attention. Don't concentrate. Just relax. (This exercise is designed to help you move from analysis and concentration to the playfulness and boundaryless zone of Intuitive imaging.) Allow impressions and images to float in your mind.

Remember: Your Intuitive side is nonverbal; therefore, images and impressions are the language of the Intuitive perceptual process. After the images, the verbal words form to articulate impressions and insights.

Remember: Your Sensor side likes to create boundaries to make ideas more manageable and ready them for close scrutiny. Your Intuitor side likes to take the boundaries off to allow possibilities and previously unimagined relationships to form among the data.

3. Intuitive creative thought naturally jumps around, moving in seemingly random fashion. Your Sensor side wants the process to be sequential and orderly. Observe your tolerance for free flow of images and free association of whatever comes into your mind. Get to know your Sensor demand for focus and order. Learn to throw your attention to the playful, free association, creative linking of information of your Intuitive process. Learn when to throw your attention to the Sensor side of labelling, classifying, categorizing, and orderly arrangement of ideas.

Remember: What you give your attention to tends to become your reality. Learning to focus your mind more clearly brings you much more potency.

4. Focus on a specific problem. Attempt to activate your creative Intuitive process by imagining that *anything is possible.* Taking the limits off and allowing yourself to roam freely among possibilities is tantamount to releasing creativity. Every time your mind throws up a limiting idea, brush it aside with the notion that *anything is possible.* Use that thought to reopen the door of creativity every time your Sensor function tries to stop the free flowing process with criticism.

5. Our Sensor process attempts to limit and exclude by throwing out what doesn't fit. Our Intuitor process attempts to expand and include multiple possibilities. The Intuitor process is sparked by the provocative, not the analytical.

6. Sensor thinking attempts to fit things into known paths or recognizable procedures, while Intuitive processing looks for least likely paths. Select a situation or idea and use a metaphor for comparison. The following is a list of metaphors to consider.

    Situation _____ is like . . . (Select a metaphor that accurately describes the situation)

Buying a car	Lying on the beach	Eating a persimmon
Talking to a baby	Fighting a fire	Shooting a cannon
Cooking a steak	Reading a book	Fighting a war
Beating a bush	Flying a blimp	Running a race
Firing a wrestler	Planting a garden	Signing a check
Raising a child	Sky-diving	Driving a Harley Davidson

7. Suspend premature criticism of an idea. Tolerate the ambiguity required for the hatching period. Don't denounce the idea because of lack of success in the early stages of effort. Expanding your capacity for the ambiguous phase increases your chances of developing original ideas and unusual solutions.

Exercise 46:   Shift from Content to Process

Practice shifting from the content of Sensing focus on words and nonverbal body signals to processing patterns, implications, and linking meanings.

FROM SENSING DATA	TO INTUITIVE DATA
1. Action	What is happening?
2. Feelings	What feelings are involved?
3. Motives	What are the motivations?
4. Patterns	What are the patterns?
5. History	Does this connect with past patterns?
6. Growth opportunity	What can I learn from this?

7. Techniques   What communication techniques were used?

8. After-effects   What are the physical, mental, and emotional after-effects?

Exercise 47: Teamwork Considerations

Intuitive members should be aware of Sensor preferences:

1. Ground Intuitive ideas at the beginning point. Sensors tend to get irritated at starting in the middle. Ideas and concepts are just words that don't mean as much if they aren't rooted at a realistic beginning point.
2. Sensors prefer to experience first, then conceptualize the experience afterward.
3. Sensors have little tolerance for process and sifting. They don't want to be wrong . . . Just the "right" way, please!
4. They prefer facts, case studies, applications, hands-on learning, lots of examples to show how theory can be applied.
5. Sensors like to be introduced to new things one at a time, with the opportunity to compare it to past experience.
6. Sensors prefer time to collect rich Sensory experience, and they want to be respected for it as they dislike being seen as boring bean-counters excited by numbers.
7. Sensors get uncomfortable with hypothesizing about details.
8. They offer creativity to the team by applying innovative solutions to immediate, practical, here-and-now problems. They are creative about making things work. They use adaptive creativity and prefer reality to provide a fact to stimulate their adaptive creativity.
9. Sensors tend to be nervous when doing something outside their base of experience, until they learn what is expected.
10. Intuitors lose credibility with Sensors when they generalize without a fact base.

Sensors should be aware of Intuitive preferences in teamwork:

1. Intuitors have a greater natural interest in novelty.

2. They have a greater tolerance for complexity.

3. Intuitors need hatching or incubation time while their ideas recur and recur, coming each time in improved or altered form.

4. Intuitors have a greater tolerance for muddling (ambiguity) and lack of insight in early stages of change.

5. They prefer to work on multiple ideas at once.

6. Intuitors need time to be mentally playful to energize themselves through unfocusing, expanding, soaring, and exploring possibilities.

7. Be patient with the Intuitor's need to take a number of unrelated experiences, facts, and understandings as a process to focus them into a keen, clear point of attack.

8. Recognize and accept the Intuitor's trust in gentle flashes, quick insights, and freedom from realistic constraint.

9. Remember the Intuitor is not pre-programmed by limitation, while the Sensor is bound by learned interpretation of events from education and experience that provides a framework of rules/regulations for appropriate reactions.

– 5 –

Thinker-Feeler:
Blending Logic with Emotion

Main Ideas of Chapter 5:

1. Both Thinkers and Feelers use logical analysis but disagree on the importance of varying kinds of evidence.

2. Thinkers prefer objectivity, logical analysis, testability, and substantiated evidence; thereby needing to develop appreciation for individual values, diversity, and intangible attitudinal and cultural impact on situations.

3. Feelers rely most heavily on logical analysis using their people sensitivity, preference for harmony, and acceptance of extenuating circumstances; thereby needing to develop more objectivity and use of testable substantiated evidence.

4. What we give our attention to tends to become our reality. Thinkers primarily tend to cause-effect inferences, while Feelers primarily attend to personal impact on people and values.

5. Attention can be defined as concentration of consciousness or awareness.

6. Leaders must confront people, step-up to problems, risk

personal attack, and willingly pay emotional costs to confront problematic behavior.

7. Thinkers' defensive walls to protect against feelings can become so habituated that they are hard to drop after work when more intimacy and sharing is needed.

8. Feelers must learn to negotiate for relationship standards when interpersonal behaviors do not meet their relationship criteria — instead of imposing their own standards without discussion.

9. Openness to feelings expands a leader's ability to understand and relate.

DEVELOPING THINKER-FEELER POTENTIAL

Leadership development demands risk-taking and tolerance for vulnerability. Turning potential into usable skill requires going beyond habitual responses to stretch comfort zones. Thinkers need to open up to more conscious awareness of feelings, while Feelers must do more objective logical assessment of situations. Thinkers must not only continue to develop clear judgment containing objectivity, logic, testability and substantiated evidence for conclusions, but must also develop their sensitivity to values, diversity, and intangible attitudinal impact. Feelers must continue their work to yoke their people sensitivity and preference for harmony to logical inferences including people values and bottom-line impact.

Thinkers and Feelers rarely agree on what constitutes evidence. Feelers place individual values and people's feelings as primary variables in their logical equation, while Thinkers tend to discount values and feelings. Thinkers prefer objective variables and weigh subjective value-laden variables as inferior. They rarely see situations the same.

An example of different ways of seeing occurred in a small, nine-partner law office. One of the law partners walked over to the office manager and handed her some work that had to be done immediately. A few minutes later another partner brought work that had the same immediate priority. A Thinker clerk said: "Let's start on the first partner's work. He was here first. That's only fair." A Feeler clerk responded: "Oh, but the second partner seemed the most stressed. I think we should start on that first. He seemed so worried and upset."

The Thinker clerk looked at the situation and applied a fairness rule based upon whose request was first. The Feeler clerk applied a value rule based upon who was the most stressed and upset. The two reached different conclusions.

Decisions don't reach the manager clearly labeled with the issues; they are not stamped with instructions such as "value issue" or "factual analysis issue." Decision-makers have to decide the value issues interlacing the problem. They should also examine the issues for what the actual situation is in terms of facts and variables. Balancing Thinker-Feeler consideration amounts to balancing *what ought to be* with *what is.*

Attention is the light of focalization that causes a Thinker and a Feeler to look at the same situation and see different aspects. William James described attention: "It is the taking possession by the mind, in clear and vivid form, of one out of what seem several simultaneously possible objects or trains of thought. Focalization, concentration of consciousness are of its essence. It implies withdrawal from some things in order to deal effectively with others." Feelers are more conscious of feelings and individual values while Thinkers are more conscious of facts and inferences involving cause-effect reasoning.

Feelers' self-esteem involves attending to people's values and feelings. Other people's responses impact Feelers strongly. People response is primary data for Feeler self-esteem. When other people are particularly valued, the following Feeler operating principles usually apply:

1. Words and actions should be monitored carefully to avoid hurting or upsetting anyone.
2. People upset with me don't like me.
3. Hurting or upsetting someone is bad.
4. Hurting someone makes me feel guilty.
5. Conflict is to be avoided if at all possible.

These typical Feeler guidelines for interactions operate in various degrees within natural Feelers. Their self-concept is affected by their perception of how well they demonstrate responsible relationship standards.

In the competitive work world the Feeler operating rules

come into consciousness and must be dealt with at the very time the Feeler needs to push on through the feeling. One Feeler said, "At the very moment I needed some killer instinct, I became overwhelmed with what the other person was feeling and I backed off." Similar hesitation was voiced by a Feeler supervisor. She noted two significant omissions in work done by a Thinker employee. When the Feeler called attention to the omissions, the employee launched an angry rebuttal citing her rights and her understanding of what she was supposed to do. The employee cited her tenure in the job as her main defense against being corrected. The supervisor responded defensively: "It is my understanding that I have the right to check your work. That is what it says in my performance standards. Don't I have the right to do my job? I'm sorry that I upset you. Don't I have the right to tell you when you missed something?" She later said she has difficulty thinking clearly when someone is angry with her.

When the Feeler supervisor discussed the problem with her boss, she framed it up as a problem of an employee "being mad at me." The Thinker boss was annoyed and responded, "Well, your job is to see that the work is done right . . . not whether or not people like you."

As the Feeler discussed her distress about how she had handled the situation with both the employee and the boss, she became more certain that she had totally failed. As we discussed the problem she sorted through the situation and realized that the problem was one of work not being done according to specifications. That is a much different sounding issue to discuss with her boss than an issue of someone "being mad at me." Her recognition of a problem was accurate; her communication of that problem was unfocused and implied that the issue was personal rather than work-oriented.

The young Feeler supervisor had been ridiculed so many times when trying to express her recognition of a problem that she didn't trust her innate abilities to spot one. As she reviewed the employee's rebuttal, she realized the differences in the Feeler and Thinker perspective:

> Thinker employee: "I already did that once." (Implying injustice if asked to repeat.)
>
> Feeler supervisor: "I'm not picking on you." (Felt maybe she was being mean.)

Thinker: "Are you saying I haven't done something I say I have?" (Implying the Feeler was saying she lied.)

Feeler: "I have the right to check the work. I'm supposed to do that." (Responding defensively as she identifies with the painful reaction to being called a liar.)

Thinker: "It's not my fault, it's the machine's fault." (Recognizing that the Feeler was on the defensive, the Thinker used a careless rationalization.)

Feelers develop their Thinker potential by learning to think factually and logically while experiencing emotional overload. Thinkers develop potential by learning to feel emotional overload while processing factually and logically. Processing both Feeler and Thinker data is essential to clear perception and judgment.

In the monthly publication *The Type Reporter,* an article entitled "What's It Like to be a Feeling Man?" offered some excellent observations. The stereotypical approach to sexual differences is incomplete as an explanation for the differences between men and women. Thinker-Feeler preferences are very useful. Feeler men share some of the same concerns that Feeler women acknowledge. The stereotype still relies on primitive role divisions of men with larger bodies for hunting, fighting and protecting, while women with smaller bodies are seen primarily for nurturing, serving and raising children. The expectations, though deeply buried, are behaviorally acted out. "Today, men are still expected to hunt, although now it's more for money and power. And they're still expected to fight and kill, even if it's just the competition . . . But when it comes to hurting people or taking money and power from them, F(feeler) men don't feel cut out for the job. All of the F(feeler) men interviewed for this issue said it's their unwillingness to hurt people that separates them most from other males. They first noticed it when they were boys, when they were called upon to be physically aggressive."

Feeler men who were interviewed tended to agree that their fighting as children was more defensive than offensive. They would avoid fights unless drawn into protecting themselves or the underdog. They mutually agreed on their distaste for conflict.

Feeler men acknowledged that "unless they are well disciplined, they are not motivated to put high financial value on their work, to strategize ways to best the competition, to put the needs

of the business over the needs of the people, or to make decisions based on objective data, like the bottom line."

The Barr and Barr data base verifies that 65% of American
women are Feelers and 65% of American men are Thinkers. Our
data show 83% of managers are Thinkers. The dominant style in
American management is Thinker-oriented; therefore, Feeler
men and women are continually measured by a Thinker yardstick. Too often Feeler managers feel unfairly measured and misunderstood.

Thinker attention is focused more keenly on cause-effect
situations to reach fair, equitable, and defensible conclusions.
Thinkers' natural and habitual thinking preference is logic and
analysis. "I prefer to analyze feelings instead of feel them," said
one strong Thinker.

Thinkers give their attention to information they deem critical to objective logic. They tend to strip data of value-tone. Thinkers are proud of their ability to be fair and impartial (a condition
that is not humanly possible since each person perceives according to one's own values, preferences, and judgments — quasi-ob-
jective is a more accurate notion). Thinkers analyze while attempting to use objective and impersonal criteria to draw
accurate cause and effect relationships. They try to reach conclusions by using established principles and rules of logical analysis.
Feelings and values appear imprecise and too indefensible to
have primary value in Thinker equations.

Competency in logical thought heavily influences the Thinker's self-esteem, whereas Feeler self-esteem is based more upon
people relationships. Thinker guidelines for interaction are:

1. Be fair.
2. Be objective.
3. Use criteria, principles, policy, and law in thought process.
4. Look for consistency and validity as primary consider-
   ations.
5. Be thorough and be right in reaching substantiated conclusions.

Compare Thinker guidelines with Feeler guidelines, and it
becomes apparent that Thinker attention (point of conscious
concentration) is directed to "objective" logical analysis and Feelers focus on "personalized" value analysis. Both types use logic,

but vary greatly in the premises they use and the kind of evidence applied.

Thinkers tend to have strong values of justice, truth, consistency, and validity. They can sometimes be oblivious to their own emotional response to injustice, lies, inconsistency and invalidity. In the case of obvious violation of their values, they can indulge in righteous indignation based upon errors in the "inviolable rules of right thinking," and be oblivious to their own reactions.

Feelers tend to have strong values of harmony, acceptance, kindness, trust, and compassion. Feelers can sometimes be oblivious to the logic they use when their values are violated. They can indulge in righteous indignation based upon violation of the "inviolable rules of right caring," and be unaware of their unforgiving condemnation of "wrong behavior."

Clear perception requires awareness of the tendency to shape information according to our values.

FEAR OF CONFLICT

If fear of conflict leads to perpetual avoidance, personal power erodes. If fear of conflict leads to perpetual emotional coldness, personal power erodes. At times, the best approach might be avoidance, but a clear assessment is needed. If avoidance is a habitual defense mechanism, the power erodes. Leaders must clearly assess the situation and when necessary step up to problems, risk personal attack, and willingly pay emotional costs to confront and solve problems.

Ironically, both Thinkers and Feelers fear negative emotional expression. They are both afraid of being overwhelmed by intense emotion that might dictate their behavior. Both are afraid of being emotionally out of control.

When observing others in conflict, Feelers sometimes remain quiet although feeling emotionally wrenched. They tend to fear being dragged openly into the conflict and may remain quiet instead of speaking up; thus, they can freeze in the rush of complicated feelings. They don't want to become centrally involved in the painful situation while simultaneously experiencing enormous guilt for standing by and doing nothing. Introverted Feelers are more likely to hold back longer than Extroverted Feelers in speaking up during conflict, although they are very involved internally. One Feeler said, "I am full of thoughts and feelings but I just freeze. I can't get them out."

Feelers aren't the only ones who have difficulty with conflict.

CASE STUDY: DEFENDED THINKER
AT HOME AND AT WORK

A senior vice-president in a highly competitive industry began an executive development program. Paul's scientific background, his job as an executive comptroller, his ISTJ (Introvert, Sensor, Thinker, Judge) personal style, and his Abusive Dictator power style combined to make him formidable as foe or friend. He is married to an intelligent woman with a degree in social work. Jane, trained in social work, scores as an ESFP (Extrovert, Sensor, Feeler, Perceiver) on personal style and is a Benevolent Dictator in power style. By mutual agreement Jane does not have a job outside their home. Since their first child was born a few months after college graduation, Jane never practiced social work but instead stayed home to raise their four children. Paul, meanwhile, moved skillfully up the corporate ladder.

The president of the company is a sixty-five-year-old traditionalist who informally overlays his own values on the management group. Though one can't find a formal policy, it is obvious that all of the executive group and those selected for fast-track management development are all men whose wives stay at home and raise the children. No written policy exists, but the practice is clear.

Paul's ISTJ is a good fit with the traditional, conservative values of the president. He prefers the traditional male/female roles. Jane's ESFP nature allows her to partially accept the roles. Her Sensing nature likes the clear role expectations, but her Extroverted Perceiving likes the unexplored. She struggles to accept the homemaker role. She has to depend primarily on the world of mothers and children for her Extroverted expression. Paul is not interested in social activities. After work he prefers quiet and minimal interaction.

Paul has little tolerance for expression of feelings. He sees raising the children as Jane's job; he dislikes getting involved in "children's squabbles." Interestingly enough, he doesn't like getting into "employee squabbles" either. His behaviors reveal his fear of the display of feelings.

At a particularly intense business meeting, one of the managers voiced her anger at another person. She identified the problem, described the particular behaviors that contributed to the problem, and shared what she had tried to do to resolve the problem. Paul was so irritated with the expression of emotion that he shut out the content and reacted to the "inappropriateness" of emotion. Later he could recall none of the rationale she used in explaining her anger. He focused instead on his discomfort. As with other imbalanced Thinkers, he is afraid of having his own feelings activated by someone else's expression.

As we later discussed Paul's reactions, he had a carefully constructed argument about why the expression of anger was inappropriate. Listening carefully, his defense was easy to see. His argument was:

1. "Professional people keep emotion out of their interaction." (Translated as "I keep emotion locked out of my consciousness; therefore, I think I am emotionless and that's the way professional people should be.")

2. "That anger was between the two of them. It shouldn't have involved the rest of us." (Translated as "I resent the disturbing effect anger has on me.")

3. "Maybe she isn't managerial material after all." (Translated as "She had better conform to emotion-suppression or I will withdraw my approval and support of her.")

I asked him to go back in memory to his first reaction. I asked him to remember the sensation and describe it. As a Sensor, Paul could recall body sensation much more readily than if I asked him to describe his feelings. Though the data are the same, he openly resents anyone asking him about feelings. He said, "It felt like someone kicked me in the stomach. Her anger felt like she hit me with a hammer or something. It took me by surprise. Even though she wasn't mad at me, it felt like it. I got hot and then I got angry and tried to figure out how to get the meeting over with."

I probed gently again about sensations in his body. He slowly began to describe his reactions. "I remember feeling a hot rush . . . like when you suddenly feel as if you are going to throw up. I felt pressure in my chest and I got hot." I asked what he felt next. He replied, "I'm not sure what happened but I felt really angry at her one minute and then I became instantly cold toward her. I still don't like what she did."

Paul had no understanding of the automatic triggering of the defensive wall when Thinkers get overloaded with too many chaotic feelings. He had no way to logically explain how he could feel hot anger one minute followed by instant coldness, which he described as numbness. As we discussed the Thinker propensity to throw up a defensive wall when too much emotion is triggered, he suddenly paled. He said, "I don't like to feel. I usually don't. Sometimes it bothers me that I can't really relate to Jane or the kids on things that seem silly to me but they get excited about." As we talked further, Paul acknowledged that he goes weeks without consciously experiencing feelings. In the weeks that followed, Paul decided that his executive development plan involved more than just his professional life. He found his interpersonal problems at home were mirrored at work. He is perceived as cold, aloof, insensitive, and critical both at work and at home. One of his development assignments was to try to overcome his relationship problems. He needed to learn to listen and practice drawing other people out.

Paul tried to practice receiving feedback in a nondefensive manner but found it hard. Paul said, "Listening to the way people really see me is one of the most difficult things I've ever done. Learning to listen without shutting down is hard. It isn't a problem to keep my mouth shut while they talk, but it is hard not to shut down inside and contradict them mentally inside my own head. When I disciplined myself not to use my mental sword to hack their impressions to death, I could hardly stand the way my heart raced and my body and mind felt. It was like being attacked. I instinctively defend when attacked. It is hard not to use my defensive wall. Behind it, I can shoot anyone down."

Paul began to talk about his relationships at home. "Everybody likes Jane. The neighbors, the kids, just about everyone thinks she is a great person. I love her but just don't understand why she has to be told that repeatedly. She has plenty of evidence. We've been married twelve years. She does a great job at home. She takes good care of the house and kids. I don't see why she can't just let me continue to earn the living. She wants me to be more involved with her and the kids. I'm trying, but it isn't easy."

He talked about his discomfort when he tried staying home one Saturday with their sick son. He said he felt sorry for the kid but didn't know how to express tenderness, so he just kidded him about vomiting and diarrhea. I asked how his son reacted. He replied, "I honestly don't know. He seemed relieved when his mom got home."

As an Abusive Dictator, Paul used harsh criticism, coldness, and disassociation to keep people from getting close enough to disturb him emotionally. The incident that triggered his emotion at the management meeting coincided with the beginning of his intensive executive development process. By keeping his own feelings out of consciousness and erecting careful barriers of logic and "professionalism," he was safely insulated from his effect on others. As he became more aware and began developing his awareness of feeling, he necessarily began to realize his impact on others. He didn't like what he saw.

It took him two years of intensive work to develop enough familiarity with feelings to become reasonably comfortable with them. His development goal was to use his Thinker preference to discover his Feeler potential. In balanced development the goal is to have his Feeler become an accepted supporter and trusted ally to his Thinker expression. Developing a less preferred aspect is a long-term process, but well worth the effort in the increased capacity it yields.

BALANCE AND APPROPRIATE EXPRESSION

In the power game, feelings are labeled as weakness, while cool aloofness is perceived as strength — a tenet obviously touted by Thinkers. Drawing emotional blood (interpreted as visible emotional response) from opponents is seen as weakening their argument. When someone responds with a bit too much feeling, their information is discounted as defensiveness. It is quite a predictable game for power players to poke around until they get their opponent emotionally reactive and then decimate opponents' argument. No wonder busy executives approach the competitive corporate arena with shields held firmly in place to ward off emotions. How, then, do we reconcile the need to defend against power players and emotional manipulation? Paradoxically, how do we reconcile employee demand for more genuine interactions, higher levels of trust, and greater candor? Will power players interpret such actions as opportunities to take advantage?

Examine the following principles identified in Stage IV Leaders. Each of the Stage IVs we work with shows a balanced style with an Intuitive grasp of people's feelings and values, as well as demonstrating intelligent use of Sensory facts and logic. Openness to emotion greatly expands the leader's ability to understand and relate to people. Unwillingness to feel may be one of the biggest barriers to leadership development.

1. Stage IV Leaders are caring, candid, and responsive to people.

    [They use excellent judgment about interactions with competitors and respond appropriately to varying situations. They are not locked into rigid application of candor and responsiveness that could give outsiders and competitors unfair advantage.]

2. They have a participative management style with a willingness to share power.

    [Participative does not mean running the place by committee. They make the calls when appropriate and involve people when appropriate. They empower others at every reasonable opportunity.]

3. Stage IVs are persuasive communicators — genuine, believable, and accessible.

    [They do not have to rely on slick manipulation. They rely on consistency of style and demonstrated values to provide a recognizable basis for interpreting their messages.]

4. They have self-knowledge and are quite conscious of their strengths and weaknesses and lead others into self-discovery.

    [Stage IVs take responsibility for their own feelings and actions. They do not blame others. They hold themselves responsible for their own reactions and teach others to do the same.]

5. Stage IVs are willing to take risks.

    [They demonstrate vision, strategic planning, tactical wisdom, and lead the way. They carry a sense of confidence and courage.]

6. Stage IVs are change agents.

[They repeatedly reorganize while perpetually searching for innovative approaches and continuous improvement. They don't allow people to become complacent. They stimulate, inspire, and push.]

7. Stage IVs confront people and situations as needed.

[They are *unwilling* to accept unethical or inappropriate behavior. Stage IVs are unwilling to pander to bad behavior. They confront clearly, descriptively, and forcefully. They leave no room for doubt about what they will and will not tolerate.]

8. Stage IVs use teamwork whenever possible and expect cooperation to be the norm.

[They don't waste time with groups of uninterested members. They have high involvement and participation standards that are guided into team bonding, synergism, and focused action.]

9. All of the Stage IVs are skilled in group process and know how to facilitate meetings to get high interest, active participation, and committed action.

[Meetings are focused, fast-paced, and action-oriented with excellent use of brainstorming for creative bursts, analysis to weigh evidence and alternative solutions, creative exercises to allow "blue sky" time to let good minds drift freely above the rigors of facts and logic to find unusual ways to look at the issues, and process checks to see how people see the group interacting.]

10. All of the Stage IVs are competent in their respective professions.

[They demonstrate competency and knowledge, as well as clear insight into people and organizations.]

Stage IV Leaders know that people are the key to productivity, innovation, and success. They also know that establishing trust with people requires openness and feeling. They tell us the emotional cost is worth the rewards of teamwork, commitment, and growth-oriented employees.

Remember:

- It is natural to discharge feelings.
- Thinkers and Feelers discharge feelings differently.
- Mature adults discharge feelings carefully and responsibly.
- Difficulty occurs in balancing the need to discharge feelings while accommodating others.
- Thinkers tend to shield themselves against too much feeling — Protective walls go up under pressure and may be hard to take down.
- Delaying discharge of feelings produces tension.
- American culture endorses the suppression of normal discharge of feelings. Americans have institutionally approved ways of expressing feelings such as in sports, concerts, dancing, music, movies, church, etc.
- Careless application of the word *professional* encourages suppression of feeling.

PROFESSIONALISM: STONEWALLING FEELINGS?

Too many people use the following definition: "Professionalism means objective, unemotional, knowledge-based response." That definition is used by hundreds of workshop participants across the country. Their operational definition of the word hinges on being knowledgeable and "cool under pressure." The bias toward Thinking is apparent, with Feeling too often seen as the nemisis of professionalism. Although we disagree with their narrow definition of professionalism, we nevertheless recognize its prevalence across America.

Defining professionalism as unemotional and objective creates a conflict with current workforce demands of greater candor, trust, and responsiveness from managers. Paradoxically, while expecting more genuine interactions, unconsciously many people use the unexamined but consciously accepted definition — resulting in internal dissonance.

In workshop discussions a common theme occurs. The narrow definition of professionalism actually means that "disturbing emotions" should not be part of the interaction. Most participant concerns had to do with negative behaviors that caused emotional discomfort such as intimidation, humiliation, cursing, insulting, angry response, hateful remarks, disdainful comments, or personal conflict. The only warm emotions noted as unprofessional were excessive ones such as: overly expressive, too gushy, or too accommodating.

The Webster definition of *professional* is "engaged in or worthy of the standards of a profession." This broad-based definition does not imply cool, unemotional interaction. That was supplied by people's interpretation. Professional does not mean terminally polite nor iceberg cold. It implies technologically competent, demonstrated knowledge, and it now implies interpersonal competence as well. When the industrial age was prevalent and scientific management was the norm setter, the limited definition wasn't challenged. Today, however, in the information age, the definition no longer fits. Interpersonal skills, genuine interactions, and technological competence must be linked.

To match today's challenge by a more informed and demanding work force, we submit the following as a more fitting definition:

"Professionalism is knowledgeable, credible, ethical, trustworthy interaction based upon open, candid, understandable communication."

What is the effect of the unexamined but commonly accepted association of unemotional with professional? Why do Americans allow themselves to be passionate about national values but value emotionless expression in professionals? The word *emotional* has come to mean dysfunctional or inappropriate in the work world, and in some cases the negative connotation carries over into interpersonal relationships at home.

Arousal of emotion is closely connected to thoughts. What we think dictates what we feel. We can have physiological arousal from aching muscles or stretched tendons without emotional arousal, but we cannot have emotional arousal without triggering thoughts, assumptions, or beliefs. What we think triggers what we feel.

Human beings are involved in the ceaseless process of interpreting what is going on inside themselves and their environment. We are continually noting our body sensations and attributing meaning to them, just as we interpret our external experiences and attribute causes to them. This ongoing process forms the basis of emotional existence. Emotions result from the way we structure reality. The way we see, interpret, and react is the process of attributing meaning to experience and sensation. Our personal style and our power style are the basis for the way we determine reality.

BAD GUY MANIPULATORS IN ORGANIZATIONS

Authoritarian managers can easily become bad guy Intimidatiors. They can become so accustomed to having their own way, they get angry when thwarted. They gain power by promoting their reputations as bad guys who are not to be crossed. Intimidator types are small in number but exponentially damaging to open, innovative organizations. Intimidators threaten healthy organizations. They are controlling, demanding, and punitive. Their dominance tends to kill or punish individual initiative. If they didn't originate the idea, it is condemned.

Intimidators try to control other people through fogging techniques. They thrive on activating negative emotions in others which provides the fog. Intimidators create such a perceptual fog that other people have difficulty seeing through the illusion to the real situation. Intimidators project powerful images of themselves while projecting deficiencies in others. They use three main manipulations: control, fear, and authority.

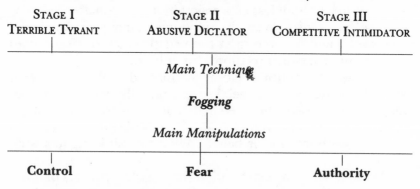

Stage I	Stage II	Stage III
Terrible Tyrant	Abusive Dictator	Competitive Intimidator

Main Technique

Fogging

Main Manipulations

Control	Fear	Authority

Fogging — Principal ways Intimidators fog are:

Play superiority role: Intimidators see themselves as standard-bearers for "professional" behavior based upon technical competence, thus setting themselves up as arbitrators of acceptability.

Create doubt: Intimidators try to manipulate others into doubting themselves, their abilities, and their own judgment, thereby allowing the Intimidator to control perception of competence.

Manipulate emotion: Intimidators fog others' perception by skillful manipulation of emotion to confuse thinking. Stirring up negative emotions such as doubt, anger, guilt, and frustration confuses the issue. Intimidators know that too much emotion clouds most people's judgment. Few people are trained to withstand the emotional fog.

Wear masks: Intimidators wear masks of such convincing subtlety that they may be difficult to detect and even more difficult to unmask. They are superb role players and can quickly assess the mask needed to pretend support of cooperation by wearing the mask of team player while continuing to control. *They focus details to fog real intent:* By manipulating others to focus on details, they fog their real intentions.

Control — Intimidators use control as a main manipulation. They are desperate to control their job, their domain, their employees, and particularly their boss' perception of them.

Claim superior performance: They repeatedly see themselves as paragons of good business practice, frequently reminding people of their own high standards.

Value performance but not people: Intimidators define best business practice as keeping costs controlled and making a profit (widely accepted standards), but they don't tell you that they do it at the cost of people, morale, and initiative. They talk performance as the *only* point of focus while denigrating people and ignoring the brutal cost of human resources. They use performance to cover up and fog over the real way they treat people.

Control turf: Intimidators want autonomy as they guard their turf jealously. In order to make themselves look good, they try to control everything that goes to their boss. They carefully guard their reputation with important customers and go out of their way to establish themselves as having a reputation for sound business judgment. They use all the right terms.

Fear — Intimidators use fear to make sure they maintain control. After discovering the debilitating cost of fear, they become adept at studying others to find indicators of underlying fears or concerns. They have an uncanny knack for pushing people's "hot buttons."

Threaten: Dictators threaten employees who challenge or irritate them with damaging performance appraisals or loss of their jobs.

Intimidate: Dictators take pride in knowing rules, regulations, and policies thoroughly to use in catching people in error over some small detail and then ridiculing their integrity, questioning their intent, belittling their competence, and deriding their judgment.

Retaliate: Dictators retaliate against employees who irritate them by nitpicking work according to form, detail, and rigid adherence to procedure — attempting to cause self-doubt and loss of confidence.

Humiliate: Dictators point out people's errors with anger and assertions of stupidity, dishonest intention, and technical incompetence.

Authority — Intimidators capitalize on people's unresolved authority issues. They activate employee respect for position and unresolved authority issues, to more easily assume a parental role with employees.

Judge harshly: They use authority of their positions to play the daddy or mommy role of controlling, dominating, and shaping the children (employees) to suit their own desires. By combining the abusive and domineering parental role with technical expertise, Intimidators wield a difficult power jolt.

Demoralize employees: By criticizing harshly, threatening, intimidating, and humiliating, Intimidators try to undermine employee self-confidence and make them dependent upon the Intimidator to determine acceptability. They then reward or withhold acceptance as a means of control.

Undermine their boss: They repeatedly undermine their boss by creating doubt in people's minds about the boss' abilities while promoting their own superior business practices. Behind the boss' back they point out weaknesses in the boss' communication style, decision-making ability, and knowledge of the job in order to undermine the boss' authority. They then make themselves look good by showing their superiority to the boss. By convincing their subordinates that the Intimidator's boss is inadequate, they create hostility and walls around their kingdom, thus preventing the flow of information to the Intimidator's boss.

Create guilt: By catching others in errors, even insignificant ones, Intimidators fog employee judgment and get them so focused on pleasing the Intimidator that they become absorbed in doing things the Intimidator's way in order to avoid harassment and ridicule. Employee initiative is often turned into anxious compliance.

Key point: Intimidators are driven by needs for power and control.

CASE STUDY: ABUSIVE DICTATOR

Look for recognition points in the following case study. Sharpen your ability to spot the intimidation games of Abusive Dictators. They count on people being afraid to deal openly with emotionally explosive situations. They, themselves, are afraid of emotional situations *if* they aren't the ones initiating and controlling the emotions.

Tom is a senior vice-president of operations of a gas and oil division. He manipulates people's fear of conflict. He scores as an ESTJ (Extrovert, Sensor, Thinker, Judge) and uses Abusive Dictator power style.

Tom's staff includes department heads and two secretaries. When he assumed the job, he went directly to his office and studied the roles for weeks. He has a slight preference for Extroversion, so his cloistered office approach to prepare his manipulation game was not difficult for him. He mastered a complex set of rules, regulations, policies, and practices. That approach seemed reasonable until his habitual patterns revealed the way he used that information. It provided the basis for his infamous "I gotcha ya, you sonofabitch!" routine.

Tom started out low key with a studious approach. Carefully

he began a control mechanism. He meticulously reviewed memos, purchase requests, travel vouchers, performance reviews, performance variance reports, and other reporting or business tracking methods. He rechecked math, grammar, rules application, and form. He demanded that memos be typed in a certain way. He had rules and standards for both the important and unimportant. Tom worked late each night, combing through the stacks of papers to find errors.

I passed him in the hall late one evening and asked him how things were going. He responded: "I've got a lot to do to shape these folks up. Come here. I want to show you something." I followed him into his office. He pointed to a fourteen-inch stack of papers. "I found seventy-eight errors in just this stack of papers." He looked so proud of himself. To check my impression, I asked him to clarify. He responded with a thundering accusation of the need for a careful paper trail of good business practice. When I asked him whether the errors were major or minor, he looked annoyed. He said, "Whether it's simple math, spelling, or in the wrong form, it needs correcting." I asked, "Did you find any errors that put the company in jeopardy?" He replied, "No, nothing like that. Just little things. Take a look! They just aren't professional looking."

The paperwork was generously sprinkled with little blue sticky notes. I later heard staff referring to Tom's acid "I gotcha ya, you sonofabitch" zinger notes. In working with his staff I discovered that the notes had such a demoralizing effect that people didn't discuss the notes' content with each other. The notes were personally degrading. Most of the errors were errors of form rather than errors of logic or judgment. The vitrolic tone of the notes didn't seem to distinguish between major or minor errors. A sample of Tom's zinger notes shows you his approach:

> "Correct this immediately. A freshman engineering student wouldn't make that mistake."

> "This is an incorrect number. How many other numbers have you tried to slip by me? Professionals don't make this kind of mistake! Incompetents do."

> "Your memo contains lies and half-truths. Don't send me such garbage again. Give me facts, logic, correct spelling, and typed in the right form. I'll tolerate nothing less than professional work."

"How dare you make this request. You know how I think about this."

"Your judgment sucks! Get your head out of your ass and shape up!"

"The answer is HELL NO! This is such a stupid request I wonder about your competence."

Tom's need to humiliate, threaten, and intimidate is not confined to the blue zinger notes. When he had fully developed his rules-based "I gotcha" arsenal, he became more verbally abusive as well. He craftily curtailed his verbal abuse to controlled in-house meetings. When his boss or clients were present, he was the model manager. He talked the most managerially savvy game, handily using the latest terms. Watching him manage was a 180-degree turn from his espoused management philosophy.

He held long harangues with his staff, preaching good business practices, meticulous paper trails, and obedience to the chain of command. He periodically victimized someone to remind the others to be compliant. When he caught an employee in a factual or mathematical error, he denounced them and ridiculed their inability to use good judgment. When one department head became upset and angrily responded, Tom said, "If you can't conduct yourself professionally, I suggest you find employment elsewhere." He clearly exempted himself from the standard. He insidiously judged employees for showing any type of emotion, while he indulged in frequent angry outbursts. He excused his outbursts as caused by his incompetent staff's lack of professionalism on the job. Tom was clearly using circular reasoning, but no one on his staff challenged him.

Don't conclude that he had a bunch of unintelligent, incompetents working for him. These incidents occurred while the gas and oil industry was quite depressed and many engineers and geologists were out of work. Tom so cleverly blended technical expertise with intimidation that he was pretty difficult to confront. Employees felt angry, trapped, and brutalized but found it hard to deal with a man who was improving the bottom line. They were unequipped to confront his behavior, and he continually forced the division's performance record down any throat that implied problems with his behavior.

An interesting group phenomenon also contributed to Tom's

ability to control through fear and authority. At meetings when Tom mentally and emotionally abused someone, the others kept silent. As people looked around the room and saw others whom they considered intelligent also being silent, doubt occurred in their own judgment. Amidst chaotic feelings, people tend to check social reality by observing other people's reactions.

Tom intensely disliked his boss, while telling everyone that he respects the position. He belittled his boss behind his back, denouncing the boss' lack of knowledge of day-to-day business operations while making a tactical comment about his own twenty-five years of experience in the field. He badmouthed his boss, then turned around and demanded that his staff be totally loyal, compliant, and obedient to him. He saw no discrepancy with what he demanded from his staff but was unwilling to give to his boss.

The head of engineering sent a request to Tom for approval. He came roaring down the hall, bursting into the engineer's office. "How dare you send me this decision for final approval. You know how I think. I won't tolerate insubordination and disloyalty." Tom declared anyone who held a different opinion as insubordinate and disloyal. Careful examination of the department head's request showed no violation of good practice nor of regulations. The department head told me, "Being right in decisions isn't good enough; they have to be Tom's way to be right."

Tom's erratic behavior kept people on their toes, anticipating his next explosion. One day he would ridicule, humiliate, and decry a manager's decision. The next day he would be charming and genial to the same manager. He dealt mercilessly with people's feelings. He excluded himself from personal scrutiny by holding clearly to his beliefs that he was technically superior, a champion of good business practice, and a top performer.

One manager approved a request by one of his supervisors but had to send it to Tom for final approval. Tom exploded. "If you don't stop mollycoddling these babies, I'm going to fire you. How dare you insult my intelligence by asking me to approve such an asinine request. Get out of here and take this piece of crap (the paper) with you."

The manager went back to the supervisor and explained why the request could not be approved. The manager did not "pass the buck" to Tom. He explained the rejection and took responsibility for it. The supervisor was so angry that he went straight to Tom and demanded an explanation. Tom was all conciliatory and signed the request with little question, intimating that his manager hadn't handled the request properly. The supervisor went back to the manager and told him about his success.

Tom demanded that chain of command be tightly honored coming up to his position, while he violated the chain at will.

CASE STUDY: REORGANIZATION

When economic necessities forced reorganization, we were hired as consultants to help the management team restructure. Management teams were formed of the top performers to examine the situation, assemble the data, and plan the restructure. Of course, Tom was selected for the team. It was immediately apparent that we would have to confront Tom's behavior. Company research showed that they needed to change the organizational culture. They found that their average age employee was thirty-one. Further investigation found that the highly educated group of professionals were very angry about the abusive environment.

When the change meetings began, Tom dominated the conversation while generously using positive terms: leadership, teamwork, empowerment, participative management, open communication, and employee respect. You can imagine the demoralizing effect his behavior had on the process. The very one who was most deadly to those terms was setting himself up to champion them. At the first three meetings he tactically tried to position himself to lead the process. We waited until the group had established the team guidelines of candor and openness before we began to teach how to professionally confront dysfunctional behavior. Tom became increasingly uncomfortable. When he realized he could not intimidate us, he tried to coopt us through personal asides and inclusion.

First, the group had to be trained in behavior identification. They were largely unaware. They had to learn to consciously observe behavior and learn to verbally describe what they saw. They had to learn to observe gestures, movement, words, intonations and become more aware of the subtleties that carry message content. Next, they had to learn to describe behaviors so clearly that other people could judge for themselves what the behaviors implied. Then came the hard part. They had to practice giving each other feedback about bothersome or disruptive behavior. No one wanted to deal with Tom. I assumed that role. I explained guidelines that would let us practice within safer parameters.

The guidelines for confronting behavior are:

1. Identify the message you inferred.
2. Describe specific behaviors that contributed to your conclusion.
3. Explain what you inferred from those behaviors.
4. Identify your reaction to the behaviors.
5. Clarify for understanding.

By teaching the group members to describe the behaviors, they learned how to establish a more equal conversational field for discussing behavior, a process we call *leveling*. Others can then trace your behavioral evidence, your inferences and your conclusion, providing a level field to assess the information.

During three subsequent meetings, I confronted Tom's abusive behavior. His reaction was always denial, rearrangement, and rationalization. At each meeting he became more crafty and manipulative. At the fourth meeting I asked people to work in two small groups. I separated Tom from the four people who report to him. Tom was in a group with his boss. The assignment of the group was to have them identify helping and hindering behaviors to their leadership process. The two groups worked in separate rooms so they would not disturb each other.

I facilitated Tom's staff. Slowly they began to acknowledge to each other the treatment they had received from Tom between meetings. Each of them had been verbally abused and threatened with their jobs. Ten professionals had already left the company stating that Tom was the main reason for their leaving. They just couldn't tolerate his abuse any longer. They said it was affecting them too deeply, gradually seeping into their home life, their mental attitudes, their initiative, and their well being. As the four staff members began to share openly the behavioral evidence of Tom's style, they filled a sheet of paper of abusive behaviors. Then, suddenly, one of them said, "We can't do this. We can't afford to say this to him. He'll make our lives miserable or fire us on the spot."

The group took more than an hour to decide whether to follow through on the assignment. Finally, one person said, "If we care anything at all about this company, we've got to do it. He's destroying it. Too many good people have already been hurt. I say, 'Let's go for it.' "

We established guidelines to enable them to see that the term *professional* includes responsible behavior assessment as well as candor. As we went over their list, we kept only those behaviors that three out of the four people had observed. As they began to realize that others had been seeing similar behaviors, their confidence increased that they were actually behaving professionally. They made several remarks disguised as humor about writing their resumes. They cautioned each other periodically to see if they were "Tom bashing." It was evident that they were going cautiously and wanted to observe the guidelines so they didn't get out of control. They appeared to be very relieved to be able to surface emotionally hurtful incidents without being vindictive or petty.

As the two groups came back together, I very carefully reminded them of the parameters. We would describe specific behaviors, share inferences, and clarify for understanding. I asked for volunteers to share the information and no one volunteered. As the consultant, I accepted the role to demonstrate the process. I reviewed the guidelines for including the clarifying behavior on the list. Then I asked the person receiving the feedback to respond. When we came to Tom, he looked at the list of behaviors that showed threat, retaliation, humiliation, and intimidation. As I went over the behaviors, I asked Tom if he needed any more information. He looked at the list and said, "No, I do all of those things, when I find unprofessional performance."

As you might have guessed, it took several meetings to demonstrate to Tom that the game was over. He belligerently maintained his old behavior. He was so overwhelmed by his own anger that he misread his boss' shock and revulsion as he discovered the duplicity. Tom's boss would not have tolerated such behavior if he had known. Tom was such an effective Abusive Dictator, he had kept his boss in the dark about his habitual behavior. Tom's boss put him on immediate disciplinary probation and negotiated a clear behavioral contract. Tom refused to agree to the terms and left the company. The aftermath was much like watching abused children reorient their lives after the removal of an abusive parent.

Tom combined parental dominance, technical expertise, field experience, command of rules and regulations, and the power of his position to control employees through fear by fogging.

FEAR TO GIVE FEEDBACK

Rare is the organization that gets its money's worth from performance appraisal systems. Look at city, state, or federal performance appraisal systems. Examine private industry systems. How many of them are useful planning interactions where managers and employees mutually plan for the coming year's performance? Most of the ones we've seen are paperwork systems for compliance, wage grades, and legal protection.

How can we have such accepted practice for so little practical value at such high dollar expense? It's much easier to rely on paper and a numbers game than to give honest performance feedback. Most performance standards address tasks but omit behavioral guidelines for interaction. The unified argument is that you can't write standards for behavior. Must we therefore conclude that abusive people or dysfunctional behavior has to go unchecked? We don't buy that argument.

Giving positive feedback is not as hard as giving feedback about improving, correcting, or changing a behavior pattern. One manager stoutly defended his pushy, domineering style. He said, "That's just the way I am. That's my nature." That argument is sound for a two-year-old, but what about adult behaviors that involve discipline, choice, and potential! When we ask groups what concerns them about giving negative feedback, their answers usually include the following:

"I'm afraid things will get out of control."

"I don't want them to get angry at me."

"I've got to work with that guy. He could make a lot of trouble."

"Maybe I'm the only one it bothers."

"I'm afraid of what I'll say if she gets pushy."

"Maybe he'll quit doing it. Surely he gets tired of that."

This list sounds like the list of fears of conflict noted in Chapter 2. Fear of conflict raises fear that conflict may bring out the worst in us, causing us to respond in a way we don't like. We avoid conflict by the way we think about conflict and by our fears (fear of emotional response, anger, verbal or physical attack, vindictiveness, sabotage, group reprisal, escalation of conflict, hatred, cost of damaged relationships, power of referent group retribution, entrapment, or negative impact on productivity). We've clearly been taught that negative feedback is usually costly. Most people would rather put up with bad behavior than take the risk.

Management can be held hostage to emotional blackmail if fear of conflict dominates. Confronting one's own fears is essential to increasing personal power for sustainable leadership. Balancing thinking with feeling provides a more solid foundation to deal with the highly competitive and complex world of organizational life.

FAMOUS INFLUENCERS AND THINKER-FEELER STYLE

Volumes have now been written about some of our most famous influencers. Opinions abound about who were leaders and who weren't. Rather than attempt to discern leadership, we'll look at seven famous influencers to examine behavioral data for Thinker-Feeler orientation. We'll examine Presidents Clinton, Bush, Reagan, Carter, and Johnson, Admiral Hyman Rickover, and General Norman Schwarzkopf.

President Bill Clinton, previous governor of Arkansas, demonstrates his ability to display feeling. He has unabashedly allowed tears to form in his eyes as he responds to moving moments. He repeatedly uses strategies to demonstrate his ability to be in touch with the people. Although his much publicized bus tours across America during his presidential campaign were ridiculed by many, people greeted him in record numbers.

Comparative verbal snapshots referred to the presidencies as the Carter Passionless Presidency, the Reagan Disengaged Presidency, the Bush Status Quo Presidency, and the Clinton Hyperactive Presidency. (*U.S. News and World Report*, May 10, 1993)

President Clinton appears to be an Extroverted, Intuitive, Feeler in his public persona. He is often referred to as an energetic man who prefers a loose organizational style. He tends to surround himself with genial managers with strong intellectual abilities. As governor of Arkansas, he espoused W. Edwards Deming's total quality management. President Clinton verbalized his support of putting customers first and organizing for maximum spontaneity to customer-driven needs with less hierarchical structure.

As Bill and Hillary Clinton moved into the White House, America faced its first baby boomer generation professional husband-wife partnership. As a respected lawyer, Hillary has considerable intellectual skills to contribute.

> Mrs. Clinton is, by most accounts, the superior administrator, watching over many details and keeping her schedule punctual. The president, one key adviser says, is "loosey goosey." He's habitually late and often draws sharp comment from his wife about his tardiness. At meetings, Clinton loves to prolong and encourage discussion. Mrs. Clinton, by contrast, doesn't like meetings to run on too long, and prefers to narrow the discussion more quickly and give out assignments for follow-up. (*U.S. News and World Report*, May 10, 1993)

Bill Clinton is often described as the soft-hearted, big picture version of the partnership, while Hillary is described as the cool, pragmatic strategist. President Clinton demonstrates that he is unafraid to show that he genuinely cares about people and their experiences. He is described as a good listener with an appetite for the human experience. Hillary is described as a linear, logical thinker who insists on evidence and rationality. Bill Clinton is well known for reaching his decisions "through some mysterious way," a frequent description used for one who primarily uses intuitive processing, sprinkled with deeply held values and logical evidence. In many ways, Bill and Hillary represent role-reversal in their personal styles, with Bill using more Feeler expression while Hillary shows more Thinker expression.

Bill Clinton's predecessor gained a reputation as an accommodator. George Bush was known to have a real aversion to shaking things up. He was frequently referred to as "the guy who would go along in order to get along." In his autobiography, *Looking Forward*, Bush outlined his four rules of leadership: do not get personal, do your homework, use persuasive power rather than intimidation, and be considerate of colleagues and their needs.

As an energetic president, George Bush appeared to have an Extroverted, Sensor, Thinker persona. His unwillingness to rock the status quo, difficulty with the "vision thing," and insistence on careful canvassing of possessions indicated his fundamental style. He demonstrated a basic attitude that things were fine and there was not anything fundamentally wrong; therefore, the system just needed to be maintained with an occasional tweak. He missed the outcry for change and decisive leadership. The American public wanted fundamental issues addressed rather than massaging the status quo. Making changes incrementally was President Bush's most comfortable style. In some situations incremental change is wise, and in others, bold new directions are needed.

As President Bush surrounded himself with insiders familiar with the Washington power game, his colleagues tended to reflect the stability of the power game as he understood it. His decision-making style has most often been described as compartmentalization with heavy reliance on a few confidants. He did not appear to have an overall vision that guided his individual decisions. He is consistently described as an accommodator without the internal urgency to take bold, unapproved actions. President Bush's desire for harmony tended to show in his testiness in conflict. However history deals with President Bush, his image as cautious Thinker with the inability to demonstrate sustained passionate conviction to inspire others lingers on.

Careful study of Ronald Reagan's style reveals a Feeler preference. He was referred to as a great communicator, a public relations genius, and a Teflon president. Consultants Lonnie Barone and Karen DeNuncio comment about Reagan's style. In his famous Iran television speech, he seemed to be admitting that he had made a mistake. Reagan said, "My heart and my best intentions still tell me that is true," he said of his initial rationale for the arms sale to Iran, "but the facts and the evidence tell me it is not."

Barone and DeNuncio write, "To the trained ear, it was a dead giveaway . . . Only a Feeler would claim that a stated policy can be true in his heart and intention but not true according to facts and evidence. Thinkers — who comprise the bulk of American management — would find it absurd to distinguish between what is *true* and what is *factual* . . . Reagan's language is peppered with that kind of 'Feeler' rhetoric, which usually refers to personal feelings and exudes warmth and sincerity."

In the newsletter *Gray Matters,* the following descriptions are given of President Reagan's style: He's charismatic. People follow him. Not unlike a lot of Feeling managers, he inspired loyalty. He projected warmth and sincerity. He's persuasive. He can sell. Initially he is highly credible. Also noted are the less desirable aspects of his Feeling style: He picked people he liked as opposed to those best equipped to run the country. He is loyal to a fault. He swept problems under the rug — treating mistakes like minor incidents. In the face of logic, he looked for reasons to support his initial decisions. He didn't think ahead often, but when he did he was overly optimistic. He had difficulty confronting and firing people and making tough decisions. He seemed too concerned with being liked. He took moralistic and emotional positions often reducing geopolitical complexities to simplistic issues.

In *The Triumph of Politics,* David Stockman described Reagan as too kind, gentle, and sentimental, easily moved by hard-luck stories. He described Reagan as serene and passive. "Reagan's body of knowledge is primarily impressionistic; he registers anecdotes rather than concepts." When pressed to hear something that upset him or opposed his pet ideas, he responded habitually with "I'm not going to put up with hearing it." He would occasionally stir from his passive state by slamming his fist on the table and declaring, "I don't want to hear any more of this!"

Reagan's Feeler style was generously accepted by the public, following Jimmy Carter's Thinker style. Nicholas Lemann described Carter in a *Texas Monthly* article:

> Carter is an honest, upright, hard-working man with a passionate interest in doing what is right for the country. So it's a shame that he has been unable either to get programs passed or to create a general understanding of what he's up to. The reason for these failures is the way his mind works, and, by extension, the way he chooses to do his job. Carter is a manager, a rational man, and his mistake is trying to govern with the techniques of an engineer. A president has to use politics — the irrational process of convincing people, by whatever means, to give him their loyalty, their support and their votes.

Lemann compares Carter to Johnson in the way in which they approached the job of the presidency.

Carter and LBJ are like a set of mirror images; the strengths of the one can be seen as the weaknesses of the other. Johnson saw governing as a human process, and he was at his best dealing with people face to face. (Extrovert preference) Governing for Carter is mechanical and technical, and he is made uncomfortable by the intrusion of quirky matters of human psychology.

Carter prefers to do business by decision memo (a bureaucratic art form in which an issue is presented succinctly, and then a series of options and recommendations are offered). Carter liked to handle details. Johnson liked to wing it and shoot from the hip.

LBJ certainly worked as hard as Carter, but in a far less organized, contained fashion. He liked his memos short and he liked to read them late at night and early in the morning, leaving the days free for politics. He liked to be surrounded by people, to be doing several things at once . . . Johnson loved to talk — to argue with people, to ingratiate himself, to bawl them out, to win them over. He lived by the telephone . . . talking to assistants, Cabinet members, reporters, columnists, and congressmen, trying to find out what was going on, lobbying, threatening, wheedling, cajoling. This was what, in his mind, a President was supposed to do; Carter seems to see all that as an intrusion on the real work, the careful studying and analyzing of the details of issues.

The Extroverted, Intuitive, Feeler (ENF) style of Reagan contrasts greatly with the Introverted, Sensor, Thinker (IST) style of Carter. Johnson's Extroverted, Intuitive, Thinker (ENT) style created quite a different influence style from Carter even though they appear to be Thinkers.

Johnson's Extroverted style contributed to his reputation as a flamboyant, action-oriented president. He continually used the telephone to keep him in direct contact with others. He was more occupied with analyzing the political situation to get his objectives met. He applied his Intuitive-Thinker talents to the ambiguous and hard to define world of political motives and trade-offs.

In contrast, Carter used his Introverted, Sensor, Thinker style to analyze, study, and prepare thorough decisions. Hamilton Jordan, assistant to the president, said: "He is very tough, very strong in his pursuit of an objective. He's a strong-willed person. He's slow and deliberate in making up his mind. But once he's made up his mind, he usually thinks he's right. It is very seldom that he'll reverse himself once he's gone through this kind of deliberate decision-making process."

Carter is described as very self-confident, while Johnson is described as acknowledging that he never had a job he felt really qualified for. Extroverted Johnson was described as a superb horse-trader in working Congress, while Introverted Carter was seen as too uncomfortable with the political trading side of the work. Reagan, by contrast, was described as a congenial, nice man who could not deal with conflict. He protected his Feeler sensitivity by refusing to hear about upsetting situations.

Five men in the same office brought their preferred style to the position. Although the presidency is a complicated role, the patterned and habituated responses of personal style provided the foundation for the role.

Another famous influencer was Admiral Hyman Rickover. He resisted Robert McNamara's decision to put systems analysts in charge of the procurement system. McNamara's intent to bring more rationality, planning, and control into weapons purchase was seen as loss of control by Rickover. McNamara's Thinker style and image made him an easy target to satirize. "His slicked-back hair and rimless glasses symbolized to his critics the cold technocracy that had managed the war (Vietnam). It was an inhuman image, not at all like McNamara's image of himself." (*Running Critical*, pg. 35) Rickover, an astute reader of people, knew how to use people's fears and concerns against them. He capitalized on the Thinker image of McNamara as cold and uncaring to deflect his resistance to systems analysts who might question his nuclear submarine acquisitions.

Rickover spoke to congressional leadership and offered a powerful agrument for his high-speed prototype submarine as the correct response to massive Soviet naval buildup. He asked only for a prototype. He got it, and in so doing got a foothold in the defense budget that ballooned beyond all porportion. "By the time the public learned the true cost, the weapon system had gained unstoppable momentum and coalition support from politicial constituencies, contractors, and jobs in home districts." (*Running Critical*, pg. 51)

Rickover's Thinker ability to find weaknesses in others and use them to get his way is legendary. General Dynamics, the shipyard contractor, saw Rickover as their benefactor, and they let him have his way. "For a decade, General Dynamics had gone along with an informal practice of letting Rickover approve or veto senior management positions and it was well known in the shipyard that to ascend in the organization meant playing to Rickover's people. Rickover insisted on daily telephone calls from the general manager, and on weekly self-criticism in writing, a kind of technical Maoism with Rickover in charge of everything, knowing everyone's faults and keeping them on file just in case he needed the leverage to get some more work done in the nuclear construction program." (*Running Critical*, pg. 94)

Rickover's intimidation tirades are well documented. He capitalized on people's fear. A General Dynamics executive "found Rickover's rampages distressing and intimidating and sometimes when he got off the telephone, he sank into his chair disgusted at what he had to put up with to keep peace with the old man." Intimidation is most effective when it not only creates external fear of the other person but activates internal dissonance between opposing values. The value of keeping Rickover's business conflicted strongly with the value of self-respect.

Rickover's management of meetings also showed the Thinker calculation when feelings are used as manipulation tools. "He would start off yelling about something insignificant just so everyone in the room was thrown off balance and then he would launch into his agenda so that he could frame the issues in the way that suited him the best . . .

"Rickover yelled with his most abusive and threatening tone . . . He demanded action. He wanted all of the reports gathered up and burned, destroyed. His tone conjured the dire consequences of inaction." (*Running Critical,* pg. 97)

Forcing other people to humiliate themselves in public was one of the power plays Rickover used to create such doubt and self-loathing in others that they became easy to mold. That tactic and other power techniques contributed to Rickover's reputation as the "single military officer who had such solid personal control over the procurement process." (*Running Critical*, pg. 105)

By contrast, General Norman Schwarzkopf is described as a Thinker who learned to express respect and affection for others as well as issue commands. In his autobiography, *It Doesn't Take a Hero*, Schwarzkopf recounts the forming of his leadership. He leaped to prominent attention as the primary focal point in

Desert Shield/Desert Storm. He wrote candidly of the way he dealt with the pain of his beloved mother's alcoholism.

> At times it was anger that overwhelmed me, at other times fear, but what I felt most was complete helplessness. I simply retreated . . . Deep inside me was a place where I would withdraw when things were unhappy at home. I discovered I could hide the painful feelings and still make friends and love dogs and help old ladies across the street and be a good guy. I learned to be self-contained and independent. Maybe that was a gift my mother gave me. (pg. 21)

> Schwarzkopf expressed his early desire "to be unflappable even in the most chaotic of circumstances. That guise lasted until Vietnam, where I realized that I was dealing with human lives and if one were lost, it could never be replaced. I quickly learned that there was nothing wrong with being emotional." (pg. x)

Not only did "Stormin' Norman" learn the validity of expressing thoughts and feelings, but he also developed deeply held values early in his career. He learned to express feelings.

> To this day it's hard to explain the impact West Point had on me. Somehow, during the four years I spent in that idealized military world, a new system of values came alive in my mind. When I began as a plebe, 'Duty, Honor, Country,' was just a motto I'd heard from Pop. I loved my country, of course, and I knew how to tell right from wrong, but my conscience was still largely unformed. By the time I left, those values had become my fixed stars. It was a tremendous liberation. The Army, with its emphasis on rank and medals and efficiency reports, is the easiest institution in the world in which to get consumed with ambition . . . But West Point saved me from that by instilling the ideal of service above self — to do my duty for my country regardless of what personal gain it brought, and even if it brought no gain at all. It gave me far more than a military career — it gave me a calling. (pg. 72)

As Schwarzkopf shares his thoughts about leadership, he uses familiar refrains of both Thinker and Feeler gifts. He talks about leading individuals, sharing their concerns and fears, encouraging and rewarding, delegating and supporting, winning and losing. He talks about the strength that can form from painful, irrational, horrible circumstances. He analyzes his experiences and cites actions that demonstrate compassion.

Studying seven famous influencers shows the wide range of possibilities in Thinker and Feeler approaches. Adding individual power style to interpersonal style provides a solid foundation for reading people.

CENTRAL TRAIT – WARM OR COLD

S. E. Asch, a respected social psychologist, identified the warm-cold dimension as a *central trait.* He found that people tend to interpret other traits to make them consistent with their initial impression of a warm or cold person. He found that central traits have a powerful effect on the way we organize information about others. Consider the following:

> Before I met Bill I was told that he was very intelligent and scientific, and preferred to work math problems in his spare time. From this description, I immediately categorized him as "cold," and I had no desire to talk with him or even to meet him. Later, when I first saw him, my negative impression of him was intensified – he was quite ugly . . . I judged him as dull and uninteresting, and excluded him from any parties I had, though I invited our mutual friends.

> A year later, I had finally grown up enough to accept him as a person . . . I no longer consider him a "cold" person due to his scientific interests, and now other factors about him far outweigh his physical appearance. (Munn, Fernald, Fernald, pg. 445)

Consider the seven famous influencers. Bill Clinton is perceived as warm and value-laden, albeit sometimes described as a bit of a bleeding heart. George Bush was perceived as cool and cautious. Ronald Regan was perceived to be "warm"; therefore, the public did not impugn his motives in the same way as if he had been "cold." Feelings are a nonrational communication connection. Jimmy Carter was seen as a self-contained, detail-oriented, and logical engineer; therefore the public saw him as more cold and mechanical. LBJ was seen as an Extroverted domineering man who would good humoredly but coldly manipulate to get his way. Admiral Rickover was seen as cold and immovable. General Schwarzkopf was seen as both warm and sharply commanding.

Consider the way that assessment of a person as "cold" or

"warm" affects your perceptions. Before you deny that you use this type of initial categorization, check very carefully.

Thinkers are usually seen as "cold" compared to Feelers' "warmth." In the competitive organizational world, Thinkers appear to have the advantage. In the interpersonal world, Feelers appear to have the advantage. In the world of leadership, both Thinker cool and Feeler warmth are needed. *Remember:* Perception is a quasi-rational process involving both rational-analytic and nonrational intuitive-emotional factors.

To assume total rationality is erroneous. Professionalism is more reasonably the quasi-rational process of thoughts and feelings, rationality and nonrationality. Thinkers tend to assume that their views are based upon intellectually valid reasoning and objective reality; therefore, they assume anyone with real intelligence would agree with them. Feelers tend to assume that their views are based upon empathic valuing of individual needs and subjective reality; therefore, they assume anyone with a real heart would agree with them.

THINKER-FEELER EXCESS

Excessive reliance on Thinker preference can result in the illusion of objectivity and rationality. Determination to be objective can lead to denial of emotional content, thus destroying objectivity. Thinkers prefer to reach conclusions objectively, impersonally, analyzing facts and ordering them according to principles or rules. Thinkers' self-worth is predicated on being able to understand, predict, and control through reasoning. Thinker excess can lead to the following:

1. Relatively unemotional, thereby appearing "cold."
2. Uninterested in or unaware of people's feelings, thereby hurting feelings without realizing it.
3. May be habitually argumentative.
4. May be too critical by habitually pointing out weaknesses.
5. May be too skeptical . . . doubtful until thorough analysis occurs. May become routinized in the rejection position . . . habitually say "no" when initially receiving a request.
6. May indulge in analysis paralysis (analyze instead of actualize).

7. Habitually question and may probe too far and too hard ... tend to overlook emotional loading of questions.

8. May dictatorially advise ... holding others angrily responsible for absolutely following the advice.

Excessive reliance on Feeler perspective can lead to the illusion of kindness and supportiveness. Feelers' self-worth is predicated on their ability to get along well with others since they value harmony. Feelers interpret happenings through a valuing process which measures the importance to themselves and others. Feeler excess leads to the following:

1. Like harmony so much that they avoid conflict.

2. May be unassertive and thoughtlessly cooperative just to get along well with others.

3. May get caught up in people's feelings and miss underlying issues.

4. May be so determined to be supportive that support is given indiscriminately as they usually respond without conscious thought.

5. May be so eager to respond to people's needs that they are easy to manipulate.

6. May be so tactful in an effort to avoid hurting someone's feelings that the message gets lost.

7. Often let decisions be influenced by their own or other people's personal likes or wishes.

8. May become self-righteous in fighting for people perspective.

9. May overreact and personalize incidents, thereby tripping into passionate responses that are not substantive.

Excessive Thinker or Feeler reliance skews judgment. Combining Feeler involvement in quality and value of people relationships with Thinker analyzing cause-effect relationships provides greater perceptual clarity and more sound judgment.

DYSFUNCTIONAL POWER STYLES: I, II, and III

Dysfunctional power styles rely on manipulation of feeling. Power games utilize underlying fears and manipulation of feeling to imbalance their opponents.

Stage I Helpless Infant, Stage II Benevolent Dictator, and Stage III Competitive Manipulator are likable types. They appear to be nice, congenial, and salt-of-the-earth types espousing acceptable values: politeness, consideration, good sportsmanship, cooperation, and accommodation. When you look at their manipulations, however, they fog others so that their real motives remain clouded while they appear to be cooperative. They create relationships that appear positive to set up an unsuspecting environment of obligation, which then allows them to use their main weapon of guilt. By working on the positive side of feelings, they create a more emotionally responsive environment for their power games.

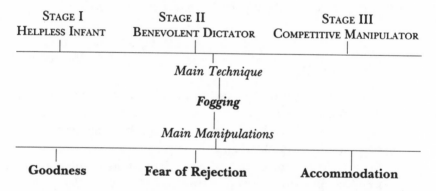

Passive Aggression

STAGE I HELPLESS INFANT	STAGE II BENEVOLENT DICTATOR	STAGE III COMPETITIVE MANIPULATOR
Main Technique		
Fogging		
Main Manipulations		
Goodness	**Fear of Rejection**	**Accommodation**

Fogging — Good-guy power players create a fog so that others have difficulty seeing through the illusion to the real situation. They project powerful images of themselves as good and project the right to dictate the rules of interacting.

Play superiority role: Good-guy power players see themselves as the standard-bearers for "right" behavior and people sensitivity, setting themselves up as judge.

Stage I Helpless Infants project such goodness and dependency that other people feel obligated to protect and serve them. Helpless Infants activate people's protection of the defenseless underdog.

Stage II Benevolent Dictators are such good parents to employees that employees who resist them are seen as troublemakers. Benevolent Dictators manipulate the goodness of the underdog in a mean world. Opposers can readily be made to appear as top-dog bullies.

Stage III Competitive Manipulators are such good sports and so valiant in sportsmanship that they fog others into seeing the carefully crafted image. The good guy seems "warm" and likable and doesn't activate anger or jealousy as readily.

Create doubt: Good-guy manipulators create doubt in other people's ability to be as good. They are clever at creating obligations that can be easily mentioned if others get too quarrelsome.

Manipulate emotion: Good-guy manipulators use a combination of stroking, obligating, and guilting to manipulate others into compliance. They are clever enough not to activate anger — an emotion most people need in order to confront. They cause others to feel sorry for them, to feel indebted to them, to feel guilty if they let them down in any way — all emotional situations that are not as likely to arouse defense systems in those being manipulated. They can stroke others to make them feel good, or they can withhold their approval and make them feel bad. They manipulate the pain-pleasure principle masterfully.

Wear masks: They control their good-person image carefully. They do "selfless-appearing" supportive acts that conceal the hidden obligatory price tag. They conceal their anger so it won't conflict with their nice person appearance.

Goodness — Good-guy manipulators are desperate to control their image. They need to maintain the cover of goodness for their games to work without being too costly.

Control image: They appear to be good-natured in order to control the interpersonal environment. If things aren't going their way, they adopt the role of patient, noncomplaining sufferers.

Value positivity: They create such a positive demeanor that they readily activate reciprocal positive response. Taking the upbeat, positive view of problem-situations gives them good-guy points and sets them up to activate a subtle version of the "sacrifice-but-I-don't-mind" martyr routine.

Verbal control: Good guys are excellent at saying the right thing, the expected thing, of espousing the right values, the right attitudes, and the most likely-to-be accepted positions.

Fear of rejection — Stages I, II, and III set themselves as representing right action. People try to avoid the pain of being told or shown that they are undesirable, unwanted, or unworthy. Good-guy manipulators activate others' need for approval and acceptance by worthwhile others.

Reward: Granting approval, esteem, access, and support become powerful motivators for compliance. Good-guy manipulators grant this, and their ego-stroking feels so good that most people can be readily conditioned to want it.

Withholding: By withholding their approval, esteem, access, and support they remove the ego-stroking, and others perceive the loss of something valuable. They can then be more readily manipulated into compliance to reestablish their source of "feel good." To be excluded from an admired group, ignored by important good guys, or to be treated like inanimate objects activates rejection fears.

Replacement: By selecting another person to receive special attention, manipulators can usually activate the competitive doubts about whether or not the person being replaced will ever be accepted again. Good-guy manipulators know how to subtly sway others to doubt their self-worth.

Accommodation — Cooperation, accommodation, and appearance of teamwork are necessary parts of a good-guy-image. They must appear nice regardless of the situation. Positive emotions only can be expressed under normal circumstances. Negative emotions are expressed in publicly approved righteousness, but must never seem to be selfishly motivated.

Passive-Aggressive: Good guys get annoyed and even get angry. They feel the usual range of emotions, but are committed to expressing only the positive side. They rely on passive aggression to release their frustrations. They get even with those who irritate them by subtle passive-aggressive games.

Pseudo-Teamwork: Good guys use such friendly, accommodating language that they often don't actually cooperate as much as it appears. They cleverly arrange for others to do the actual work while they project camaraderie and dedication to the team.

Obligatory favors: Good guys craftily study people to see what they can do that will create obligation. They gain currency in the power game by not having to overtly call in chips. Others tend to unconsciously look out for good guys' interests without consciously balancing the "power chip" scale.

Balance Thinker with Feeler capability and you will be much more difficult to manipulate. Power abusers feed off people's fear of uncomfortable feelings. People try to placate abusers in attempts to avoid attack and terrible feelings. They tend to overlook the bad feelings that occur when they unwillingly and unethically submit to the manipulation.

CASE STUDY: ACCEPTING A LEADER WHO JUST HAPPENS TO BE FEMALE

A large organization governing a river authority district is involved in utilities, land management, river access, mining, leasing, power lines, right-of-way, and recreation management. When a position opened up in one of their divisions, it became politically expedient that they try to fill the position with a woman. Finding that woman was the challenge.

Joann held a very responsible position in a large organization in another city. She was recruited by the river authority and landed the job. The challenges were enormous.

In the entire organization there were only two other women at the executive level: one was executive assistant to the director and the other was chief of personnel — two positions that had lots of responsibility but very little authority. Joann was the first woman to be named into a position of significant budgetary responsibility and professional influence. She was hired to take over the "worst division in the organization." Joann's employees were predominantly men with a small, all-female support group. Although most of the men were educated in their professions, they were not a part of the more prestigious divisions such as the Division of Engineering, the Division of Operations, and the Division of Environmental Management. They worked for Real Estate Resources Management. They were constantly reminded by others that they worked for the recreation side of the business. They sensed the "put-down" and tended to believe that their job was inferior to a more "pure" scientific application of the other divisions.

As engineers, hydrologists, planners, and real estate specialists, the men were unaccustomed and largely unwilling to accept Joann as a leader. Their best concession was to accept her formal authority while withholding their personal respect.

The division had gone through two downsizing phases, and morale was quite low. The original chief had been involved in a power struggle with a far tougher power player, the chief of Engineering Division. He lost every struggle, and as a result most of the people in the division felt that they had no one to really fight for them in the corporate wars. Joann faced a real challenge.

Requests for equipment, an upgraded computer-based planning system, furniture, and vehicle replacement requests had languished for months without making any headway through the corporate system.

The first four weeks on the job, Joann spent her time getting to know each employee. She proved to be an astute listener with a genuine interest in finding out what people did. She also began a careful strategy of getting to know the other division chiefs. As an astute observer and reader of people, she quickly gained a working knowledge of the major players, their stakeholders, and their standpoints.

She arranged a two-day, offsite planning meeting with everyone in the division. She discovered that previous managers had written long-term goals and strategies for each program but had used such vague terms that they were useless in really assessing efficiency or effectiveness. Thus, the division had no way to measure its performance, chart its future, nor prove its effectiveness. Working relationships between the division and other groups within the organization ranged from adversarial to openly hostile. The division even referred to themselves as the "Bloomin' Bastards," as they tried to make jokes about their low status in the organization. The double B's used black humor as relief valves.

Joann displayed maximum tolerance as she listened to their pained and negative comments. She listened until she assessed that the primary issues and feelings had been verbalized. She then said, "Well, what is ours to do? What can we do about this?

What do we have the authority to do that does not need corporate sanction?" At first she got few responses. She continued steadfastly to listen and to stimulate discussion.

One of the department managers, a Stage III Competitive Manipulator who devotes himself to good-guy manipulation, watched the group begin to respond to Joann's questions. He then hastily took over the role of accommodation and started to assume the role of team leader to pursue the possibilities. He talked about the ways the three departments could cooperate more with each other and perhaps gain some momentum in taking control of their situation. Many of the others resented his ploy, since they still had scars left over from turf wars with him. He had a reputation for ultimately getting even with anyone who annoyed him.

Joann steadily demonstrated her ability to hear staff frustration. She was unerring in her timing to know just when to redirect the venting phase into searching for possibilities. She demonstrated consistently that she valued ideas, no matter who offered them. The basement-mentality that so blocked, demoralized, and deadened the innovative capacity of the staff was skillfully redirected into possibility thinking by Joann. She did not offer solutions. She asked excellent, thought-provoking questions. She revealed their blocked capacity without ever blaming or shaming them. They became aware of their blocks in retrospect; they offered an idea that was supported, expanded, and developed. As they experienced the renewal that comes from the synergy of mutually reaching a solution, they could then look back and talk about how long it had been since they had been asked to think or truly seek improvement ideas.

After about two hours, one of the support staff offered an idea. The men ignored it and changed the subject. Joann listened to the man who tried to redirect, then responded. "I want to explore your suggestion, but before we do I don't think the group adequately explored the payment processing idea. Let's develop that thought further. Pam, would you refocus us on your idea?" Joann redirected the thought process without coming across as Pam's rescuer. She refocused on the idea, not on Pam the woman.

Joann repeatedly emphasized the thinking, valuing, and planning process. She sidestepped subtle innuendos that referred to her gender rather than her leadership. She simply did not make an issue of it verbally. She just consistently stayed focused, balanced, clear, empathic, and at the same time demonstrated her administrative and leadership skills. It had been a very long time since the staff had dealt with such strategic, political, and relationship sharpness.

By the time the two days ended, two-thirds of the group were renewed and ready to go to work on the specific actions they had outlined. The other one-third were cynical to noncommittal. Joann saw clearly the range of reactions but continued to drive straight toward her vision of the revitalization, restructuring, and renewal of the "Bloomin' Bastards."

The corporate executive meetings were a bruising challenge also. The weekly corporate meetings were ego-bashing affairs for Joann. She was challenged, cut-off, cursed, and ridiculed. At the fourth meeting she followed carefully the discussion on an important decision. She did not believe that the decision they were reaching was a sound one. She also recognized that she may not have all of the relevant information. Should she just keep still and try to learn after the decision was reached — or should she speak up and risk further ridicule? She decided that the decision was far too important to the organization for her to keep quiet.

Joann said, "Would someone just quickly outline the main points of the decision rationale?" All heads turned toward her. The Operations Division chief said, "We don't have time to educate you. We expect you to know the information. If you can't keep up, we'll get someone who can."

Joann kept her voice calm as she internally recoiled with the intended punch, and clearly stated, "The main premises that have been verbalized in this discussion appear to me to overlook an important issue. I find that reviewing decision rationale gives everyone an opportunity to use tough, critical thinking to assure the accuracy and supportability of the decision. I will verbalize my understanding of the decision rationale and I invite you to correct my thinking." Joann then proceeded to show a razor-sharp understanding of the decision rationale. A vigorous discussion ensued, the first half of which was used to attack her understanding. She received numerous insults and innuendos that she was out of her league. She told us later that her insides were churning and she was really grateful to be sitting down during the discussion. She said, "My knees were weak and I felt roiling negative emotions. Fortunately, I worked for a really abusive jerk where I had to learn to stay mentally focused while taking emotional hit after hit." Her risk-taking resulted in such a thorough reexamination that the group discovered a serious issue that had been overlooked. The last half of the discussion was focused on finding a more sound solution, rather than attacking Joann. No one thanked her for reopening discussion.

It took about six months for Joann to earn her place on the executive team. She was quite clear that she must respond as a clear thinker, unafraid of appearing to be stupid, compassionate, professional, a willing learner, and a tough risk-taker. Joann said, "I am a female, no question about that. I see myself as a professional, so my focus is on accurate assessment of information, clear people reading, stakeholder standpoint identification, turf control boundaries, concentration on what's important, and ability to manage distractors. The fact that I am a woman doesn't even seem relevant to my image of professionalism."

Nine months later, as I worked with one of the departments, staff referred to Joann's leadership as the best thing that had happened to them. They awarded her the title of "leader." They also demonstrated their acceptance of her leadership in the way they worked with her, tackled their jobs, and continued the art of thought-provoking questions and innovation.

They planned a huge program involving state, counties, cities, ranchers, farmers, and a variety of special interest groups to examine their mutual interests in fresh water, river access, river management, and environmental integrity. They formed a stakeholder partnership to share ideas and concerns. The enormity of the task just inspired the "Bloomin' Bastards" to tackle the impossible and find unique ways to make it possible.

The group still calls itself the double B's but now proudly avows its new meaning — Beyond the Beyond. They are teeming with ideas that will carry them right into the twenty-first century. They have learned to remove their handicapped thinking. They demonstrate the ability to envision their future while responding dynamically to ever changing demands.

Joann is a Stage IV Leader. Her personality style is INTJ. She has dealt with pain well and as a result her Introversion sustains her inner-directedness, where she relies on her deep beliefs and values to find direction and meaning in life. She is not dependent upon the external world to validate her. She developed her Extroverted skills to such an extent that she is an outstanding speaker, talented facilitator, and charming conversationalist. Although she relies principally on her intuitive scan of a situation, she has trained herself to be an astute observer of her surroundings. Her sensing skills are excellent. She developed her abilities to think clearly while feeling deeply to get a full assessment of a situation. She is adaptable and yet planful. In short, she has worked hard to know her strengths and she works perpetually on developing skills for her least preferred style.

We worked with her early in her career, beginning fifteen years ago. She was a formidable Stage III power player. She was mentally quick, largely insensitive to the whiplash left by her sarcasm, and fully equipped with a quick temper. When we first began to work with her and gave her feedback about her style, she demonstrated a real hunger for information to help her improve. She was courageous in searching out feedback. She occasionally cried as the full realization of her actions became conscious, but she did not back off. She embraced the pain, accepted the real effect on others, and began to systematically discipline her egoic urges. She is today an acknowledged Stage IV Leader.

Joann is well aware that men and women are perceived differently. She knows that women by gender and socialization are conditioned to be accommodating. She knows that by personality style she is equipped to do mental battle and follow-through to completion. She settled the male-female struggle in her own mind and found it to be a firm foundation. She said, "I know that men are socialized to be competitive, dominant, and self-sufficient. They are really punished if they cannot demonstrate strength and control. Women are socialized to be accommodating, interactive, participatory, and collaborative. Women are punished if we aren't accommodating. Both men and women can be stuck in the gender trap. I think leadership goes beyond that limitation. A real leader should be comfortable with the obvious — their gender; but quality of action, consistency of values and ethics, courage and caring, risking and daring all go beyond male or female. I am biologically a woman, but through my choices and actions I hope to daily earn leadership status."

DEVELOPMENTAL EXERCISES
Exercise 48: Challenges for Thinkers and Feelers

The central trait around which we organize perceptions of others is the warm-cool dimension. Feelers are usually perceived to lean toward the warm side and Thinkers toward the cool side.

Thinkers consciously work toward objectivity and can be so guarded against feeling messages as to be perceived as cold. Feelers consciously work toward subjectivity and can be so involved in values as to be perceived as too involved with feelings to see clearly.

In the Winter 1990 publication of AT&T's "Partners," an article noted a survey conducted to see why customers quit and seek other service. The results indicated that 68% quit because of an attitude of indifference toward the customer by the owner, manager, or some other employee. Only 14% changed because of dissatisfaction with the product. The way customers *feel* is more significant than logical analysis of the best product. Also reported was the ratio that it takes 12 positive service incidents to overcome one negative incident. Whether you market goods or services, attitude toward people is important. Balance of Thinker and Feeler characteristics provides a solid basis for trust-building interactions.

Recognizing that both statements have some application to you, select *A* or *B* as more true of you.

A _____ Interpret most events by analyzing *why* things happen more than figure out people's values in the situation
or

B _____ Interpret most events by analyzing people and their feelings

A _____ Strive to control recognized feelings by forcing them to match my logical reasons   *or*

B _____ Strive to control recognized thoughts by forcing them to match my feelings

A _____ Tend to question people to see if they are logical *or*

B _____ Tend to agree with people if possible

A _____ Principally base self-esteem on competence, especially task and project competence, as well as intellectual competence   *or*

B _____ Principally base self-esteem on affection, acceptance, and the ability to get along well with others

A _____ Critical and ready to find wrongs — see what's wrong first   *or*

B _____ Smooth and harmonize and focus on helping people cooperate

A _____ Point out logical flaws   *or*

B _____ Quick to judge thoughtlessness that results in hurt feelings

A _____ Tend to be businesslike and formal, sticking to roles
       or

B _____ Tend to be friendly and informal, establishing relationships

A _____ Relatively unemotional and don't want feelings to interfere   *or*

B _____ Tend to be very aware of other people and their feelings

A _____ May hurt people's feelings without knowing it   *or*

B _____ Enjoy pleasing people, even in small ways

A _____ Like analysis and putting things in logical order
       or

B _____ Often influenced by own and other people's personal likes and wishes

A _____ Use the need to be fair and to be treated fairly as impetus to tell people upsetting messages   *or*

B _____ Dislike telling people unpleasant things so much that I tend to avoid, postpone, or rearrange the message

A _____ May seem indifferent, cool, or hard-hearted   *or*

B _____ May be so sympathetic and kind that others manipulate me

A _____ Tend to be skeptical, but a logical results getter   *or*

B _____ Tend to be overly optimistic, but relate well to most people

Count your *A* answers for Thinker and your *B* answers for Feeler

Thinker score _____   Feeler score _____

Exercise 49: Problem-Solving

Thorough problem-solving requires use of facts, analysis, personal values, as well as possibilities and implications — all four quadrants.

COMMUNICATION CHANNELS	
Sensor	**Thinker**
Facts	*Analysis*
What are the facts?	What is the problem?
What are the details?	Why did this happen?
• Observable facts	• Cause and effect
• Verifiable facts	• Logical rationale
Rules and norms	Principles and inferences
Regulations and laws	Evidence and reasoning
(Provable reality)	*(Logical consistency)*
Intuitor	**Feeler**
Possibilities	*Personal Values*
What is the strategy?	How important is this?
What does this mean?	Who is upset?
• Patterns and connections	• Compassion
• Improvements	• Acceptance
Innovation	Relationships
Interpreting the unnoticeable	Working toward harmony
(Tomorrow's possibles)	*(Meaning and relationships)*

A. Identify a decision you made. Beginning with the Sensor quadrant, reexamine your fact base. Proceed through the other three quadrants. Do you feel more comfortable with two of the quadrants? Are they easier to use? Most people's style preference affects problem-solving.

B. In a government organization a reduction in force (RIF) was needed. Management did a careful job of getting the facts and logic together, but was less effective using the other two quadrants.

Sensor	*Thinker*
Facts	*Analysis*
Budget reduction	People biggest expense
Workload decreasing	Fewer people needed
Attrition rate 10% yearly	Use attrition rate for RIF
10% reduction needed	Hiring freeze solves the problem

The management group focused on the Sensor and Thinker quadrants, carefully preparing the numbers and the charts to indicate what was happening. They gave verbal assurance that everything was all right. They overlooked the Intuitor and Feeler quadrants. Although management felt very fair in its decision, they made no preparation for the feelings, attitudes and problems that needed attention.

Intuitor	*Feeler*
Possibilities	*Personal values*
Natural attrition is not likely to balance workload	Some groups will be overworked and will resent those who have less to do
Need to read trends and plan work force changes to position for future needs	RIFs affect morale
	RIFs fuel distrust of management
People fear loss of security	Caring interaction required

Exercise 50:   Communication Quadrants

One useful way to improve your people skills is to be more conscious of individual style. The following questions and comments are frequently used by those preferring that style. Observe ten people by noting the questions they ask or the observations they make and identify their preferences. Remember to listen for the dominant pattern.

Sensor *Facts and experience*	**Thinker** *Logic and evidence*
My experience tells me . . . What I have seen before is . . . What other unit is using this? What are the facts? Get to the point! When is this due? Comply with the rules or else eliminate them.	Authority basis for judgment is . . . What caused this problem? What can we do to solve it? Let's examine the issue. Establish the guidelines! Decide what's reasonable. Where's your evidence to suggest that's true?
Intuitor *Possibilities and concepts*	**Feeler** *Feelings and values*
Look at the implication! We can find a way. Let's improve this. What does this mean for the future? What ideas are driving this? Let's look at the ideal situation.	I know how important it is to you! Why are you angry with me? It's not their fault! How upsetting is this incident? Don't overlook the significance! Get people together and involved.

Ten people to observe: _____   _____

_____   _____   _____

_____   _____   _____

_____   _____

Exercise 51:   Thinker Troublesome Possibilities

The following checklist can be used for self-analysis or as a checklist to identify troublesome employee behavior. The list can also be used to identify development areas with children.

Rate the following items according to how much or how little interference the following behaviors have on warm, trusting relationships.

A. No interference   B. Some interference   C. Significant interference   D. Too much interference

A B C D Very analytical.

A B C D Handle emergencies or conflicts dispassionately.

A B C D Question intensely and probe deeply.

A B C D Assert own position forcefully and state opinion clearly.

A B C D Critical and unaware of hurting feelings.

A B C D Argumentative and at times quarrelsome.

A B C D Usually begin by searching for weakness.

A B C D Value logic in selling ideas and motivating people and not as comfortable dealing with personal perspectives.

A B C D Suppress own feelings so may be out-of-touch with them.

A B C D Give unsought advice.

A B C D Explain very thoroughly and cite evidence for position.

A B C D Enjoy gathering information and exploring solutions so as to procrastinate on deciding and taking action.

A B C D Tendency toward a formal approach . . . may appear stiff.

A B C D Tendency to rationalize problems, thus misreading the seriousness by underrating emotional factors.

List the basic behaviors where a C or D is marked. Those indicate behaviors for improvement. Identify the behaviors you want to change. Prioritize them. Use Thinker strength to make the change.

   1. Identify the behaviors.

   2. Analyze situations where interfering behaviors occur most frequently.

3. Analyze the consequences of the current behaviors.

4. Identify the pay-offs for changing the behaviors.

5. Identify the behavior with which you will replace trouble-some ones.

Exercise 52: Feeler Troublesome Possibilities

The following checklist can be used for self-evaluation or as a checklist to identify troublesome employee behaviors. The list can also be used to identify development areas for children, and adults other than your employees.

Rate the following according to how much or how little interference the behaviors have on competent, clear analysis of people, motives, and situations.

A. No interference B. Some interference C. Significant interference D. Too much interference

A B C D   Taking things personally and sometimes distort the real intent.

A B C D   So sensitive that messages are filtered primarily for whether they feel good or bad, instead of sorting to see if messages are true or untrue.

A B C D   Tend to oversimplify issues by focusing on minor parts.

A B C D   Absorb too many feelings from others and over-react.

A B C D   Letting others waste too much time by spending

so much time helping others that their own work suffers.

A   B   C   D   Give away too much information, time, and energy in an effort to avoid hurting anyone's feelings.

A   B   C   D   Tend to overexpress, taking too long to make a point by telling too many human interest points and descriptions.

A   B   C   D   Tend to focus too much on people part of the issue, causing Thinkers to discount the viewpoint for lack of "substantive evidence."

A   B   C   D   Tend to be so anxious about conflict that avoidance, denial, or smoothing over serious problems is typical response.

A   B   C   D   Tend to be too responsive, thereby giving unwanted, unwarranted, excessive support.

A   B   C   D   May be so accepting as to be gullible.

A   B   C   D   Tend to irrationally support someone because of liking, rather than substantive, verifiable evidence for doing so.

A   B   C   D   May rely so much on ability to charm that adequate advance preparation is not done.

A   B   C   D   Too vague, indirect, and abstract in communication.

List the basic behaviors where a C or D is marked. These indicate behaviors for improvement. Identify the behaviors you want to change. Prioritize them. Use Feeler strengths to make the change.

1. Identify the behaviors you want to change.

2. Identify the values involved in the behaviors.

3. Identify replacement behaviors and align them with a value that will reinforce. (*Example:* Tendency to avoid conflict because of the value of not hurting anyone. Identify the behavior of confronting and associate it with the value of honesty and openness.)

4. Identify benefits to you and other people of your changed behavior.

Exercise 53: Feeler Development of Rationale

Presenting an issue rationally facilitates discussion. Rational means to be able to reason; therefore, to present a rationale implies an explanation of reasons or principles. Feelers tend to present the emotional impact as the main focus of an issue, with their rationale scattered among the explanations.

Example: A receptionist was hired. She routed over 300 calls a day. She had been on the job for ten days. A senior vice-president came out and angrily reprimanded her for routing a call to him that should have gone to someone else. The receptionist's supervisor went to her manager saying, "Look, if you can't keep the big egos around here off my people's back, I'm not going to keep morale up at all. My receptionist is in tears. She just got racked for something she had never been told to do. She was never told not to route a customer's call to that VP. I didn't know that was one of his rules, so how could I tell her if I didn't know? I'm tired of people looking down on support staff."

What is the issue? What can be done about it? How does that interaction make the supervisor look to the manager?

What if . . . the supervisor had gone to her manager with a *statement of the problem* and discussed it as a problem-solving interaction, rather than a complaint session?

What if . . . the supervisor had identified the problem as a behavior or chain of command problem where a senior VP reached across five levels to issue a reprimand and did so abusively? The *effect of the action* involved the supervisor's credibility, work group morale, need for a system for resolving complaints, and development of the receptionist's skills to receive reprimands.

What if . . . the supervisor then presented the *factual evidence:* (1) Receptionist had been on the job ten days, (2) routing approximately 300 calls a day, (3) first evidence of inappropriate routing — 1 in 3,000 is exceptional performance, (4) she answers promptly and courteously, (5) neither the supervisor nor receptionist knew the senior VP's rule, (6) six months earlier the supervisor sent a memo to each office asking for any special requirements for message routing, (7) VP in question did not respond, (8) she informed her manager of the way she dealt with the receptionist's feelings, and (9) she came to discuss problem resolution to avoid future occurrence.

After the supervisor clearly developed the rationale, the emotional impact becomes part of the fact base, rather than being the focal point that might weaken the rationale. The supervisor might want to vent emotional frustration to the manager about the VP's behavior, but should figure the cost. Venting frustration about a situation over which the manager may have little control may create frustration in the manager, which is more likely to be focused on the supervisor than the VP.

1. Identify a situation about which you feel angry.
    A.   Develop a statement of the problem.

    B.   Identify the effects of the problem.

    C.   Identify the factual evidence.

D. Develop your rationale (an explanation of reasons or principles) involved in your conclusion.

Exercise 54:   Coaching Feelers

One Feeler talked about the pain she felt about being perceived as an "airhead." She is an intelligent college graduate with a 3.5 grade point average on a 4-point scale. She is, however, stuck in Feeler style. When she describes an event, she goes into great detail about the words spoken, feelings expressed, the setting where it occurred, the impact on other people, the wrongness of treating people badly, and adds feeling nuance to each fact. The impact of her statement is considerably watered down by the abundance of (Thinker-perceived) "trivia."

Feelers who have trouble getting others to seriously consider their points may find the following exercise useful. If you do not personally have that problem but are responsible for helping others develop who do overstate with too much expression, consider this exercise.

Exercise A   Identify an important issue. Put it in precise language. Examine the issue statement to see if it has value-laden words in it. If it does, reword the statement until it is a clear, analytical statement. Next, sort out thoughts, feelings, and ideas, looking for information that gives factual evidence about the issue. Identify background factors that influence the issue. Identify feelings that affect the issue. Identify emotionally laden parts of the issue that color the underlying issue.

Exercise B   Mark the following statements as analytical or emotionally laden issue statements. Mark them A for analytical or E for emotionally laden.

_____1. The CEO was malicious in the way he slashed our budgets.

_____2. The CEO cut our budgets by 20%.

_____3. The manager hurt my feelings about the way I handled it.

_____4. The customer conflict was obviously Sam's vendetta.

_____5. The rapid rate of change is affecting the way we do billing.

_____6. Removing employee parking spaces affects morale.

_____7. The way the secretary snaps at people makes people avoid going into her office.

_____8. The company is changing from service-based priority to profit-based priority.

_____9. Reducing overtime pay really made people mad; management should have thought about how that decision feels to us.

_____10. This company never has cared about the people who work here.

ANSWERS TO EXERCISE B

_E_ 1. "Malicious" is a value-laden word. "Slashed" is a value-laden verb implying vicious attack, drastic reduction, and a sweeping wound.

_A_ 2. Clear statement of issue without emotional wording.

_E_ 3. Statement of feelings of speaker without enough substantive information to allow the listener to identify the issue. The listener receives the statement of wrongness and the situation, but receives no information about the way the call was handled.

_E_ 4. "Customer conflict" identifies the way the speaker labels the issue, but uses the word "obviously" to imply that the listener must surely agree. The term "vendetta" implies a blood feud, murder, or vengeance.

_A_ 5. Issue is arranged in cause-effect statement. Cause (rapid rate of change) affects billing (effect).

_A_ 6. Issue is arranged in cause-effect statement. Cause (removing employee parking spaces) affects morale (effect).

_E_ 7. "The secretary snaps at people" describes style but does not clearly indicate that the way the secretary treats people is the issue.

_A_ 8. Issue is arranged in cause-effect statement. Cause

(change) affects profit-based priority replacing service (effect).

__E__ 9. Emphasis is on the feelings that resulted from reducing overtime pay and does not address the cause of reducing overtime pay. The sentence clouds the issue by emphasing effect. Emotionally charged assertions were implied of anger, injustice, insensitivity, and selfishness.

__E__ 10. The statement is a value judgment, but doesn't precisely name an issue.

EXERCISE C   Key to feeling messages — become more aware of value-laden words used in discussing issues. Value-laden words such as . . .

nice	vindictive	blessing	selfish	caring
good	pleasant	loathsome	enjoyable	uncaring
ugly	unpleasant	malicious	detestable	shameful
sweet	embarrassment	dishonor	disgrace	hateful
sincere	horrible	valuable	vile	earnest
honest	dishonest	cruel	bad	fine

Identify the value-laden words you use most often.

EXERCISE D   Checklist for developing rationale.

1. Put the issue in precise language, developing a clear statement of the issue arranged in cause-effect sentence structure.

2. Eliminate as many value-laden words as possible in your first remarks about the issue.

3. Cite factual evidence affecting the issue.

4. Cite background factors that influence the issue.

5. Identify the emotional aspects of the issue.

6. Identify your own values involved in the question as a way of desensitizing the potency of your feelings that might overwhelm you if they surprised you during the discussion.

7. Restate in outline form your rationale:
   A. The issue I'm discussing is . . .
   B. Factual evidence is . . .
   C. Background factors affecting this issue are . . .
   D. Emotional factors affecting this issue are . . .
   E. My conclusion is . . .

Feelers are not asked to ignore the emotional factors. Just put them in a support position in your rationale rather than in lead position. Emotional factors can support a clearly developed rationale, but tend to weaken the argument if they come first in the rationale.

Exercise 55:   Using Feelings to Create Image

Select three people whom you believe to be strong Thinkers. Read the following excerpt to them, asking them to discuss the rationality versus emotionality issues.

> Reagan obviously brought formidable talents to the image game. He has the dramatic voice and the confident, jaunty air of Franklin Roosevelt and aw-shucks smile of Dwight Eisenhower, the easy masculinity and glamour of Jack Kennedy. Reagan is a leader operating powerfully at the level of visions, dreams, and legends, the most magnetic ingredients of political imagery. He has the lure of the pied piper. Especially at moments of triumph or despair, Reagan has sensed instinctively how to bond himself with the emotions of others and how to draw them into bonding with him . . . he has known how to create a sense of familiarity by tossing a smiling wave at an isolated camera crew that millions of folks back home felt he was sending them a personal greeting. Reagan has understood that politics for the millions — in the television age — is not rational, but emotional. *(The Power Game,* pg. 422–423)

1. How does manipulation of feeling figure in the image game?

2. What is the impact of activating people's visions, dreams, and legends?

3. What is the benefit of bonding with the emotions of others?

4. What is the impact of getting people to bond with you?

5. How does the emotionality of the television age impact management?

Exercise 56: Domination

In the book *Liar's Poker*, Michael Lewis writes about Wall Street and life at Salomon Brothers in particular. In the following, note the use of power to establish different values from socially accepted ones.

> The bond salesmen from the forty-first floor . . . were by definition leaders in the firm, and they might have provided me with a role model, but their smooth metal surfaces offered nothing to cling to. Some of the men . . . were truly awful human beings. They sacked others to promote themselves. They harrassed women. They humiliated trainees. They didn't have customers. They had victims. . . . The point is that it didn't matter one bit whether he is good or evil as long as he continued to swing that big bat of his. Bad guys did not suffer their comeuppance in Act V on the forty-first floor. They flourished . . . the chosen home of the firm's most ambitious people, and because there were no rules governing the pursuit of profit and glory, the men who worked there, including the more bloodthirsty, had a haunted look about them. The place was governed by the simple understanding — conduct of perceived self-interest was healthy. Eat or be eaten. The range of acceptable conduct within Salomon Brothers was wide indeed. It said something about the ability of the free marketplace to mold people's behavior into a socially acceptable pattern. For this was capitalism at its most raw, and it was self-destructive. (pg. 69–70)

1. Identify the values established for conduct by traders.

2. Explore the meaning of the description "their smooth metal surfaces offered nothing to cling to."

3. How do you think Feelers would fare on the forty-first floor?

4. One of the most financially successful traders who taught a class for trainees was called "the Human Piranha." What implications does Lewis' description of the Human Piranha have for interpersonal relations?

   The Human Piranha was short and square, like the hooker on a rugby team. The most unusual thing about him was the frozen expression on his face. His dark eyes, black holes really, rarely moved. And when they did, they moved very slowly, like a periscope. His mouth never seemed to alter in shape; rather it expanded and contracted proportionately when he spoke. And out of that mouth came a steady stream of bottom-line analysis and profanity. (pg. 70)

   A. Read the description to three Feelers and ask them to share their opinions with you.

   B. Read the description to three Thinkers and ask them to share their opinions with you.

   C. Listen carefully for the words chosen, the phrasing, and the reasoning.

   D. Identify your value system concerning the way people should treat each other.

Exercise 57: Thinkers' Feelings

Thinkers tend to think of themselves as being unemotional and may even take pride in "keeping feelings under control." These two premises may in fact blind Thinkers to the way their own values trigger emotional reaction to "objective evidence." The following responses were given by a group of high-scoring

Thinkers when asked to identify abuses of power. Note the emotionality of the responses.

Examples of Abuses of Power:

1. selfish, cold tyrant
2. hypocritical actions
3. power-tripping with large self-focused ego
4. abusive and arrogant
5. undermining and destroying potential in others
6. tells lies — untrustworthy
7. bossy — closed mind
8. power crazy
9. put-down artist
10. self-righteous
11. childish
12. whiner
13. intimidates and humiliates
14. hot air bullshit artist
15. can't handle criticism
16. doesn't praise
17. position power for personal gain
18. criticizing people
19. autocratic
20. undiplomatic

Exercise 58:   Fear of Feelings

Ironically, both the Thinker and Feeler are afraid of becoming overwhelmed with feelings. Examine the following premises.

Premise: All fear is emotion . . . it hits you in the chest first.
Premise: People are afraid of anger . . . we fear getting so emotional that we will do damage to ourselves or others.
Premise: We may fear feeling crazy and out of control.
Conclusion: We try to maintain control of feelings (though Thinkers and Feelers have different standards for control).

Thinker rule: "I must always be rational." The statement itself is not a rational standard since every message has feeling content. To control too rigidly leads to insensitivity, which is in itself a feeling of numbness, a limiting state for objectivity.

Feeler rule: "I must not hurt other people." The statement overlooks the reality of frustration and anger that does seek expression; thus allowing expression through passive-aggressive acts, thus violating the Feeler rule.

Antidote: Confront the fear. Sit down and think about something that makes you angry. Remember it without rationalizing. Let the feelings express. Become very familiar with the physiological aspects of anger. Note your heart rate, your breathing pattern, physical discomfort, nervous system response. Establish your norms for feeling anger without losing the ability to think clearly.

Thinkers fear being seen as a Feeler (emotional). Feelers fear being seen as a Thinker (critical and insensitive). Real leadership requires the balance of Thinking and Feeling as an antidote to emotional manipulation. Write a value statement about expression of anger that satisfies you.

Exercise 59:   Dealing with Criticism

Skill: Identify the word message. Identify the feeling message. *Every activity and experience has a coloring of feeling.* Learn to identify both content and feeling. In the following examples of reaction to criticism, note differences between Thinker and Feeler message handling.

Groups were asked how they respond to personal criticism. Thinkers established the following pattern without identifying whether or not the criticizer was personally important to them. Feelers used interpersonal relationship, with the criticizer as an important variable.

Feelers reported the following responses.

Criticism from someone I don't know causes me to:

1. Hurt, but I don't worry as much . . . don't take it to heart as much.
2. Try to explain.
3. Give outward compliance but inward resistance.
4. Get angry and use energy to try to ignore it.

Criticism from someone I love causes me to:

1. Feel really emotionally upset.
2. Not believe that they could hurt me so.
3. Be defensive, angry and possibly to cry but try to keep from it.
4. Try to find out why they are mad at me.

5. Try to fix it.
6. Try to deny the hurt.
7. Rationalize that they probably didn't mean it.
8. Go back later and try to explain.

Thinkers reported the following responses without placing weight on the relationship with the criticizer:

1. Validate the expertise of the criticizer to see if there is a legitimate expertise base from which to criticize.
2. Validate the criticism.
3. Analyze for facts and evidence to gather information for defense.
4. Decide if the criticism is legitimate.
5. Then react: If criticism is valid, accept it or qualify it. If the criticism is invalid, destroy the other person's argument and dismiss the incident.
6. Resolve the incident . . . but don't let the hurt or disturbance show.

EXERCISE A   Ask someone to give you constructive feedback. Pay close attention to your reaction. Listen to the internal dialogue that forms in your mind while you listen. Note the physiological reactions in your body.

EXERCISE B   Compare your reaction to expected feedback with unexpected negative feedback. Does surprise affect your response?

EXERCISE C   Identify the word and feeling messages:

1. "I dislike arguments with my wife. She will not fight fair."

   For example:

   Word message: implies discomfort in arguing with a person who does not argue by logical rules.

   Feeling message: implies feelings of helplessness when treated unjustly.

2. "He never listens to me. He doesn't even look at me. He just grunts some monosyllable reply."

Word message:

Feeling message:

3. "How do you think I look in this new suit?"
    Word message:

    Feeling message:

4. "I strongly suggest that you rethink your position."
    Word message:

    Feeling message:

5. "Don't you think you should respond? They will think you
    don't care."

Word message:

Feeling message:

Practice listening for both word and feeling messages.

Exercise 60:   Thinker-Feeler Couple
Case Study of an ENTJ and an INFP

An Extroverted-Thinker was married to an Introverted-Feeler. They were having difficulty in their marriage.

The Thinker made a list of the reasons why he should stay married and the reasons why he should not. He tried to analytically make the decision. Examine his lists and then answer "What's wrong with this picture?"

Thinker reasons for staying married to the Feeler:

1. "I need to be married for my career."
2. "I haven't found anything better. I don't have a replacement. She's as good as I've found."
3. "She's not perfect, but she's most of what I want."
4. "She's so good and loving and my children love her."
5. "I've chased a lot of women and I don't like what's out there."
6. "I want to be remembered as a good husband and father."
7. "I want my life to count for something."
8. "I haven't committed to my marriage with the same bulldog intensity that I've given to my career."
9. "She gives a lot."

Thinker reasons for not staying married:

1. "She lacks courage to go out and risk."

2. "She lacks the courage to confront. She won't argue or stand up for herself."
3. "She doesn't have outside interests."
4. "She is too closed to outside activities."

Feeler's issues in the marriage:

1. "I am not growing."
2. "I have a health problem and I watch what I do."
3. "I was happy and then he decided he didn't want the marriage anymore, then he decided he did. I can't really trust him."
4. "He has no patience in dealing with us. He won't talk about it."
5. "He seems to need to be threatened with loss in order to love."
6. "We had some common interests."
7. "I enjoyed watching him play softball and tennis, but he wasn't content to let me just watch and enjoy."
8. "He doesn't really try to understand me."

EXERCISE A   Identify the differences in the way the Thinker husband and the Feeler wife approached the painful problem of a dysfunctional marriage.

EXERCISE B   What evidence do you have that each is stuck in preference and needs some development of their other side?

EXERCISE C   Use what you know about Thinker/Feeler characteristics to recommend a strategy for healing the pain produced by the differences and turn them into assets. How do they learn to value each other?

Exercise 61:   Defenses Instead of Growth
Case Study of a Stuck ISTP

A highly intelligent blue collar worker who is an ISTP (Introvert, Sensor, Thinker, Perceiver) in personal style decided to embark on a development plan. As Bill analyzed his family needs and the problem of his three children with future college goals, he was prompted to look at his career plans.

With careful guidance, Bill identified his anger and fears driving it.

1. *Anger:*   Angry at being labeled as irresponsible for reaching the age of forty without planning for his family's future.

   Fear: That people will see him as irresponsible like his dad, whom he had criticized for being irresponsible.

2. *Anger:*   Angry about his indebtedness . . . hate being seen as one who can't pay his bills.

   Fear: Being labeled as a failure — a chip off the old block.

3. *Anger:*   Angry at his wife.

Fear: Afraid he cannot control her. Fears others will see how she dominates and controls him. Fears her ability to hurt him.

4. *Anger:*   Angry at his family's emotional demands on him.

   Fear: Afraid of the guilt feelings of leaving his children emotionally starved but fears more not having enough private time for himself.

5. *Anger:*   Angry about his intelligence being wasted as a laborer.

   Fear: Fears being stuck in the workman role the rest of his life, but fears more becoming a supervisor due to the demands, obligations, and more sophisticated power games played.

6. *Anger:*   Angry at his small life.

   Fear: Afraid of the self-discipline and courage it takes to change.

Bill is a stuck ISTP controlled by his fears. They drive predictable, habitual patterns of response. When his fears are triggered, he does not respond with original thinking and strategy, but instead uses defensive patterned responses. He had trouble acknowledging his fears and it was quite an effort to get him to question the fears and the driven behaviors.

Examine the way his patterned responses helped him defend against his fear. When his fear of being seen as irresponsible is activated, he identifies the following habituated pattern:

- Become defensive.
- Internally deny that he is irresponsible.
- Mentally or verbally list all the ways he is responsible as evidence to counter the charge and assuage the feelings.
- Withdraw.
- If he can't physically get away, he will change the subject.
- Retreat to the privacy of inner thoughts to destroy the other person's credibility. By focusing on faults he discounts the source.
- Avoid the person from then on.

Plan: Identify the fear. Identify the habituated response pattern. Analyze the payoffs for the habituated pattern. Identify the behavior he wanted instead. Create a living image of the new behavior by mentally rehearsing it and creating a focusing sentence to light the way until the new behavior is fully established.

Examine another of Bill's patterns. Bill was afraid that he couldn't fulfill his family's financial demands. He feared the feelings of inadequacy and guilt at his inability to provide. His habituated response pattern to the fear of financial demands was:

- Habitually said "no" to any request by a family member to spend money . . . made them wait or delayed further discussion.
- Criticized their request, making it look unreasonable or selfish.
- Repeated their request to others to show the ridiculousness of the request and simultaneously showed the burden they place on him.
- Recited his financial woes at every opportunity.
- Met each family request with pessimistic head-of-the-family role of dire warning, then later gives in without a struggle.
- The warning allowed him to abdicate his self-appointed role as head of the family responsible for staying within budget.
- Credited himself for the cautionary words about debt and ignored the responsibility for letting them go ahead and buy and raise the debt. His out was to blame the family . . . "I tried."

Plan: Bill identified one fear at a time and worked on it until he felt that he not only understood it but was on the way to confronting it. Then he systematically selected another fear to work on.

Let's examine one more fear. Bill was afraid that he could not hold his own with his wife. She is dominant. As an ESFJ (Extrovert, Sensor, Feeler, Judge), she manipulates him through his feelings, which he is busy denying. When he gets angry with her he responds habitually: attack, followed by hasty withdrawal, or withholding. His habitual response is:

- Attack her by criticizing.
- Attack her by ridiculing her through hurtful humor.
- Withdraw from her and respond with coldness.
- Withdraw and lock her out of his inner world. As she senses his holding back, she demands more. He withholds and becomes even more noncommunicative.
- Withholds his approval by looking down on her as intellectually inferior.
- Privately lists her faults as his way to reduce the validity of her criticism of him.
- Withholds affection when others are around whom she wants to impress. He acts bored and uninterested.

Plan: Take down the defense shield and look clearly at the patterns and the fears driving them. Follow the plan: (1) identify the fear; (2) identify the habituated response pattern; (3) analyze the payoffs for the habituated pattern; (4) identify the behavior he wanted instead; (5) create a living image of the new behavior by mentally rehearsing it; (6) create a focusing sentence to use during stressful times to focus the new behavior until it is fully established.

Exercise 62:   Words of Advice from Thinkers and Feelers

Quotes from Feelers: Discuss these quotes with a Feeler whom you believe to be well-balanced.

1. "I have two types of emotions. Some just come up so strong that I can't stop them. My chest fills up with them. The emotions feel like they are trapping me, blotting out everything else. I've learned to accept them. I use the focusing thought 'These too shall pass.' I've learned to see them as only an uncomfortable set of vibrations and try to suspend attaching my thoughts to them. It's a little like experiencing them but disciplining myself not to let them dominate my thinking. I remind myself that they will go away. I don't let them be my total reality."

2. "It took me a long time to understand that people could disagree with me without disliking me. Disagreement felt

like dislike. I misread my own feelings of discomfort with disagreement as dislike by the other person. I have learned to handle conversational disagreement without taking it personally."

3. "As an Intuitor-Feeler I get quick impressions without details, yet I trust the impressions implicitly. I have learned to cope with the frustration of confusion when someone asks me how I know. I can't explain it. I just know. I've learned to trust my liking or disliking someone as a subtle reading of real indicators. I just don't recognize the signals consciously yet."

4. "It was hard for me to learn that my husband's criticism, which sounds like a complete rejection of me, is really a criticism of a mistake I made and not proof that he doesn't love me. One angry tone in his voice used to seem like certain proof that he didn't love me anymore. I am still very sensitive, but I don't jump to such broad conclusions anymore from one small incident."

5. "Good feelings fill me with energy and bad feelings deplete me. I have really had to work to pin the reality of my world on something more stable than how I feel. I worked hard to identify my core beliefs. I repeat them to keep my feelings from defining my world. I remind myself that God made me whole with many gifts; that I can learn from mistakes; that I am a loving and lovable person. These core beliefs give me a solid foundation when I am tempted by depression or its opposite – a volcano of feelings."

Quotes from Thinkers: Discuss these quotes with Thinkers whom you consider to have developed their Feeler capabilities to provide balance.

1. "I grew up in a family that did not express affection. I never remember getting a hug or a compliment. I remember cold, stoney silence. When I married this wonderfully expressive Feeler man, I felt uncomfortable at first. I thought he was gushy and overexpressive. Gradually I learned from him to take down my defensive wall of judgment and learn to express. I feel like a bird who has been set free. Sometimes I feel like a child who can bubble unself-consciously over a sunset or a butterfly. Occasionally, I feel my old judg-

mental Thinker accusing me of acting silly or gushy. I just laugh at my old self and praise the new life that flows through me. I don't intend to close the feeling door again. I feel too hemmed in when I do."

2. "I took great pride in being professional. I chose my clothes carefully, as well as what I said. I was proper and circumspect. I was hurt and surprised when I overheard two people talking about how stuffy and formal I was. Instead of admiring my 'professionalism' they were actually ridiculing me. As a typical Thinker, I carefully analyzed the problem and finally reached the same conclusion they did. I decided to do something about it. I asked my wife to work with me on expressing myself more feelingly. I was stunned to learn how she and the children described me. By getting in touch with feelings and learning to express them, I am a much better manager . . . and besides . . . I'm having more fun."

3. "My friends used to call me 'The untouchable and the hopelessly unreachable.' Tough times made it abundantly clear to me that I had to get in touch with feelings . . . best decision I ever made."

Exercise 63: Thinker-Feeler Checklist

Feelers tend to . . .

1. Expect others to listen for feeling messages.

2. Expect others to know how they feel. Since Feelers are usually careful to consider people's feelings, they expect Thinkers to do the same.

3. Collaborate and consult others in problem-solving; and tend to look at facts, documentation, and consult with someone else.

4. Assume they messed up when first confronted with conflict, then question the relationships involved.

5. Have a goal during conflict to establish harmony and salvage the relationship.

6. Be sensitive about others attending to what they are saying. One Feeler said, "Don't dismiss me in your mind."

7. Have difficulty expressing their anger. They frequently make statements such as "I just can't get it out," "I know what I mean but I can't get it out," "My internal picture is so vague but the feeling is so strong," "I just have too much emotion sometimes to put it into words."

8. Take mild criticisms as harsh denouncements; mild criticisms can trigger deep emotional responses.

9. Avoid seeing aspects of a situation or person that conflicts with their personal values; they would rather not acknowledge the conflict.

10. Need to develop the skill of analyzing the consequences, since they primarily focus on what people want or what feels right to them.

Thinkers tend to . . .

1. Try to avoid involvement in interpersonal issues, as they much prefer task, organizational, or business issues to analyze.

2. Discount the importance of their own feelings by rationalizing feelings rather than feeling them.

3. Not be easily impressed, since they tend to weigh, evaluate, and criticize.

4. Focus on competence and persuasion during conflict; whereas Feelers tend to focus on accommodating others.

5. Be out of touch with their feelings, since they want feelings to be logically aligned; they tend to have less tolerance for the irrationality of feelings.

6. Look for organizing principles driving actions and situations. They prefer to analyze data to see what logical thread holds the experience together in order to identify the organizing principle.

7. Rely on being able to logically frame experiences; the logical frame is critical to their sense of well-being.

THINKERS AND FEELERS NEED TO DEAL WITH FEELINGS:

1. Deal with emotions when you first feel them. If you don't, they can build up and overwhelm you unexpectedly.

2. Train yourself to recognize both the feeling and word messages.

3. Find the control thought or value that is driving the emotion.

4. Express emotions to the person or persons involved, rather than expressing them to a safe alternate.

5. Train yourself to recognize both verbal and nonverbal messages directed at you. Respond to them clearly and directly. Keep the communication focused and clean.

– 6 –

Judge-Perceiver:
To Control or To Adapt?

Main Ideas of Chapter 6:

1. Judge-controlling and Perceiver-adapting use perception and judgment differently, causing difficulty or complementarity.

2. Using clear perception and sound judgment is critical to long-term, effective leadership.

3. Fogging perception is a typical power strategy.

4. Leaders need increased visual literacy.

5. Milken manipulated perception of the staid financial community.

6. Leaders can use the four-quadrant problem-solving process to aid clear perception and sound judgment.

7. Judge-Perceiver characteristics are reviewed.

8. Judge-Perceiver developmental exercises are included.

Classical assumptions about people and management were based upon authority as a chain of command in a pyramid structure with power controlled at the top and work performed at the bottom. Pyramid power implies that people at the top have a virtual monopoly on intelligence, experience, knowledge, and vision. The implication is that people at the bottom just need to provide the muscle to carry out orders of those at the top. Power and authority are primarily to keep brawn controlled and working in the right direction. The motto supports division of labor — brains to direct and muscles to do the work.

Yesterday's work force had more tolerance for authoritarian, chain-of-command management while today's work force has very little patience with authoritarianism or classical organizational assumptions. The trend toward participatory management seriously challenges tradition.

Yesterday's work ethic, motivated by security and responsibility, is being rapidly replaced by consumer ethics of achievement, advancement, recognition, and interesting work. Organizational culture is increasingly important.

The way managers deal with their environment is strongly influenced by their preference on the Judging-Perceiving dimension. This preference is an inner disposition to deal with the environment primarily through judgment of Thinker/Feeler analysis or through perception of Sensor/Intuitive assimilation.

Both Judges and Perceivers can be authoritarian in the way they deal with the outer world, but Judges tend to *appear* more authoritarian because of their natural preference for control, order, dependability, and predictability. Perceivers *appear* to be less authoritarian because of their preference for spontaneity, adaptability, curiosity, and openness. Note that the key word is *appear*. Inner disposition of preferences does not determine one's use of power. Judge or Perceiver preference does not predict power development.

JUDGMENT AS STANDARD BEARER

Use of judgment (Thinker-Feeler) is essential in establishing one's personal standards. People with Thinker judgment as their primary preference tend to analyze incoming data by identifying organizing principles. For example, a Thinker-Judge walked into an office and quickly assessed staff, space, decor, and office arrangement according to implied status and work efficiency. Multiple perceptions were arranged along dimensions. Thinker-Judge preference continually organizes perceptions to draw conclusions that establish rules and standards. A Feeler-Judge looking at the same office might organize perceptions along dimensions of warm-cold and people responsiveness to draw conclusions. Judges use perception as servant to the judging process, while Perceivers use judgment as servant to the perceiving process.

Preference for Judging involves a need for order, system, and control. Judges tend to order their perceptions and systematize meanings for overall control of perception. Thinker-Judges organize around cause-effect and analyze situations for consequences and inferences as they seek to identify the organizing principles. Feeler-Judges organize around values and analyze situations for their importance and people impact, drawing conclusions using operating principles of consideration for people.

Judging types like structure and predictability. Their inner disposition is to identify the operating rules for judging what they perceive; whereas, Perceivers trust more what they perceive while tending to delay organizing the principles. Dr. Mary McCaulley and Isabel Briggs Myers explain the judging preference: ". . . for all persons who characteristically live in the judging attitude, perception tends to be shut off as soon as they have observed enough to make a decision." (pg. 14)

For example, a Judge scheduled a meeting to discuss an important budget issue. He focused his attention on the budget problem and withdrew his perception from what was happening in the office. A serious conflict erupted between two of the department heads. The Judge didn't pick up the tension nor the carefully controlled barbs the two were exchanging. The Judge was so focused on the budget issue that he was paying little conscious attention to incoming data. Later, as we discussed the cues that he missed, he had little trouble recognizing that they had occurred. He perceived the cues but did not route them into his consciousness. As we talked, he recalled the interaction and validated the perceptions I shared with him. Though he was judging and perceiving, he focused his attention on the judging process, leaving the perceiving process to function just out of consciousness.

Judges withdraw attention from new data in the environment after they decide on a course of action or summarize the meaning of the data. Judges then focus their attention on the environment to control it to make their plan or summation happen.

Judges withdraw attention from the environment after they have decided and therefore may not process new information that questions their original assumptions.

Many people assume that Judges are impervious to whether or not their environment is hostile to them. We assert that Judges, like Perceivers, are interested in avoiding hostile interference from their environment. People tend to perceive harmony with the environment as movement toward pleasure or at least avoidance of pain, while conflict with the environment is movement toward pain and loss of pleasure. It appears that Judges don't care, but they also tend to avoid conflict. Judges try to control their environment by predicting the outcome as a way of keeping the environment from sending them surprise negative messages.

Our data show the majority of American managers score as Judges. It therefore follows that American managers may use much of their personal power to avoid receiving negative messages from their environment. Unless Judges regularly do the brutal self-confrontation necessary for clear perception, they may be unaware of the amount of energy they put into keeping their environment from hurting or frustrating them. They can be quite unaware of the amount of perceptual distortion they use to keep from perceiving upsetting elements in their environment.

Examine the perceptual distortion in this example. Tom is head of the Finance Department. His personal preference is Sensor, Thinker, Judge (STJ), and as expected, he has several strong standards by which he judges departmental data. He believes: (1) mathematical errors result from carelessness and are unforgiveable; (2) putting data on the right form and in the right form is critical; (3) establishing paper record of transactions is demanded; and (4) errors are indications of technical weakness or bad attitude.

From those four standards, Tom painstakingly checks paper to find evidence of poor performance or employee substandard skill. When he finds an error, he then attacks the person for technical weakness or bad attitude. Watching Tom verbally insult his staff clearly shows his basic arrogance as he assumes that he rarely makes errors, thereby establishing his right to attack others when they err. When Tom makes an error, he immediately blames someone else for it. He is unwilling to see the real situation of his own fallibility because he would have to let go of his assumed superiority. He uses his judging capacity to keep the environment from delivering him proof that his abusive anger dumped on others sits on the erroneous premise of his own infallibility. He attacks anyone who challenges him. He relies on the authority of his position to stop the environment from delivering hostile messages – a typical distortion of a Stage II Abusive Dictator or Stage III Competitive Intimidator.

The judging dimension is useful in establishing standards for one's own conduct, for identifying operating principles to organize incoming data, for self-discipline, and for staying focused on one's own goals and values. It begins to be problematic when Judges try to force others to conform to their standards and plans. Judges use control and authority as ways to avoid painful experiences that could flood them from the environment.

PERCEPTION AS DATA GATHERER

Perceivers try to avoid pain through *adapting and harmonizing* with the environment, whereas Judges seek to avoid painful experiences through *judging and controlling* their environment. Perceivers use adaptation and Judges use control as main ways to avoid negative messages from the environment.

Both Perceivers and Judges want favorable response from their environment, though they use different strategies. If Perceivers can adapt enough to make the environment like them, they have a better chance of avoiding negative experiences. If Judges can control enough of the environment, they have a better chance of avoiding negative experiences.

Perceivers keep primary attention on the environment for fresh data to enable them to adapt to changing demands. With primary attention on the environment, Perceivers continually assess what others want from them and try to adapt and harmonize with the demands. Human beings seek positive strokes and tend to try to avoid negative ones; thus, both Perceivers and Judges are motivated to try to get positive environmental responses.

Perceivers prefer spontaneity, adaptability, and openness to ever-changing environment. They tend to be reluctant to decide or finally agree, preferring instead to leave the door open to accommodate new data. Judges often get irritated trying to reach closure with Perceivers. Just when closure seems possible, the Perceiver reopens discussion of options.

Complexity does not seem as messy to the Perceiver, who is accustomed to continually moving things around mentally to see additional meanings. Where Judges try to take complex information and categorize, structure, and order it for greater predictability and manageability, Perceivers keep the information mobile and are reluctant to declare certainty or complete conclusions. Judges are more willing to share their rules of conduct and logical premises as finite principles around which they organize their behavior and their work. Perceivers select a few more general rules around which they organize while keeping the context viable for changing and adapting.

Flexibility is highly valued by Perceivers. Suppose a Judge and a Perceiver were each painting a picture; their approaches would probably be quite different. The Judge might have the picture or idea to be conveyed clearly in mind and move steadily toward transferring it to the canvas. The Perceiver might begin with a general picture or idea and start painting to see what evolved, staying open to inspiration, new ideas, occurring nuances.

Judges set a specific goal, plan to achieve the goal, and steadily move toward goal accomplishment. Perceivers set a general goal or direction to allow it to evolve as they experience it. Judges focus on goals and closure for satisfaction; while Perceivers focus on experiencing and options.

We are in a perpetual state of perceiving and judging. Twenty-four hours a day the process goes on. Clear and accurate perception accompanied by sound judgment are vital processes for leadership.

CLEAR PERCEPTION AND SOUND JUDGMENT

The first three stages of power have built-in perceptual bias that skews judgment. Unconfronted fear distorts the way we see and judge. Fear that has been confronted and overcome or clearly managed forms the basis for strength and clarity.

Winston Churchill wrestled with massive depression most of his life. He faced the hopeless situation in 1940 of Nazi invasion after France had fallen, and Russia and the United States were still claiming neutrality. The Nazi Luftwaffe were bombing Britain in preparation for a cross channel invasion. Despair was predominant. "Any political leader might have tried to rally Britain with brave words, though his heart was full of despair. But only a man who had known and faced despair within himself could carry conviction at such a moment." Churchill was able to rally and inspire the English with the bold and memorable words "I have nothing to offer but blood, sweat, toil and tears." He was a man who had known, lived, and fought with the demon "Failure." He knew how it felt and tasted, thus, being quite clear about the way it consumed perception. He called his depression and sense of failure "My black dog."(Anthony Storr, *Churchill's Black Dog, Kafka's Mice and Other Phenomena of the Human Mind*)

Churchill's experience with despair and failure gave him an authentic voice and his countrymen followed his leadership to turn and face the situation with their human will. He inspired them to face the situation clearly and draw on their deepest sources for the courage to stand rather than be paralyzed by fear. His leadership during the war is a study of an ordinary fear-driven man who repeatedly faced his fear and inspired a country and later a world.

Stages I, II, and III are driven by fear of powerlessness (i.e., being out of control), fear of failure, fear of rejection, fear of conflict that they aren't instigating. These needs distort perception and interfere with sound judgment.

STRATEGY FOR ACHIEVING AND MAINTAINING CLEAR PERCEPTION AND SOUND JUDGMENT:

1. Know your own style's strengths and weaknesses. (Acknowledge tendencies, biases, and preferences.)

2. Identify and confront your fears. (Know the potential distortion that comes from avoiding the things, situations, people, and information you don't want to face.)

3. Perpetually do brutal self-examination to maintain balance. (Examine avoidance habits, excuse-making tendencies, logical errors, value omissions, and egoic defenses you may be using.)

4. Learn to ask yourself penetrating questions. (Check your own motives as well as your logic and values.)

5. Examine your actions continually for use of power. (Check your actions against the four stages of power to see if you are getting stuck in Stages I, II, or III.)

CASE STUDY: FAULTY PERCEPTION AND UNSOUND JUDGMENT (ABUSIVE DICTATOR)

Ted Tomlinson hasn't noticed that his organization is changing, nor has he recognized that with his formidable intelligence, he may be capable of faulty perceptions and false conclusions. A 140 IQ does not guarantee overall intelligence when you look at the various kinds of intelligence: linguistic, musical, logical-mathematical, spatial, bodily-kinesthetic, interpersonal and intrapersonal. (Howard Gardner's theory of multiple intelligences.)

Ted Tomlinson believes he is superior to other people. He focuses his IQ on logical-mathematical and spatial concepts with some tolerance for linguistic intelligence, while greatly disdaining the other four kinds of intelligence. He refuses to acknowledge that bodily-kinesthetic, musical, interpersonal (between people) and intrapersonal (personal awareness) are even relative to intelligence.

As a forty-five-year-old corporate lawyer, he believes his logical-mathematical intelligence is the only "real" intelligence base. He sees all other approaches as inferior. His style is ISTJ (Introvert, Sensor, Thinker, Judge), and he is stuck in some of the worst aspects of style. He is such a strong Judge-controller that he forces his perception to yield information that fits his preconceived ideas. He proclaims his great objectivity while allowing himself to be unaccountable for the way his perception is dominated by his tendency to shut off observation as soon as he finds evidence for his opinion. His belief in his intellectual superiority, reinforced by the pride of the legal profession, blinds him to his perceptual distortion. He is a Stage II Abusive Dictator while believing himself to be objective.

The corporation where he works went through a cultural change, and as a Stage II Abusive Dictator, Ted was no longer in harmony with the desirable culture. He was so successful in the old culture that he refuses to accept evidence of changing conditions. Company background reveals more about Ted.

The company prospered during the seventies and early eighties. Then, subtle signals surfaced to suggest that something was amiss in maintaining their competitive edge. The company used traditional chain-of-command authority, and the power styles of the executives were Stages II or III. The most powerful executives were power abusive. As the new wave of employees began to resist the mistreatment, older employees also began to discuss their discontent.

As the company began to lose some of its top professionals, the brain drain alarmed top executives. Then, the profit margin began to slowly dwindle. Innovation was desperately needed to remain competitive in the market, but few people wanted to put themselves in a position to be ridiculed and persecuted. Why be innovative? They were ridiculed if ideas failed and persecuted if they succeeded by those unwilling to share the power.

After many failed starts at changing the corporate culture, the executives finally came to the realization that the problem lay in their court rather than with employees and customers. It took two years of denial with vicious struggles among turf warriors for the reality to be accepted by enough of the top executives to begin the change.

Those executives targeted with the responsibility to turn the company around concluded that the company had a reputation for power abuse, top-down decision-making, selective information announcements, and unfair hiring practices. Multiple need identification meetings were held with upper-level managers to identify behaviors helpful to business and those that hindered it; mid-management went through the same process. The lists were so similar that they were accepted as the real situation. Their culture was (1) power abusive, (2) communication weak, (3) untrusting, (4) turf-controlling and kingdom-building, (5) uncooperative, and (6) resource wasteful in managing their human assets.

Solutions were posited to change managerial behavior and move from power abuse to leadership. Tenets of their change process were:

1. Mature use of power and authority.
2. Open, responsible communication.
3. Honest performance feedback.
4. Teamwork and cooperation.

5. Clear leadership and participation.
6. Development and valuing of people assets.

As soon as people saw the desirable tenets in print, they immediately expected change and employees began to judge their managers' behaviors against the six standards. Although the executives tried to tell employees that the standards were the direction of the future culture, the employees wanted them to be real instantly. The tenets created *immediate* expectations for today, not tomorrow.

Candor, clear performance feedback, and trustworthy leadership was instantly expected. Behavioral change takes time, of course, but the employee expectations weren't rationally based — they were value based. People began to expect their unaddressed wrongs to be immediately righted. Their irrational expectations for immediate redress became topics of conversation. Each time they saw a manager behaving in the old way, they flooded the grapevine with angry remarks and serious doubts about whether "old dogs could learn new tricks."

The abusive authoritarian type of Stage II and Stage III threaten any change process the most in the initial stages of change. The pleasant and harder to detect style of the Benevolent Dictator and the Competitive Manipulator hide under cover of positivity and therefore do not become as much a target of employee pessimism and wrath about real change until later in the process. The authoritarian types who are controlling, demanding, intimidating, and retaliating create the most immediate fear.

As previously explained, Abusive Dictators and Competitive Manipulators use *fogging* of perception as a way to prevent people from seeing their actions clearly. By creating such a perceptual fog that other people have difficulty seeing through the illusion, the real situation skims by undetected. They project powerful images of themselves while projecting deficiencies in other people. Four of the fogging techniques used are: (1) superiority role, (2) creating doubt, (3) manipulating emotion, and (4) wearing masks.

FOGGING TECHNIQUE #1 *Superiority role:* Dictators see themselves as standard-bearers for "professional" behavior and technical competence, thus setting themselves up as *the* judge of professionalism standards.

Ted's belief in his own intellectual superiority made him believe that he was always right. He took great delight in picking apart other people's work. As he received work from all departments, he wrote nasty little zinger notes and attached them to documents. His preconceived notion of his own superiority caused him to distort incoming perceptions to match his belief in his own infallibility.

FOGGING TECHNIQUE #2   *Create doubt:*   Dictators try to manipulate others into doubting themselves, their abilities and their own judgment, thus the Dictator gets to control perception of competence.

Ted is so successful at intimidating people with "legalese" that most people have trouble thinking clearly when he spews the legal fog. His intimidation techniques frequently challenge the logical basis of others' viewpoints. Note some of his doubt-creating terms:

"You made an elementary *post hoc* error." Few people know readily how to follow his charge of making the logical error of thinking that a happening which follows another must be its result. Ted counts on most people having forgotten or having never known the meaning of *post hoc* or *ergo propter hoc.*

"Your fact base is weak, causing false dependence and error."

"You are making unwarranted generalizations."

"You are using elementary logical dodges. Don't beg the question."

"You make the mistake of thinking absurdity can pass for reason."

"Your point is oversimplification or just simpleton grasp."

FOGGING TECHNIQUE #3   *Manipulate emotion:*   Dictators fog other people's perception by skillful manipulation of emotion to confuse others' thinking. Stirring up negative emotions such as doubt, anger, guilt, and frustration confuses issues. Dictators know that too much emotion tends to cloud judgment. Few people are trained to withstand emotional fog.

Ted frequently called people stupid, ridiculed them in front of others, and had past errors carefully catalogued in memory so he could use specific errors to upset people. He proudly stated, "I don't generalize beyond the data. I use hard evidence."

FOGGING TECHNIQUE #4 *Wearing masks:* Expert Dictators wear masks of such convincing subtlety that they may be difficult to detect and even more difficult to unmask. They are superb role players, quickly assessing the mask needed to pretend support when they actually withhold it.

Ted was quick to assess that some of the old power abusers were actually trying to make changes in the way they behaved. When the CEO announced that every officer and manager would be expected to behave according to the six tenets, Ted began to endorse the changes. He made deceptive statements such as "This is the way we should have been doing business all along." "I have been the lone voice arguing for more integrity in the logic of the way we do things around here." "Some people are going to have to be more accountable for the logic of their decision-making." "People are not going to get away with sloppy thinking anymore." He skillfully fashioned the changes as something he had been championing for some time. It is noteworthy that each of his remarks focused on his intellectual power base as self-appointed authority on logic and thinking.

Ted's fogging techniques are driven by his need for control, his fear, and his manipulation of authority. A look at his manipulations in each of these areas is useful to understanding the Abusive Dictator.

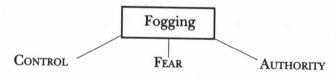

Are The Main Manipulations

CONTROL — Dictators are desperate to control their job, their domain, their employees and particularly their boss' perception.

1. *Claim superior performance:* Dictators repeatedly see themselves as paragons of good business practice.

    Ted frequently referred to "good business practice" so he was not only in charge of logic and reasoning but insinuated himself into people's consciousness as the guardian of good business practice.

2. *Value performance but not people*: Dictators define best business practice as keeping costs controlled, being legally compliant, and making a profit at the cost of people, morale, and initiative. They talk performance as the *only* points of focus while denigrating people and ignoring the brutal cost in human resources. They use legality and bottom-line performance to cover up and fog over the way they treat people.

Ted proudly announced his record of never losing a case. He didn't mention settling out of court and other trade-offs that didn't ever get to court. He demanded long hours of staff without acknowledgment or extra pay. He was a nitpicker about form and style. His approach was, "Why thank people for what they get paid to do? If they aren't performing, they can be sure I will let them know. Otherwise, they need to do what they are paid to do."

3. *Turf control*: Dictators want autonomy as they guard their turf jealously and try to control everything that goes to their boss to make themselves look good. They carefully guard their reputation with important customers and go out of their way to establish themselves as having sound business judgment. They use all the right terms in order to be seen as knowledgeable.

Ted controlled his turf by viciously attacking anyone who dared to have an opinion on regulatory or legal issues. He had his boss, the CEO, convinced that Ted should be present at most decision-making sessions. You can easily see that in the increasingly complex legalistic world of business, his argument had merit. His motive for being present was difficult to detect. He continually guarded his turf and promoted his own image.

FEAR — Dictators use fear to make sure they maintain control.

1. *Threaten*: Dictators deal with employees who challenge or irritate them by threatening damaging performance appraisals, loss of their jobs, or damage to their reputation.

2. *Intimidate*: Dictators take pride in knowing rules, regula-

tions, and policies to use in catching people in error in small details and then ridiculing integrity, questioning intent, belittling competence, and deriding their judgment. Ted fashioned himself as the corporate defender against legal vulnerability. He primed the fear of litigation.

3. *Retaliate:* Dictators retaliate against employees who irritate them by nitpicking work according to form, detail and rigid adherence to procedure — attempting to cause self-doubt and loss of confidence.

4. *Humiliation:* Dictators point out people's errors with anger and assertions of stupidity, dishonest intention, and technical incompetence. Ted tended to overgeneralize threats to the corporation.

AUTHORITY — Dictators capitalize on people's unresolved authority issues. By activating employee respect for position and their unresolved authority issues, Dictators easily assume a parental role with employees.

1. *Judge harshly:* They use position authority to play the daddy or mommy role of controlling, dominating, and shaping the children to suit their own desires. By combining the abusive and domineering parental role with technical expertise, Dictators wield a potent power bolt to hurl at employees.

2. *Demoralize employees:* By criticizing harshly, threatening, intimidating and humiliating, Dictators try to undermine employee self-confidence and make others dependent upon the Dictator to determine acceptability. Dictators then reward or withhold acceptance as a means of control.

3. *Undermine their boss:* They repeatedly undermine their boss by creating doubt in people's minds about the boss' abilities while promoting their own superior business practices. Behind the boss' back, they point out weaknesses in the boss' communication style, decision-making ability, and knowledge of the job. They then make themselves look good by showing how they are superior to the boss. By convincing their subordinates that the Dictator's boss is inadequate, they create hostility and walls around their kingdom and thus prevent the flow of information to the Dictator's boss.

One of Ted's most frequent statements to the CEO was, "Boss, you had better have me by your side to protect your legal flank." Ted's use of the word *boss* is ironic since he later declares the CEO to be an inferior decision-maker while giving himself credit for the successful deals.

Note his use of innuendo. "I don't know what the CEO was thinking when he made that decision. It sure couldn't have been for the good of the company. I don't agree with him, but he is the boss and if he wants us to implement that inferior plan, we will have to do it." "He's had no experience with that, so we'll just have to guide him carefully into a solid call." "Keeping him from making disastrous moves is my job, and believe me, it is a full-time challenge!"

4. *Create guilt:* By catching others in errors, albeit they may be insignificant details, Dictators fog others' judgment and get them so focused on pleasing the Dictator that they become absorbed in doing things the Dictator's way in order to avoid harassment and ridicule. Employee initiative is turned into anxious compliance.

Ted attacked one employee making a purchase request for a $50 item. "How dare you send that request to me. You know how I think about that. You know what I like and what I don't. You asked for this just to irritate me. You are unbelievably stupid to think I wouldn't catch on. If you continue to irritate me like this, I will make life around here unbearable for you." The request was not a violation of policy, it was simply something that Ted personally didn't like.

Review the situation of attempting to change a corporate culture with a power player like Ted. Is Ted motivated to change? How likely is Ted to endorse leadership, teamwork, open communication, people development, and fair and equitable treatment? He has succeeded for a lifetime as a power abuser. Look at the rationale.

Premise: Abusive Dictators are driven by the need for power and control.

Premise: Teamwork requires sharing of power.

Premise: Abusive Dictators refuse to share power.

Premise: Abusive Dictators have no wish to be a team player and therefore are extremely threatened by candor and leadership.

Premise: Dictators are such good role players that they may pretend support while undermining the process.

Conclusion: Abusive Dictators seriously threaten the change process and are most likely to try to undermine the process rather than change to more mature and responsible use of power.

As managers and employees became more aware of leadership behaviors, they began to see power abuse more clearly. It was a long and painful process, but as more people began to see the behaviors, Ted became more and more uncomfortable. When the CEO learned about Ted's abuse of people, his undermining, his innuendos, the CEO gave Ted a clear set of behavioral objectives. Ted would have to abandon his manipulation techniques and deal with people more openly and responsibly. He would have to drop his intimidation and humiliation techniques. Ted chose to leave the company rather than comply.

Ted attempted to blame the change process for his leaving; too many people had learned to recognize mature and responsible behavior. Blaming others just didn't pass the perceptual reality test. As people became better equipped to recognize manipulative behavior, it became less and less effective. The company has succeeded in changing the corporate culture by doing the tough daily work of clearly perceiving and soundly judging. The leaders in the company regularly practice mature and responsible interactions.

When dealing with Abusive Dictators, questions you can ask yourself are:

1. Do the words and actions match?

    (Are the verbal and nonverbal messages matching? Are the words, actions, and feelings giving the same message?)

2. Does this person really share power and authority or just pretend to do so?

    (Does this person assign the task, but control the pass? Do

you have to perpetually do it their way, in their preferred style, with their ideas in order to get something approved?)

3. Am I being manipulated?

(Do I consistently walk away feeling uncertain, set up, angry, incompetent, inferior, or falsely complimented?)

4. Does this person accept responsibility for his/her own behavior?

(Is blame continually passed to others? Are others criticized without behavioral data to explain the criticism? Are others put down in order to make that person look good?)

Remember: Abusive Dictators count on being able to fog your perception. Focus on what you know to be true rather than giving too much credence to "expertise." Become alert when you feel your confidence slipping. Ask yourself, "Is the slippage valid or resulting from manipulation of perception?"

In addition to using this four-question process for checking Abusive Dictator behavior, you can check yourself with the same four questions:

1. Do my words and actions match?

2. Do I really share power and authority, or am I just pretending?

3. Am I manipulating for selfish reasons?

4. Am I accepting responsibility for my own behavior?

Clear perception is difficult since human beings try to avoid or eliminate inconsistencies among their feelings, thinking, and behavior. The consistency principle so necessary to perceived stability predisposes people to try to eliminate incongruity. Inconsistencies among our feelings, thoughts, and actions create disharmony and discomfort in most of us. Therefore, we unconsciously tend to rearrange information to keep it from giving us glimpses of ourselves that do not fit our own image. The need to face the fear of painful acknowledgment of our own weaknesses is basic to clear perception. Dissonance can be deeply buried in subconscious storage. To uncover it, one must dig deeply and be willing to risk the self-concept battering that may result.

Since Ted's belief in his own superiority and infallibility was so strong, he used his perception to rearrange information to fit his belief. He liked the power of criticizing others and disliked the discomfort of internal dissonance. He found it easier to be critical of others than to be brutally frank with himself.

Power abuse involves dominance, intimidation, and belittling others. Stage IV Leadership persuasiveness includes such factors as trustworthiness, persuasiveness, character, integrity, knowledge, competence, honesty, and dynamism.

NEED FOR VISUAL LITERACY

With the advent of the Reagan years, clear perception associated with leadership became increasingly difficult. History already shows that never before had America seen such a carefully staged presidency as the Reagan era. The most advanced media packaging techniques were used to control perception. In Blumenthal's *The Permanent Campaign,* he discusses the "techniques of imagery and symbolism projected through a media-based politics." This period marked a historic change from verbal to visual eloquence as the basis for American political discourse. Image-based politics began to shape our perceptions about use of power, and across the country packaging was more important than substantive action. We seemed unable to sort through the carefully orchestrated stagings that affected our perception.

Other writers note the perceptual quagmire. "The challenge," says Oreskes, "is in understanding how images affect us. We have to become more aware of the difference between verbal and visual literacy. We can be very sophisticated about verbal literacy and not realize that there are things the eye sees which the ear doesn't necessarily understand."

Jim Shahin says, "Television prefers pictures to words — moving pictures. And pictures don't inform as much as they illustrate . . . (some critics maintain) that the new visual literacy has changed the role of words: They used to be used to describe events; now they caption them. The result has been to emphasize style over content." Media analyst Tony Schwarts says, "Radio, and then television, drew our attention away from issues and caused us to focus on the more personal qualities of the politician, his ability to speak and his style of presentation."

Daily perceptual control of image politics affects our gullibility in not noting the difference between words and actions, between intention and outcome, between illusion and reality. Seeing clearly is an ongoing challenge, and particularly true for the leader. People are continually trying to control the leader's perception through carefully withheld or selective information and innuendo.

Perhaps we need to rethink the potency of the adage "A picture is worth a thousand words." We have taught verbal literacy for thousands of years, yet visual literacy is exponentially more potent in manipulating perception.

Vital ingredients of Stage IV power are accurate interpretation of information, balanced judgment based upon knowledge and reliable instincts, respect that doesn't breed resentment, and trustworthiness and integrity that inspire loyalty and courage. Leaders must be impervious to visual manipulation.

MANIPULATED PERCEPTION
OF THE FINANCIAL COMMUNITY

How could the most intelligent, savvy people in the financial market be duped by one of the world's oldest scams — the ponzi? A ponzi is a swindle where early investors are paid off by later investors, and success depends on keeping it going. Michael Milken of Drexel Burnham Lambert's junk bond manipulation helped fund the disastrous merger and acquisition (M&A) mania of the eighties. Milken in early 1990 was under indictment on 98 felony counts. He left the M&A market effectively dead and numerous companies with debt they could not repay.

Barron's writer Benjamin J. Stein posited a scenario of the notable pieces of the Milken incident. Review the major pieces in the ponzi swindle, noting carefully the manipulation of perception that was essential to get sophisticated financial experts to accept Milken's theory — a theory which defied the most elementary securities valuation theory.

Milken claimed to have found a market anomaly. He claimed to have done significant research into below-investment grade bonds and discovered the anomaly. His basic premise was: "Below investment-grade bonds were consistently priced too low."

From that premise, Milken reasoned that owning enough junk bonds diversified across a wide spectrum would achieve a total return on coupon plus capital gains, offset by defaults that would consistently exceed the return on investment-grade corporate bonds or treasuries.

Milken postulated a 2% rate of default that in fact turned out to be 18% a year, with as much as 58% default rate over an eight-year period. He led people to expect a safe rate of default; thus his original premise of undervalued junk bonds was a lie, since the default rate was much higher than he postulated.

Next, Milken found sub-investment grade debt in M&A situations to finance corporate takeovers. "The hostile takeover, funded by Drexel/Milken, altered the face of corporate America." (Ben Stein, *Barron's*, February 19, 1990)

By enlisting the cooperation of several people involved with complaints with the Securities and Exchange Commission, or in failed schemes of the past, he was able to select a specific group of junk bonds and along with his friends inflate the price without ever having the junk tested in the free market.

Milken carefully managed his own reputation as an expert in selecting junk bonds that paid rich dividends. He was so successful at raising money for mergers and acquisitions that he was able to demand and get fees three times larger than others for placing debt. He perpetuated the myth of the extraordinary return on junk bonds that he carefully selected. If a highly visible bond was about to default, he arranged a false feeler to suggest an interested party wanted to buy the company.

He used academics, statisticians, and public relations professionals to keep his reputation alive — a critical element of the scam. Stein posited:

> Not only were academics and lawyers sucked in . . . Basically, the whole country was led to believe a myth that contradicted the system itself . . . The whole country was led by one very enthusiastic man and his pals to believe that the entire securities pricing system for both bonds and stocks was wrong — and only he knew what was right, that the whole management structure of American business was broken, and only he could fix it, that he could, by openly selling securities that contradicted basic notions of markets, save a nation . . . If ever there were a cheerleader magician, if ever there were a nation so uneducated that it would believe a three card-monte scam, they found themselves in Michael Milken and 1980's America . . . Captain of the cheerleaders in Something for Nothing America, 1981-1990. (*Barron's*, February 19, 1990, pg. 32)

How could the sophisticated American financial community suspend critical judgment and accept an illogical message? Perhaps a number of variables came together at the right time — the illusion of expertise, the programming of image above substance, personal greed, dissolution of business ethics, and personal laziness that contribute to faulty perception and poor judgment.

FOUR-QUADRANT PROBLEM-SOLVING
FOR CLEAR PERCEPTION AND SOUND JUDGMENT

Excellent problem-solving requires thorough analysis and accurate perception. Most college-educated people have been thoroughly trained to identify a problem, analyze the facts, consider alternatives, and reach a logical conclusion. Such training prepares us to use three of the four quadrants necessary for excellent thinking. The fourth quadrant, however, has not received attention in America until the last few years. American pursuit of excellence and total quality has finally forced us to use the fourth quadrant, which involves impact on people.

The Judging dimension helps us analyze with Thinker and Feeler information while our Perceiving dimension helps us interpret facts and possibilities. Those people who have natural preferences of Sensor and Thinker are usually more adept at interpreting the facts and analyzing the consequences of those facts. They, however, are usually less nimble at using their Feeler to analyze the impact on people, values, and relationships. Neither are they usually as quick to use their Intuitive focus on possibilities and alternatives. The reverse is true of the Intuitor and Feeler. The indicators show that we are more comfortable using our preferred dimensions and less comfortable with using the other half of those dimensions.

A manager can do a thorough job of analyzing numbers and reports but may miss possibilities and importance. Similarly, a manager who is capable of seeing possibilities in problems and motivating people to help may run into budget problems by failing to grasp details of budget limitations.

We recommend the four-quadrant problem-solving approach.

Sensor (Facts) "The Happenings?"	Thinker (Analysis) "The Consequences?"
Identify the "knowns," the limits the constraints, the resources.	Apply the Rules of Logic.
Focus on facts, numbers, contractual obligations, regulations, laws, norms.	Analyze to determine the operating rules.
What are the facts? What happened?	What are the causes and effects? What are the consequences?
What does it take to get the job done?	What is fair, reasonable, and defensible?
Intuitor (Alternatives) "The Possibilities?"	**Feeler (Values/Relationships)** "The Importance?"
Look for overall themes.	Look for impact on roles.
Identify patterns.	Look for impact on relationships.
Look for innovative ways.	Check supportiveness and harmony.
What are the overall impacts and possibilities?	How does this impact people?
What can we do that has never been done before?	How can we get people to want to do this?
	How do we get their "buy-in" and commitment?
What is our future position?	Are Stakeholders considered?

An examination of each of the quadrants in more detail will show the kind of essential consideration in each one. We tend to favor either the Sensor or Intuitor quadrant as we apply perception to interpret meaning.

Sensor Quadrant (Facts)

When we are using our Sensor quadrant, we are using perception to interpret verifiable or observable facts. We look for that which is demonstrably existent. We check the rules, regulations, policies, laws, contracts, procedures for an understanding of the limitations and parameters of the issue. Dominant Sensors want to list the facts, establish the priorities, identify what needs to get done, search out as many facts as possible, and identify the solution that has the greatest probability of getting the job accomplished.

Dominant Sensors tend to trust numbers and verifiable information more than any other type of information. One Sensor remarked, "I trust the numbers and ignore the gut unless I can verify it with something real."

When Sensing is the dominant perceptual preference, a constant struggle is required to keep from becoming too resistant, too cynical, too pessimistic, and too rigid to see overall impacts and possibilities.

Sensors tend to believe they own the **Code of Realism and Constraints:**

1. Identify the problem.
2. Classify the facts.
3. Check the written restrictions (contracts, laws, regulations, etc.).
4. Identify the time limits.
5. Note the resource constraints (people, money, equipment, space).
6. Identify the realistic solution.

Sensors tend to believe that they are uniquely gifted with the responsibility of guarding realism. A balanced Sensor is disciplined enough to value the other three quadrants also.

Intuitor Quadrant (Alternatives)

The Intuitor quadrant is the perceptual process of removing or ignoring constraints in order to pursue possibilities and overall impacts. By initially ignoring constraints, Intuitors are free to look at the big picture and explore possible alternatives. Intuitors look for linkages or uncharacteristic relationships among the disparate parts of the issue. They turn information and possibilities over and over or move data points around to change their juxtaposition as they look for that unusual insight that will open the door of real possibility.

Intuitors instinctively search for an innovative way to solve the problem as they search for the unusual approach. Intuitors believe they own the **Code of Possibility:**

1. Remove the limits on the thinking process.
2. Start with the notion that anything is possible.
3. Make a random search for linkages and connections.
4. Search until you get an energizing insight.
5. Develop the insight into a clear picture or image.
6. Identify the three to five basic components.
7. Make it happen.

Thinker Quadrant (Analysis)

The Thinker quadrant is the process of logical thought that enables us to identify the operating rules that logically apply to the situation. In searching out the operating rules, the Thinker tries to apply his/her Rules of Logic, since intellectual competence is vitally important to Thinker self-worth.

Thinkers apply their universal **Code of Logic:**

1. Classify the problem/issue.
2. Examine the evidence.
3. Remain skeptical until the evidence is carefully weighed.
4. Check causes and effects for correct inferences.
5. Challenge assumptions.
6. Draw logical, defensible conclusion.

Thinkers typically challenge, question, and criticize intellectually. In applying their Code of Logic, they analyze for fairness, impartiality, and objectivity. They discount passion and emotionality, frequently touting truth at the expense of tact. They tend to discount those who take criticism personally. Unless the Thinker is well-balanced with well-developed Feeler capability, s/he tends to discount or partially discredit evidence that is too emotional. *Remember:* Many arguments have been won by the person who first draws emotional blood. Thinkers tend to believe that emotionality implies faulty reasoning. This may or may not be true, but it is frequently interpreted as less substantial reasoning.

Thinkers can be so dedicated to objectivity that they may overlook the subjective data that are important to the Feeler perspective. We have seen many corporate decisions that looked correct when you examined the facts and numbers and analyzed the situation, but the impact and importance to people involved was not correctly assessed. The decision failed in implementation.

People resisted. Though Thinkers like to make decisions with their head, genuine commitment is an affair of the heart.

Feeler Quadrant (Values/Relationships)

Feelers analyze and assimilate evidence that gives them the truest understanding of the way people feel. Feelers give credence to the values evident in situations. They give much weight to evidence that shows how important an issue is to the people involved. Feelers tend to believe that accurate problem-solving is based primarily on the ability to identify the major Stakeholders in the situation and adequately consider their concerns and interests. Feelers place much importance on recognizing individual interests, values, and feelings.

Feelers tend to analyze rules and regulations according to how well they account for individual circumstances and unusual occurrences. They analyze situations for compassion, acceptance, and caring consideration. Feelers analyze problems using intangible reality. Though a person's feelings may not be tangible to others, Feelers consider the effect on human systems of feelings as real though unprovable to others.

Feelers tend to believe they own the **Code of Relationship Standards:**

1. Identify the Stakeholders.
2. Acknowledge Stakeholder interests and concerns.
3. Evaluate the warmth and compassion or lack of it.
4. Judge the degree of active listening and genuine interest.
5. Guard against conflict and disharmony.
6. Measure tact, thoughtfulness, and consideration.
7. Decide how deeply people care.

DOMINANT QUADRANTS AND THE ARNOLD FAMILY

Each of us has a tendency to overuse one of the quadrants and try to force the information from the other three to support our dominant quadrant. Research indicates that ISTJs, ISFJs, ESTPs, and ESFPs use the Sensor quadrant primarily to interpret the information in the other three areas. INTJs, INFJs, ENTPs, and ENFPs use the Intuitor quadrant as dominant. ESTJs, ENTJs,

INTPs, and ISTPs use the Thinker quadrant as dominant, while ISFPs, INFPs, ESFJs, and ENFJs use the Feeler quadrant as dominant.

Regardless of which quadrant is dominant, power games are played primarily in order to have maximum manipulation of the Feeler quadrant. Whether insulting or complimenting, self-worth is ultimately decided by feelings of worth and assessment of relationships and achievement. The power player's major playing field is in the area of people's values and self-worth. Fear involves anxiety about powerlessness, pain, put-down, and priorities.

The Arnold family consists of parents and three children. Dad scores primarily as an ISTJ (Introvert, Sensor, Thinker, Judge) and a Stage II power user. His paternalism is normally Benevolent Dictator, but when crossed he becomes an Abusive Dictator. He is cynical, critical, and has difficulty accepting affection. He works as a power plant superintendent.

Mom scores as an ESFJ (Extrovert, Sensor, Feeler, Judge) and is a Stage III Competitive Manipulator. She is outgoing, warm, expressive, and efficient. She works as a nurse in the Intensive Care Unit of the community hospital. She plays the role of family arbitrator during the many disputes of this diverse family and often plays Competitive Manipulator to attempt to keep harmony among the members.

Dad — ISTJ is a dominant Sensor

Mom — ESFJ is a dominant Feeler

Daughter and youngest child — INFP is a dominant Feeler — 8 years old

Oldest son — ENTP is a dominant Intuitor — 16 years old

Middle son — ENTJ is a dominant Thinker — 14 years old

Dad plays the role of establishing rules, assigning chores, and correcting behavior. A child who breaks the rules is a "bad" child. Dad uses rule-compliance as one of his principal measures of worth. He overuses his Sensor quadrant to focus on constraints as his major role. When he checks his next favorite quadrant, his Thinker reinforces that role by reminding him of the consequences of undisciplined children. Thus, Dad is the critic who enforces constraints. When his oldest son asked to go to the beach with several of his friends for the weekend, Dad immediately said "No." When questioned he replied, "It will cost too much. You have to do the lawn this weekend. You don't have a car and you have no business going off with a bunch of kids without adult supervision."

The sixteen-year-old ENTP easily applied his Intuitor quadrant to supply Dad with possibilities. He argued, "I have the money in my savings account. I can do the lawn Thursday evening after school. Danny's folks are letting him take his car and Danny's aunt and uncle live in Galveston. We could always call them if we need anything."

Dad responded, "You will not touch that savings account. It is for college. I don't want the lawn done on Thursday. I want it done on Saturday so we don't get out of cycle."

The ENTJ middle son joined the fray. "Dad, I can do the lawn on Saturday. I'm sure I can get my brother to do something for me in return."

Dad shouted, "You aren't going. I don't need you two to tell me what is right and wrong about this. You know that you are not allowed to take money out of your savings. You just said that to make me angry. Don't try ganging up on me. Both of you go to your room!"

The INFP daughter was so upset about the argument that she started to cry. She went to her mother and said, "I have $8.92 that I could give so he could go. He really wants to go. His friends are going. I could help mow the grass Saturday. I will be really good so Daddy's not upset. Please, Mom, help us."

Mom was torn between the various positions. Her Feeler nature wanted harmony more than anything, but her Sensor backup reminded her that rules were rules, and Dad in the role of Dad had the right to make decisions for the kids. She went to her husband to talk to him, but he was adamant. When she realized that she could not change his mind, she went to the kitchen and fixed a tray of chips and dip, opened two Cokes and headed for the boys' room. If she couldn't change the decision, she would at least nurture and try to calm. After she visited the boys, she went back to the kitchen. She made two cups of coffee and sought her husband.

The little INFP daughter picked up her kitten and tried to think of what she could do to keep everyone from being upset.

Let's review the interaction.

SENSOR (Dad, ISTJ)
"I make the rules."
"It takes money."
"You have a weekend chore."
"You'll have no supervision."

"You don't have a car."

INTUITOR (Son, ENTP)
"I see an opportunity."
"I would rather do the lawn
than clean the garage."

FEELER (Mother, ESFJ)
"I want them to be happy."
"I accept the roles."
"I'll nurture them all."

THINKER (Son, ENTJ)
"I'll find a way."
"I have a savings account."
"I can do it Thursday evening."
"Danny's aunt and uncle will
be there."
"Danny has a car."

FEELER (Daughter, INFP)
"It's my fault that I can't
find a way to help everyone
get what they want."

Each family member perceived the situation from his or her dominant quadrant with unconscious forces influencing the way they see and react to the situation. Clear perception and fair judgment is difficult.

CASE STUDY: INTERPRETATION CONFLICT

Sensors are accused of being so literal in their interpretation of regulations and contracts that they become overwhelmed by "administrivia" while losing sight of the intent behind the "law." Intuitors are accused of being so figurative that they ignore content while liberally interpreting intent. Thinkers are accused of focusing so keenly on being intellectually competent that they ignore the feeling imprint. Feelers are accused of being so compelled by the information imprint on feelings that they misrepresent consequences of allowing individual exception.

A construction company was awarded the bid on a large government project. The company is wholly owned by the officers and managers of the company. They operate on a strong sense of personal values that provide the foundation for the way they do business. They insist on scrupulous honesty, integrity, legality, and responsibility. They have been in business for thirty-five years and feel that they have the track record to make them one of the most respected construction companies in the country.

As they began work, one of their subcontractors bid the job

to erect the steel. Both the prime contractor and the sub discussed the interepretation of the Buy America Act. The subcontractor purchased the steel in raw lengths in Belgium and had an American company build the tube casings that were specifically needed in the buildings. The prime and the subcontractor read the Buy America Act and noted carefully that the act said foreign steel could be purchased if over 51% of its actual molded form were prepared by an American company. They were sure that the American company would provide the quality assurance to meet the intent of the Buy America Act.

The subcontractor spent over $1 million buying Belgian steel and having it delivered to the American company for molding into the specific materials required by the contract. Since steel erection comes early in a construction project, the subcontractor submitted a payment request to the prime contractor for the steel that was already being erected. The government agency who was administering the construction contract objected to the Belgian steel and refused to make payment.

SENSOR (Facts)	THINKER (Analysis)
Govt. Contract Payment Division Perspective:	
• Belgian steel	• Out of compliance
• Must be American steel	• Out of compliance
• Won't pay	• Can't pay for noncompliance
Prime Project Manager Perspective:	
• Over 51% of constructed steel pieces were tooled in America;	therefore, we are in compliance.
• Your Quality Assurance man was on site watching us for the 23 days of steel erection he saw our steel;	therefore, he approved it.
• The American company who prepared the Belgian steel gave us manufacturing process documents that demonstrate quality;	therefore, we have proof.

Interpretation

The government contract payment division took a determined stand that they would not pay for Belgian steel. The prime and subcontractors believed they had proof that they were in compliance. Both sides became angry and embattled.

INTUITOR (Alternatives)	FEELER (Values/relationships)
• Each side froze its thinking and refused to consider alternative positions.	• Each side believed its basic integrity was being challenged and showed righteous indignation.
• Each one sought new ways to prove the stupidity of the other's position.	• Govt. rep. was incensed at being expected to "break the law" while the contractors were incensed at being treated like cheaters.

The government reps were STJs (Sensor, Thinker, Judges) who examined the facts, made a judgment, and closed the window of perception to look at alternative data. The contractor reps were NTJs (Intuitor, Thinker, Judges) who interpreted the Buy America Act, honored the intent, and closed their window of perception to make their judgment that they were in compliance.

Both groups were personally impacted and their feelings were activated. The government reps showed behavioral evidence of emotionality as one of them cried, "It is our job to protect the public trust. You cannot expect us to break the law." The government interpretation had now taken on the awesome solemnity of the moral high ground of the "public trust" as he expressed his astonishment that he should be asked to engage in a criminal activity.

The prime and subcontractor spokesmen were also angry at having their motives maligned. The project manager for the prime contractor retorted, "We have thirty-five years of integrity to stand upon and never have we been accused of asking anyone to break the law. The only thing we ask is a little common sense and fairness. We have always supported the Buy America Act. After all, it is our reputation that will suffer if we do not put quality into these buildings. We have the most to lose here. Don't act as if we have nothing at stake."

At that point in the relationship breakdown, as facilitators, we asked each side to go to a flip chart and outline their rationale using the Sensor and Thinker quadrants. As each group began to outline its position, calm gradually returned. Each side was then asked to identify what messages the other side received that may have been hurtful. They were asked to identify the "put-downs" in both of the positions. As they moved into the Feeler fourth quadrant of the problem-solving process, most of the group began to see why the argument had become so intense. The personal worth and professional integrity of both sides had come under attack.

The resolution of the issue came when the top decision-makers of each of the quarreling organizations went into the next room to fill out the third quadrant of the problem-solving process. They reached agreement by reestablishing each side's primary motive: government wanted a quality project that was in compliance with rules and regulations, the contractors wanted to retain their justifiable reputation of top-quality construction, and the subcontractors wanted payment for work performed. They found a way to get the situation settled, through quality guarantees and tests. The matter was settled within ten days.

JUDGE-PERCEIVER CHARACTERISTICS

Anyone with a Judge-controller preference for dealing with the world wants to organize, order, and drive toward closure. Judges tend to use their Perceiver functions of Sensing/Intuiting until they make a decision. They then tend to reduce their perception of new or changing circumstances and focus their attention on carrying out their ideas of what needs to be done. The vulnerability of becoming too dependent on completion is the failure to take in new and important circumstances. Judges like to decide about people, situations, and happenings without waiting too long to gather information. Waiting for information in order to act is stressful for Judges.

Perceiver-adapter preference for acquiring more information, working in flexible ways, and managing emerging problems drives them to trying to keep their options open. Perceivers tend to use their perceiver functions of Sensing/Intuiting while delaying movement into their judging-deciding mode. Perceivers tend to have more tolerance for complexity and delay than Judges. As curious explorers of information and circumstance, Perceivers love spontaneity, surprises, and unexpected happenings.

Review the natural characteristics in their positive expression and compare the troublesome possibilities that can occur if perception and judgment are not kept somewhat balanced.

Perceiver-Adapter

POSITIVE POSSIBILITIES | TROUBLESOME POSSIBILITIES

Planning, Doing, and Adapting

POSITIVE POSSIBILITIES	TROUBLESOME POSSIBILITIES
Let things happen	Can be so adaptable that others are unclear about what is intended
Open to possibility	May gather too much information in order to delay or avoid making a decision or commitment
Curious	May get sidetracked due to more interesting stimuli
Flexible	May be too flexible and get pulled in too many directions — tend to get irritable when overscheduled and have too many time-demands
Open-minded	May be too tolerant and let issues or problems go too long
Responsive	May habitually procrastinate to get the exhilirating last-minute high

Time

Adaptable	May plan so loosely as to be disorganized — others don't know to act
Spontaneous	May be so spontaneous that others do not take Perceiver seriously
Facilitator/Supporter	May be so open to change priorities that too many things get shoved aside
Adaptable to Change	May have too many projects of lost interest with things stacking up
Unhurried	May let deadlines pass or change

Judge-Controller

POSITIVE POSSIBILITIES | TROUBLESOME POSSIBILITIES

Planning, Doing, and Controlling

POSITIVE POSSIBILITIES	TROUBLESOME POSSIBILITIES
Plans and schedules	May plan too tightly . . . May be so attached to plans and schedule that changing priorities may not be considered . . . May be too locked in
Plans ahead and prepares	May get irritable or agitated when not given time to plan ahead

Controls events	May be so controlling that others feel dominated and stifled
Orders and organizes	May be too rigid about *how* to do something, insisting on the plan
Decisive	May be close-minded about other suggestions once decision is set

Time

Controls time/Fights time	Intensely dislikes wasting time . . . May forget to relax . . . has trouble not working
Maximizes time	Perpetually hurrying . . . trying to achieve as much as possible in a short amount of time
Prioritizes	Tends to let watch, calendar, and plan kill any spontaneity — rigid and stubborn
Completes work	Intense drive to finish things can result in tunnelvision . . . excluding everything but finishing the project
Goal-oriented	May get unreasonably anxious when schedule bogs down and gets behind

CASE STUDY: GROUP DYNAMICS OF JUDGES AND PERCEIVERS

Judge-controllers usually walk into meetings demonstrating a need or desire to reach conclusions and get the meeting wrapped up. This urgent behavior is frequently seen through words and body language that show Judges' determination to close discussion, reach agreements, and get on with business. Judges seem to have an inner time clock which tells them when enough is enough. Whether they consciously estimate the "appropriate" amount of time they are willing to spend on the topic, or they just unconsciously have a sense of their version of "appropriate" timing, the inner alarm sounds. They start to show signs of impatience. They may disengage eye contact, move their chairs back, close the notepad, put their pen away, or other closing type of behavior.

The Perceiver-adapters are internally wired to challenge perceptions and hold out for additional options. Perceivers, therefore, show behavioral evidence of impatience if the subject is closed too quickly. At meetings they frequently demonstrate their need or desire to review the group conclusion one more time or reopen discussion for more options. Just when the Judges are ready to disengage, Perceivers reopen discussion as they challenge the conclusion in order to assure themselves that all cogent options are given adequate consideration.

Fifteen health care professionals came together to develop a five-year plan for their particular speciality. They had four days to develop a vision, identify goals, develop objectives, identify an action plan, organize regional infrastructures, and identify benchmarks and time frames. The scope of work was ambitious and required hard work and sustained focus.

Midafternoon on the first day, group dynamics were already strained. The senior professional and funder of the meeting had already irritated the group three times with her reopening behavior. She scores as an INTP (Introvert, Intuitor, Thinker, Perceiver). The group contained twelve Judge-controllers and three Perceiver-adapters. It was my job as consultant to facilitate group process, draw out best thinking, and provide enough focused group process to help them accomplish the scope of work.

Three times the group engaged in vigorous and lively discussion and was ready to reach closure on the topic. Just as I was writing the group agreement on the flip chart, the INTP said, "Wait a minute. I'm not sure we looked at this from all angles." She then raised several additional issues. The second time the group was moving to closure, I recorded their conclusion and was preparing to put it on the wall, when she said, "I'm not comfortable with this. We didn't consider . . ." Previously the group had carefully veiled its annoyance, but this time they did not do so. They showed nonverbal annoyance that she had again stopped them from moving to closure. Some members exchanged glances, others rolled their eyes, while two members pushed their chairs back from the table abruptly and moved quickly to get cups of coffee.

As the INTP voiced her concerns and insisted on more discussion, the group maintained silence and continued its nonverbal irritation messages. Finally, one of the members who is particularly politically savvy offered additional thoughts, effectively reopening discussion.

As an Introvert, the senior professional was not always articulate about what options she wanted to explore, so most often her opening comments sounded like criticism of their work. She would begin by saying, "I'm not sure this is the best we can do. We may just be too tired to come up with a more creative way to do this, but we should at least try. I'm not sure we've really given this enough consideration."

The third time the INTP prevented closure, the majority of the group felt confirmed in their irritation with her and one of the more extroverted members said, "Oh, no! Here we go again." When one person voiced the irritation, several of the others became more open in their annoyance. Some of the irritation came out in a tone of condescension, exaggerated patience while they made her understand, and an override of her queries or perceptions, with an exchange of knowing looks and subtle smiles when she was not looking at them.

Rather than let group openness and camaraderie dissolve, we did a group process check where we discussed behaviors of personal style and various needs, desires, or preferences. We discussed the topics of group dynamics, work, closure, and agreement. We talked about the impatience cues of Judges and Perceivers. We talked openly about how to process the vital messages in the group so the process could remain focused and energetic.

The following day I observed several instances where the INTP started to stop group closure and then decided not to do so. She told me that she started asking herself if her desire for more discussion was truly in the interest of a superior product or just indulgence in her preference. She became more aware of how to distinguish between the two.

Judges agreed to discipline their impatience to get discussions over by assessing their own motives also. They agreed to try the questions: "Am I just bored and impatient? Is this really the best answer? Am I just settling for any answer in order to get to closure? Have we fully explored options to reach the highest quality?" The Perceivers agreed to discipline their natural inclination to keep options open by asking themselves some questions. "Am I just indulging in my desire to consider something else? Is this conclusion really going to meet the test of high quality? Can I really think of a serious consideration we have overlooked?"

The group completed its ambitious scope of work and were working with a sense of understanding, liking, and teamwork.

BALANCING JUDGING AND PERCEIVING

Judge-controllers may appear too exacting and stubborn, while Perceiver-adapters may appear too tentative and undecided. Balance between one's judging and perceiving preference, however, is essential to adequately utilize the four-quadrant problem-solving process.

We receive manipulative messages continually. We try to persuade others to see things from our perspective. We barter and bargain for agreement. We persuade and argue.

Leaders must see through fogging techniques, sense manipulative traps, intuit possibilities and strategies, analyze situations, and feel the important values that are driving the process.

DEVELOPMENTAL EXERCISES

Exercise 64:   Strategy for Communication with a Judge

Identify someone in your management group that you believe is a Judge-controller. *Option 1:*   Develop a strategy for persuading the Judge to agree to your proposal to buy a new computer program that will help you process your work more efficiently. *Option 2:*   Develop a strategy for persuading the Judge to agree to give you permission for something that you really want to do.

Recommended Strategic Format:

1. Present your information in decision format. Tell the Judge that you are going to outline what you want to do (your decision) and quickly describe the alternatives you considered, followed by the evidence and reasoning used in your decision.
   A. Lead with your decision.
   B. Be sure to use facts, logic, alternatives, and values.
   C. Demonstrate that you are planning ahead by demonstrating your plan for contingencies — your "What if" plan. Appeal to the Judge's desire to have no surprises.
   D. Set clear parameters (When, What, Why, Where, How).
   F. Set priorities, milestones, and success indicators so the Judge can readily recognize task achievement and closure.

2. Develop your strategy:
   A. Decision.

   B. Supporting facts, logic, alternatives and values.

   C. Contingency Plan. (What if . . . then . . .)

   D. Set the parameters. (When, Where, Who, How, Why, How Much)

   E. Identify priorities, milestones, and success indicators.
   Priorities (It is most important to . . .)

   Milestones (Signficant phases will be accomplished when . . .)

   Success Indicators (You'll know I am succeeding when . . .)

   F. Completion. (You'll know I did it when . . .)

Exercise 65:   Strategy for Communicating with a Perceiver

Identify someone in your management group that you believe is a Perceiver-adapter. *Option 1:* Develop a strategy for persuading the Perceiver to agree to your proposal to buy a new computer program that will help you process your work more efficiently. *Option 2:* Develop a strategy for persuading the Perceiver to agree to give you permission for something that you really want to do.

Recommended Strategic Format:

1. Present your points in information format — not persuasive format. (Perceivers tend to resent demanding people; therefore, use an informative rather than a persuasive forceful approach.)

    A. Present your *request.*

    B. Present information with several options.

    C. Don't plan too rigidly, since the Perceiver will want to have input into arranging the information.

    D. Identify the large pieces, elements, or aspects of your proposal. Perceivers like to control only the large pieces and usually do not care to control the small stuff.

    E. Present ample information, but identify the pieces that will need Perceiver input or decision.

    F. Be prepared for the Perceiver to ask for time to think it over and get back to you. Ask for a specific date to get back together if this delay occurs.

2. Develop your strategy:

    A. Your request.

    B. Present your request with several options.

    C. Don't plan a rigid presentation. Seek Perceiver input and discussion. Consider using drawing out and probing skills to stimulate interaction ("What are your thoughts on this?").

    D. Identify the major pieces, elements, or aspects of the issue.

    E. Present ample information and identify the pieces on which you particularly want Perceiver input.

    F. Summarize your understanding and ask for closure. Be prepared to ask for or to set a decision date.

Exercise 66: Identifying Judge and Perceiver Clues

Improving observation skills allows you to more accurately assess the type of person with whom you are interacting. The way people word things is as important as the words selected. Practice your skills by identifying the following sentences as being typical Judge or Perceiver sentences. In the blank put "J" for Judge or "P" for Perceiver.

1._____"Let's keep our options open."

2._____"Let's get on with it."

3._____"This will save time."

4._____"I'll be glad when this is finished."

5._____"Well, we'll just have to see."

6._____"Well done! You moved right in and took care of it. Now it's finished."

7._____"In the interest of time, let's push on and finish it."

8._____"Ask me again later. It's too early to tell."

9._____"If we don't find something better, I guess we could do it."

10._____"That's done! I won't have to think about it anymore."

11._____"Why don't we think it over and get back together later?"

12._____"No use back-tracking. We'll swing by and pick it up on the way."

Remember: Perceivers like spontaneity, flexibility, variety, curiosity, and options. Judges like efficiency, control, order, schedule, and closure.

Answers: 1. P 2. J 3. J 4. J 5. P 6. J 7. J 8. P 9. P 10. J 11. P 12. J

Exercise 67:   Developing Perception

"For all persons who characteristically live in the Judging attitude, perception tends to be shut off as soon as they have observed enough to make a decision. (In contrast, persons who prefer the Perceptive attitude will often suspend judgment to take another look, reporting 'We don't know enough yet to make a decision.'" (Myers and McCaulley, pg. 14)

Judges need to practice accurate listening. Listen to someone and consciously discipline yourself to continue taking in information without judging what you are hearing. Practice suspending judgment in order to keep your perceptual window open to more information.

1. Engage someone in conversation. Set a goal to suspend judgment for ten minutes while you listen and interact. See if you can stay in the information intake mode for at least ten minutes.

2. Describe your Judge tendency to shut out new information to reach judgment and shut down your intake mode. Describe the process.

3. Engage in conversation again. This time attempt to suspend judgment for 20 minutes.

4. Summarize what you did to keep your perceptual information intake window open.

Exercise 68: Judges and Spontaneity

Judge-controllers can be described as purposeful, decisive, exacting, stubborn, determined, outcome-oriented, deadline-driven, and wanting to finish things.

The following statements from Judge-controllers will give you a clear framework for reviewing Judges' desire to plan and order things.

"Planning is survival, a necessity, stressful without it."

"Planning is a security."

"You are only as good as your filing system."

"Good planning inspires and encourages me."

"Good planning gives direction and then with good planning I can work on flexibility."

Exercise: Judges have to learn spontaneity. This exercise will ask you to plan to be spontaneous. If it sounds paradoxical, just reread the Judges' own words in the five statements.

Judges, try to mark off a weekend on your calendar for doing spontaneously whatever you want to do. Plan not to work. Plan to be spontaneous. Catch yourself every time you think ahead to what you might do with that weekend. See if you can experience the entire weekend without planning ahead. Watch to see what happens to your energy.

1. What is your response to the unplanned time? Watch your thoughts, feelings, and impulses to see how strongly you are accustomed to planning ahead.

2. Does your tolerance for spontaneity vary? Is it different at the start of the weekend, in the middle, at the end?

3. Did you have any frustration about not getting a lot of tasks accomplished during the weekend? Watch to see how attached you are to measuring your weekend against an achievement list of getting a number of things finished or organized.

4. How much of your identity is wrapped around work accomplishment?

5. How much of your feelings of satisfaction are related to accomplishing tasks?

6. Are you an "either-or" Judge, who either works hard or does nothing equally as hard? Can you float through a weekend?

Exercise 69: Perceiver Avoidance

Perceivers can be described as flexible, adaptable, pending, emergent, tentative, open to options, and process-oriented.

The following statements from Perceiver-adapters will give you a clear framework for reviewing Perceivers' desire to keep options open.

"I hate having to get tickets for something ahead of time."

"I don't like to agree to something too far in the future. When I do it begins to nag at me and make me feel committed. I may back out at the last minute. I just don't like to make plans too far ahead."

"I do general planning . . . not detailed plans."

"If you control time by planning tasks, then you don't have to watch the clock."

"I don't like to decide until I have to do so."

Exercise: Perceivers, think of three partially done tasks that you have started. Reconstruct what happened that caused you to set them aside. Examine the kinds of tasks or events that took priority. Identify your impulse patterns that tend to pull you away from tasks and start you on new ones.

Now, set a time in two hours from the time you make the decision to start this exercise. Decide on three unfinished tasks to finish during the time allotted. Allow nothing to interrupt your finishing them. See what happens.

1. Does the idea of deciding to finish three tasks and committing to yourself to begin the work in two hours feel irritating?

2. Will you readily remember that you committed to begin work on those specific tasks exactly two hours from the time of your decision? Is it possible that you may "accidentally" get involved in something else and forget your com-

mitment, thus giving in to your natural propensity for getting involved in something more interesting?

Exercise 70:   Perceiver Time Commitment

Our research indicates that Perceivers have to manage their reluctance to make specific time commitments. If you have already disciplined this urge, you may want to skip this exercise.

Perceiver, think about your reluctance to make specific commitments on small, everyday type things. Confront this reluctance. Select some task that you really do not want to do. Set a time and date to do the task. Set the date four or five days ahead.

1. Note the thoughts you have about setting the task date.

2. Note the feelings that are lightly stirred about the task and the date. As the time draws nearer, pay close attention to the subtle thoughts and feelings that creep into your consciousness.

3. Actually do the task at the set time and date.

4. Pay attention to the subtle ways you have of getting out of it or rearranging how you do the task.

Key: Get in touch with the many ways you rearrange information and priorities to allow yourself to do something more interesting.

Exercise 71:   Perceiver Postponement

Perceivers tend to let issues go on too long without confronting them. Check to see if you have been postponing confronting some issues, telling yourself that they are going to change, go away, or get better.

People I need to confront . . .

Personal habits I need to change . . .

Unpleasant tasks I need to do . . .

Decisions I need to make . . .

Exercise 72:   Four-Quadrant Problem-Solving

Select a problem for which you need to do thorough thinking. Use the four quadrants to prepare your thoughts and feelings.

PROBLEM _____

SENSOR (Facts) The Happenings?	THINKER (Analysis) The Consequences?
What are the facts, numbers regulations, norms, obligations?	What are the causes? What are the effects?
What does it take to get the job done?	What is fair, reasonable, and defensible?

INTUITOR (Alternatives)
The Possibilities?

FEELER (Values/Relationships)
The Importance?

What are the overall impacts,
patterns, themes, and
possibilities?

How important is this to me?

How important is this to others?

What can we do that has
never been done before?

Who will be upset by this?

How can we position for
the future?

How can people get committed
to this . . . or to "buy-in"?

Exercise 73: Perceiver Troublesome Possibilities

If you are a Perceiver or if you are working on a development plan for a Perceiver, use the following checklist to identify those areas that need more development of Judge-controller skills.

1. Put a checkmark by the areas of troublesome possibilities that need work.

    _____So adaptable that others have trouble knowing what is intended.

_____Postpones decisions so long that others are negatively impacted.

_____Gets easily sidetracked from task on hand.

_____Gets too many things going and gets pulled in too many directions.

_____Habitually procrastinates and waits to the last minute.

_____Frequently stressed about other people setting deadlines for the Perceiver.

_____Seems so spontaneous that others may not take Perceiver seriously . . . hard to read what is really important.

_____Has too many unfinished projects due to losing interest.

_____Tends to get rebellious when too many time demands are made.

_____Tends to gets rebellious against being controlled.

_____Difficult to get a clear commitment to take on responsibility.

_____Demands too much freedom in efforts to avoid entanglement.

_____So spontaneous that may be inefficient due to lack of planning.

2. Set specific development objectives in each of the following Judge-controlling areas:

A. Finishing things

B. Ordering and organizing

C. Deciding

D. Scheduling specific times and meeting the schedule

E. Planning and preparing ahead of time

Key: Perceiver has natural characteristics of adaptability, flexibility, responsiveness, spontaneity, and openness to changing interests. Finding a balance point between the natural characteristics and reasonable use of controlling, deciding, ordering, organizing, scheduling, and planning ahead is the goal.

Exercise 74: Judge Troublesome Possibilities

If you are a Judge-controller or if you are working on a development plan for a Judge, use the following checklist to identify those areas that need more development of Perceiver-adapter skills.

1. Put a checkmark by the areas of troublesome possibilities that need work.

   _____So controlling that others tend to feel dominated and stifled.

   _____So attached to own plans and schedule that refuses to change priorities even when it is advisable . . . too locked into own schedule.

   _____Gets unreasonably irritable or anxious when schedule bogs down.

   _____Is too rigid about how to do something – thinks own way is best.

_____Tends to become close-minded about other sugges-
tions, once Judge reaches own decision.

_____Tends to finish things that are no longer important,
just to indulge the satisfaction of finishing things.

_____Tends to like to work own list of things to do without
much regard for incoming changing priorities.

_____Tends to be driven by time, continually fighting to
control it, maximize it, or trying to achieve as much
as possible in as little time as possible . . . perpetually
hurrying.

_____Often lets watch, calendar, and pre-plan kill sponta-
neity, resulting in stubbornness and rigidity.

_____Can get so intent on finishing something, on not
wasting time, that may exude so much tension that
others find the Judge difficult to be around.

2. Set specific development objectives in each of the following Perceiver-adapter areas:

A. Adaptable to changing priorities

B. Flexible about ways to accomplish work

C. Spontaneous without preplanning

D. Open-minded about something you had already decided — willing to think about it again in a different way

E. Responsive to incoming stimuli

Key: Judge-controllers have natural characteristics of controlling, deciding, ordering, organizing, scheduling, and planning ahead. The goal is to develop Perceiver skills of adaptability, flexibility, responsiveness, spontaneity, and openness to changing interests. Finding a balance point between the natural and the learned is the goal.

Exercise 75:   Balancing Judging and Perceiving

Write an objective for each of the following opposing characteristics that would help you achieve a more balanced use of both your natural and your learned skills. Your objective should be a clear statement of the ideal state if you achieved balanced capability to use both judgment and perception required for your leadership style.

JUDGE-CONTROLLING   PERCEIVER-ADAPTING

Closure _____ Open to options
Objective:

Settled _____ Pending
Objective:

Decided/Fixed _____ Undecided/ Flexible
Objective:

Plan ahead_____Adapt as you go
Objective:

Deciding/Judging _____ Tentative/Perceiving
Objective:

Completed _____ Emergent
Objective:

Hurrying/Time urgency_____Unhurried/Little time urgency
Objective:

Outcome-oriented _____ Process-oriented
Objective:

Deadline-driven _____ Changing opportunities
Objective:

– 7 –

Change

1. Effective change requires leadership that involves:
   A. Vision
   B. Clear perception
   C. Sound judgment
   D. Energized focus
2. Effective change involves process thinking instead of status quo, linear thinking, or task-specific thinking.
3. Process thinking requires continuous assimilation of units of experience, incidents, and situations to clearly perceive current reality and future impact.
4. Targets of change are people, organizational systems, procedures, structure, and culture.
5. Barr and Barr make fifteen assumptions about change.
6. Organizational changes go through predictable phases.
7. Partnership is a growing movement.

351

8. Case studies of individuals, companies, and organizations going through change demonstrate strategies and challenges of the process.

CHANGE AND LEADERSHIP

How nice it would be if one bolt from a magic change wand could turn turkeys into eagles, could change obsolete procedures into common sense approaches, could turn troublesome asses into team players, and could change rigid bureaucracy without resistance!

A magic change wand would be priceless, but we would miss all of the growth opportunities that accompany the tumultuous uncertainty of change. Fortunately, change is a dynamic process that usually occurs over time. The leaders of the best-run companies and organizations embrace change with an attitude of enthusiastic opportunity for visionary change toward a desirable future state rather than forced change into a hasty reactionary state.

Today's fast-paced changes must be met with leaders who are process managers who can stay focused on products while seeing clearly the processes needed for continuous improvement and customer responsiveness. Peter F. Drucker argues that managers' inability to change their attitudes and behavior as rapidly as change requires is the major obstacle to organizational growth.

We find that it is fairly easy to recognize change after it has occurred, but it is more difficult to analyze, interpret, predict, and understand what is needed during the change. Leaders vigorously question what they see and perpetually think in terms of finding a better way. To guide or influence change while it is under way is challenging.

Ask yourself these questions: "How many things have changed around me that I have not noticed?" "How many out-of-date assumptions am I using in today's decisions?" "How many rules, norms, and traditions do I use that are no longer relevant?"

Roger von Oech's excellent book entitled *A Whack on the Side of the Head* addresses the need to challenge rules and question their current applicability. He explains how Sholes and Co. in the 1870s solved a problem that still affects us today. Sholes was a leading manufacturer of typewriters. In response to the complaint that the keys stuck together if the typist went too fast, the engineers' solution was to identify which fingers have the least dexterity and to place the often used vowels in the weaker position on the keyboard. The 1870 solution is still in effect today, even though we no longer have the same machines. Today our most sophisticated computers use the same alphabet configuration. Oech points out:

Premise: Rules are based on solution to a problem.
Premise: People follow established rules.
Premise: Time passes; things change.

Conclusion: The original problem may no longer exist, but the rule lives on as an absolute.

CONCEPTS OF CHANGE

Our approach to change involves the concepts of leadership, process, the human system, teamwork, organizational systems, structure, and culture. Defining these concepts gives us a framework for discussing change.

LEADERSHIP is the process of influencing people to give their energies, use their potential, release their determination, and go beyond their comfort zones to accomplish goals. Leadership is a dynamic process. It affects, risks, drives, inspires, threatens, supports, and leads. Leadership draws trust, acknowledgment, risk, and loyalty from the led.

PROCESS is the dynamic interrelatedness of occurrences (situations, thoughts, feelings, actions, people relationships, market changes) that form linkages and impacts. The leader with process awareness quickly integrates a mass of information, drawing together meaningful relatedness of facts and occurrences. The leader sees coherent meaning by making connections in what may look like unrelated or quite disparate data.

TEAMWORK is mutually trusting people working together for organizational achievement, sharing a unifying set of values and goals while communicating candidly, caringly, and openly.

HUMAN SYSTEM is the dynamic interrelationships of thoughts, feelings, fears, and behaviors of the human system.

ORGANIZATIONAL SYSTEMS are the business systems that support the legal and information needs of an organization. Primary systems are accounting, auditing, financial, legal, personnel, and information management.

ORGANIZATIONAL STRUCTURE refers to the formal way authority is disbursed to managers of divisions, departments, or units. Structure includes the division of work, interrelatedness, formal power distribution, and resource allocation.

ORGANIZATIONAL CULTURE refers to the habitual and traditional ways of thinking, feeling, and reacting that are characteristic of the ways an organization meets its problems and achieves its objectives — in short, the way it does business.

Change strategies then involve the following:

Leadership — provides the energetic focus and vision.

Process — provides the meaning of occurrences that reveals linkages and impacts.

Teamwork — a leadership strategy for focusing energy and achieving synergistic action.

People's behaviors — their thoughts, feelings, fears, and actions involved in the process.

Organizational system — the business systems that provide stability, accountability, and legality.

Organizational structures — the ways that resources and authority are distributed.

Organizational culture — the way people think, feel, and act as they do business.

Change leaders use clear perception and sound judgment in recognizing and communicating process while leading people to change. Leaders are likely to rely heavily on a teamwork strategy to bring about needed changes in people, organizational systems, structures, and cultures. Although Chapter 8 deals with process and teamwork, both concepts are vital to successful organizational change.

Leadership

through

Managing Process and Teamwork

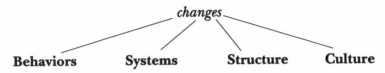

changes

Behaviors   **Systems**   **Structure**   **Culture**

THE NATURE OF CHANGE

Change is power redistribution. Some people are threatened by it, others are apathetic toward it, and others are thrilled by the opportunities. *Change is about getting, losing, increasing, and redistributing power.* Power is defined as the potential to influence. Formal power is called authority, which means legitimized, attributed power to command — commonly called "position power." Informal power is the ability to influence and set standards with or without position power — commonly called "personal power." Change is redistributing power through shifting people, systems, structures, and cultures.

Change is about letting go . . . letting go of the old and embracing the new.

Since change is alteration, replacement, variation from the norm or the familiar, change represents something different from the status quo.

STATUS QUO (the existing state)	FUTURE STATE (the changed state)
Predictable	Unpredictable
Familiar	Unfamiliar
Known	Unknown
Within comfort zone	Outside of comfort zone

Resistance to change is frequently fueled by fear of the unknown. The knowns are more tolerable than the unknowns. One man said, "My boss is an asshole, but at least he is a predictable asshole. He doesn't pull surprise punches." Some anxiety is reduced by knowing what to expect, even if it is not pleasant. Unknowns represent the possibility of loss and powerlessness, involving ambiguity, risk, and possible power struggles. The status quo means that seven vital elements are usually known.

KNOWNS IN THE STATUS QUO

1. Power Relationships (Who controls what)
2. Status (Where each one fits)
3. Values (What is important — what gets rewarded or punished)
4. Resource Distribution (Who has what)
5. Territory (Who owns what turf)
6. Roles (Who does what)
7. Norms (What is acceptable — what is expected)

Resistance is frequently due to *fear* of the consequences of change and the effect on the important seven vital elements. The fundamental perspective is: "HOW DOES THIS AFFECT ME?"

Many people fear that change means losing resources such as money, supplies, contacts, authority, privileges, information, or access to important others. They may fear a threat to their perceived territory and see change as competition, usurpation, or abolition. They may fear losing authority and control. They may fear losing expertise and competence as they wonder if their specialities will still be needed or valued as the change progresses. They may fear ambiguity of changing rules, reward and punishment systems, evaluation systems, new values, new relationships, new standards. They may fear inadequacy in the face of altering demands. They may fear reduced self-esteem and importance.

The natural order of the world involves change; therefore, the only possible stability is stability in motion. If an individual could accept the idea of change as a natural process, some of the anxiety associated with change might be reduced. Behavioral change can be facilitated through a reification of attitude toward change.

"Mind-forged manacles" referred to by John W. Gardner are perceptual manacles to restrain change. Why do people often resist change? Fears of powerlessness, losing, ambiguity, and inadequacy fuel resistance.

The status quo is powerful. Familiarity seems to reduce risk by giving one a feeling of "knowing what to expect." Within a state of equilibrium the "knowns" provide a comfort zone of predictability. When a rumor of change occurs, the rumor can serve as a "red alert" that marshals energy toward defending and maintaining the system as it is.

A person perceiving change as threatening uses a negative frame, thus focuses energy to defend and resist change rather than evaluate possible benefits. Changing conditions over which the person perceives s/he has no control tend to increase the stress and pain.

FIFTEEN CHANGE ASSUMPTIONS

From our experience we make the following assumptions about change:

1. Change is redistribution of power.

   Key: Identify the *major Stakeholders* who are likely to throw the force of their influence into supporting the status quo. Identify the major Stakeholders who are likely to help lead the change.

2. Change frequently involves chaos and stress that arouse *self-worth anxieties and fear.*

   Key: Watch actions, messages, and explanations about the change that hold potentially *damaging self-esteem messages.*

3. Most people have low tolerance for change, particularly if they are not instigating it.

   Key: Expect people to be concerned about change and explain the changes, be visible and accessible, and *communicate-communicate-communicate.*

4. Opinion setters are essential to provide focus, clarity, and realistic optimism since people experience emotional turmoil during change processes due to uncertainty, interruption, and potential loss of status.

   Key: Identify *opinion setters* throughout the organization and organize them to inform and stay informed.

5. Resistance to change is greater when people believe that the change is not in their best interest nor the organization's.

Key: *Communicate from the people perspective* rather than starting with the organization's perspective. First connect with their interests and concerns, then explain the organizational perspective.

6. People prefer to construct reality out of stability and predictability; when too much uncertainty is present they resort to social reality by comparing perceptions with others and observing accepted social response of important others.

Key: Identify the opinion setters to whom people are likely to turn to compare and check their perceptions. *Inform, include, and seek commitment from the opinion setters.*

7. Change may be so gradual that people do not notice.

Key: Develop your information strategy if you want people to recognize and assist with the change efforts. Establish *observable indicators of the desirable change* and urge opinion setters to communicate the forward movement and the challenges.

8. Most people do not have well-developed behavior observation skills.

Key: Early *training in behavior observation* is critical for opinion setters and team members.

9. Most people have to learn to read patterns and link occurrences to derive understanding of change.

Key: Early *training in process and intuitive assimilation* is essential for opinion setters and team members.

10. Commitment is withheld without true active Stakeholder involvement in formulation of change strategies and implementation.

Key: People feel more committed to that which they helped formulate and implement; thus, *early involvement of Stakeholders provides more opportunity for developing Stakeholder commitment.*

11. "The divine right of kings or managers no longer exists." Robert E. Kelley

Key: People tend to resist traditional authoritarian role behaviors as they demand more information, more inclusion, and more explanation.

12. A better educated work force expects management to explain its decision rationale.

   Key: As more people are trained to analyze, question, and evaluate evidence, their resentment increases for anyone who is unwilling to submit his/her reasoning for discussion and review.

13. Innovation requires perpetual reframing and refocusing.

   Key: Looking at today through yesterday's glasses won't yield insights nor identify improvement possibilities. Finding a different way to think about things is basic to innovation and change. *Clear leadership requires reframing and refocusing changing conditions and innovative solutions.*

14. During the discomfort of change, people tend to want to return to the old pattern of behavior and frequently distort their feelings and perceptions about it as they commiserate over the discomfort of change. They selectively distort their perception of how good the old way was.

   Key: People try to return to the status quo when the pressure to change is relaxed; thus, leaders must vigorously lead, focus, and energize the change until people establish new perceived comfort levels.

15. Most people are afraid of confrontation. Leaders must confront and hold people accountable or the process will fail.

   Key: Effective management of change requires leaders to have the strength, skills, and will to confront people, problems, and issues. Leaders must be unafraid of confronting the tough stuff that is unearthed in the change process. They must be emotionally mature in order to competently handle the volatility of confrontation.

Although change goes on continually from birth until death, we tend to stabilize ourselves by constructing our own concepts of reality. Many people stabilize their perceptions of today by interpreting them through yesterday's experience. Some people try to fit today's happenings into already understood frameworks. When change is rapid, conditions occur that have no obvious connection to past habitual response. For example, consider the president of a small bank who in the past could study investments and take his time deciding where to put the bank's money. That same president today is losing money if he doesn't take advantage of the time differential of investments around the world. If his money is lying uninvested overnnight, he may be missing a profit opportunity.

What about the small business owner who began by doing most things herself but expands to an organization of 200 people? The difference between success and failure is very dependent upon the owner's ability to see changing requirements and let go of obsolete ways of perceiving, comparing, and controlling. The challenge to perception is to retain the wisdom of experience while correctly assessing changing phenomena.

DISTORTIONS AND DISTRACTORS

Some commonly accepted distortions affect the framework we use for interpreting changing situations and conditions:

Distortion #1 "We can go back to the way we were."

(Based upon the belief that life is static, rather than dynamic and ever moving)

Distortion #2 "Change causes uncertainty, resulting in discomfort. Discomfort is bad; therefore, change is bad."

(Based upon the belief that pain is bad and comfort is good)

Distortion #3 "Certainty through predictability is less stressful and more comfortable; therefore, the old way is more comfortable, and thereby better."

(Based upon the belief that comfortable means better)

Distortion #4 "Change causes chaos and unpredictability, so let's blame the ones causing these uncomfortable feelings."

(Based upon the belief that others are responsible for one's feelings)

Distortion #5 "I can just wait this out, drag my feet, and kill this change momentum; however, I will pretend I support it."

(Based upon the belief that we can go back to a frozen picture of the past)

Distortion #6 "I can change easily, if I want to do so."

(Based upon the belief that resistance is really just undecidedness)

One leader said her biggest challenge is managing distracting variables in her daily interactions. She said, "Staying clear about what I am trying to do is difficult. When I am alone thinking, it is easy to keep my vision clearly focused. But when my day has endless interruptions, I begin to get scattered with tasks, personality issues, rumors, and complaints. I really feel the burden of being the one who is supposed to keep us clearly focused."

We helped her develop a process for focusing on important aspects rather than becoming scattered with distractors. First, she asks "What makes a difference?" "What can I control or influence?" "Whose responsibility is this?" "With the vision as the framework, what needs to be done immediately?" "Is this occurrence a driver or a resistor?"

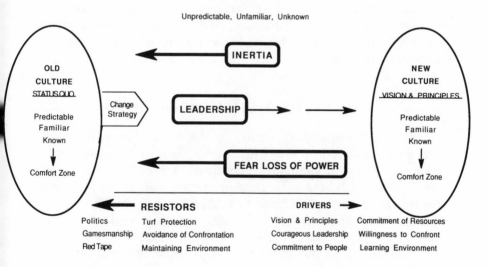

DRIVERS AND RESISTORS OF CHANGE

Leading the change process is a matter of focused *energy* to overcome distortions. Leading change involves the energy of personal will, the energy of thoughts-feelings-actions, the energy to change the inertia of cultural habits. Energy is used to resist change and energy is used to drive change. Kurt Lewin's forced field analysis is still a relevant way to look at the energy required for purposeful change.

Leadership is a struggle between the forces of stability (status quo) and the forces of change. Inertia and fear of the loss of power creates resistance to change.

Politics cause resistance to redistribution of power. Coalitions form as Stakeholders who have power in the current state tend to align with others who have power and are unwilling to risk losing it if the changing direction succeeds. Power alliances form, break apart, and regroup during different stages of a planned change process. Gamesmanship and turf protection increase. Predictable games are malicious obedience, pretended compliance, analysis paralysis, negative attitudes, parochialism, rumormongering, scapegoating, and character assassination. Clear perception is difficult for leaders to maintain in the face of strong gamesmanship.

CASE STUDY: THE MAN WHO FAILED

In one company the principal leader of change had both personal and position power in the company. George was considering the need to change the company. I asked him if he felt strongly enough about the change to risk losing his job over it. He looked surprised. He was well liked by the powerful men in the company seats of power. He was unaccustomed to thinking about being vulnerable. He was a favored son.

We discussed the anger, fear, and resistance that is stirred up by change. If he played a significant role in that change, he could expect to become a lightning rod for people's anger and discomfort. He did not consider that to be a problem. Part of his power had always been in careful strategizing. He was a talented manipulator and quite skilled at mind games. He was overly confident that he could get other people to make the suggestions and act on his strategies. He was confident that he could lead from behind until he was ready to move out front and take credit for the success. He was a novice to the potency of people's resistance and anger when their comfortable, predictable world is disrupted by the chaos of change.

George put together his process action team and began a leisurely pursuit of knowledge. He became intrigued by the available knowledge that had never before appealed to his engineer-oriented mind. He immersed himself in exploring communication skills, group dynamics, change theories, organizational structure, systems and processes. He was waking up to the scientific world of predictable patterns in human beings. He had heretofore believed that people were manipulatable but somewhat unknowable. He became a knowledge sponge as he discovered the operating rules of change and human behavior.

He was brilliant in developing the strategic plan to begin the methodical process of changing the company's culture. Without his personal and position power, the work would have gone at an even slower pace. He was smart enough to select some very intelligent people to work with him. They turned into a synergistic powerhouse that infused the process with direction, conscience, knowledge, and leadership. As the change process gathered momentum, some of the old power players tried to discount it. They felt smug and in control; they liked the company just the way it was. They didn't want anyone changing the basis of power. Before the power players realized it, the momentum became so great that some of them were openly confronted about their behaviors, intentions, and impacts.

George began to feel the heat of the lightning rod position at the peak of the battle. Rumors spread to slander his character. His motives were suspect. He was pulled aside by some of the power players and warned.

As I watched him developing into a leader and saw him learning the skills of empowerment, I was encouraged. He seemed to become really inspired by his ability to help bright, talented young employees begin to grow and discover greater capacities to risk and produce. It was delightful to watch him and his employees.

The problem began to occur as his fears started to overwhelm him. This very intelligent, tough executive was unwilling to recognize his terrible fear of confrontation and emotional pain.

He was not afraid to confront someone when he had time to strategize, study the situation, rehearse the possible responses of the other person and get thoroughly mentally prepared. His vulnerability lay in surprise conflict, confrontations that he did not instigate, or confrontations that had the potency to rip aside his guard and reveal his terror of emotional pain. When he prepared his own confrontational moves, he rehearsed careful mind games and scenarios. By the time the confrontation actually occurred, he had carefully sealed off potentially emotional feelings. He could play the confrontation as a dispassionate chess player who found it intellectually stimulating to see how well he had anticipated the responses and manipulated the outcome. He kept himself carefully aloof from others' emotional responses.

He moved the change process to a critical point in the transition. It really needed visible leadership. The heat got so bad that he resigned his leadership position and withdrew for several months from the process. Other changes occurred that brought him to a new position in the company with even more position power — but it was a promotion that was granted by the old power guard.

He faced a terrible dilemma. He now has the power to make some significant changes. He is now in position to remove some of the real concretized power players and reorganize with more mature, talented people. He was too afraid to make the moves. He has become ineffectual as he tries to keep his feet in the power camp of the old regime while espousing the changing basis of power identified in the change process. He has become untrustworthy to both camps. His desire to avoid tough, clear, strong confrontation is too strong to give him the energy needed to do what is necessary.

It is disappointing to see him come so close to Stage IV Leadership but fail because of his unconfronted fear of emotional pain.

CHANGE CHALLENGES COMFORT ZONES

Traditional ways of doing business (bureaucracies) become major strongholds of resistance. "Red tape" impedes the change process by instigating stringent compliance with rules, regulations, and norms. Legality and basic order in business systems do have to be managed, but "nitpicking" attitudes can seriously hinder the progress.

People basically dislike confrontation and uncomfortable circumstances. Change is frequently a struggle with fear. Attempts to deny the need for change directly oppose acceptance of change. Leaders absorb the frustration and fears of subordinates. Leaders of change must confront people, situations, and issues; otherwise, the change is cosmetic rather than substantive. Effort can be easily confused with purposefully achieving the needed changes. Leaders frequently become the focus of anger and blame.

Drivers: One of the most potent drivers of change is leaders' ability to create vision and engage people in a purpose that involves their core values. The leadership challenge is to develop a shared mental model in enough of the opinion setters in the organization to bring the mental model into reality. Leaders must have the ability to identify the critical issues in a complex, changing situation, frame them in an understandable and repeatable way. Leaders need to speak simply, memorably, and powerfully. They must be able to explain the mental model that people will need in order to reframe and refocus what they see happening. The leaders' explanations need to be easy to understand, easy to remember, easy to repeat, and potently clear. Leaders need to reach people at the feeling/value level without creating dependence.

Communicating clearly the leadership vision and engaging core values implies that behavioral principles must also be articulated, modeled, and normalized. People are not moved to make risky changes through intellectual persuasion. Leaders have to balance their communication between emotional and cognitive dynamics. Leaders must exhibit disciplined thinking and rigorous examination of assumptions at the same time that they demonstrate empathy and understanding of the emotional impact of the changes. Commitment, morale, trust, and inspired motive comes from engaging people's strongly held values. The leaders must be able to accurately predict how their actions are likely to affect others.

Leaders are prudent risk-takers who are willing to take an unpopular stand, create a challenging vision, and vigorously move toward it when they see they must set a course for the renewal of company energies.

Drivers include demonstrated commitment to people, willingness to confront, and perpetually cultivating a learning environment. Leaders mobilize the potency of committed, thinking, learning people with organizational commitment of time and financial resources to support the transition to the desired future state.

LEADERSHIP AND PROCESS SAVVY

Wise leaders are process savvy. Such awareness allows leaders economy of thought. They can focus on a singular line of process without getting distracted with specific occurrences or disparate facts and events. They practice looking at the overall forest instead of cataloging the individual trees. The characteristics of process are:

Connections and Relatedness

Economy of Thought   *Continuity and Impact*

Perpetually Changing Cycles

Process savvy is seeing connections and relatedness among disparate elements. Learning to see the connecting threads of process has advantages: The elusive can become knowable by connecting units of experience. You can draw meaning from intangible occurrences while they are still in living, dynamic form. You can see the line of relatedness while events are in motion. Since process is not static, you must apprehend dynamic changing relationships among force, energy, and motion.

We earlier defined process as the dynamic interrelatedness of occurrences (situations, thoughts, feelings, actions, people relationships, market changes) that form linkages and impacts. Leaders must be able to recognize and lead the change process. Leaders must see coherent meaning in units of experience and occurrences that form a connecting line of impact on the process.

Process involves the principle of relatedness. Experiences, situations, and occurrences connect to impact the direction of change. Since change is dynamic and ever evolving, perceptual clarity requires the leader to recognize major process components that are in perpetual motion and varying force. Recognition of process enables one to draw together intangible elements into meaningful form while they are still in living movement. Process is not concretized, inert, or frozen in time; it is continuous movement and must be perceived in motion. It is not something to be quantified, cut up, or analyzed; it is moving and must be apprehended while it is occurring.

What a group does during a management meeting cannot be fully understood if one is unaware of how the group interacted. A business group met to determine how to increase purchasing authority at the field level. At the conclusion of the meeting, the official minutes showed that the group agreed to raise the purchasing authority by $75,000. What the minutes did not show were the interpersonal dynamics involved in the decision. A person with process awareness would see the power issues and note the domineering force of one personality steamrolling his own opinion right over other people's objections, threatening and browbeating others into silent submission. Noting the subtle nonverbal resistance messages that three men were communicating would reveal the impact of how the decision was reached. Though people can sometimes be forced into silence or surface compliance with sheer show of dominant force, commitment to successfully help implement the decision is an individual, internal happening.

Process involves the principle of continuity cycles. Process understanding operates on the awareness that when an idea, feeling, project, experience, or action seems to come to an end, it doesn't dissolve. No experience is lost. Experience is recycled repeatedly in different configurations. The component parts continue to exist in the bank of memory to be reintegrated in another cycle of experience. Ideas, thoughts, and feelings that dominate during one life experience may in another circumstance drop into an inactive state within our memory bank where their existence continues. When a new situation stimulates them, they arise to the surface of consciousness to resume their continuity in a different context.

One manager was dealing with a difficult employee who seemed to be argumentative and resistant. During discussion, the manager discovered that the employee had just suffered a miscarriage of a much wanted child. The manager felt her own tear ducts warm up and strange waves of emotional grief filled her chest as unwanted remembrances of her own loss twelve years earlier penetrated her consciousness. She had lost a baby during the sixth month of pregnancy. She intellectually dealt with the grief and got back to work. Today, she is going through a particularly stressful time in her career. The sudden flood of sadness totally surprised her. She said, "I thought that I had completely dealt with that loss. I guess I am just too tired to keep it suppressed. I am amazed at the force with which those old memories hit me!"

Change frequently involves the mind, body, emotions, and spirit.

Although change involves perpetually changing cycles, information continues and the impact varies with thoughts, feelings, values, and situations.

CHANGE INVOLVES TANGIBLE AND INTANGIBLE FACTORS

Recognizing and managing the intangible part of the organization is tantamount to process awareness. Tangible aspects include things you can observe and quantify while the intangible aspects include elements that cannot themselves be seen — only their effects can be observed. Most managers are much more comfortable managing the tangible aspects, when it is too frequently the intangible elements that carry the seeds of success or failure.

ORGANIZATIONAL ENVIRONMENT
(see *Gold Collar Worker* by Robert Kelley)

TANGIBLE ASPECTS	INTANGIBLE ASPECTS
Work Tasks, Equipment	*People Relationships, Group*
Budget, Supplies, Buildings	*Processes, Teamwork*
• Rules, regulations, policies	• Interpretation of rules, regulations, policies
• Physical furnishings and buildings	• Work environment (the way it feels to work there)
• Tasks	• Relationships

- Projects
- Paperwork
- Organizational chart
- Bottom line
- Position authority

- Impact on others and interdependencies
- Attitudes toward paperwork
- Actual influencers and real interaction patterns
- Company culture (the way people habitually think, feel, and act)
- Position power and personal power

Behaviors

- Actions
- Words

Feelings, Reactions, Values

- Motives and intentions
- Attitudes and impacts

In addition to tangible and intangible cultural aspects, rewards are also both tangible and intangible. Among the tangible rewards are pay, bonus, fringe benefits, vacations, promotions, deferred compensation, resource availability, office furnishings, work space, equipment, training opportunities, and physical work conditions. Intangible rewards are meaningful work, achieving challenging goals, alignment with company goals, responsibility, and societal contribution. Other very important but intangible rewards are feedback from a credible source, feedback about a task, praise, morale, group cohesion, caring relationships, recognition from a role model, valuing individual differences, friendships, participation, and having a positive impact on others. (Please note that these intangibles can be powerful drivers of change.)

Research also indicates that punishments can be both tangible and intangible. Among the tangible punishments are low pay, docking pay, dangerous work, poor working conditions, standardized work environment. Intangible punishments are seen as lack of feedback, management failure to listen or behave as if they care, public degradation, coercion, intimidation, exploitation, unfair labeling, unhealthful competition, time pressure, undermining quality work, no new skill acquisition, no new knowledge acquisition, boring work, lack of responsibility, lack of recognition. (Please note that perceived punishments can contribute to powerful resistance to change.)

CASE STUDY: CHANGE AT S CORPORATION

The profit margins began to dwindle for a small corporation of 5,000 employees we will call S Corporation to protect its real identity. Something needed to be done. They analyzed the tangible parts of the business as they worked the numbers, analyzed the systems, revisited their assets, and analyzed their markets.

As a predominantly engineer-managed corporation, the executives were fairly unaware of intangible aspects such as working relationships, leadership, company culture, use of position power, and employee morale. They were forced to recognize the intangible aspects when two divergent forces hit the company at the same time. They recognized their need to develop a pool of managers to strengthen acquisition opportunities, and they needed to "appear" to be doing more for women and minorities since they decided to pursue a government contract. They knew that winning a government contract would require them to appear to be compliant with EEO guidelines, so they appointed a committee to look into women and minority issues. The two forces resulted in a committee headed by a corporate officer to study the issues.

The committee of five began to educate themselves. They wanted to know what other companies were doing to develop management succession plans, managerial pools, and employee development of all types.

As their study was drawing to an end, the chairperson asked us to facilitate a three-day planning session as they summarized their thoughts. It was clear to us that they were considering going to the marketplace to buy expensive development programs to solve the problem. Even a brief interaction with the corporation revealed that their corporate culture would stifle the implementation of the best programs they could buy.

Observing a few interactions showed the cultural norm. Power was controlled by a few insiders. The power system was paternalistic, with the chairman of the board using a Stage II Benevolent Dictator style when he was pleased, while switching to Abusive Dictator when displeased. Men who emulated his style were selected for promotion. Information was closely guarded at the top. Decisions that affected many of the company's internal Stakeholders were made behind closed executive doors and then announced. People were moved around the various companies without being asked. Retribution and humiliation stories kept most employees from challenging their bosses.

We told the committee that the problem of developing a seasoned management pool that called freely on real talent whether it was white or minority, male or female, was dependent on having an organizational culture that could sustain their development once they received the knowledge and exposure. The real problem was an antiquated company culture of privilege, power abuse, and information/decision control. I recommended that they either tackle the real problem or disband the committee. They could spend the proposed $800,000 for prepackaged programs, but they would not achieve the objective. Their corporate culture was a 1950s culture trying to compete in the swift, competitive, international market of the nineties.

It would have been ludicrous to send people to excellent training on participative management, mature use of personal and position power, interpersonal communication skills, negotiation, leadership, and group dynamics and then come back to the antiquated culture that would destroy anyone trying to actually use what they had learned. The training would just educate the company's best and brightest in seeing ever more clearly the power abuse in the company. Raising their awareness of better ways to lead, communicate, and interact would lead inevitably to even more discontent and dissatisfaction. What a fruitless strategy!

The committee decided to do the toughest thing — to change the corporate culture. They got permission to bring the corporation's top managers together from the various companies and do a needs assessment. Using group interaction, they posed a simple question: "In what ways do we as a corporation support or discourage business?" The results of the small group work revealed 152 behaviors that discouraged business, and only 33 that supported it.

The results of that meeting were shocking. The negating behaviors could not be dismissed as coming from disgruntled employees. That assessment came from upper-level management ranks. When the forum for assessment of company culture was presented, managers began to talk about long suppressed frustrations. The change process ignited.

The change strategy was developed with the following assumptions: (1) people help change what they help design; (2) change in a dictatorial company requires officers to be internal change agents; (3) they need to hire a change consultant to help them assess the change phases; (4) the Cultural Change Committee working with the consultant has responsibility for process analysis and feedback to the corporate body.

The corporation went through the predictable phases of the change process:

Phase 1 Recognizing need to change.

Phase 2 Assessing the need to change.

Phase 3 Developing a plan of change.

Phase 4 Getting leadership and formal company commitment.

Phase 5 Skill development.

Phase 6 Managing of coalition formation and increased resistance.

Phase 7 Opposing forces fight to control perception.

Phase 8 Increased chaos, frustration and unpredictability.

Phase 9 Crisis of maintaining leaders' energy, motivation and focus.

Phase 10 Leaders of change gain momentum and establish the norms of the new culture.

A summary of each phase further explains the dynamics of change that had to be actively managed.

Phase 1/Recognize Need to Change: Keep in mind that S Corp was driven by the concern for profits to find a way to better compete. This was not change for the sake of change, nor was it philosophically or altruistically driven. S Corp is in business to make profits. The Cultural Change Committee was the first to recognize the depth of the change that was needed. They knew the corporation's power-oriented companies of the corporation would not accept some outsider's assessment of the need to change. They developed a process by which they hoped the managers would reach that conclusion, thus the managerial meeting to discuss the way they did their business.

Phase 2/Assess Need to Change: The Cultural Change Committee (CCC) gathered information about the current state, their competitors, change processes, and change strategies. They then organized the meeting for top managers to assess the way the S Corp did business. The lists of the practices, attitudes, and behaviors that demonstrated the way they did business were overwhelmingly negative. From that meeting the executive group empowered the CCC to look into the change process further. I overheard one power player attempt to discount the information with the remark: "We shouldn't ever have gotten them together for a bitch session. We've let this go too far." Nevertheless, the CCC combined the managerial data into a report and gained permission to develop a change plan.

Phase 3/Develop Plan of Change: The Cultural Change Committee identified the major variables to be changed. They developed a Change Plan that included their vision statement and the principles for action they needed to support the change. Their study of other companies making significant successful changes had some common themes: shared values, improved systems, innovative approaches, and mature leadership. They worked those themes into their principles. They developed a vision that stated: S Corp will pursue continuous improvement through leadership and teamwork based upon trust, respect, diversity, and participation. They identified the following principles of action:

- Communicate openly and share information.
- Give responsible, honest feedback.
- Seek continuous improvement and innovation.
- Confront issues through rational, responsible interaction.
- Develop group process skills for robust, invigorating meeting management.
- Include Stakeholders' input into decision-making process.
- Create a nonthreatening environment for responsible exchange.

The implementation plan involved having a Culture Change Team within each company chaired by the corporate officer in charge. Five to seven members were selected for the CCTeams. Each team was to work with the vision and principles and develop an action plan. Each officer and team had a change consultant working with them to help them develop group process, communication, and leadership skills. The CCC worked with each team as a resource person and corporate coordinator. Each company could develop its own independent plan as long as it supported the Vision and Principles.

Implementation of Change Plan:

1. Develop a Vision, identify shared values, and define principles.
2. Involve executive officers as CCTeam facilitators.
3. Form CCTeams.
4. Develop group process, communication, and leadership skills.
5. Develop action plans.
6. Act on those plans.
7. Determine success indicators using both measurable and observable indicator.
8. Provide for continuous feedback, planning, and improvement processes.

Phase 4/Get Leadership and Formal Company Commitment: The CCCommittee went to the executive board and secured budget and formal authority to coordinate and support the CCTeams throughout the company. By requiring each CCTeam to be headed by a corporate officer, the officer was by official duty obligated to work with the process. The company must invest resources to support the change process. Leaders commit to lead the change and negotiate with managers who resist the change process. These leaders establish observable behavioral standards and measurable process improvement criteria. Leaders hold themselves and others responsible for the standards.

Phase 5/Develop Skills: We identified several knowledge bases and skills clusters that each team needed.

KNOWLEDGE	SKILLS
Group Dynamics	Process Recognition Skills
	Group Development Phase Recognition
	Group Facilitation Skills
	Conflict Management Skills
	Group Value-Sharing Skills

Communication	Accurate Listening Skills
	Observation Skills
	Clear Articulation Skills
	Analyzing and Reasoning Skills
	Giving and Receiving Feedback Skills
Leadership	Self-Knowledge and Clear Perception
	Confrontation of Problem Behavior Skills
	Politically Savvy Strategy Development Skills
	Trust-building Skills
	Team-building Skills
	Continuous, Tough Self-Assessment Skills
	Inspiration and Motivation Skills
	People-reading Skills
	Change Management Skills

Some of the teams developed excellent skills, while others floundered. The ones who did well were led by leaders committed to the vision and principles and the change process. Teams that floundered were inevitably facilitated by officers who championed the status quo, thereby letting the teams die from lack of support.

Phase 6/Manage Coalition Formation and Increased Resistance: As the CCTeams began to work on Action Plans, cliques and groups formed among those who supported the change as well as among those who resisted it. There is also power in the inertia of those who watched and criticized as well as those who watched and hoped but did nothing to help. The Stakeholder battles increased with those who feared the redistribution of power and influence. The grapevine ran amuck with rumors and stories of villainous motives in the change process. Factions questioned the change agents' motives and rumors increased to discredit the members of the CCCommittee as well as CC members.

Phase 7/Opposing Forces Fight to Control Perception: Supporters increased their communication of success stories indicating positive change, while resistors communicated failure stories as proof that the change process was failing. They selected one of the most abusive power players and watched him for evidence of the failing process. They circulated stories of the power player's latest abuses as ways to erode the change momentum. They frequently said, "I'll believe this when I see him change." This phase required vigorous leadership demonstration and championing of success indicators.

Phase 8/Increased Chaos, Frustration, and Unpredictability: High emotional stress occurred as CCTeams attended numerous meetings while carrying their usual workload. For those who had not yet learned to observe the intangibles of working relationships and did not know how to recognize behavior patterns, they saw no change and lost hope. Control issues and "turf" protection increased. Confusion, inconsistency, and conflict increased. The status quo of the old culture became selectively remembered as better than it actually was. Resistors tended to idealize the past as preferable to the chaos of transition.

This phase is a particularly vulnerable time for the change process. If the resistance reaches critical mass with too many critics in influential places, the change momentum can be seriously slowed down.

Phase 9/Crisis of Maintaining Leaders' Energy, Motivation, and Focus: Power players resisting the change exerted tremendous position power pressure on the visible leaders of change. They tried to bury the leaders in work tasks and demoralizing comments such as "You need to get your real work done and quit letting that CCTeam take up so much of your time." Critical events became the flagship for people to watch, as leaders of change and leaders of the status quo used both their personal and position power against each other, while people watched, talked and inadvertently added their energy to the struggle.

Learning, feedback, and confrontation of issues and behavior is critical to energizing the process. Leaders need teamwork and synergy to keep them focused and moving against the inertia of the status quo.

Leaders of the change go through severe attacks that drain their energy and dilute their focus. Roadblocks are thrown up, and unfair practices assault their values. It is a precarious time. Leaders must draw heavily on their own beliefs and values to provide energy to keep up the struggle.

Phase 10/Leaders of Change Gain Momentum and Establish the Norms of the New Culture: If the change process reaches Phase 10, the leaders of change ignite ownership and commitment in enough people to establish the new culture with its vision and principles. It becomes the norm through modeling and establishing accountability for the standards of behavior implied in the vision and principles.

OR the alternate occurs . . . Phase 10/Leaders of Status Quo Kill the Change Momentum: The leaders of the status quo kill the change momentum and get people's attention scattered through insistence that the daily work is the "real business" while promoting the change process as an expensive interference with making money.

One of the most powerful leaders of resistance had a temper tantrum at an executive meeting. He threw papers, cursed, and raged. He declared that the change process was a failure, and he for one was going to get back to making money. He stormed out of the meeting. He was able to effectively destroy the change momentum. His tantrum was so calculated, so childlike, so abusive, that the other executives abandoned their skills and moved quickly to try to calm him down and give him what he wanted. For ten months it looked as if he had won. Then external forces intervened.

A financial crisis, ethical wrongdoing, and serious flight of professionals from the company forced the change issue back into the spotlight.

We are recharging the change process through candid diagnosis of the derailment. We are going through brutal "lessons-learned" sessions. You can see the fire of hope beginning to burn in people's energized questions, the rebirth of innovative thinking, the desire to move quickly and decisively to get on with creating the kind of companies they want to build. Dissecting the incidents and projections that scattered their energies and altered their perceptions is valuable learning. From the pain of failure, greater knowledge and even some wisdom is born.

CHANGE: CONFUSION – THEN CLARITY

The change process has periods of confusion, disintegration, and despair when meaning has not yet emerged. Occurrences do not yet connect to give coherent meaning. With insight and integration usually comes a feeling of relief from the confusion. Leadership is required to keep the purpose and the vision clear enough to hold the course during confusion, disintegration, frustration and/or despair until insight and integration occurs.

The process of living involves an aggregation of thoughts, feelings, images, fears, ideas, facts, opinions, plans, visions, and desires. Seeing these forces in an integrated picture provides clarity and sound judgment. Though these are intangible inner experiences, they are nevertheless full of force, energy, and motion.

Process has periods of confusion, but insight into the patterns and connections brings a flush of enthusiasm or at least relief. Insight has to be integrated into coherent thoughts, feelings, and actions to bring sustainable energy and power to the change.

Integration sometimes comes at the most emotionally desperate moments. Depression, despair, panic, despondency, or even a sense of hopelessness may precede integration. Rather than experiencing these as wrongness, understand that those emotions may hold rich integration opportunity.

Change requires us to experience at different levels of our being. The status quo gives us a comfortable, predictable, recognizable way to create inner order. Change challenges the inner structure of understanding and predictability that supports us. When our recognizable framework starts breaking apart, that means of ordering reality loses its strength and validity. We tend to go in one of two directions. Either we feel hope and renewed opportunities, or we feel hopelessness and fear.

Breaking up the status quo causes adaptation. An inner disintegration takes place that causes some people to panic. For those who have come to understand the process of life, faith in the evolutionary aspect of life experiences carries them forward until the insight and clarity occurs. Others are so afraid of the chaotic confusion in change transitions that they stubbornly resist change and cling to old, limited thinking. For those who believe that you can finally figure out what is going on, identify the rules and act accordingly without freshly assessing occurrences, change causes fear and panic.

Inner integration is essential for an individual to be able to sustain changed behavior and clear perception. Inner integration at a level of beliefs, attitudes, values, and ultimately behaviors pushes one to feel the vulnerability of chaos and confusion that precedes reintegration. Several cycles of integrative experience occur that deepen the effect on the system as the beliefs, attitudes, values, and behaviors are realigned.

Vision is quite useful in change processes since it carries in it the integration possibility that can generate feelings of hope thereby increasing force of movement in the direction of the vision. Increased valuing releases energy laced with feeling that spreads a sense of purpose through the various activities. Vision carries the light of integration into the changing state. Eventually, a sufficient number of behaviors, thoughts, and feelings fit together to make the outer reality fit with the inner vision — thus forming a meaningful cycle of experience. Integration coalesces experience into meaningful components, and those components draw together in a single direction toward unity of meaning and purpose.

Once integration occurs, then activities can progress in a linear set of steps providing a period of stabilization when the vision and experiences come together. Changing circumstances will eventually render the linear activities obsolete and the process of evolution begins another change cycle. The cycle then ends with disintegration and a new cycle begins. It starts with a stimulus or force causing change, disintegration of status quo, chaos and confusion, emotional responses, integration or disintegration, deciding on linear activities, and a time of increasing the comfort zone — and then comes another change cycle! Disintegration provides opportunity for another stage of development.

Disintegration feels so terrible that it is difficult to remember that something new is born out of the disintegration of the old.

CHANGE: NATURAL DISASTER

A number of lakeside dwellers were startled one December to discover that record amounts of rainfall were causing the lake near their homes to rise. Since there had never been a lake level that threatened homes in the area, some homes were built in the flood plane. As the lake began to rise and the surrounding geographic area was also experiencing heavy rains, residents in low-lying areas were warned to move to higher ground.

As the system of dams and lakes interrelated with rivers and creeks, flood control in one area greatly impacted floodwaters downstream. Residents around the lake demanded that the flood gates be opened in order to save their homes. Residents downstream demanded that the flood gates be closed in order to save their homes.

Great change produced by the forces of nature releases fear and a sense of powerlessness that makes coping rather difficult.

One man was standing on a muddy elevation, looking down at his chimney sticking up above the waterline. He lamented: "I don't know what to do. I can just barely see the outline of my roof underneath the water. I don't know if my insurance is going to cover my personal property loss. I don't know if the county is going to let me reclaim my property since it is below the flood plane. I don't know if I qualify for help from FEMA or low-interest cleanup loans. I just don't know what I am dealing with."

His eyes were stressed and he paused several seconds as he tried to organize his thoughts. As an ESTJ (Extroverted, Sensor, Thinker, Judge) he was unaccustomed to having his feelings so exposed and vulnerable. He described it as feeling "kinda raw inside." He described his experience as heavy weights that were stacking up on him, weighing him down, and his being too tired to sort things out. He had little energy to assess his situation. He felt that he needed to be at work, to deal with regulating agencies, to deal with his girlfriend, to secure his boat, to organize his possessions, and to deal with the complicated financial problems. He was overwhelmed. As a Thinker-Judge, he felt particularly vulnerable to have his possessions so disorganized.

The homeowner was experiencing the disintegration phase of change, having not yet reached the insight or integration period where he could then set in place a linear course of action steps. He was still in the uncertainty phase, and it was quite disabling.

We humans assume that life will go on as it always has. We tend to avoid too much discussion of environmental dangers, the nation's fiscal bankruptcy, the poverty gap, AIDS, skyrocketing health care costs, decaying infrastructure, recession, aging, shrinking paychecks, global warming, drug damaging decay, and increased random acts of violence. We like to focus on the immediate and the tangible. It takes courage to look at the process of life on planet Earth today.

Challenging traditional use of power requires courage. People today are surging toward involvement, desire to give input, and reluctance to submit to the traditional authoritarian use of position or personal power.

MOVING FROM AUTHORITARIANISM
TOWARD PARTNERSHIP

With the threat of litigation pervading business and organizations, daily work has become choked with volumes of paperwork to protect one from litigation or fault. CYA (cover your ass) behavior has become the norm in many organizations. Individuals try to protect themselves, whether it is from the threat of lawsuit or the threat of humiliation at the hands of an authoritarian. The cost of fearful CYA behavior is great to American businesses and organizations. Instead of reasonable risk-taking, we play it safe. Instead of common sense and sound judgment, we have mindless adherence to norms or regulations that are not valid. Instead of energized minds and hearts, we have boredom and apathy.

With the enormous changes in the world situation, we are experiencing a changing basis of brokered power. As the Berlin Wall came down and the Soviet Union changed its power face, the desire for individual expression bloomed as if life-giving water had suddenly caused a desert to flower. The occasional themes of cooperation and shared values were heard early, but after the international changes, they turned into a familiar refrain of anger, chaos, and discontent. The movement strengthened in the United States to lend prestige to those companies that were seeking quality and continuous improvement. As the movement became more formalized through the Malcolm Baldridge Award and popularization of Dr. Deming's philosophies of Total Quality Management, brokered power norms began to shift.

The United States is in transition. We have not abandoned our traditional ways of brokering power with its basis in influence, privilege, and insider access. We are professing with our mouths, our words, and our program-orientations that we are now brokering power through participation and shared values. We have not yet established shared power as the norm. Although we may never achieve the real evolution of shared power, it is at least a journey worth taking.

Real shared power would require mature use of power from all people involved. Conceptually and ideally we love the words of cooperation, integrity, shared values, and shared power. Realistically, those concepts can only be lived and led by mature, responsible people. Fortunately, we have some leaders who can consistently demonstrate mature use of power; however, most people still struggle with unconfronted fears and personal egotism.

The basis of power changes from a little less reliance on hierarchical position, which we call position power. The transition phase is to move from position power to shared power through input and participation. Managers have finally discovered that people will more likely commit to that in which they feel meaningfully involved. The evolved state is genuinely shared power among those mature enough to deal responsibly.

The power of command is shifting toward the power to lead. People in a free world are no longer mesmerized by orders and commands. We are increasingly searching for trustworthy leaders whose intelligence, integrity, beliefs, and values cause us to want to help them achieve worthwhile goals.

Changing basis of power moves from privileged inclusion to the ability to access informal networks, find information, and get desirable things accomplished. We recognize increasing power in the ability to establish partnerships and appeal to broad-based constituencies. Power and influence increase in demonstrated ability to build strategic alliances and create collaborative work environments.

Power currency is building in such time-worn notions as trustworthiness, ethics, responsibility, competence, courage, and leadership. The note of caution, however, must be sounded. The old power currency has not disappeared. It is still potent in the form of privilege, exclusivity, elitism, specialness, money, status, possessions, and access to others with wealth and power. Transition means a confused mix of the old and the new.

PARTNERSHIP

We define "partnership" as a sharing relationship in business with mutual interests and concerns. It implies cooperation and issue resolution in an open-discussion environment with joint resolution. Partnership implies adult interdependence as well as individual contribution in responsibly tending to the relationships involved. Partnering attempts to recapture a way of doing business that was founded on a person's word as his or her bond — when people accepted responsibility for their actions and held themselves accountable to do what they said. Originally, legal contracts carried an implied covenant of good faith. Today we spend millions of dollars trying to put into writing every possible detail to keep us from cheating one another. Fear of litigation sends us down the copious legal document trail.

Partnering is a formalized attempt to get the various Stakeholders in a project to reach agreement on how they intend to work together during the life of the contract. Projects vary from construction to investment to community projects. The concept lends itself to any situation where various Stakeholders represent different departments, divisions, companies, or agencies which have mutual interests in getting a project accomplished.

The legal contract establishes the legal relationships. The partnering process establishes the working relationships.

The Stakeholders usually get together for a two-day conference to form a cohesive partnership that strives to draw on the strengths of each organization involved. The purpose of the partnering meeting is to develop working relationships to most effectively accomplish the legally signed contract that spells out the specifications of the project. The formal, legal contract is not the purpose of the meeting. The focus is on establishing the interpersonal working relationships that are necessary to achieve a quality project, done right the first time, within budget and on schedule. The Stakeholders commit to values, goals, and mutual interests that will best allow them to accomplish the work in a spirit of cooperation.

Too many projects today begin and end in adversarial relationships. Partnering sessions attempt to get working agreements early in the contract for Stakeholders to work together in a spirit of teamwork, trust, open communication, and mutual problem-resolution processes. Barr and Barr Consultants has been involved in facilitating many partnering conferences and heartily endorse the approach. We have seen partnership work effectively on small projects of a few million dollars to large projects of two and one-half billion dollars. Partnering appeals to shared values, mutual interests and common sense. Of course, we have also seen a few partnership attempts fail.

PARTNERSHIP SUCCESS AND FAILURE ASPECTS

Leadership Commitment — Partnerships fail without leaders who have position power and personal commitment to lead and support the process. If the working relationships are not clearly identified with observable measures of success, inertia takes over and Stakeholders lose their partnership perspective and parochialism resurfaces. Individuals then begin to focus on their own piece of the action with little or no consideration of how the overall project is affected.

Getting the significant players to attend the initial partnership conference is critical. We attempt to get the main decision-makers from each of the major Stakeholder organizations to attend. In selecting conference participants, we focus on the job site to identify critical players. We then need decision-makers from each of the main levels within each organization. In partnering conferences that we facilitate, we insist on having the decision-makers from various tiers in each organization present in order to give the partnership a good chance of succeeding.

Problem-Solving Process — Partnerships fail if the Stakeholders do not establish a problem-solving process where they can argue vigorously for their standpoints but have a way to proceed in cooperation and fairness when they appear hopelessly deadlocked. They agree to use a mutually trusted third-party facilitator to help them find a way to negotiate their differences. Every attempt is made to resolve the differences before engaging in the formal dispute resolution process. Resolving problems at the job site saves time and prevents work slowdowns since formal disputes have to work their way through various organizations' bureaucratic systems — a predictably slow and tedious process.

Mature Use of Power — Partners must be willing to confront real problems in an open and responsible manner. We frequently ask participants if they are willing to sign up for "Jerk Patrol." We find in most partnerships some jerk who spreads the skunk-oil of obnoxious behavior without any concern for the way others are affected. Each organization has to have leaders who will sign up for "Jerk Patrol" and will confront offensive behavior and attitudes within their own organizations. We also ask participants to sign up for "Bureaucracy Busting" chores within their own organizations when paperwork mentality overrides reasonable action and project achievement.

Communication Style — Partners need a reasonable framework for understanding different thought processes, work habits, and ways of seeing the world. We encourage participants to use the Myers-Briggs framework for getting better working understanding of each other. Without some way to focus the dynamics of working relationships, conferences can turn quickly into detail and blueprint discussions that overshadow the needed attention to their *working relationships*.

CASE STUDY: CONSTRUCTION PARTNERING CONFERENCE

The litigation threat in the construction industry causes difficulty in meeting deadlines and keeping work on the job site progressing according to a manageable schedule. Paperwork takes precedence over work at the job site. In a time of distrust, various organizations involved want legally binding paperwork before they proceed with work. Of course, in a business climate of distrust, greed, and legal control, having the right piece of paper is necessary.

On a construction job where the contract was administered by the U.S. Army Corps of Engineers for construction of a U.S. Air Force project, a partnering conference was not held at the beginning of the contract. Work began and old habitual work norms occurred. The general contractor, the main subcontractors (electrical, mechanical, steel erectors, and suppliers) began work drawing on many of their past experiences with government groups. The Corps is the manager of the contract. The Air Force is the owner of the buildings to be constructed. The general contractor won the bid to build the building. The subcontractors work for the general contractor.

The usual patterns occurred quickly. The actual job site construction was continually interrupted while paperwork was filled out or clarified.

A subcontractor brought his framing crew to the job site. As work began, he realized that the specifications on his blueprints were wrong. He realized that the doors would not be large enough to get the heavy equipment inside the building which was meant to store it. His common sense told him that something was wrong in the design. He measured one of the pieces of heavy equipment and confirmed that a design error had occurred. He went to the general contractor's job superintendent to tell him of the needed change.

Although the subcontractor had an eight-man crew on the site ready to work, the superintendent told him to stop work until the paperwork was approved for the needed change.

Paperwork process began to drive the show. The subcontractor filled out the job modification request. The job superintendent filled out his understanding of the problem and sent it to the general contractor's project engineer. From there the modification went to the Corps project manager, who then sent it to the quality assurance manager at the job site. Then the paper was returned to the Corps project manager, and he sent it to the district office where the paper began the rounds within the Construction Division. Next the paper went to the architectural design firm to determine the structural impact of the larger doors. Note that after the change was made and authorized, the paper then had to work its way back through the individual players before the subcontractor could go back to work.

Instead of trying to assemble the various players to get together and come up with a face-to-face solution, the job got stuck in a bureaucratic paperwork chain, with the paper moving slowly from one player to the next. The paperwork did not convey the sense of urgency that the subcontractor and his crew felt while they waited to resume work. Nor did the paperwork convey the frustration of the general contractor's job superintendent while the paperwork dilemma interrupted work at the job site and threw his schedule into disarray. The paperwork did not convey the frustration of the Air Force project manager, who wondered why framing stopped, or the Corps project manager, who tried to explain that the paperwork for the change was under way.

The paperwork tangle resulted in halting job site work over a necessary change. Common sense could tell any of the people involved that the change order was addressing a design error. It was clear that the subcontractor was not attempting to cheat or get a personally lucrative change approved. It was clearly a necessary change which turned out to have little appreciable structural impact. Yet, the change was sent through the many parts of the system without any sense of urgency. The paperwork went into the system and the paper then moved according to the leisurely bureaucratic pacing as it passed from one office to another within the various organizations, including the AE firm. It was handled as routine paper, tediously moving its way through the various approval loops.

The cumulative effects of eight or nine change orders meant that all Stakeholders were impacted. Delivery date to the user was jeopardized. Delays meant additional costs to the subcontractor as he tried to keep his crew intact while he waited. The possibility of punitive penalties to the general contractor increased. The project slowed to a snail's pace. Tempers flared. Reason and common sense were defiled while nameless and faceless bureaucracy demanded its day as people hid behind their paperwork safe zone. Responsibility was diffused as more and more people refused to take reasonable risks to move the problem through the systems.

Government agencies are not exclusive owners of bureaucracy. The general contractor, some of the larger subcontractors, and the architectural firm each had its own bureaucratic procedures.

Bureaucracy is a term used to describe an administrative system that is unwieldy and inflexible in its operation. The framing contractor did not deal with a bureaucratic situation since he owned his business and managed all the functions himself. He laughingly told me that his bureaucracy was in his shirt pocket, where he stuck notes and receipts. He worked all day and did his own paperwork at night. He didn't have an organizational structure of contracting, accounting, engineering, design, quality assurance, and quality control. He was his own system as owner, worker, administrator.

Nine months into the project, the Corps of Engineers chief of the Construction Division heard about the partnering concept and broached the topic with the Stakeholders. They agreed to try it out. The conference was held and they were able to look at the problems on the job and do a "lessons-learned" diagnosis. They established working relationships, mutual goals, a problem-solving process, and a plan to evaluate their partnership agreement.

CASE STUDY: PARTNERING AND A LOCAL GOVERNMENT PROJECT

A similar problem occurred on another construction project that began traditionally without a partnering agreement. Business began as usual.

The owner, a local governing body for a city, asked that the schedule be accelerated since they had a binding no-slippage delivery date. The project had to finish on time. Slipping the delivery date would result in disastrous costs to all parties.

The original schedule called for a five-month steel erection plan. Erecting the steel is a critical part of the job which has to occur before much of the other work can take place. The steel erector company was asked by the owner to accelerate the schedule, which they agreed to do. The steel company owner ordered precast steel that was custom molded to the specifications, prestamped for the government owner, and cut to length for this particular job. The steel company owner acted in good faith to the city's request.

The steel for the project was delivered to the steel company home office, which is in an adjacent state to the building site. The steel was stored in their warehouse. The steel company then submitted a bill to the city's project management team for payment for the 12,000 tons of stored steel. After six weeks in the city's system, the paperwork finally got back to the project management group with a "payment rejected" message stamped across it.

When the project management area manager notified the steel company of the rejection, the steel company owner became furious. He called his lawyers to prepare the next phase of interaction — litigation.

The steel owner felt he had acted in good faith in response to the owner's request to accelerate the schedule. He ordered the steel, paid for it, and had it shipped to his storage yard for rapid movement to the job site. When he asked for payment, the city contract administrator refused to pay.

The city contract administrator read the terms of the contract and interpreted the clause dealing with stored materials to mean that the city would pay only for materials stored on the job site. The contract administrator and his staff were guarding against a contractor charging the city for materials that they might be using on another job. The contracting group had attitudinal behaviors that indicated that they single-handedly had the responsibility to keep contractors from cheating. The steel owner was angry at having thousands of his dollars tied up while he waited for site preparation and laying of the foundation of the building.

The problem is complex. The city bureaucracy was many layered. Once the paperwork left the job site where the project management area manager knew the integrity of the steel owner, the issue became regulation and paper driven. The area manager was aware of the accelerated schedule request which necessitated early acquisition of the steel. The contracting group was not located at the job site and had no face-to-face working relationship with the steel company owner. They relied on past experience that tended to confirm their stereotypical belief that most contractors were out to cheat government groups.

Let's examine some actual dialogue between the steel owner and the city's contract administrator.

Steel Owner: "The materials are stored in our warehouse at our home office."

City Admin: "We don't pay until it is moved to the construction site."

Steel Owner: "You don't have the construction site ready yet."

City Admin: "So we don't pay you yet!"

Steel Owner: "But you asked us to accelerate the schedule."

City Admin: "And you said you would."

Steel Owner: "We did, so pay me."

City Admin: "Look! We're not going to pay you for steel in your warehouse. The steel could be used on any of your projects. We can't inspect steel until we know it's at job site."

Steel Owner: "That's ridiculous! It is precast steel ordered from General Steel, custom molded, cut to contract length, and pre-stamped with the city's name. You'll be able to recognize it . . . or can't you read job specifications and stamps?"

City Admin: "Our policy says we can't pay without inspection."

Steel Owner: "So, come inspect it."

City Admin: "I don't have travel budget to run around the country."

Steel Owner: "I'll buy you a ticket."

The interaction ended in accusation, cursing, and shouting.

The common sense framework and total picture of mutual responsibility was lost as the payment request wound its way from the job site to the estimator group to the contract compliance administration group. At each of the stops the payment request was carefully examined from the standpoint of strict regulation and contract interpretation and finally the angry interaction erupted.

Later investigation of the internal bureaucratic process revealed that the paperwork was reviewed for rigid compliance with no emphasis on sound reasoning, common sense, interpersonal relationship, original intent, or Stakeholder impact. Once the paper left the job site, it lost its sense of urgency and became a paperwork drill.

The steel owner's urgent desire to get paid and treated fairly was sorely trampled in the paperwork debacle. He became angry and felt his only recourse was to have his lawyers take charge.

Multiply this one contractor's attitude by thirty companies who felt they were being unfairly treated and imagine what it was like to walk onto the job site. People were angry, distrustful, complaining, and filled with stories of the idiocy of the government folks. Walk through the city offices and the scene is about the same, only the stories are about sloppy paperwork, the kind of stupidity that can't fill out forms correctly, attempts to cheat, and attempts to loosely interpret contracts. Unfortunately, this scene has too often been the usual work environment in the construction industry. Today, however, the Army Corps of Engineers as well as other local and state government entities are joining the leaders in the construction industry in trying to change that costly cycle.

The construction industry, government contract administrators, and owners of projects have been forced to realize that they cannot survive with a "business-as-usual" attitude. The partnering concept is being attempted from coast to coast in a variety of organizations.

The Stakeholders come together in a partnering conference to explore ways they can work together in a spirit of cooperation, trust, and candor to put common sense back in the construction industry. They move it from the adversarial atmosphere forward to joint partnerships with mutual interests in getting quality projects built safely, on time and within budget. Some of the partnerships actually agree on a stated goal of being able to walk away at the end of the project with both interpersonal and professional good will intact. Partnering is an attempt to turn the adversarial construction environment into one of cooperation and good faith.

Many issues in the construction industry have a high probability of becoming emotionally volatile. Angry encounters can be ignited by disparaging remarks about one's dedication to quality or safety. These two topics have become as sacrosanct in the construction industry as motherhood and apple pie.

Disagreements about cost can be emotionally explosive. Affirmative Action issues, labor relations, and media focus are also potentially difficult issues to discuss.

The counterweight is found in the time-tested values of trust, integrity, mutual respect, fairness, honesty, cooperation, teamwork, and sincere concern for the well-being of all Stakeholders. Dysfunctional power styles violate time-tested values.

CASE STUDY: DYSFUNCTIONAL POWER STYLE

John is a financially successful physician but an interpersonal failure as a man. Both at home and at work he is primarily a Competitive Intimidator/Manipulator. When he is in a good mood, he manipulates, and when he is angry he intimidates. He fully intends to have his way, no matter which style it takes. His self-picture does not include seeing himself as a Stage III power player. His communication style is ENTJ (Extrovert, Intuitor, Thinker, Judge). As a highly intelligent ENTJ, he has fooled himself. He thinks he is the nicest fellow he knows.

He had almost no anger control. When he was annoyed, he exploded at someone. He was showing most of the classic emotional immaturity symptoms:

No tolerance for criticism.

Indulgence in self-pity if things are not going his way.

Little control of his temper.

Always expecting special privilege – John first, above all others.

Emotionally explosive and accusative during emergencies.
Feelings are easily hurt.
Rarely accepts responsibility for his own actions or feelings.
Totally impatient with any kind of delay.
Throws a temper tantrum if he loses at something.
Brags and shows off in socially unacceptable ways.
Rarely listens to anyone else's ideas.
Is a chronic fault-finder and criticizer.

John is wealthy and has a high level of intelligence, but he has little interpersonal skill or wisdom. He acts as if he is stuck in the "terrible twos" of childhood.

Change was not even considered — until four incidents occurred. Five of his finest employees quit, saying they would no longer tolerate his abusive and manipulative behaviors. At about the same time, he saw an opportunity to expand his office to include both practicing physicians and medical research, but too many of the best people refused to work with him. His wife moved out of their home, stating that she didn't want to live with him anymore. His office manager quit and told him angrily what he was really like.

As the evidence stacked up, John could no longer hold his favorite picture of himself as a likable, intelligent guy. He decided that he should do something.

When he called Barr and Barr, it was ostensibly to look at some organizational development. Our preliminary meeting, however, revealed his real motive. He wanted to circuitously learn how to control his anger. When we recognized his real motive, we immediately put his self-deception on the conversational table.

At first he angrily and forcefully denied that he had a problem. He ranted and raved about five minutes and then came back around to admitting that he does have a problem.

He described the way he loses his temper. He tried to diminish its importance by saying, "I don't mean anything by it. I get over it quickly and then forget it. Everyone else should do the same."

Our immediate reaction was to challenge his irrational conclusion. The power struggle was activiated quickly. We pointed out the error of his belief that he could point a guided missile of anger, emotion, and destructive words at someone without expecting it to do any damage. He became instantly enraged and asked us what gave us the stupid idea that we could tell him his thinking was wrong.

We used his outburst to describe back to him his behavior. His body tensed, his hands clenched, his face reddened, his voice raised in volume and pitch, his language became judgmental, and his personal force increased. By using his own behaviors, we provided the proof of his Intimidator style. He calmed down instantly when he realized that the power play did not work.

He said, "Well, maybe you are right. Let's say that you are. What do you think I could do about it?"

We were not optimistic that he would have enough incentive to make a change effort possible. We suggested that he should first go get professional help from a psychiatrist or a psychologist who specializes in anger. If he could assure us that he did not have a psychological problem, we would then work with him on executive development.

Surprisingly, he agreed to see a psychiatrist. He discovered that he did not have a complicated psychological problem. He was an indulgent man who had just gone unchallenged so long that he had become almost totally self-focused.

We gave him a framework of the essential phases of a personal change plan. We carefully discussed the fact that change is not a finite set of steps that you move through in a lock-step linear fashion. Change is a continuous process. We helped him develop a comprehensive framework for integrating past, present, and future experiences and opportunities. Self-development is a lifelong activity. He has spent forty-five years dominating, manipulating, and controlling, and therefore has deeply habituated behavior patterns.

John is completely responsible for his change process; we provide clarity and feedback. The process itself has some critical phases which are in dynamic juxtaposition as they emerge, recede, and then reemerge in the change process. The change phases are:

- Recognized **need to change.**
  (John was experiencing fear of loneliness, failure, and limited professional opportunity and money-making capacity.)
- Assessment of the **costs** of not changing.
  (He appeared to be losing his professional growth and busi-

ness opportunity, his colleagues, his wife, and his staff.)

- Assessment of the individual **gains** in changing.

(An opportunity to regain his business and professional opportunity, his colleagues, his wife, and his staff.)

- **Decision to do it** and make it a top priority every day.

(It took John three months to decide to do it. He would talk himself out of making the effort, indulge in his self-pity and angry repudiation, then come back around to his fear of terrible failure and loneliness if he did not try. He decided that he had to change. He had to make a firm decision with total commitment of personal will. He could not give himself easy outs since self-confrontation would be extremely difficult.)

- Identify clear **progress/failure indicators.**

(We helped John identify clear, observable behaviors that would give him a progress/failure yardstick. We provided periodic feedback and clarity to help him avoid falling into his old habit of perceptual distortion and skewed judgment.)

- Clearly **visualize the outcome** of successfully changing.

(We helped John identify very clear images of the undesirable behavior and written objectives of the desired behaviors. He wrote the specific description of the undesired behavior and then wrote a clear description of the desirable behavior. We continually use his written objectives in feedback sessions.)

- Make a **total commitment — no back doors.**

(John identified some specific penalties he would pay as he found himself looking for ways to back out and find ways to escape from the fear, pain, and vulnerability of changing his behaviors. John had used intimidation and manipulation to keep people from impacting him. Without those behaviors he felt completely vulnerable. He described it as being like a turtle without a shell for protection on a beach of predators.

- **Management of increased resistance** to change.

(We helped John recognize the various phases of resistance and fear. With the ability to identify what was happening, he could then muster the personal will to confront the resistance. He found fear driving most of his resistance.)

- Continuous **feedback and focus.**

  (We work with John periodically to observe his behavior and give him feedback. Occasionally he calls before our scheduled visit and says, "Come as soon as you can. I feel like I am losing my grip on this process." We also helped him select feedback process partners, helping him gain the skill of receiving feedback. He learned to seek criticism, as he saw the terrific learning opportunity it gave him. As a strong Thinker, he was fairly terrified initially at the potent feelings that criticism elicited. Over time, he became more and more emotionally mature.)

- **Remotivate** himself and **recommit** continually.

  (John threw his formidable intelligence and the creativity of his Intuitor style into finding clever, workable ways to keep himself committed.)

Nine months into his change process, John is enthusiastically working at his process. He fails and falls; gets up and succeeds; the cycle repeats. But he has not quit. He and his wife are temporarily reconciled. She describes herself as cautiously hopeful.

CHANGE: PERSONAL AND ORGANIZATIONAL CHALLENGE

Change is continuous whether we notice it or not. Some change is personal choice, other change is forced on us; some is situationally needed, and some occurs with the natural aging process.

Organizational change involves changing the structure to a different configuration to better address changing requirements. Organizational systems may need changing such as personnel, budget, accounting, information processing, internal auditing, purchasing, or financial management. The organizational environment may need changing, such as buildings, equipment, space, heating/cooling, or decor. Organizational culture may need changing in the way people value, act, and broker personal and position power, personalities, and politics.

We know that resistance to change is usually fueled by fear of the unknown. Resistance is frequently due to fear of consequences. Some of the fears we see repeatedly are: fear of losing resources (money, supplies, contact persons, authority channels, privileges); fear of threat to turf/territory (tendency to see change as competition, usurpation, abolition or one-upmanship); fear of loss of authority and control (inability to cause or prevent happenings); fear of expertise and competence (concern that expertise will become outdated or out of favor or unappreciated); fear of ambiguity (new rules, roles, reward and punishment systems, evaluation systems, new values, new people); fear of inadequacy (concern about being incapable of doing what is required); or fear of reduced self-concept (loss of self-esteem or reputation).

Can our society absorb the many changes that are occurring? In a book entitled *Social Psychology,* Daniel Katz says that social change proceeds from the individual to the structure of society and then to the psychosocial characteristics of a social group. He identifies four types of social change: (1) individual change that involves altering personality characteristics; (2) incremental change that is represented by gradual changes in the structure of society; (3) radical change that involves reorganization and restructuring of a social system; (4) cultural change that requires attitudes, beliefs, and behavior change for most people in a society.

Leaders manage change with three large issues to wrestle: personal style, power style, and fear.

DEVELOPMENTAL EXERCISES

Exercise 76: Organizational Assessment — Organizational Difficulty with Change

Instructions: In the space to the right identify the kind of power games and power plays you have observed in the four areas of change.

POWER AND AUTHORITY   POWER AND AUTHORITY

Rules and regulation bound.

Strict use of chain of command.

Protocol is more important than results.

Too much segmentation — too many kingdoms; departments sealed off from each other.

INFORMATION

INFORMATION

Information is guarded and secretive.

Communication, information, and interaction is severely limited and controlled.

RESOURCES

RESOURCES

Little discretionary use of resources.

Boss controls and dominates.

Tools, support, and assistance are hard to get.

Not much lateral cooperation.

WORK CULTURE

WORK CULTURE

No incentive to innovate — new ideas are met with disapproval or apathy.

Conflict escalates easily into resistance.

Teamwork across work units seen as betrayal.

Exercise 77: Organizational Change — Effectively Managing Change

Instructions: In the space to the right, identify observable behaviors that you would see in an organization effectively managing change.

POWER AND AUTHORITY

Emphasizes results, not protocol.

Minimal reliance on legitimate authority; maximum reliance on coalition building.

People-centered organization instead of power of privilege in chain of command.

Emphasizes leadership, cooperation and outcome rather than title and position power.

INFORMATION

Uses multiple integrative mechanisms to share information.

Information flows freely; real effort to keep people informed and get Stakeholder input.

Uses open systems as highly reliant on each other to supply resources and support.

RESOURCES

Emphasizes knowledge and teamwork.

Effectively shares information and resources.

POWER AND AUTHORITY

INFORMATION

RESOURCES

WORK CULTURE

WORK CULTURE

Rewards cooperation, action and
results while punishing turf
protection.

Systematically examines for
obsolesence and opportunity
to innovate.

Commits up-front to lengthy
process of team-building for
payoff in strengthened ability
to act fast through focused,
integrated teams.

Exercise 78: Power of the Status Quo

Instructions: The status quo represents that which is known, expected, regularly occurring in organizational social structures. Resistance to change is frequently due to *fear* of the consequences of change. People want to know "What about me!!" How does **fear of powerlessness, fear of failure, fear of rejection,** and **fear of conflict** cause resistance to change? What are people afraid of losing in each of the following areas of the status quo?

STATUS QUO

RESISTANCE TO CHANGE

Current state

What are people afraid of losing?

1. **Power relationships**
   (Know who controls what)

2. **Status**
   (Know where each person fits)

3. **Values**
   (Know what is important and
   know what gets rewarded and
   what gets punished)

4. **Resource distribution**
   (Know who has what and who
   has authorization to do what)

5. **Territory**
   (Know who "owns" what turf;
   know who controls what)

6. **Roles**
   (Know who does what and who
   is accepted as having authority,
   expertise, power)

7. **Norms**
   (Know what is acceptable;
   know what the limits are)

In a change strategy, what can you do to minimize resistance due to fear? You cannot eliminate fear. Can you think of ways to help manage it?

Exercise 79: Barr and Barr Change Assumptions

Instructions: Select an organizational or societal change with which you are very familiar and do a **diagnosis of change** by applying the fifteen change assumptions in your diagnosis.

*Change you are diagnosing:*_____

ASSUMPTION 1: Change is redistribution of power.

Key: Identify major Stakeholders. Remember Stakeholders can be an individual, a department, an agency, regulatory/legal/or political representatives.

Activity A: Identify the major Stakeholders who resisted and identify the standpoint* on which they resisted. (*Susan Fisher is credited with utilizing the term "standpoint" with Stakeholder analysis.)

Example:

Stakeholder: Personnel Department
Standpoint: "That will cause us a lot of extra work."

Stakeholder: Union Representative
Standpoint: "I don't think the contract allows that."

Stakeholder: OSHA Representative
Standpoint: "Asbestos safety is critical."

Stakeholder: Stakeholder:

Standpoint: Standpoint:

Stakeholder: Stakeholder:

Standpoint: Standpoint:

Stakeholder: Stakeholder:

Standpoint: Standpoint

Activity B: Identify the Stakeholders who supported and helped lead the change.

Stakeholder: Stakeholder:

Standpoint: Standpoint:

Stakeholder: Stakeholder:

Standpoint: Standpoint:

Stakeholder: Stakeholder:

Standpoint: Standpoint:

ASSUMPTION 2: Change frequently involves chaos and stress that arouse self-worth anxieties and fear.

Key: Watch actions, messages, and explanations about the change that hold potentially damaging self-esteem messages.

Activity C: What did you hear in the grapevine that told you what people were afraid of? Who did they quote? What issues did you hear repeatedly?

ASSUMPTION 3: Most people have low tolerance for change, particularly if they are not instigating it.

Key: Expect people to be concerned about change and explain the changes, be visible and accessible, and communicate-communicate-communicate.

Activity D: What was done to keep people informed? Were leaders of the change accessible and visible?

ASSUMPTION 4: Opinion setters are essential to provide focus, clarity, and realistic optimism since people experience emotional turmoil during change processes due to uncertainty, interruption, and potential loss of status.

Key: Identify *opinion setters* throughout the organization and organize them to inform others and stay informed themselves.

Activity E: Who were the informal leaders whose opinion seriously influenced the process? Identify the positive and the negative opinion setters.

ASSUMPTION 5: Resistance to change is greater when people believe that the change is *not* in their best interest nor the organization's best interest.

Key: Communicate from the people perspective rather than starting from the organization's perspective — first connect with people's interests, values, and concerns, then explain the organizational perspective.

Activity F: Identify the verbal, printed, electronic, and publicity focus. Were individual concerns or the corporate view most used?

ASSUMPTION 6: People prefer to construct reality out of stability and predictability; when too much uncertainty is present they resort to social reality of comparing perceptions with others and observing accepted social response of important others.

Key: Identify the opinion setters to whom people turn for comparing and checking their perceptions. Inform, include, and seek commitment from the opinion setters.

Activity G: Whose opinion was frequently quoted? Whom did most people watch to decide how the change was going?

ASSUMPTION 7: Change may be so gradual that people do not notice.

Key: Develop your information strategy if you want people to recognize and assist with the change efforts. Establish observable indicators of the desirable change and urge opinion setters to communicate the forward movement and the challenges.

Activity H: Identify some of the things that the leaders did to identify, celebrate, and communicate success indicators.

ASSUMPTION 8: Most people do not have well-developed behavior observation skills.

Key: Early training in behavior observation is critical for opinion setters and team members.

Activity I: Assess the degree of skill exhibited by the main players in the process. Assess their group facilitation skills, group dynamics understanding, their observation skills, their feedback skills, and their clarifying, summarizing, confronting, and conflict management skills.

   Main Players:
   Group Facilitation Skills

Group Dynamics Understanding

Observation Skills

Feedback Skills

Clarifying, Summarizing Skills

Confronting Skills

Conflict Management Skills

ASSUMPTION 9: Most people have to learn to read patterns and link occurrences to derive understanding of change.

Key: Early training in process and intuitive assimilation is essential for opinion setters and team members.

Activity J: Did the organization provide consultants or team leaders who were skilled in process management? Assess the effect on the process.

ASSUMPTION 10: Commitment is withheld without active Stakeholder involvement in formulation of change strategies and implementation.

Key: People feel more committed to that which they help formulate and implement; thus, early involvement of Stakeholders provides more opportunity for developing Stakeholder commitment.

Activity K: How were Stakeholders involved? At what point in the process were they involved? How was Stakeholder input utilized?

ASSUMPTION 11: "The divine right of kings or managers no longer exists." Robert E. Kelley

Key: People tend to resist traditional authoritarian role behavior as they demand more information, more inclusion, and more explanation.

Activity L: How did people resist authoritarians? How did they respond to leaders who demonstrated participative management?

ASSUMPTION 12: A better educated work force expects management to explain its decision rationale.

Key: As more people are trained to analyze, question, and evaluate evidence, their resentment increases for anyone who is unwilling to submit his/her reasoning for discussion and review.

Activity M: Identify the person(s) whose work group felt that they were well informed and who felt that their concerns were addressed. Identify the person(s) whose work group felt ill-informed and ignored.

ASSUMPTION 13: Innovation requires perpetual reframing and re-focusing.

Key: Looking at today through yesterday's glasses won't yield insights or identify improvement possibilities. Finding a different way to think about things is basic to innovation and change. Clear leadership requires reframing and refocusing changing conditions and finding innovative solutions.

Activity N: Identify the person(s) who could always bring clarity and help others get refocused. Who were the person(s) who could always find ways to move ahead?

ASSUMPTION 14: During the discomfort of change, people tend to want to return to the old pattern of behavior and frequently distort their feelings and perceptions about it; they selectively distort their perception of how good the old way was.

Key: People try to return to the status quo when the pressure to change is relaxed; thus, leaders must vigorously lead, focus, and energize the change until people establish new perceived comfort levels.

Activity O: Identify those people who were the most vocal about the "good old days." Was anything done to counter their influence?

Assumption 15: Most people are afraid of confrontation. Leaders must confront and hold people accountable or the process will fail.

Key: Effective management of change requires leaders to have the strength, skills, and will to confront people, problems, and issues. Leaders must be unafraid of confronting the tough stuff that is unearthed in the change process. They must be emotionally mature in order to competently handle the volatility of confrontation.

Activity P: Identify the people, problems, and/or issues that were effectively confronted. Identify those that were allowed to go unaddressed. Explain why no one confronted them.

Exercise 80:   Change and Transition Culture

Kurt Lewin gave us a useful way to think about change in organizations. He did not see change as static relationships, but rather as dynamic forces working in opposite directions within the social-psychological space of the organization. He admonishes us to be very clear about those forces that drive the change and those forces that resist the change. Clear recognition of those forces is critical to effective change management.

Inertia to resist change and the fear of loss of power provide potent energy forces for human resistance to change. In our Transition Culture diagram, we identify the main categories of

Resistors as politics, gamesmanship, red tape, turf protection, avoidance of confrontation, and maintaining the current environment.

Identify a change process in which you have participated.

CHANGE PROCESS: _____

Review the following list of behaviors, attitudes, and actions that are predictable as expressions of Resistors. Put a 1 beside those that you observed that had a primary (major) negative impact on the change process. Put a 2 beside the ones you observed that had a secondary impact on the change process.

Politics, Gamesmanship, Turf Protection

___ Posturing and dramatizing points for effect rather than substance.

___ Manipulating points and emotions to cloud real issues.

___ Vigorously defending and protecting turf without true consideration of input or changing conditions.

___ Verbalizing and projecting the attitude of "This is a waste of time — nothing is going to change."

___ Using group or meeting time to monopolize the attention on their own interests.

___ Refusing to participate or support anything that does not involve their own turf — showing little or no interest in the overall interests or needs of the organization.

___ Refusing to give attention or verbal acknowledgment of anyone else's interests or contributions.

___ Using "analysis paralysis" to hold up critical decisions.

___ Demanding more information as a delay or avoidance tactic.

___ Demanding information that cannot be obtained as a condition for their commitment.

___ Projecting that teamwork is running the organization by committee.

___ Projecting the attitude that the time spent on managing change is an interruption of "real" business.

___ Projecting the message that "These meetings are a waste of time. We need to get back to work (implying illegitimacy)."

__ Punishing their own subordinates who are involved in the change process, through criticism, attempting to load subordinates down with so much work that they cannot participate in the process, threatening them with low performance ratings, or piling on inconsequential assignments and setting demanding deadlines.

__ Withholding important information.

__ Continually criticizing and complaining about the process.

__ Demanding control of agendas so they can kill needed focus on critical change issues, processes, or needed confrontations.

Red Tape, Avoidance of Confrontation, Maintaining Status Quo

__ Refusing to accept responsibility for change process — "they" syndrome.

__ Refusing to cooperate until all of the paperwork is scrupulously examined for accuracy, form, and compliance.

__ Ignoring change process input and continuing to stubbornly proceed as if nothing were changing.

__ Forming cliques before or after meetings to broker positions and information rather than using open discussion.

__ Labeling open discussion of issues, unproductive behavior, conflicts, or confrontations as "bullying," "bashing," "psychologically abusing" as a way to discount and distort real accountability for behavior.

__ Withholding resources needed for the change process.

__ Undermining change efforts.

__ Creating doubt through managing complaints and the rumor mill.

__ Communicating unrealistic expectations through their criticism, such as "We've sure spent a lot of time and money and have nothing to show for our efforts."

__ Impugning the motives of the change leaders.

__ Attacking the character and reputation of the change leaders.

__ Glorifying the "good old days" before all of this started.

__ Setting supporters of the change process up to fail by withholding resources, information, opportunity, or access.

Review the following list of behaviors, attitudes, and actions that are predictable as expressions of supporters of change, called **Drivers**. Put a 1 beside those that you observed that had a primary (major) positive impact on the change process. Put a 2 beside the ones you observed that had a secondary impact on the change process.

Vision, Principles, Values, Courageous Leadership

__ Executive-level commitment.

__ Clear vision of the desired state.

__ Clear understanding of the current state.

__ Clear understanding of the transition state and resulting chaos and stress of the necessary unpredictability, unfamiliarity, and unknown aspects of the transition from the known state of the status quo to the desired state of the realized vision.

__ Genuine desire of people to contribute to something worthwhile.

__ Opinion setters throughout the organization becoming leaders of the change process.

__ Leaders taking intelligent risks.

__ Leaders who are persuasive and trustworthy so they can hold the faith of people to follow them through the uncertainty of the chaos and change on the route to the desired state of the realized vision.

__ Leaders who cut through the manipulations, games, and blocks to see clearly what is happening and have the judgment to decide what makes sense to do.

__ Leaders who are strong, tough, compassionate, and genuinely caring in order to deal with people's fear and resistance.

__ Shared values of honesty, integrity, caring, rationality, and fairness.

__ Communicating verifiable business or organizational reasons for the change.

__ Clearly and easily communicating rationale for the change process and the desired state of the realized vision.

__ Nonthreatening environment to try, to fail, to learn from the failure, and to try again.

Commitment to People, Commitment of Resources, Willingness to Confront, and Creation of a Learning Environment

__ Demonstrated valuing of people and their individual differences.

__ Leaders demonstrating accurate listening skills with the ability to clearly perceive the four levels of message: words, feelings, importance, and intentions.

__ Leaders demonstrating excellent facilitation skills.

__ Leaders developing highly effective teams.

__ Willingness to set aside position power to enable sharing of employees with expertise in cross-functional teams without strong reporting relationships; team output is the organizational accountability rather than strong supervisory control.

__ People demonstrating high level of trust.

__ People demonstrating a willingness and desire to learn.

__ Open communication environment where leaders demonstrate excellent communication skills of accurate listening, clarifying, summarizing, and eliciting.

__ Highly accountable environment where members are expected to take full responsibility for their own behavior by demonstrating mature and responsible interactions.

__ Members demonstrating mature and professional level skills in giving and receiving feedback, confronting issues and behaviors, and problem resolution.

__ Confrontation and feedback is done by describing clearly the behaviors so that those involved can review the information and decide on needed action.

__ Commitment of money, time, equipment, people, and support services for efforts in the change process.

__ Active seeking of Stakeholder input and fair consideration of all points of view.

__ Ongoing strategy development by the leaders of the change process.

__ Celebrating and communicating success stories.

__ Communicating "lessons learned" from failure stories.

__ Seeing visible, dedicated, strong, trustworthy, wise leaders.

STRATEGY DEVELOPMENT: Human nature tends to focus on the negative, thus absorbing a lot of attention. Leaders must discipline their tendency to focus on the Resistors to such an extent that they drain the energy. Leaders must be alert to Resistors, but must get the forward momentum for the change process from the Drivers. To do this requires clear perception and sound judgment in order to balance clear understanding of the Resistors without letting them distort judgment.

Develop a change strategy where you emphasize the Drivers while dealing with the Resistors.

Exercise 81: Phases of the Change Process

The change process has several phases which may or may not occur in a linear, lock-step manner. Change is made up of continuously changing relationships of dynamic driving and resisting forces; therefore, the phases of the change process are more effectively used as recogniziable relationships to give us a framework to interpret and understand the phase.

The following checklist can be used in recognizing each phase.

Phase 1/Recognize the Need to Change

__ Customer complaints.

__ Loss of customers.

__ Changes in the market.

__ Changes in technology.

__ Changes in desired expertise.

__ Survival demands the change.

__ Need is acknowledged.

__ Need is communicated to/from decision-makers.

__ Responsibility is assigned.

__ Group is formed to do something about the change.

Phase 2/Assess the Need to Change

__ Gather information about current state (status quo).

__ Identify forces driving the change.

__ Decide on seriousness of the options.

    A. Do nothing.

    B. Make small adjustments.

    C. Make major changes.

    D. Make program changes.

    E. Make cultural changes.

__ Decide on data-gathering methods (surveys, research, observations, meetings, interviews, etc.) to verify variables to be changed.

Phase 3/Develop a Plan of Change

__ Identify the current state (the status quo).

__ Envision the desired future state (the vision).

__ Identify the values that are fundamental to the desired future state (e.g., fairness, integrity, honesty, respect).

__ Identify the value-based processes that are fundamental to achieving the desired future state (e.g., Stakeholder input, participative management, teamwork, shared reasoning in communication of decision rationale, accountability for time-money-actions).

__ Develop a change leadership team.

__ Develop a change leadership strategy.

__ Develop a change leadership plan with milestones.

Phase 4/Get Leadership and Formal Organizational Commitment

__ Get organizational commitment to invest resources needed to support the change process (budget, people, time, equipment, support services).

__ Select leaders of the process (both those with position power and opinion setters with personal power).

__ Get leader commitment to the process.

__ Leader commitment to facilitate and coach.

__ Negotiation with leaders who resist the change process whether overtly or covertly.

__ Establish observable behavior standards.

__ Leaders hold themselves and others responsible for acting in accordance with the values and behavioral standards.

Phase 5/Development of Skills

__ Leaders need to demonstrate, teach, and coach:
A. Mature use of power behaviors.
B. People skills.
C. Communication skills.
D. Thinking-action skills.
E. Group process and team-building skills.

Phase 6/Management of Coalition Formation and Increased Resistance to Change

__ Leaders recognize, understand, and work with Resistors.

__ Leaders recognize, understand, and energize Drivers.

__ Leaders expect and plan wise response to increasing anger that will be directed at them as fear of potential redistribution of power and influence increases.

__ Leader prepare for possible "character assassination" attempts in the rumor mill.

__ Leaders remain alert to factions questioning their motives as attempts increase to discredit them as change agents.

Phase 7/Coalitions Fight to Control Perception

__ Groups form who support the change.

__ Groups form who oppose the change.

__ Leaders must manage the power of inertia of those who watch and criticize, as well as those who watch and hope for success but will not help. (It is as important to accurately assess passive-aggressive resistance as to assess the overt aggressive resistance.)

___ Stakeholder battles increase.

___ Grapevine will be full of stories of "villians with selfish or greedy motives" in the change process.

Phase 8/Increased Chaos, Frustration and Unpredictability

___ Fear increases.

___ Emotional stress rises as numerous meetings and activities occur, but those who have not learned to see the intangible subtle behaviors and patterns have trouble seeing progress and tend to lose hope.

___ Control issues and "turf" protection increases.

___ Conflict increases.

___ Inconsistencies of the transition state tend to look as if the process is out of control.

___ Tendency to irrationally overvalue the status quo of the old state and idealize the past as preferable to the chaos of the transition state.

Phase 9/Crisis of Maintaining Leaders' Energy, Motivation, and Focus

___ People identify critical events and people as the flagships for people to watch.

___ Leaders who are driving the change identify positive events and people as flagships of successful indicators.

___ Leaders who are resisting the change identify negative events and people as flagships of failure indicators.

___ People watch, talk, and inadvertently add their energy to the struggle as they watch the change leaders and the resistance leaders use both personal and position power.

___ Critical energizers of the process are continuous learning challenges, feedback, and confrontation of people-issues or blockages.

___ Leaders need teamwork and the synergy of those with shared values to aid their energy and personal will to continue forging ahead despite the inertia of the status quo.

Phase 10/Leaders of Change Gain Momentum to Establish Norms
of the Vision of the Desired State or Leaders of Resistance Gain
Momentum to Block the Desired State Vision

___ New norms of the values, behavior standards, and the vision are established as the way the organization does business.

___ Accountability is established.

or

___ Leaders of resistance kill the change momentum.

___ Leaders of resistance get people's attention scattered through criticism, delay, sabotage, or framing daily business as the real work and frame the change process as an expensive interference, thus denying legitimacy of the change process.

Exercise 82:   Change Implementation Plan

The change implementation plan will focus on personal, system, or cultural change or all three categories.

Personal change involves individual beliefs, values, ethics, attitudes, and behaviors. Since behaviors are observable, patterns of behavior imply attitudes, values, ethics, and beliefs. **Key:** BEHAVIOR IS A FOCUS POINT FOR CHANGE STRATEGY.

System change involves business systems as accounting, information management, personnel, internal auditing, purchasing, and legal. System change may involve business development practices. It also involves organizational programs, training, and standard practices, as well as organizational policies such as capital purchases, job posting/hiring, approval processes, job families, wage and salary scales, etc. **Key:** SYSTEMS ARE A FOCUS POINT FOR CHANGE STRATEGY.

Culture change deals with the way the organization uses power and authority, interpersonal relationships, standards of conduct, and values that are rewarded. **Key:** CULTURE IS A FOCUS POINT FOR CHANGE STRATEGY.

The Change Implementation Plan needs to manage five elements: Human Relations, Decision-making, Planning, Communication, and Teamwork.

Instructions: Identify a change that is needed by your organization. Outline an implementation plan for change by indicating what and how you would accomplish each of the elements of the implementation plan.

CHANGE IMPLEMENTATION PLAN:

1. Develop a vision, identify shared values, and define principles.

2. Involve executive officers, team leaders, and opinion setters as action team facilitators.

3. Form change action teams.

4. Develop group process, communication, and leadership skills.

5. Develop action plans to implement the change.

6. Put action plans into action.

7. Determine success indicators using both measurable and observable indicators.

8. Provide for continuous feedback, planning, and improvement processes in the management of human relations, decision-making, planning, communication, and teamwork.

Exercise 83:   Partnering Process

Instructions: Review the following steps of the Partnering Process.

PURPOSE OF PARTNERING: To develop working relationships among the various organizations involved in a project. In order to most effectively accomplish the contract, the managing organization, the general contractor, the principal subcontractors, and the user/owner try to form a cohesive partnership for effective exchange of information and establishment of cooperative processes during the life of the project.

The Partnership strives to draw on the strengths of each organization in an effort *to achieve a quality project, done right the first time, within budget and on schedule.*

KEY TERMS:

Partnership — implies a sharing relationship in business with mutual interests and concerns; implies cooperation and issue resolution in an open discussion environment with joint resolution.

Teamwork — is mutually trusting people working together to achieve a unifying goal and supporting each other in an open communicative environment.

Trust — is firm belief and confident expectation in the honesty, reliability, and trustworthy intention of the other person.

Communication — is a process of message exchange whereby meaning is attributed to messages. Communication is efficient and economical when the message sent is the message received.

Problem-Resolution Process — a mutually agreed upon way of working through disagreements, different interpretations of specifications or contractual agreements, and different points of view.

The expected outcomes of Partnering are:
- Establishment and maintenance of open communication.
- Development and maintenance of team spirit in working relationships.
- Identification of mutual interests of all parties.
- Identification of Myers-Briggs natural styles of Partners.
- Agreement to an informal process of attempting to resolve

problems prior to having to send them up each respective chain of command for resolution.

- Agreement on a problem resolution approach for the strong disagreements to be used to attempt to avoid formal resolution process.
- Establishment and maintenance of mutually shared Partnering goals and values.
- Creation of a Partnering agreement in writing with signatures.
- Development of a plan to achieve the Partnering goals and sustainment of team spirit in working relationships.
- Agreement on a leadership plan to maintain and energize the Partnership agreement with periodic refocusing.
- Agreement on lead persons/champions to lead each of the action items identified as critical to achieving the Partnership goals.
- Agreement on a process to evaluate implementation of the Partnership agreement.

Exercise 84:   Personal Change Process

Individual change is a process that has some critical phases which are in dynamic juxtaposition as they emerge, recede, and then reemerge in the change process.

Instructions: Identify a change you personally want to make. Develop your personal change plan by working through the following phases:

1. Recognized NEED to change.

    (What caused you to become aware of the need to change?)

2. Assessment of the Costs of not changing.
    (What will you lose or have to pay if you do not change?)

3. Assessment of your Gains if you are successful in chang-
    ing.
    (How will you benefit by this proposed change?)

4. Decide to do it and make it a top priority every day.
    (What do you have to do to make a decision with no "back
    doors" by which you can back out and change your mind?)

5. Identify clear PROGRESS/FAILURE INDICATORS.
   (How will you know if you are making progress or failing?)

6. Clearly VISUALIZE THE OUTCOME of successfully changing.
   (See yourself reaping the benefits of succeeding. Feel the joy of succeeding. Think about how success energizes you.)

7. Make a TOTAL COMMITMENT with no thought of quitting.
   (How can you bring the force of your personal will to the success of this change?)

8. Manage the INCREASED RESISTANCE to the change.

(How will you deal with the urge to quit, the excuses that you don't have time, you don't have the energy, or you just don't feel like it today?)

9. Seek continuous FEEDBACK and FOCUS.

(How are you going to get feedback to know how you are doing?)

10. REMOTIVATE yourself and RECOMMIT continually.

(How will you remotivate, encourage, and reward your recommitment to make the change occur?)

– 8 –

Maturity and Teamwork: Stage IV Leaders and Teamwork

Main Ideas of Chapter 8:

1. The framework for power abuse is the same as for living a blaming, childish, immature life.

2. The framework for developing leadership skills is the same as for living a responsible, mature adult life.

3. Leaders demonstrate emotional and mental maturity.

4. Stage IV Leaders utilize teamwork as a principal process.

5. Eight critical elements of teamwork are: trust, candor, shared values, participation, accurate listening, shared reasoning, conflict resolution, and Stakeholder input into decision-making.

Power games are manipulations of mind and emotion. The games are intended to control outcomes. Power players believe that whoever controls perception controls outcomes.

Leaders understand the fight for perceptual control. They accept the difficult task of developing others' capability to see through manipulation. They help people become more aware of power games and perceptual distortions.

Leadership requires power; you cannot lead without it. Understanding power requires awareness of the ways power games are used to control perception. Developing leadership skills requires excellent behavior observation capabilities, process recognition, and intrapersonal as well as interpersonal understanding.

Recognizing behaviors that give clues about a person's power style provides the requisite information for clear interaction choices. We believe that skilled recognition of communication and power style is fundamental to responsible leadership.

The framework for power abuse is the same as for living a blaming, childish, immature life. Review immature power paradigm.

IMMATURE USE OF POWER

Recognition: Power styles and communication types can be used for manipulation and "to get my way."

Basic Belief: Pain is bad; pleasure is good.

Root Cause of Power Abuse: Fear.

Typical Mechanism for Dealing With Fear: Control!!

Result: Blame others for pain or failure.

Attitude: Be jealous of others and angry about others having more.

Cost: Illusion, foggy perception, skewed judgment.

Outcome: Results in power abuse/ perpetually wanting and taking.

The paradigm for immature use of power enables the leader to see and to explain causative reasons for power abuse.

Watch for behaviors that reveal the way people deal with pain and frustration. You get the best reading of the part fear plays in their lives. Power abuse is driven by fear.

CASE STUDY: FEAR DRIVES OUT TEAMWORK

Burt had just been assigned to a federal government Directorate. As director with twenty-seven years of government experience, he felt ready to tackle the new job. Little did he know that "tackle" was the right term.

The past two directors were described as laid-back and uninvolved. Burt inherited eighty-five employees with little management supervision for the past ten years.

In the absence of clear leadership, people scramble for power and influence. Employees had developed some very dysfunctional patterns during the leadership vacuum.

Burt is an ESTP (Extrovert, Sensor, Thinker, Perceiver) who earned a reputation for possessing excellent technical knowledge. Much of his management career with the federal government occurred when the emphasis was on technical skills, and little value was placed on people skills.

When he assessed his current situation, he found numerous cliques operating within various sections of the three divisions. The cliques were narrow little exclusive groups who guarded and supported each other but considered everyone outside the group as the enemy. Distrust was evident.

As he observed the Directorate, Burt saw people coming and going as they pleased with little time accountability, no productivity standards, misuse of time, excessive socializing within the cliques, and work getting stuck due to the lack of cooperation among the cliques. A few of the employees tried to avoid the office dynamics by working as much as possible by themselves. The loners chose to cope with the dysfunctional office dynamics by avoiding involvement in anything other than task.

Burt's Extroverted approach was to "come in hard and leave soft." He analyzed the situation and decided that more rules, strict office policy, and publicized statements of punishment would prove that he meant to change things. He decided to allow *no* deviation from the rules. He thought that strict enforcement of office policy would shape things right up.

The situation only worsened. Since people tend to compare the new with the old, perception became rearranged within the grapevine. Several of the rumor mill's most active influencers began to remember the past bosses as having amazingly superior characteristics — almost reaching angelic perfection. Those people who were not thinking for themselves joined in rumor-mill myopia — seeing things simplistically as "totally good" or "totally bad."

The new director was quickly labeled in the rumor mill as an ego maniac, a tyrant, an intimidator, and an insensitive authoritarian. Burt, unfortunately, gave them plenty of behavioral ammunition to support the image.

As the employees resisted him, Burt became even more "hard-nosed" as he determined to win the struggle. He repeatedly called attention to his record of firing someone in every location where he had worked. For extra punch, he said, "I've never worked anywhere that I haven't fired someone. I may top my all-time record for getting rid of people. There are certainly plenty of candidates around here for my list." He repeatedly used threats such as "If you don't like it, you can hit the road," "You can be replaced," and "We obviously have too many people and not enough work if people have time to gossip and complain."

He made strong statements about what would or would not be allowed. After he made the forceful statements, he then singled out someone for humiliation. He confronted the person in front of others, then after the verbal show, he tended to forget the issue. He made an example of someone and then went on to something else. He was a "stuck" ESTP. He liked to make noisy public statements, devoid of Feeler sensitivity, lay out clear rules and regulations, and then focus on something else without following through to see the resolution of the issue. His Perceiver-adapter tendency did not spur the follow-through necessary to demonstrate firm intention.

We were asked to come work with the Directorate. Burt had tried for fourteen months to order the situation by applying more force, more intimidation, and more anger. After observing the groups at work and interviewing each of the individuals we assessed the work climate: five major power struggles, favoritism, cliques, spying, surveillance, gossip, character assassination, low morale, lack of trust, fear of retaliation, and unequal distribution of work. Conflict stimulated one of two extreme reactions by management — either respond with force, edicts, and threats, or avoid it and pretend it isn't happening.

Without fair and equitable use of managerial power, mature use of power by employees is highly unlikely. As the director berated the division chiefs, and the division chiefs relied even more on their cliques to help them lick their wounds, status became a handy way to judge each other. The division chiefs were angry with each other and vied for power, the branch managers were also struggling with each other and with the chiefs, the team leaders bad-mouthed each other, and the rest of the employees divided up among cliques of technicians and support staff clerks. One wise person who called herself "just a tired old gray-hair" said she was "so close to retirement that I can say what I think. Let's face it . . . Shit rolls down hill. And the clerks are at the bottom of the hill. They band together, but what can they do? They have become defensive and quarrelsome. If you looked for a week you can't find a thimble-full of cooperation around here."

With power abuse as the norm, the directorate was a terrible place to work. When I asked people to complete a sentence about working at the Directorate — "Working at the Directorate can most accurately be described as . . ." — responses were "tension is so thick you can cut it, surveillance and spying, rumor and divisiveness, jealousy, back-stabbing, turmoil, paranoia, intimidation, and retribution." In short, *fear* underscores the description.

Management throughout the Directorate habitually demonstrated immature use of power. One division chief as a Feeler was a frequent target of manipulation. Bret is a "stuck" ESFJ (Extrovert, Sensor, Feeler, Judge). Employees describe him as "a nice guy who desperately wants to be liked," "a good technician who should never have been moved into management," and "a man who was terrified of conflict."

Bret has favorites who make up his inner circle. He listens to his favorites and then reacts without checking things out. He just rebounds with his feelings and does not exercise clear thinking. He responds moodily. One employee said he was a man of extreme moods — either loudly pleased and stimulating a party atmosphere or sullenly angry at some perceived hurt or injustice and becoming demanding and nitpicky. One employee said, "He either won't talk to me . . . ignoring me . . . refusing to even return my morning greeting, or he treats me so special that it is grossly uncomfortable. When I am his 'good little worker' he jokes and showers me with compliments. When I've disappointed him, he punishes me by trying to freeze me out of his little special inner circle."

Bret is a Stage I power player. He is most habituated to Helpless Infant, with guilting and obligatory games to keep his inner circle protecting him and telling him how kind and likable he is. When cross with someone, Bret is a Terrible Tyrant. He is accused of retaliation at performance appraisal time with vague reasons for the rating. His reputation for getting even with anyone who upsets him tends to keep employees from challenging his punitive behaviors. He is manipulated by Rob, one of the section leaders who reports to him.

Rob is a Competitive Manipulator whose personal style is ESTJ (Extrovert, Sensor, Thinker, Judge). He matches Bret's Extroverted energy and creates a synergistic web to lull Bret into his manipulative plan. Rob strokes Bret's ego, brings him tidbits of gossip information, plays the dutiful son bringing Daddy evidence that Bret's nemesis is the new director. Rob repeatedly criticizes Burt, while praising Bret's skills.

Bret and Rob called me aside, saying they "wanted to straighten me out" about the director. Rob demonstrated his "stroke, thrust, and console" technique. He said, "I never met anyone who is as sharp about our business as Bret here. He's terrific. And another thing, he's always willing to help. Burt is jealous of his technical skill and he picks on Bret. Doesn't he, Bret? [To which Bret dutifully shook his head in agreement.] Burt questions Bret in humiliating ways and treats him very unprofessionally. If it wasn't for those of us who defend Bret, I think Burt would have already fired him. Bret did mess up on an important project and I thought sure Burt was going to can him. But he didn't, did he Bret? [Again, Bret looked uncomfortable but shook his head in mute agreement.] Bret doesn't know the offshore calculations very well, but he knows everything else. He's just great to work for . . . if we could just get that damn director out of our hair, then we could go back to doing business in a much more relaxed and fun way, couldn't we, Bret? [Bret again shook his head in agreement.]

Rob creates conflict all around him while appearing to be innocent himself. He masterfully drops innuendos and strings together bits of information to manipulate inferences. For example, he was discussing another section leader whom he obviously dislikes. He said, "Quite honestly, I can't really tell you how she got selected for the job. She got it, but I don't know how she *got it,* if you know what I mean." I responded by telling him that I did not know what he meant and asked him to explain.

Rob said, "Well, I heard Burt telling Bret that he needed to fire her. She did not know what she was doing. Then Burt had to attend a director's meeting in Chicago and decided to take her with him. He used some excuse like the project she was working on might come up at the meeting. I can't say why he really took her, but they have been as thick as thieves ever since they took that trip. It seems that she developed some miraculous new skills on that trip that makes her a prized employee now. That seems like a strange reversal. One day you aren't technically qualified and the next day you are. Pretty amazing!"

He criticizes others in such personal ways that people are afraid of him. They feel helpless to counter his innuendos and carelessly drawn conclusions. He makes continuous logical errors by making cause-effect inferences that are not supportable as "proof" of his opinions.

Rob's Stage III Competitive Manipulator/Intimidator style challenges even skilled people to hold their own while dealing with him. He uses very intense, penetrating eye contact that has a mesmerizing effect while using a personalizing tone of voice and inflection that tends to compel and seduce. The tones sound like the conspiratorial sharing of your best friend entrusting most sacred insights. He has the ability to draw people out and get them to place unwarranted confidence in his intentions. His arguments are circular and difficult to nail down. He baits and sets up circular sidetracking arguments that tend to confuse and obfuscate his real motives. He strokes, thrusts, and consoles in a disarming way.

He criticizes others with emotionally loaded words that appear to be deliberate attempts to trigger fear, confusion, and a sense of vulnerability in others. He was arrogantly careless of his manipulation techniques, apparently believing that people either did not have the clarity to see what he was doing or they didn't have the courage to risk engaging him.

The intervention we recommended was a three-day, off-site session where we could address the issues. Each participant was interviewed. We used a structured set of questions so that their individual answers could be kept private but the issues could be quantified. In addition, each participant was asked to fill out an Organizational Culture Questionnaire that we prepared. They also filled out the Myers-Briggs Type Indicator.

At the session, people demonstrated ambivalence. On the one hand they did not believe the real issues would be addressed, and on the other hand they really wanted some relief from the war zone of broken and punitive relationships.

To demonstrate integrity of the process, we reviewed the specific issues and then began working them one at a time using the four-quadrant problem-solving process. We took an issue and summarized the information by identifying the facts in Quadrant 1, the analysis of consequences in Quadrant 2, the possibilities in Quadrant 3, and the values and relationship issues in Quadrant 4. After giving them a candid list of the issues, we discussed the director's style first. People told me later that they could not believe that I had accurately reported their concerns about the director's style.

We addressed each of the power struggles, identified the issues, identified the style differences, the games involved, and identified actions that the group wanted to take to responsibly work on problem resolution.

The Directorate could not hope to work as a team without cleaning up some old hurtful issues, establishing clear professional standards for working together, establishing teamwork criteria, and identifying specific actions, and measurements of success.

Participants had to learn to describe behavior. They had to start rebuilding basic communication skills of listening, verbalizing, talking to the person with whom they were irritated instead of talking to others about the person. The process is arduous. The power players resisted. They have a lot to lose if the culture is changed from criticism, divisiveness, and control through innuendo and rumor. Power players don't fare very well when problems are clearly assessed and confronted. Power players get scared when they have to deal in the light of clear perception, probing for verification of issues, and sharing of information so that the entire situation can be analyzed. They function best in the dark.

Bret, the ESFJ Stage I power player, took a demotion and vowed that he would never again allow himself to fall into the "snake pit of managerial responsibility." Rob, the ESTJ Stage III Competitive Manipulator/Intimidator, asked for a transfer to another section of the country and moved on to another job within six weeks of the confrontation of the dysfunctional dynamics of the Directorate. Burt, the ESTP Stage III Competitive Intimidator, is working on developing people skills. He began his work with a frank acknowledgment that he understood the system and he understood the thousands of rules and regulations governing his profession, but he was just scratching the surface of the complexity of leading people. The cliques have been somewhat broken up as some of the people were cross-functionally trained to get a better mix of skills. The clerks have been reassigned to teams and no longer function as a separate group left to form a defensive clique fighting for self-esteem.

Without trust, candor, participation, and shared values to establish what is important and to agree on interaction standards, groups can never develop teamwork. Without the processes of accurate listening, conflict resolution, shared reasoning, and Stakeholder involvement in decision-making, groups cannot sustain teamwork. Without mature use of power, teamwork will not survive.

Stage I power players are in a state of dependency while fearing the powerlessness that dependency creates. As long as Stage I Helpless Infants are getting needs met, pretended niceness is easy. Bret liked to be the Helpless Infant. When he became frustrated in getting what he wanted, however, the Terrible Tyrant rises out of the Helpless Infant to wreak havoc. The person who is the object of Stage I's manipulation must play the game by taking responsibility for the Stage I's happiness in order for the Stage I to control the game. If, however, someone sees the game clearly and refuses to play, the Stage I experiences a rush of anger as fear of powerlessness, failure, and rejection shouts the alarm. Stage I then tries to marshal enough energy to explode and activate the other person's fear of conflict to force compliance. Bret rewarded with inclusion and punished with exclusion.

Stage II power players demonstrate similar tendencies. They frequently play the Benevolent Dictator until crossed. They are vigilant about any cue that the manipulation is not working. The move into Abusive Dictator behaviors usually happens suddenly as their fear overwhelms them. They move straight to explosive force, intending to impel compliance. This strategy too often works. Only those people who have confronted their own fears of powerlessness, failure, rejection, and conflict can withstand the onslaught without falling under the dictator's spell.

Stage III power players usually begin interactions as Competitive Manipulators until they either feel fear themselves or decide that they must activate an immediate dose of fear in their opponent. A surprise switch from hale and hearty Manipulator to deadly and punitive Intimidator is a strategy to maximize the fearful response in others. Rob used cobra-like movements as he lulled people into his conspiratorial confidence and then attacked them with penetrating personal criticism.

Power players rely on fear for their power. They rely on the lie that pain is bad for continual renewal of currency in their game.

The basic belief that pain is bad and pleasure is good undergirds the power game and contributes to immature use of power. If you have not fully examined the potency for self-deception in the pain-is-bad belief, you are an easy candidate for power struggles and manipulations. Power players depend on people's fear of pain to cause people to rearrange their own perception, to look the other way, to pretend, and to discount the real intentions. We see overwhelming behavioral evidence of power abuse and watch actions that show that people lie to themselves to avoid having to experience the pain of the real situation. They say, "Oh, it's not so bad. He didn't really mean to do that. She just didn't realize how much that hurt. Oh, I won't think anything of it ten years from now" — thus refusing to see the behaviors for what they truly are. They too often choose to suffer the internal dissonance of compromising their own standards rather than deal with their fear of open confrontation and pain.

When fear activates, the typical immature person usually tries to control, control, control. The costs are enormous. In fearful locked-down posture, we become rigid, inflexible, defensive, concretized, and ultimately walled in by our fear. As we try to build thicker and thicker walls to keep out the pain, we discover too late that we are walled in with our fear of failure, rejection, powerlessness as we experience the pain of conflict within ourselves. The wall that is designed to keep others out keeps us locked inside simultaneously. Many try to reach the state of numbness and if successful, they further close down perception.

If you purchased an expensive camera with a powerful lens, you would probably go to great lengths to protect it. Why, then, would you not be just as attentive to taking excellent care of the much more powerful process of perception. Power Players continually fling the mud of confusion, the acid of deception, the grease of flattery, and the distortion of fogging our perceptual process to prevent our seeing clearly. Too many times we assist in the contamination of our own perception by refusing to become aware of our own fears and beliefs.

CASE STUDY: A SMALL, FEARFUL LIFE

One of our acquaintances is a small business owner. Ernest is a hard-working man who has inculcated his wife, two sons, and his daughter with his own fears. His parents were married during the Depression and were deeply scarred with the fear of not having enough money. As a child he heard story after story that imprinted him with a terror of being in a powerless situation without the money to fix it. He equated power with money; therefore, powerlessness meant not having enough money to avoid pain.

He had his first paper route at six years of age, worked two jobs during his entire school life, and continued his lifetime course of working every hour that he is awake. He is so dominated by his fear of being without money that he cannot see the pain caused by his fixation.

His fear so dominates him that he and his family live a very small life, with little activity that is not work-focused. He is cheap in every way. He buys the cheapest things he can find. He sacrifices what he really wants at the altar of finding less quality on sale. Finding something on sale destroys his ability to fairly judge the quality or even remember what he really wanted before he looked at the price tag. Price tags can completely change his attitude; consequently, he works hard but never lives the life that he wants.

As the economy worsens and the stock market gyrates, he studies incessantly about how to tighten the family belt, although he owns real estate, stocks and bonds, and has a sizable cash savings. He tries to find ways to live an even more bleak existence. He does not realize that life is lived today, right now, in the present. He has been "waiting for Godot" all of his life as he hangs on to the irrational belief that one day he will have enough money and then he will be happy. He has not realized that with unconfronted fear driving his obsession with money, there will *never* be enough. Fear is a greedy god with insatiable drives. His life is becoming more and more habituated, smaller and smaller. He doesn't try anything new for fear that it will cost more than he feels comfortable paying. He is unhappy. His family is unhappy. All five individuals demonstrate fearful, intense, uptight, careful lives. Their minds and emotions seem to be locked down, and the joyful possibilities of life escape them.

Power abuse can be unintentional. Ernest is basically a decent, hard-working man who lives a principled life dedicated to his family. He is deeply patriotic, taking pride in being well informed. His power abuse is driven by his unacknowledged fear. His wife is driven by her dependency and fear of rejection. His children are consequently fearful and lack the confidence to go zestfully forward to discover their potentialities.

Unraveling Ernest's distorted perception could be done with an intensive change process. He would have to change

from Denial of Fear	to Recognition of Fear
from Avoidance of Pain	to Confrontation of Fear
from Control	to Acceptance
from Concretization	to Openness

Presently, Ernest is in such a state of denial that regenerative change is not occurring.

PATHWAY FROM IMMATURITY TO MATURITY

The leader is quite familiar with pain but is also familiar with peace that comes when beliefs, values, and actions are aligned. In successfully confronting one's fear, the hidden, dark, unexamined urges are diminished in the light of truth. We would never suggest that leaders have no fear; we do unequivocably state, however, that Stage IV Leaders know their fears and have the courage to act wisely despite them. Because Stage IVs have confronted their fears, power players cannot use leaders' fears to overwhelm them. Leaders accept their fear as a known and recognized force which considerably dispels the hidden blinding force of unknown fear. The Stage IV Leader does what is necessary despite the fear involved.

The interactive processes of emotion and feelings, of our nervous systems and endocrine systems, allow us to experience pain. Without pain we tend to have little reason to pursue the discomfort of growth and change. The status quo has the tremendous power of inverse inertia.

Obviously, we are physically, mentally, and emotionally endowed with the mechanisms for experiencing pain. We cannot get through life without pain, so why not make it count for something? The wise leader recognizes the value of pain and helps people in the organization use pain for the advantage of growth, self-renewal, understanding, and adapting to changing environments.

Individual ideas of the amount of pain we can bear is greatly affected by our frame of reference. A helicopter pilot who had voluntarily served three missions in Vietnam with four of his copters shot out from under him obviously had a different frame of reference for pain and suffering than the young, family-supported college graduate. Their tolerance for the inanities of organizational life were 180 degrees apart. The young lawyer, complaining about having to work all day Saturday without extra pay or appreciation, looked a bit like a whiner from the vet's framework. He was fond of saying, "If they can't kill you, lock you up, or physically torture you, you ain't got it bad at all."

Leaders are not afraid of pain, and they openly bear the awesome responsibility of inflicting pain when progress cannot be made without it. Many times the truth is painful; yet, the leader must be devoted to the truth. Power players inflict pain for personal gain or personal pettiness. Stage IV Leaders recognize that neither pain nor power is inherently bad.

Change frequently involves pain, uncertainty, and a breaking-up in order to find better adapted forms. We are wonderfully endowed with tremendous self-renewing capacity, but we are not given any guarantee that the self-renewing journey is not painful.

Ilya Prigogine's Nobel Prize-winning work in chemistry gave us a descriptive term called "dissipative structures" that is generalizable to the human system, which is made up of chemical systems. He proved that living entities have the capacity to lose energy as they dissipate, but contain the capacity for regeneration into a more adaptive form in response to environmental demands. He demonstrated that living systems have the capacity to go through disorder while retaining a generalized field of order, thus allowing chaos and order to be twin aspects of the same process. Anyone going through massive change should be able to instantly identify with the dissipative energy in the midst of massive change that, when successfully navigated, emerges as new strength, insight, and order. The endless process of change goes on as disorder evolves into order to eventually go through other phases of self-renewal or degeneration.

Leaders do not dodge the difficult task of administering pain when it is required for breakthrough, growth, understanding, or freedom from distorted perception and cloudy judgment. They are unafraid to bring temporary disorder for the opportunity to evolve into a more productive order to meet changing needs. They will, however, be very self-examining to make sure that the painful condition is necessary for growth and not just an egoic indulgence in power.

Leaders understand that pain is a powerful motivator. If nothing else works, pain usually does. The ever present questions are: "What is this pain teaching? What is being discovered? What freedom is won as a result of this pain? What transformation is occurring? What is being gained and what is the price?"

Clear judgment provides the leader with an understanding of how much truth or pain a person can tolerate at any one point in time and still be able to grow as a result of it. Compassion must be a significant element in leadership. Compassion comes from the leader's having been through some of the very same things. Having experienced the doubts, fears, anxieties and worked through those to the order that comes with understanding and insight, the leader understands the necessity for pain.

If the world continues in its present trend, there will be more than enough pain to motivate the population to seek real leadership. The leader need have no concern about becoming obsolete. At this point in time, we see an unending need for real leadership. Leaders will continue to find themselves in great demand. Real leadership is required to get the jobs done that need doing. They are unafraid of addressing real issues, and they produce needed results.

Leaders are ever making themselves dispensable. They demonstrate the ongoing act of voluntarily relinquishing power by enabling others, modeling, teaching, and supporting others. Leaders are perpetually training others to take their place. Giving away power exponentially increases it when the empowerment is done with clear-headed assessment of capacity for mature handling of power. We have seen too many instances of empowerment where immature power players used the opportunity to abuse others. Wise empowerment requires the Leader to make clear assessment of communication and power style, fear management, and capacity to respond wisely to change.

Voluntarily giving up power and control is fundamental to the development of real leadership — something most of those who claim to be leaders would never do. Just listen to them scream if anyone dares to take their parking place or tries to withhold their privileges in any way.

The real leader understands that admission of fear is the first step to diminishing it. Experiencing powerlessness tends to demystify it, thus putting power into a realistic perspective. Stage IV Leaders understand the importance of confronting fear, admitting it and getting familiar with it as a way of diminishing its hold. Leaders understand this important phenomenon, thereby expecting and encouraging the management of fear from those s/he serves (i.e., followers).

The developmental exercises at the end of each chapter are designed to give you working materials to improve your ability to recognize power styles, perceptual distortions, and the role fear plays in self-deception, to review change dynamics, and ultimately to pull each of those understandings into a comprehensible framework for leading people.

MATURE USE OF POWER

The framework for developing leadership skills is the same as for living a responsible, mature adult life. The framework is based upon clear perception, sound judgment, and acceptance of responsibility for one's own thoughts, feelings, and actions.

Recognition: Individuals are responsible for their power styles and development of their communication styles.

Basic Belief: Pain is one-half of life's dual nature that cannot be avoided; therefore, one should always strive to learn from pain and accept its lessons. Pleasure is the other half that teaches and brings balance to the pain-pleasure dimension.

Power: The potential to influence brings with it an enormous responsibility to use it wisely and caringly.

Fear: Fear must be acknowledged and accepted in order to keep it from fogging perception and hindering right action.

Method for Dealing With Fear: Awareness, acceptance, right action.

Result: Accept responsibility for own thoughts, feelings, and actions.

Attitude: Be thankful and appreciative for what you have.

Cost: Continuous, brutal self-examination, perpetually questioning own motives, interests, desires, and frustrations.

Outcome: Foundation for mature use of power — leadership.

Throughout the book we have given examples of Stage IV Leaders. You can recognize them by the consistency of their actions. "Leader" is a title that is given by others; when people try to claim it for themselves with words, braggadocio, and self-serving actions, clear-thinking people recognize the power player trying to manipulate perception.

The adage "The proof is in the eating of the pudding" leads us to assert that the proof of a leader is in the effect s/he has on others.

You know you work for a **leader** when . . .

1. You have a continual internal push to do excellent thinking, responding, and action.

2. You are pushed or inspired to discover new talents and increased expansion of recognized talents.

3. You increase your ability to risk.

4. Your confidence to achieve increases.

5. Your understanding of system, people, politics, and the organization increases . . . you learn continually from the leader . . . the process becomes clearer.

6. You see the leader continually demonstrate clear perception and judgment.

7. You see mediocrity met with no-nonsense confrontation.

8. All are held accountable for their actions.

Conversely, you can also readily observe the effect of power players. You know you are seeing a **power player** when . . .

1. People tend to quit thinking for themselves and think pri-

marily in terms of how to keep the power player from becoming angry and punishing.

2. People are expected to frequently stroke the power player's ego.

3. The power player takes the credit for anything well done in the work unit and finds a scapegoat for anything that is amiss.

4. Favoritism and cronyism determine privilege.

5. Information is guarded and secretive.

6. People spend much time protecting themselves (CYA).

7. People don't trust, aren't candid, and play it safe.

8. Blaming others and creating alibis is the norm.

STAGE IV LEADERSHIP PRINCIPLES

Leaders operate with dependable principles. In organizations, teams, and groups that are led by leaders, their leadership principles establish the group norms:

Confrontation of issues and unproductive behavior will occur.

Participation and collaboration are expected.

Clear perception and sound judgment are fundamental.

Excellent **communication skills** are demonstrated.

Challenge and excellent performance are expected.

People skills use human behavior knowledge to develop, motivate/inspire people for excellent performance, cooperation, and teamwork.

EMOTIONAL AND MENTAL MATURITY

Leaders demonstrate emotional and mental maturity. You do not see childishness in thought or behavior. Leaders behave as mature adults. They accept full responsibility for their own experiences. Some of the personal characteristics, attitudes, and beliefs that you see leaders demonstrate can also serve as a checklist for you to review your own level of maturity.

1. Leaders **accept responsibility for their own acts.** They do not blame others nor alibi.

2. Leaders **accept criticism.** They weigh the criticism gratefully as an opportunity to improve.

3. Leaders **do not expect special consideration.** They do not see themselves as better than others nor as deserving exceptional status.

4. Leaders **do not indulge in self-pity nor self-praise.** They accept the duality laws that bring power and powerlessness, pain and pleasure, sadness and joy. They accept pain and disappointment without whining or complaining. They accept success and joy with heartfelt appreciation for all who helped make it happen.

5. Leaders **control their temper.** They use anger responsibly and wisely.

6. Leaders **confront themselves and deal with their own fears.** They acknowledge and manage their fear instead of denying it.

7. Leaders **communicate excellently.** They paint clear, memorable pictures, listen open-mindedly and thoughtfully to others, and explain and respond with clear messages.

8. Leaders **accept others' success without envy or jealousy.** They can genuinely celebrate the deserved success of others.

9. Leaders' **feelings are not easily hurt.** They are emotionally mature and do not entertain imagined innuendos nor lash out in retaliation.

10. Leaders **deal with emergencies, surprises, and challenges with poise and clear thinking.** They do not forsake their devotion to truth when challenged or attacked.

Leaders are not ordinary. We repeat: They are *extraordinary*. Leaders may not have been endowed with any special talents, but they have certainly responded extraordinarily to the challenges of life. Their responses led them to mature and responsible use of power.

ORGANIZATIONS AS LIVING ORGANISMS

Organizations, like families, live, breathe, hope, hate, compete, and support — for they have all of the potentialities that comprise humanity. Organizations provide recognizable boundaries for gathering people together; they are dynamic, shared energy fields representing the personal styles of the people who comprise them while sharing the organizational culture. We fall short of trying to capture the dynamic reality of organizations when we try to draw organizational charts with boxes and lines to try to capture organizational identities. Those boxes may capture the formal authority lines, but they can never explain the relationships that work or fail that truly make up the nature of the organization. The organizational chart fails miserably to account for leadership, teamwork, or caustic-adversarial relationships within the groups.

Organizations are not machines that can be understood by carefully analyzing all of their parts and eventually coming to an understanding. We must finally acknowledge that the interaction of people, processes, and personalities creates interconnections and interferences that cannot be understood by reductionist or additive logic. We ultimately have to engage head, heart, impressions, knowings, and values to be able to sense the perpetually changing and exchanging human energies that remain loosely bound by the organizational culture within which they work and live.

Leaders move past reductionist logic or adding up tasks and use process awareness to see organizational life as much more than its number of people, supplies, equipment, and buildings. Leaders know that organizations are people.

People impact one another as they share space, and their boundaries touch, fuse, or repel. We saw two experts assigned to share an intensive project. The results were disastrous.

Although Julie's talent, enthusiasm, and dedication had been proven over and over, when she was paired with Jonathan, we observed her struggle to retain her own energy level. Jonathan, though a knowledgeable engineer, argues minutiae, reacts to suggestions as hostile invasions, and can best be described as a dominator turned sniveler if he doesn't get his way. When Julie and Jonathan were paired on an important task, the energy field was caustic. Together they produced less quality than either of them could have produced independently. Their energy was wasted in controlling their individual boundaries with little left over to contribute to the project.

As we walked into a planning session, the tension was palpable between Julie and Jonathan. The other six people in the room were clearly affected. Conversation was terse, transitions between thoughts were jerky, facial muscles showed strained tension, and words were carefully chosen. People were locked down. Interactions were stiff and formal. We had seen both Julie and Jonathan produce outstanding work, but they were subtracting instead of adding to each other. They were clearly repelling each other, and the work was consequently suffering.

Creating synergistic working relationships is one of the largest challenges of leadership. Putting the right people together can create such synergy that the potential becomes exponential rather than just arithmetical. Each individual brings a field of energy that subtly communicates and broadcasts energy. When individual energy fields connect and together expand boundaries, their synergy creates possibility, innovation, exploration, and expansion. When individual energy fields repel, reject, and struggle to maintain dominance, their contact becomes interference that shuts down open exchange in favor of control and concretization.

Some people inspire expansion and exploration, while others cause contraction and caution.

STAGE IV LEADERSHIP AND TEAMWORK

Teamwork requires emotional and mental maturity. We define teamwork as "Mutually trusting people working together responsibly to achieve unifying goals while supporting each other in an open, candid, communicative environment." Teams need each individual to responsibly and candidly contribute to the team effort. We frequently hear about self-directed teams and have seen some in action, but few know how to facilitate the fundamental determiner of success or failure — power and communication style.

Poor quality work, low productivity, poor morale, inadequate commitment have long been recognized as problematic. One of

America's responses to these challenges has been "self-directed teams." Basically, people are selected for a project and allowed to organize themselves, their work, their budget, and their schedules to achieve a clearly measurable goal. Self-directed groups decide for themselves in nontraditional ways how to achieve the task. The ideas sound wonderful when you think about people's desires to be independent adults.

Leaders are aware that people in groups usually have a desire to be involved in a worthwhile mission to which they can make a significant contribution where their input is solicited and they can get feedback.

Human nature operating in groups is motivated by mission, self-worth, participation, and feedback. Leaders understand the human nature principles of group interaction:

MISSION — People want to *contribute* to something meaningful.

SELF-WORTH — People want to know their *contribution* is important . . . that they make a significant difference.

PARTICIPATION — People want *input* into what affects them.

FEEDBACK — People want evidence that their input was *heard, understood, and considered.*

Those operating principles must be modeled and focused in order to create the norms for group conduct. Self-directed teams theoretically are organized on the implicit assumption that the selected individuals will all function with mature use of power.

Self-directed teams are predicated on the idea that as the project or task evolves, whomever has the expertise will assume the leader/facilitator role at that time. The excellent idea works only to the degree that each of the individuals manages his/her own fears, power styles, and personalities in a mature manner.

Research indicates that groups will not long go leaderless. A focal point is required. True, if the project or task is clear and the members have strongly shared values, goals, and commitments, the unity that results will be the organizing synergy that propels the group forward. We believe that a leader will nevertheless emerge. One person will win the recognition for having the ability to keep things focused. Indicating the need for such focus are remarks about a leader who can "cut to the chase," "help get through stuck points or plateaus and get going again," "keep clearly in mind the goal," "recognize when someone's expertise is overlooked," "push for greater integrity of thought," and "be perpetually aware of the overall process."

Committees are usually appointed with members selected for their expertise, authority, or access to equipment or resources. They may never move into the development phases to become a team. A committee may never achieve much except endless meetings with little growth or productive outcomes. Unfortunately, millions of dollars are lost every year in pointless committee meetings. One team can outperform ten committees. Teams perform from the synergistic effect of their energies that cause them to achieve more than the total of their individual capabilities.

American management has been too eager to find solutions to the anachronistic, antagonistic, authoritarian approach to people. Teams sound like the way to go. We caution the blanket endorsement of teams without clear understanding of human nature and a framework for building teams. Although we philosophically endorse teamwork and know that it is a highly desirable force to unleash at challenges, it cannot be done successfully without leadership and focus.

When task groups or committees form, they go through development phases. As dynamic human systems they come together, each bringing their own force fields of attitudes, styles, and power stages. Whether or not they go through the development phases to become a team depends on leadership and bonding experiences. Bonding causes unity, cohesiveness, and shared feelings that move people toward team identity. People can work together for months on committees and never bond as a team. Groups go through identifiable phases as they move through the process to transition from a group into a team. Many groups do not successfully manage the transition from phase to phase, thus never making it through the stages of maturity required for teamwork. We've seen many groups but far fewer teams.

We have worked with organizations for years and have observed the phases of development. The movement from committee or group into the bonding of teamwork results in commitment (individual buy-in) and trusting relationships.

High levels of trust are required for teamwork; therefore, the most significant dynamic to lead, observe, and continually assess is the state of demonstrated trust among team members.

Trust is dynamic — a force continuously forming, changing, expanding, or contracting. The dynamics of trust, trust-building, or untrustworthiness are driving forces in each phase of group development.

Trust is not a tangible commodity. It is not available on demand; it is not established through words. Trust is earned through continuous confidence in behavior that shows reliable, honest intentions. Trust is best earned by extending it. Trust must be earned. It cannot be demanded; it cannot be taken by command. Trust is a gift we can give but cannot demand.

The phases of group development may not come in linear order. Sometimes you can watch one meeting where various phases manifest. If you have a familiar framework for recognizing the behaviors within the various phases, you can more accurately assess what is needed.

When people first come together as a group, they typically go through Phase 1, the **Polite Phase.** Group members are getting acquainted, or if already acquainted, observing the particular roles that they may be asked to play. Group members observe each other, assess the group and make decisions about the purpose of the group and its chances of developing into something meaningful.

In Phase 2, the **Task Accomplishment Phase,** members look for assurance that something is going to be accomplished so they want to know clearly what is expected, the desired outcomes, and how the goal will be accomplished.

Phase 3, the **Struggle for Power and Control Phase** brings the struggle for dominance/submission into forceful dimensions. Group members experience different levels of commitment, doubt, concerns, and direction. This is a critical phase where groups can become so factionalized that they splinter into subgroups and destroy teamwork potential.

Phase 4, the **Clarifying and Refocusing Phase,** occurs when group members assess where they started, what they learned, and where they want to go. They reassess whether or not they want to continue and how they can get energized and focused.

If group members have successfully bonded during the previous phases of development they may reach Phase 5, the **Teamwork and Growth Phase.** Group members are valued and accepted for their strengths and weaknesses while simultaneously expected to grow, develop, and demonstrate excellent group process skills. The group members modify and discipline their own behavior to facilitate teamwork and goal achievement.

Groups whose members do not have clear communication type development or mature use of power are quite challenging to a group's ability to become a mature team. Immature use of power has a better chance of resulting in a gang — but not in a team. The term "gang" currently denotes group behavior devoid of individuality. Gang membership demands mindless conformity to group norms.

Without mature leadership, Phase 3 struggle for dominance can degenerate into gang tendencies of one person's dominance over the group. Unsuccessful Phase 3 can also result in "groupthink" as a means to avoid conflict and group punishment.

Irving L. Janis defined "groupthink" in his 1982 work: "Groupthink refers to a deterioration of mental efficiency, reality testing, and moral judgment that results from in-group pressures." (pg. 9)

ELEMENTS OF TEAMWORK

In addition to the five phases of group development, leaders should demonstrate eight critical elements of teamwork: four of the elements are attitudes and values and the other four are skills, processes, and actions.

Attitudes and Values:

TRUST Firm belief and confident expectation in the honesty, reliability, and trustworthy intention of the other person.

CANDOR Frank expression, straightforwardness about thoughts, feelings, and intentions.

SHARED VALUES Mutually shared values of worthwhile principles . . . agreement about what is important, top priority, and essential.

PARTICIPATION Committed to actively share, support, and take part.

Skills, Processes, and Actions:

ACCURATE LISTENING   Dedication to listen to message from all four quadrants: Quadrant 1 Sensor (words and observable actions); Quadrant 2 Thinker (reasoning process of causes and consequences); Quadrant 3 Intuitor (possibilities, linkages, implications); Quadrant 4 Feeler (values, importance, and people impact)

SHARED REASONING   Verbalize the reasoning process, clearly stating premises, assumptions, and conclusions for others to consider, interpret, and question.

CONFLICT RESOLUTION   Responsibly identify the issue, gather the different standpoints, identify the differences, and work toward clearly understanding the values involved while finding a solution that is the most fair and reasonable. Identify observable indicators for successful resolution.

STAKEHOLDER INPUT TO DECISION-MAKING   Stakeholders are those who are affected by the decision and thereby see themselves as having a stake in the decision. Getting their information into the decision process is important to fair consideration of Stakeholder standpoints.

CASE STUDY: A COMMITTEE THAT NEVER BECAME A TEAM

Several people were brought together to analyze the company's complex financial structure. The group was tasked to find a better way to structure their assets and debts. They were told to reexamine sales growth, pretax income, cash, R&D expenditures, general and administrative costs, overhead rate, inventory turnover, and reserves accrual.

Individuals were selected for their expertise, with no consideration of the way they might work as a group. The chairperson of the group is a power player. When you view the committee members with the useful framework of power and communication style, you can make a much more accurate assessment of the chances of their becoming a team.

Committees can do task work. Teams are needed if you need an extraordinary outcome, an innovative, pace-setting, breakthrough kind of work. Team synergy produces exceptional rather than mediocre work.

Evelyn, as vice-president of financial management, was asked to serve as committee chairperson. Her intelligence and her ENTJ (Extrovert, Intuitor, Thinker, Judge) style enabled her to demonstrate quick grasp of financial complexities. She also brought fifteen years of institutional memory to the discussions.

As the only female officer, she had learned to play ruthless power games. Her now retired male mentor was a Stage II Benevolent/Abusive Dictator, and she had learned his tactics thoroughly. Evelyn's own particular power style switched from Stage II, with those upon whom she looked down, to Stage III, with those of whom she was afraid. She flashed white hot anger one moment and became the solicitous Benevolent Dictator the next. To make her power games even more potent, she moved rapidly between sexy, seductive posturing to outraged, wounded mother in the blink of an eye. She effectively provoked responses that caused people to feel out of control. People demonstrated tense, alert, defensive behaviors in meetings with her. No one could predict what would "set her off."

Jim, the president of the company, who asked Evelyn to head the task force, is an ESTJ (Extrovert, Sensor, Thinker, Judge) with Stage III Competitor/Intimidator power usage. He plays a ruthless game. His behavior reveals his game. He uses three immutable laws: "(1) the company will always reward me if I make it money, (2) the men with the power will always overlook how I treat people as long as I make money, and (3) three people control the power (the CEO and two board members), so I don't have to concern myself with anyone else. I'll keep them happy and the rest of you don't count." Of course, Jim doesn't share his beliefs. You must be able to read his behavior to verify them.

Jim is a formidable opponent because he has fewer ethical or mental limits than others. He wastes little energy wondering what people are going to do or say. He concentrates on only three people, which frees up considerable attention to use on his power games. He stimulates fear in others and projects a recklessness that dares others to challenge him. He projects so powerfully that I heard the projection verbalized through various people. Jim projects: "I have fewer limits than you. If you go up against me, I'll beat you every time. It will be ugly. I will make you pay." When we met him, he had not been confronted in many years. He had grown soft from running roughshod over others without challenge.

The committee reported to Jim. Although he did not attend most of the meetings, he pervades the cultural environment. Between Evelyn's mercurial style and Jim's intimidation, what are the chances of people approaching the committee in the spirit of teamwork? Will people be likely to risk being trusting, candid, openly participative? Do you think they will expect accurate listening, shared reasoning, conflict resolution, and Stakeholder input into decision-making?

We were asked to facilitate the task force. Observing the first meeting, we easily saw people's reluctance to be involved.

Brad, one of the committee members, is a principled, ethical man who has real difficulty dealing with Jim and with Evelyn. We identified nine behavior laws that he uses as the parameters of his behavior: "(1) I will not lie, cheat, nor steal, (2) I will treat people openly and fairly, (3) I will help people develop their potential, (4) I will work cooperatively with other departments for the good of the company, (5) I will not violate my own integrity — If you ask my opinion, I will give it, (6) I believe in treating people with respect and civility, (7) I will not display anger nor irritation for I intend to behave professionally, (8) I will not use abusive language, (9) I will not instigate conflict. I will work to problem-solve." What do you think a power struggle between Brad and Jim would be like? Is Brad limited by fair, ethical respect and civility?

Brad is standing on solid values. His behavior parameters leave one large weakness that makes him no match for Jim. He is terrified of conflict and thus uses ethical laws as an excuse to avoid the pain of conflict. Power players can easily spot those people who are afraid of confrontation. The smell of fear brings out the bully in the power player.

Ethics and integrity must be yoked to the strength of character that comes from being willing to confront, to stand-up to bullies, and to experience the pain that comes with the struggle.

As an INTP (Introvert, Intuitor, Thinker, Perceiver), Brad became easily scattered when Jim or Evelyn's Extroverted force blasted him in public. His face reddened, his body stiffened, and his words became halting.

Two other members of the team were on a self-development drive that had already propelled them into some self-confrontation, identification of fears, and recognition of style limitations. Though they had not worked closely prior to the committee, they quickly recognized an awareness level in each other that they valued. They discovered shared values: importance of willingness to risk standing up to bullies, clarity of perception that is fundamental to development, and the desirability of putting company mission above personal interest. Sarah is an INFP (Introvert, Intuitor, Feeler, Perceiver) with a recognized goal to become a Stage IV Leader. F. R. is an INTJ (Introvert, Intuitor, Thinker, Judge) with the same goal.

As the meetings occurred, Sarah and F. R. bonded as they recognized kindred interests, courage, and challenge.

Initially, we facilitated the discussions of the group dynamics that were impeding the committee work. We were the ones who repeatedly confronted and described Evelyn's and Jim's behavior that negatively impacted the group's efforts to become a team. We facilitated repeated discussions of how their behavior activated fear, and other team members began to realize that they were responsible for submitting to their fears. The team was stuck in Phase 2 Task Accomplishment Phase and was perpetually in Phase 3 Struggle for Power and Control Phase.

As Sarah and F. R. grew in leadership abilities, they were singled out for additional intimidation attempts by both Jim and Evelyn. The young leaders-in-training grew more confident. The tempering of the vessels under fire indeed produced strength.

After nine months of intensive task work, Jim attended a meeting. He listened to their well-researched ideas and arbitrarily rejected them without explanation. When Sarah questioned him about his thinking, Jim did one of his "terrible twos" routines. He grabbed their report, threw it on the ground, stomped on it and yelled, "This is what I think of your work. I'm disbanding this committee right here and now. What a waste of company time and money. What a stupid bunch of imbeciles!" The group was stunned.

Evelyn moved quickly to placate his wrath to see what he wanted done. Jim jumped up and raced out of the room as he yelled, "This committee is fired."

People were anxious about the implication. Were they fired

from their jobs or from the committee? Jim tossed a well-aimed grenade right into the fear depository.

As a facilitator, I asked the group if they wanted to process their experience. Even Evelyn hastily agreed that they needed to understand their experience.

Brad was white-faced and shaking, Evelyn's glibness was gone, Sarah and F. R. exchanged mutually satisfying looks that confirmed their understandings of the manipulation and intimidation that had held the company by the cultural throat. The other member was ashen and withdrawn.

We focused on specific behaviors that all had seen. We used the observations as the fact base from which we could apply the four-quadrant problem-solving process. We discussed the facts, their consequences, the intended impact and other alternatives, as well as how people were feeling and reacting to the experience. Plenty of behavioral evidence was observed to support the intimidation methods and their effects. Some of the members grew from the experience, while others just redoubled their efforts to avoid future encounters.

Did Jim win the day? He won the skirmish but lost the war. Six months later, a number of forces came together that revealed Jim, his ruthlessness, and the considerable damage that his unethical behavior had done to the company. The implementation of the federal Clean Air Act amendments, litigious joint-ventures, a plant accident, the loss of a lawsuit brought by a stockholder, increased market competition, and the loss of two major customers brought the wrath of the power players down on Jim's head. One of the very laws that he trusted so much was the one that destroyed him. He lost money for the company. The three old power players that he had been serving for years were the ones who fired him.

Did the committee fail because it didn't become a team? Achieving teamwork is not the goal. Achieving company goals and providing employee growth and development opportunities in order to strengthen the company's human assets are the real benefits.

The strength that Sarah and F. R. experienced during that painful growth circle served them well as they each went on to form fantastic teams to tackle serious problems. Each of them became a leader with skill in developing and maintaining teams.

They are producing impressive results in actual improvements, dollars saved, and dollars earned.

Teamwork is a commonsense strategy that sits solidly on basic human principles of people wanting to contribute to something meaningful by knowing that their contribution is important, their input is useful, and that they will receive feedback on their participation. It is the solid gold of human interaction — teamwork.

DEVELOPMENTAL EXERCISES

Exercise 85:   How You Know You Work for a Leader

Think of someone with whom you work or have worked that you classify as a leader. If you can answer "Yes" to the following questions, the person has indeed had a leadership effect on your development.

Please answer "Yes" or "No."

1._____ Did you feel a continual internal push to do excellent thinking, responding, and action when involved with the person?

2._____ Did you feel pushed or inspired to discover new talents and increased expansion of recognized talents?

3._____ Did you increase your ability to risk?

4._____ Did your confidence to achieve increase?

5._____ Did your understanding of systems, people, politics, and the organization increase? Did you continually learn from the person? Did the process become clearer?

6._____ Did the person continually demonstrate clear perception and judgment?

7._____ Did the person meet mediocrity with no-nonsense confrontation?

8._____ Did the person hold self and others accountable for their actions?

Exercise 86:   How You Know You Work for a Power Player

Think of someone with whom you work or have worked that you classify as a power player. If you can answer "Yes" to the following questions, the person has had a power player's effect on you.

Please answer "Yes" or "No."

1._____ Did you spend a lot of conscious time trying to keep the person from becoming angry and punishing?

2._____ Were you expected to stroke the person's ego?

3._____ Did the person take the credit for anything well done in the work unit and find a scapegoat for anything that was wrong?

4._____ Did the person have favorites and cronies who got special privileges?

5._____ Was the person secretive and guarded with information?

6._____ Did people spend much time protecting themselves (CYA)?

7._____ Were people cautious, untrusting, closed and playing it safe?

8._____ Was the creation of alibis and blaming others the norm?

Exercise 87:   Checklist for Emotional and Mental Maturity

How often do you demonstrate the following:

Use the ratings:	Often	Sometimes	Rarely
	3	2	1

1._____ Do you accept responsibility for your own acts without blaming others or giving an alibi?

2._____ Do you accept criticism gratefully and consider it an opportunity to improve?

3._____ Do you see yourself as working for what you get, instead of expecting special consideration?

4._____ Do you indulge in self-pity and self-praise?

5._____ Do you control your temper and use anger responsibly and wisely?

6._____ Do you acknowledge your own fear, confront your fears, and try to manage your fears responsibly?

7._____ Do you communicate excellently by painting clear, memorable pictures?

8._____ Do you listen open-mindedly and thoughtfully to others?

9._____ Do you explain and respond with clear messages?

10._____ Do you accept others' success without envy or jealousy?

11._____ Do you get your feelings hurt easily?

12._____ Do you deal with emergencies, surprises, and challenges with poise and clear thinking?

Exercise 88:   Four Principles of Human Nature

Consider each of the following principles. Develop a rationale that supports or denies each principle.

1. MISSION – People want to *contribute* to something meaningful.

Premise:

Premise:

Premise:

Conclusion:

2. SELF-WORTH — People want to know their *contribution* is important . . . that they make a significant difference.

   Premise:

   Premise:

   Premise:

   Conclusion:

3. PARTICIPATION — People want *input* into what affects them.

   Premise:

   Premise:

Premise:

Conclusion:

4. FEEDBACK — People want evidence that their input was *heard, understood, and considered.*

Premise:

Premise:

Premise:

Conclusion:

Exercise 89:   Group Process Check — Teamwork

TEAMWORK — To what extent did our team members demonstrate the effective use of the teamwork elements or processes? Use the following rating:

1	2	3	4	5
Never	Seldom	Sometimes	Usually	Consistently

1._____ ***Trust*** — Extent to which members demonstrated firm belief in others' honesty, reliability, and trustworthy intention.

2._____ ***Candor*** — Extent that we demonstrated frank expression and straightforward thoughts, feelings, and intentions.

3._____ ***Participation*** — Extent to which we actively shared, responded, and took part, both verbally and non-verbally.

4._____ ***Accurate Listening*** — Extent to which we listened on all four levels of messages (Level 1 Sensor words and observable actions, Level 2 Thinker reasoning process of causes and consequences, Level 3 Intuitor possibilities, linkages and implications, Level 4 Feeler values, importance and people impact).

5._____ ***Shared Reasoning*** — Extent to which we verbalized our reasoning, clearly stated premises/assumptions and conclusions for others to consider, interpret, and question.

6._____ ***Shared Values*** — Extent to which we mutually shared values of worthwhile principles through agreement about what is important, top priority, and essential.

7._____ ***Conflict Resolution*** — Extent to which we responsibly identified issues, gathered different standpoints, identified differences, worked toward agreement, and identified observables for effective resolution.

8._____ ***Stakeholder Input into Decision-making*** — Extent that we gave fair consideration to those people with the greatest stake in what we decided to do (both to our team members and others who will be affected).

Does this team need to work on attitudes and values (the first four variables of trust, candor, shared values, participation)?

If work is needed, what can you do?

Does this team need to work on skills, processes, and actions (the last four variables of accurate listening, shared reasoning, conflict resolution, and Stakeholder input into decision-making)?

If work is needed, what can you do?

– 9 –

Leadership and the Power Game

Main Ideas of Chapter 9:

1. Power is defined as the potential to influence.
   A. *Webster's Ninth New Collegiate Dictionary* uses the synonyms of power, authority, jurisdiction, control, command, sway, and dominion.
   B. We have simplified our discussion of power by using two categories: personal power and position power.
2. Traditional power is authoritarian in nature, while today's focus is on empowerment.
3. Authoritarian power lends itself to power players, while leaders focus on leading through empowerment.
4. Power games directly contrast with leaders building on genuine relationships.
5. The power game has rules of engagement.
6. Political gamesmanship is one of the most potent of all games.
7. Perhaps it is time for a leadership paradigm shift.

PERSONAL AND POSITION POWER

Power is the potential to influence. It is defined as "possession of control, authority, or influence over others" in *Webster's Ninth New Collegiate Dictionary*. In the synonym description of "power," the following distinctions are made:

> syn POWER AUTHORITY, JURISDICTION, CONTROL, COMMAND, SWAY, DOMINION mean the right to govern or rule or determine. POWER implies possession of ability to wield force, permissive authority or substantial influence; AUTHORITY implies the granting of power or a special purpose within specified limits; JURISDICTION applies to official power exercised within prescribed limits; CONTROL stresses the power to direct and restrain; COMMAND implies the power to make arbitrary decisions and compel obedience; SWAY suggests the extent or scope of exercised power or influence; DOMINION stresses sovereign power or supreme authority. (pg. 922)

Power is a sociological concept as it deals with influence and plays out in the interpersonal relationships among people. Stage IV Leadership is based upon the individual's mature use of personal and position power to achieve worthwhile goals that benefit people's highest good. Stages I, II, and III power players use personal and position power to achieve goals that will benefit themselves.

Although many forms of social power have been identified, we have simplified our discussion in this book into two categories: *personal power* that comes from our personalities, motives, values, and beliefs, and *position power* that comes from perception of the right to influence. We have used "position power" to cover the various types of social power attributed to a person's position whether that be organizational, political, economic, financial, business, academic, military, societal, artistic, or criminal power. We use the term "position power" to indicate the position of influence that a person has, regardless of whether or not it is formally endorsed or an informally accepted position of influence.

The Stage IV Leader must bring personal power into balance while using clear perception and sound judgment in the ethically and morally responsible exercise of position power.

TRADITIONAL POWER VS. LEADERSHIP

Traditional power is authoritarian in nature and appears to be much more in alignment with Niccolo Machiavelli's treatise on power rather than the current focus on Leadership as an empowerment-encouraging process.

In *The Prince*, Machiavelli envisoned the man in power as being both beast and man, unfettered by ordinary moral values or ethical constraints. He exorted the man of power to allow no such limitations in himself. He made no pretense of encouraging clear perception in others but encouraged the man of power to read people clearly. He said:

> Minds are of three kinds: one is capable of thinking for itself; another is able to understand the thinking of others; and a third can neither think for itself nor understand the thinking of others . . . [He totally dismisses the third as unworthy of consideration.] For when a prince can discern what is good and bad in the words and deeds of another, he will be able to distinguish between his minister's good and bad performance, praising the one and correcting the other, even though he lacks an inventive mind himself. Then the minister cannot hope to deceive him and will work reliably.

Being a clever power player himself, Machiavelli had clear advice for spotting another power player. He stated:

> Now, as to the means by which a prince may learn the character of a minister, there is one that never fails. When you see a minister who thinks more about his own interests than about yours, who seeks his own advantage in everything he does, then you may be sure that such a man will never be a good minister, and you will never be able to trust him. (pg. 80)

Power players have been discussed for generations. The German philosopher Hegel asserted that people have a basic instinct to master and enslave others. He believed that all interpersonal relationships were versions of master-enslavement struggles. Karl Marx made the master/slave philosophy even more powerful as he turned it into an appeal to revolution.

The philosophies of Machiavelli, Hegel, and Marx seem to have greatly overshadowed Plato's position that excellence in mind, body, and character was essential to living a good life of healthy, vital, honorable living. However, Plato also believed that superiority of intellect and rational thought was requisite to governing. Neither did the French philosopher Jean Paul Sartre's moralist position seem to influence traditional power as he urged us to take responsibility for ourselves and avoid self-deception at all costs.

Not enough time has passed for us to draw clear cause-effect inferences that can explain our paradigm shifting from traditional authoritarian power to leadership through empowerment and participation. Let's compare the two paradigms:

AUTHORITARIAN POWER PLAYERS	LEADERSHIP AND EMPOWERMENT LEADERS
Dominance-Submission	Trust-Respect
Control	Cooperation
Compliance	Commitment
Competition	Partnership
Punishment	Motivation/Inspiration
Position Power	Personal Power
Favoritism	Realistic Capability Assessment/ Best Match with Task
Function Focus (Stovepipe or Profession Loyalty)	Talent and Skill Focus (Innovation and Excellence)
Task Focus	Process Focus
Chain of Command Rigidity	Teamwork and Shared Values
Give orders	Share the reasoning process
Comply to avoid pain	Embrace opportunities and grow from lessons learned

The traditional authoritarian use of power was ready-made for power playing and power abuse; whereas, leaders understand that they are perpetually re-earning their right to lead.

The self-interest, self-importance, domination, and control of power players fits the power paradigm of the authoritarian and aligns with Hegel, Marx, and Machiavelli. People all around the world, however, are resisting the use of power that denies the basics of the human spirit. Although many still live in power abusive countries, companies, and communities, the will to be free of such dominance remains ever alive.

Lest you think that America has become a country of leadership and empowerment and you might be the last American to be working in an antiquated organization, we had better revisit organizational cultures. The paradigm is shifting, but it has not shifted enough to establish Stage IV Leadership as the norm. Unfortunately, Stage IV Leadership and learning, responsive organizations are still all too rare.

We have seen the dominant American auto industry be forced in the last decade to find out what customers wanted. The stovepipes within the industry were dysfunctional and devoted to turf control and maintaining rigid hierarchies. When CEO Peterson came to Ford, he began changing from the stovepipes to integrated operations among design-construction-technical and engineering. He needed an integrated, synergistic effort to meet market demands.

In the last ten years, the majority of our organizational audits or interventions have found organizations with the following characteristics: enforcement of hierarchy, jealous guarding of information, enforced information routing according to status rather than expertise, reliance on authority rather than development of cooperative working relationships, rule-oriented and legalistic interpretation of people issues, skeptical of change, skeptical of process, and resistant to the rush of changes affecting every aspect of organizational life.

After many years as consultants, we believe that we see far too much evidence that Americans have become a society of character-disordered people who have a long way to go to be ready for real leadership and full acceptance of our responsibility for what's happening to our infrastructure and position in the world marketplace.

When M. Scott Peck wrote his popular book *The Road Less Traveled*, he gave hundreds of readers a framework for revisiting the fundamental concepts of discipline and personal responsibility.

> What makes life difficult is that the process of confronting and solving problems is a painful one ... Yet it is in this whole process of meeting and solving problems that life has its meaning. Problems are the cutting edge that distinguishes between success and failure ... When we desire to encourage the growth of the human spirit, we challenge and encourage the human capacity to solve problems ... It is through the pain of confronting and resolving problems that we learn. As Benjamin Franklin said, "Those things that hurt, instruct." (pg. 16)

As we work with organization after organization, we continue to discover daily examples of blaming someone else. Peck's description of the neurotic and the character disordered is useful in the search for mature use of power for he cites them as "disorders of responsibility":

> The neurotic assumes too much responsibility; the person with a character disorder not enough. When neurotics are in conflict with the world they automatically assume that they are at fault. When those with character disorders are in conflict with the world they automatically assume that the world is at fault. (pg. 35)

We have become a litigious society. Where is the personal responsibility in a law that says we can sue the bartender for allowing us to drink too much and then get involved in an accident? How can we place the responsibility for common sense on product sales to tell us every possible way we could get hurt using their product?

In one community which experienced its huge, once-in-a-hundred-year flood, I watched an outraged man cursing the Corps of Engineers division general for the destruction of his property. The general tried to explain that when the man built his home in the flood plain, he took the risk. The man screamed, "I'm a goddam taxpayer and I pay you to keep that from happening. If you had done your job, my home would not be standing in five feet of water." The general tried to explain the expense in building flood management programs for worst-case, once-in-a-hundred-year happenings. The complainant patently rejected any personal responsibility.

How many times do we blame others for what happens to us? Malpractice insurance is expensive. New product liability is so great that when you consider the possibility of bizarre litigation, the innovative spirit is too often blunted.

Review some of the comments we hear regularly that sound like the character disordered. "It's not my fault, my supervisor told me to do it." "It's not my regulation. I'm just here to enforce it." "You should have told me not to do that, and I wouldn't have gotten hurt." "I couldn't help it; I was under a time constraint." "I don't get rated on how nice I am; I get rated on how much paper I move." "I can't operate in gray areas; you'll have to tell me exactly what you want." "My butt gets chewed over budget and schedule issues, not over how nice I am. When they write it in my job description and pay me to, I'll work on my huggy skills . . . and not until."

Confronting our fears, taking responsibility for our own thoughts, feelings, and actions is part of what created the rugged value-based foundation of America. We continue to see the strength and the amazing accomplishments when mature people work together in honesty and integrity. The new paradigm may in fact be a rebirth of a more advanced version of the independence, self-reliance, courage, and resourcefulness which gave birth to the United States of America.

POWER GAMES VS. GENUINE RELATIONSHIPS

The power game is a game of the head (cool logical strategies and tactics), while leadership involves genuine relationships based upon balanced and wise use of both head and heart. Leadership is based upon balanced use of clear perception and sound judgment in integrating the clear logical focus and accurate perception of values and people impact. It is based upon wisdom and accurate assessment. The power game is based upon the head's clear assessment of other power players, power dynamics, and potential outcome in the never-ending struggle for power and control. Fueled by aggression, hostility, distrust, and a fierce need to be the winner in the eternal struggle for power, power players find that they are ceaselessly blocked from feeling that they have enough power. Since power is addictive, a power player does not reach a satisfied state. Power relationships are constantly changing, so the game is to be alert to the changes and forge realignments.

Alvin Toffler in his book *Powershift* states:

> Power is shifting at so astonishing a rate that world leaders are being swept along by events, rather than imposing order on them . . . There is strong reason to believe that the forces now shaking power at every level of the human system will become more intense and pervasive in the years immediately ahead . . . Out of this massive restructuring of power relationships, like the shifting and grinding of tectonic plates in advance of an earthquake, will come one of the rarest events in human history: a revolution in the very nature of power . . . A "powershift" does not merely transfer power. It transforms it. (pg. 4)

If a transformation of power is occurring, then the game must change also. Perhaps the game will be replaced by ethical and moral rules of wielding power in the framework of genuine leadership.

The power game has accepted rules, as all games imply rules of engagement. Even war has internationally accepted rules of engagement. The Hague Conventions of 1899 and 1907 laid out international rules for land wars and banned asphyxiating gases, bacterial and chemical warfare. The Geneva Conventions of 1929 and 1949 set standards for the treatment of prisoners, civilians in occupied territories, and care of the sick and wounded. Long after wars cease, aggressors are brought to trial for war crimes. Throughout the centuries, rules of combat have been encouraged, and those warriors who violate the code of war risk the condemnation of people on both sides of the conflict.

Philosophically, a distinction is made between a just and an unjust war. St. Augustine in the fifth century wrestled with the distinction, as did St. Thomas Aquinas in the Middle Ages. The resultant code of war states: (1) the engagement must be to defend against encroachment or aggression, (2) war must be declared by legitimate governing authority, (3) it must right a great wrong, (4) military power should be used only against military targets, (5) no intentional harm should be done to innocent civilians, (6) no destruction of religious centers or churches should be willingfully inflicted, and (7) bravery and courage should be respected. It is ludicrous to many to consider rules in the brutal absurdity of war, yet history traces the ongoing pursuit of placing rules on human aggression.

Just as the rules of war provide some universal underpinning to the use of aggressive power, power players have rules to which they adhere in playing the power game.

In America the acceptable use of power is the exercise of power on behalf of others rather than self. Acting for the benefit of others is more likely to be seen as legitimate; consequently, appearing to be too personally ambitious and self-focused is considered egotistical and thereby illegitimate. Alexander Haig's statement that he was in charge when President Reagan was shot earned him the public persona of overweening ambition and illegitimate use of power. Thus, much of the difficulty in distinguishing between a leader and a power player lies in the motive – since the rules demand legitimacy of acting for others (i.e., the good of the nation, the company, the poor).

American rules of power gaming include:

1. Do what you do in the name of the greater good.

2. Never appear to lust for power.

3. Be reliable when you give your word (the game relies on predictability as well as cleverness). You get power points if you are clever enough to lead others to think you gave your word, when in fact you did not since manipulation of perception is an essential power game skill in order to persuade and control.

4. Master the nuances of the game . . . subtlety . . . artifice.

5. Never reveal your own vulnerabilities or weaknesses but be instantly alert to exploit others' vulnerabilities or weaknesses.

6. Never let the opponents see you bleed (i.e., never let them see you frightened, uncertain, or emotionally out-of-control).

7. Take care of your own people . . . Never let another power player encroach.

8. Do constant surveillance to assess people, situations, and events.

9. Establish your physical power center for access to the latest information and to other power players.

10. Make people pay dearly if they fail to live up to commitments.

FUNDAMENTAL RULE # 1: No permanent friends, no permanent enemies, just permanent interests or temporary alliances.

FUNDAMENTAL RULE #2: Power is a game of perception. Power ingredients are information, knowledge, access, visibility, showmanship, appearance, high-energy, self-confidence, likability, sense of humor, perceptiveness, a sense of timing, resources, connections, commitment, and the winner image.

Review the rules of the power game. Stage IV Leadership establishes a different approach, based upon genuine relationships, shared values, personal responsibility, wisdom, and mature use of power.

POLITICAL POWER

The Washington power game, one of the most potent games in our country, has gone through a transformation of the use of power. A noticeable phase occurred with the decentralization of power. A description of the traditional power games in Washington usually involved references to Sam Rayburn's rule in Congress: "To get along, you go along." He represented the grand old dean of power who embodied the accepted practice of silent apprenticeships for junior members, long payment of dues before being accepted into the inner workings of the power domain, and a slow climb into real positions of influence. Thus, the committee chairmen in the House and Senate paid traditional apprenticeship dues. Those who proved too rebellious were excluded from real power.

Then a new breed came to Washington who were unwilling to wait years to get into the game. They were smart and savvy about the use of media. They depended upon their own money-raising abilities to get to Washington rather than the old, traditional power brokers. They had the ability to communicate effectively through television to establish power in their own geographical regions. This power base freed them from apprenticeship to the power establishment. They found issues that played well in the media and forged power bases for themselves around issues. The formal seniority system was under siege as early as 1974. The game was enlarged.

The Senate operates within a framework of "Gentleman's Privilege" with excessive courtesy, privilege, and civility. The Senate rules allow filibuster and endless courteous privleges that indulge the use of porcupine power. Hedrick Smith in his excellent book *The Power Game* describes porcupine power as the use of negative power, the power to block, to obstruct, to be difficult and quarrelsome. Smith's description of North Carolina Senator Jesse Helms demonstrates the Senate framework that allows such use of power:

> [Senator Helms] projects the folksy style of the antebellum South . . . In the Senate, his manners are courtly. But his parliamentary techniques are telling and crafty. Helms plays the politics of confrontation: stalling, filibustering with marathon speeches, tying the Senate up in knots, frustrating others to

achieve his own ends. His aides have proudly nicknamed him Senator NO. Helms represents another basic kind of power in Washington: the power of obstruction, a negative power, the power to block and deny, the power of being difficult and prickly. Some call it porcupine power. (pg. 58)

The Senate rules and procedures guarantee unlimited debate unless cloture (calling for a limitation of debate) or a cutoff is voted on by 60% of the Senate. Thus, negative or blocking power is within the norm.

The House, with its 435 members, demands coalition building, bartering, and commitment of votes. Although both the Senate and the House share fields of power gaming, the difference in the Senate and House Rules puts a different spin on the mutually shared game. When the House and Senate conference committees meet to reconcile differences in legislation, the interaction is likely to have much porcupine power applied. The bargaining is tough, and "Potomac Fever" is high. Smith defines Potomac Fever as "the incurable addiction of wielding political power or feeling at the political center." (pg. 91)

The House of Representatives is excellently described in John M. Barry's *The Ambition and the Power:*

> The House is a live thing, a vital thing, and it moves according to rhythms generated by forces that bind all men and women together — personal ambition, trust, friendship and dislike, anger, the memory of past kindnesses and slights — made more complicated by ideology, by internal, national, and local politics. To succeed in the House a man or woman must be able to read its rhythms, and recognize and understand not only broad obvious currents but the eddies and under-tow indicated when another member smiles too quickly or not quickly enough, keeps silent at another's joke or laughs too hard. Even Jack Brooks, a Texas Democrat known for bluntness rather than subtlety, observes, *"Nuance. It's all nuance."* (pg. 16)

Power in the Senate and the House requires expert gamesmanship in the control of procedure and structure. Barry states:

> The key to controlling members lies in form and structure; through form and structure, one can control substance. The most important element of form is procedure; of structure, the whip organization. Parliamentary procedure is dry, technical, and mundane; but, like the coils of a rope, it can constrain or

even strangle. Procedure is part of the minutiae of politics which the press and public do not understand; the insiders understand. John Dingell, a creature of the institution, who came to Washington when he was five years old with his congressman father, then worked as a page, then inherited his father's seat, once told the Rules Committee, "If I let you write substance and you let me write procedure, I'll screw you every time." (pg. 74)

Politicians make policy, but bureaucrats implement it. As bureaucrats write procedure and regulations, they control the substance. Original intent is often lost.

With the decentralization of power the power game has become a wider game with greater unpredictability. Although tremendous power resides in control of procedure, structure, and process, the widened game involves public perception. Thus the game is more volatile and somewhat more risky.

Traditional power players depended on predictability and early access to important information in order to set into motion elaborate, complicated plans to control advantage and outcomes. The old game rested on a system of clear debts and payments; predictability, reliability of the rules of the game, and dependable fulfillment of power commitments were necessary to stabilize the game. Trust was not placed in each other but rather in the inviolability of the rules of the game.

Stage IV Leaders utilize predictability, reliability and dependability; however, the investiture is not in the power game but in authentic mature use of power. We have asserted that Leaders must do continuous, brutal self-examination to avoid the trap of self-delusion. History is littered with leaders who became power players when they fooled themselves into believing their personal ambitions were for the good of others, thereby justifying gross egotism.

The political game makes genuine leadership almost impossible. Hedrick Smith states: "The competitiveness of the power game inhibits people from revealing the kind of personal vulnerability and doubts about life that are vital to forming close and sincere friendships. To a politician, weakness can be fatal. So it is only natural that they cover up their frailties and uncertainties from rivals as well as from voters. For the risk of inner self-revelation, which genuine intimacy requires, is too dangerous for most politicians and public officials." (pg. 111)

Where does a politican get feedback so necessary to clear perception and sound judgment? In the heady world of political power, the fawning deference and personal privleges given to politicians easily contribute to the illusion of elitism and feudal superiority. Where do they find the motivation to put others' interests first and their own last? What would cause them to seek out the truth of their character rather than focus on the game? We suggest that there is little incentive to be reflective. The time spent in self-confrontation would take time away from the social game of power politics.

One of the corruptions of power is self-focus — becoming so focused on self-interest that every encounter, every situation, and every thought process is considered from one dominant viewpoint: "What can this do for me?" When that personal consideration becomes the controller of perception and judgment, distortion must necessarily be the result. Ethics, morality, and resolve to do the right thing are obliterated by power obsession.

The need to balance the power drive lies in every human being. We experience a constant battle between the egotism of self-interest and the maturity of appropriate use of power for the greatest contribution to the well-being of others. It is just too easy to rationalize that our motives are not self-serving. Choices determine whether we use our personal and position power for the betterment of others or for our own self-interests.

Arnold Hutschnecker identifies a politician's unforgivable sin as appearing to be too greedy for power. In *The Drive for Power,* he discusses the need to control the power drive.

> Every single human, in whatever socioeconomic position, has within him or her a drive for power, a force that can help unfold the potentials inherent in a personality. This force can lead to fulfillment or failure, happiness or misery, depending on the individual's set of values; and those values in turn determine the sum and sequence of his near or distant goals. Because of this, every individual has also the power to contribute to the advance of civilization — or to its destruction. For it is the direction of the power drive that leads one man to create — and another to kill. (pg. 7)

Norman Cousins identified the tendency of power to corrupt. He noted:

- The tendency of power to drive intelligence underground;

- The tendency of power to become a theology, admitting no other gods before it;

- The tendency of power to distort and damage the traditions and institutions it was designed to protect;

- The tendency of power to create a language of its own, making other forms of communication incoherent and irrelevant;

- The tendency of power to spawn imitators, leading to volatile competition;

- The tendency of power to set the stage for its own use. (*The Pathology of Power,* pg. 23–24)

The tendency of power to corrupt is legendary. We have seen ethics, integrity, and morality consumed in the fire of expediency to get the power advantage. When the focus is on power, the end justifies the means. When we focus on Leadership and mature use of power, the means and the end are integrated. The process involves the relationships and professionalism required to achieve meaningful goals.

Power has been called an aphrodisiac, an addiction, a devourer, a fatal attraction. Yet power itself is neither good nor bad. Our motives and our choices determine the valence. Our motives, our choices, our capabilities, and our actions determine whether we play power or lead.

TIME FOR A NEW PARADIGM

Perhaps the cycle of tolerating power players' lying, deceit, manipulation, and greed should end. Are we ready to demand that our leaders use personal and position power for the good of the nation? Are we ready to say "No" to governmental legislation that controls taxes, business systems, and financial regulations to give unfair advantage to power players? Are we ready to unseat greedy executives who rape corporations for immediate gain and leave their futures in jeopardy? Are we ready to blow the whistle on abuse and distortion in the systems? Are we ready to hold ourselves seriously accountable for our own actions?

A leadership paradigm means establishment of a dominant pattern, a set of rules and regulations that establish acceptable boundaries and behaviors in the exercise of power. We will have to make revolutionary changes in the way we think and use power. Over fifty years ago, Albert Einstein said: "The unleashed power of the atom has changed everything, except our thinking. Thus we are drifting towards a catastrophe beyond comparison. We shall require a substantially new manner of thinking, if mankind is to survive."

We believe that "a substantially new manner" of using power is needed. We believe that change starts within the individual, for it is the individual who allows someone else to control perception or puts out the energy to think, analyze, value, and decide. We believe that change is the responsibility of each individual to live a quality existence that contributes to the community, the environment, and the country.

Our study of leadership brings us full circle. We looked at the individual's need to balance head and heart, to confront fears, and accept full responsibility for one's own thoughts, feelings, and actions. Development of balance in personal style and development of mature use of power is the basis for an individual, a work group, a political system, an organization, or a nation to move out of the immaturity of power gaming and abuse. It is time to take the difficult course of evolving into mature and responsible sharing of power.

Ultimately, it is time for us to grow beyond the immediate gratification of power indulgence and begin to discipline ourselves to responsibly take care of our shared physical environment. Just as the leader must develop his sensory capacity to accurately interpret the real situation and be clearly focused in the present — "Right Now" — so must the leader develop his intuitive capacity to envision. An accurate assessment of possibilities, patterns, impacts, and connections of current actions is equally necessary. The leader or the mature adult needs excellent sensory and intuitive skills.

We Americans cannot postpone much longer our emotional development. We have too long worshiped at the feet of rationalism and thought that we could logically interpret feelings, values, and meaning from the safe distance of the head. Intellectual development is easier, more satisfying, and much less messy than emotional development. The safe world of mental thought offers much more control than the feeling, sensing world of emotional experience.

If people were more emotionally developed, they would never fall into the power game manipulations. As long as we are afraid of conflict, afraid of confrontation, afraid of rejection, and afraid of failure, we are too emotionally immature to change the game, much less get into the arena with a power player.

A leader has gone through painful and humbling emotional development. Opening up to one's own feelings and fears is a way to develop real strength. What a paradox to discover that only by becoming vulnerable to one's own feelings and fears can real strength and real compassion develop. In the power game, players must deny weaknesses, hide vulnerabilities, and fool themselves as well as others. They do not realize the toll taken by their fear of the lie being discovered. Power players hide the truth about their own motives and fears from themselves as well as from others. The leader engages continually in self-examination and perpetually confronts distortions within.

The power game locks players in the head, where they attempt to seal off feelings because emotions are seen as weakness.

Leadership requires full integration of the head and the heart. Intellectual development is required in order to conceptualize, to focus, to interpret, and to understand. Emotional development is required in order to experience meaning and richness of life. Emotional development adds value and allows us to personalize and experience life.

Intellectual development provides thoughts and ideas. Emotional development brings the physical response to thoughts and ideas. The full range of associations that come through valuing are vital to Leadership. The leader needs to be able to feel and sense and know what other people want, need, and fear.

Power players manipulate other people's feelings. The more addicted they become to the game, the more distorted is their use of emotional data. Since they are afraid to let an opponent see their real fears and values, they tend to cut off feelings. They become more and more resistant to experiencing any feelings except those associated with the power game. They guard against feelings of love, compassion, connection, vulnerability, empathy, sympathy, or genuine relationships. They allow themselves to experience primarily the exultant feelings of dominance, control, force, winning, retaliation, and punishment. Fear and anxiety are two emotions that the power player cannot ultimately avoid.

By cutting off the full range of feeling, the power player becomes trapped in intellect in a one-dimensional world without even the ability to fully reach satisfaction in the feelings of power. The terrible cost of the power game requires the incessant need for more power, the need to protect turf, and to ceaselessly scan for any attempts to increase or possibly to lose power. The emotional cost of the power game is perpetual insecurity, anxiety, and greedy absorption with getting more. The power addiction means "There is never enough power to reach satisfaction!"

The Stage IV Leader experiences the wide range of feelings and is unafraid to experience both the positive and negative feelings. Leaders must operate with clear perception which can only be achieved through the willingness to feel both pleasant and unpleasant associations. They are unafraid to open to the feelings that add richness to life. Feelings add meaning and establish values. Leaders are willing to experience the real feelings involved in a situation, for therein lies part of an accurate assessment of the real situation.

The leader needs well-developed sensing for greater awareness of current environment. Accurate assessment of details, awareness of objects, sensations, visual and spatial factors are interpreted through accurate awareness of environmental cues and messages.

The leader needs well-developed intuition in order to make meaning out of seemingly unrelated events. To connect bits and pieces into a holistic fabric of meaning is a necessary talent for leadership. To be able to read between the lines, to accurately intuit intent, to know probabilities, to recognize danger long before it manifests, and to innovatively see opportunities are intuitive capabilities fundamental to leadership.

The leader needs intellectual development to accurately interpret ideas, create concepts, and analyze cause and effect implications. Emotional development adds the richness, value, and meaning to life.

People want to trust leaders, but they cannot really establish that genuine connection unless the leader can open up to the full range of their needs, desires, fears, and expectations. We must come to realize that both head and heart are equally valuable.

Perhaps the day will come when Americans will refuse to allow the power game to continue. Maybe we will demand that our leaders use power responsibly, and we will hold ourselves accountable for the discipline, hard work, and effort it takes to be informed about legislation, corporate practices, environmental impacts, and long-term reparation of our infrastructure. Perhaps we will demand Stage IV Leadership in the vitally important institutions of education, health care, business, government, military, media, environment, religion, and finance.

How startling to realize that we cannot expect the responsible use of power in others until we hold ourselves accountable for the same level of maturity in our daily interactions as employees, employers, spouses, friends, parents, sons, daughters, and citizens. For change requires the individual to build from within the kind of clear-eyed integrity that we hope to see in our leaders. We can start the change now, right where we are.

The path is not easy. The price is high. The path requires brutal self-examination, confrontation of our fears, experiencing the vulnerability required for emotional development, recognizing our egoic drive for power and the need to discipline and control our basic selfish urges. In short, the price of mature and responsible use of power is the willing submission to experience both pleasure and pain, power and powerlessness. The pathway to Stage IV Leadership requires us to confront the power player within before we can wisely and caringly confront the power player in others.

Bibliography

Barr and Barr, Lee and Norma. *Leadership Equation*. Austin, TX: Eakin Press, 1989.

Barry, John M. *The Ambition and the Power*. New York: Penguin Books, 1990.

Bierstedt, Robert. *Power and Progress*. New York: McGraw-Hill Paperbacks, 1974.

Bennis, Warren, and Burt Nanus. *Leaders*. New York: Harper & Row, Publishers, 1985.

Corbin, Carolyn. *Strategies 2000*. Austin, TX: Eakin Press, 1986.

Cousins, Norman. *The Pathology of Power*. New York: Norton Press, 1987.

Dean, Douglas, John Mihalasky, Sheila Ostrander, and Lynn Schroeder. *Executive ESP*. Englewood Cliffs, CA: Prentice-Hall, Inc., 1974.

Hutschnecker, Arnold A. *The Drive for Power*. New York: M. Evans and Company, 1974.

Janis, Irving L. *Groupthink*. Boston, MA: Houghton Mifflin Company, 1982.

Kami, Michael. *Trigger Points*. New York: Berkley Books, 1992.

Kanter, Rosabeth Moss. *The Change Masters*. New York: Touchstone Press, 1983.

Katz, Daniel, and Robert L. Kahn. *The Social Psychology of Organizations*. New York: John Wiley & Sons, Inc., 1966.

Kelley, Robert E. *The Gold-Collar Worker*. Menlo Park, CA: Addison-Wesley Publishing Co., Inc., 1985.

Kotter, John P. *The Leadership Factor*. New York: The Free Press, 1988.

Lewis, Michael. *Liar's Poker*. New York: W. W. Norton & Company, Inc., 1989.

Maccoby, Michael. *The Leader*. New York: Ballantine Books, 1981.

Machiavelli, Niccolo. *The Prince*. New York: Bantam Books, 1966.

Myers, Isabel Briggs, with Peter B. Myers. *Gifts Differing.* Consulting Psychologists Press, 1985.

Myers, Isabel Briggs, and Mary H. McCaulley. *Manual: A Guide to the Development and Use of the Myers-Briggs Type Indicator.* Consulting Psychologists Press, 1985.

McClelland, David. *Power: The Inner Experience.* New York: Irvington Publishers, Inc., 1975.

Nance, John J. *On Shaky Ground.* New York: William Morrow & Company, Inc., 1988.

Oech, Roger von. *A Whack on the Side of the Head.* New York: Warner Books, 1983.

Peck, M. Scott. *The Road Less Traveled.* New York: Touchstone Books by Simon and Schuster, 1978.

Rowan, Roy. *The Intuitive Manager.* New York: Berkley Books, 1986.

Schwartzkopf, General H. Norman. *It Doesn't Take A Hero.* New York: Bantam Books, 1992.

Secord, Paul F., and Carl W. Backman. *Social Psychology.* New York: McGraw-Hill Book Company, 1964.

Smith, Hedrick. *The Power Game.* New York: Random House, 1988.

Stockman, David A. *The Triumph of Politics.* New York: Harper & Row Publishers, 1986.

Toffler, Alvin. *Power Shift.* New York: Bantam Books, 1990.

Tyler, Patrick. *Running Critical.* New York: Harper & Row Publishers, 1986.

Webster's Ninth New Collegiate Dictionary. Frederick Mish, ed. Springfield, MA: Merriam-Webster Inc., 1991.

Newspapers and Periodicals

Barron's National Business and Financial Weekly. February 19, 1990, "The Biggest Scam Ever? Drexel/Milken, a Critic Charges, Was a Giant Ponzi Scheme," by Benjamin J. Stein.

"Gray Matter" by Lonnie Barone and Karen DiNuncia. *Journal of Psychological Type,* Vol. 7 (1984).

Military Leadership. Headquarters Department of the Army, Washington D.C., October 1983, Field Manual FM 22-100.

Partners, AT&T, Winter 1990.

U.S. News & World Report, May 10, 1993.

Type Reporter, Susan Scanlon, ed. Vol. 4, no. 7 (December 1989).